The Challenge of **Effective Speaking**

The Challenge of

Effective Speaking

Twelfth Edition

Rudolph F. Verderber / Kathleen S. Verderber

University of Cincinnati / Northern Kentucky University

THOMSON
WADSWORTH

Australia · Canada · Mexico · Singapore · Spain · United Kingdom · United States

THOMSON

WADSWORTH

Executive Editor: DEIRDRE ANDERSON
Publisher: HOLLY J. ALLEN
Assistant Editor: NICOLE GEORGE
Editorial Assistant: MELE ALUSA
Technology Project Manager: JEANETTE WISEMAN
Marketing Manager: KIMBERLY RUSSELL
Marketing Assistant: NEENA CHANDRA
Advertising Project Manager: SHEMIKA BRITT
Project Manager, Editorial Production: CATHY LINBERG
Print/Media Buyer: TANDRA JORGENSEN
Permissions Editor: ROBERT KAUSER

Production Service: CECILE JOYNER/THE COOPER COMPANY
Photo Researcher: TERRI WRIGHT
Copy Editor: KAY MIKEL
Action Steps Illustrator: PETER COATES ILLUSTRATION
Text and Cover Designer: JOHN WALKER DESIGN
Cover Image: PETER COATES ILLUSTRATION
Compositor: NEW ENGLAND TYPOGRAPHIC SERVICE
Printer: R. R. DONNELLEY AND SONS, WILLARD
Photo credits are on page 367.

For more information about our products, contact us at:
Thomson Learning Academic Resource Center
1-800-423-0563
For permission to use material from this text,
contact us by:
Phone: 1-800-730-2214
Fax: 1-800-730-2215
Web: http://www.thomsonrights.com

Library of Congress Control Number: 2002103357
Student Edition ISBN 0-534-56385-6
Instructor's Edition ISBN 0-534-56387-2

Wadsworth/Thomson Learning
10 Davis Drive
Belmont, CA 94002-3098
USA

Asia
Thomson Learning
5 Shenton Way #01-01
UIC Building
Singapore 068808

Australia
Nelson Thomson Learning
102 Dodds Street
South Melbourne, Victoria 3205
Australia

Canada
Nelson Thomson Learning
1120 Birchmount Road
Toronto, Ontario M1K 5G4
Canada

Europe/Middle East/Africa
Thomson Learning
High Holborn House
50/51 Bedford Row
London WC1R 4LR
United Kingdom

Latin America
Thomson Learning
Seneca, 53
Colonia Polanco
11560 Mexico D.F.
Mexico

Spain
Paraninfo Thomson Learning
Calle/Magallanes, 25
28015 Madrid, Spain

Brief Contents

Contents

Chapter 7   Organizing and Outlining the Speech Body   116

Chapter 8   Organizing the Introduction and the Conclusion and Completing the Outline   136

Part Four ■ Adapting to Other Occasions and Formats

Chapter 15   Adapting to Special Occasions   314

Chapter 16   Increasing the Effectiveness of Problem-Solving Discussions   326

Preface

Welcome to the newest edition of *The Challenge of Effective Speaking*. As it was when it was originally written, the goal of this leading textbook is to share with students a well-tested process for effective preparation that enables them to quickly master public speaking skills. The speech preparation process that serves as the basic framework for this book has six Action Steps:

1. Determine a speech goal that meets audience needs.
2. Develop a strategy for audience adaptation.
3. Gather information.
4. Organize and develop your material in a way that is best suited to your audience.
5. Create visual aids to clarify, emphasize, and dramatize verbal information.
6. Practice speech wording and delivery.

As students complete each Action Step, they learn and master a variety of skills that they will be able to draw upon when they leave campus and encounter professional or community occasions requiring them to speak.

Speakers in the twenty-first century face numerous new challenges as they seek to competently communicate in public settings, and textbooks designed to instruct novice speakers need to address these challenges. So we are excited to present you with a 12th edition that clarifies, updates, and refines the speech preparation process to reflect the speaking challenges likely to be encountered by today's students when they move outside of the classroom. The changes to this text reflect not only our own perceptions but, more importantly, reflect the insightful feedback we have received from our colleagues across the country. In this 12th edition, you will find these special features:

Improved Skill Development Activities That Coach Students in Effective Speech Preparation and Are Available Online. This edition provides revised and expanded Speech Preparation Activities related to each of the six Action Steps. By completing each activity, students master a systematic process that enables them to create and present effective speeches. Each Speech Preparation Activity is accompanied by an example of the activity as prepared by a real student in a beginning speaking course. Students can complete these activities online using Speech Builder Express on the Challenge of Effective Speaking Web site at Wadsworth's Communication Café. Completing activities online through Speech Builder Express creates efficiencies by enabling students to use the output of one activity as the input to a subsequent activity.

Greater Emphasis on the Effective Use of Electronic Resources. The text provides expanded and updated practical information on locating and utilizing electronic resources and the criteria for evaluating the quality of information found online. In addition, specific guidelines for creating and using computer-generated visual aids are explained.

New Sample Speeches by Today's Students Are Available to Be Read, Seen and Heard, and Critiqued. *The Challenge of Effective Speaking* was the first text to use real student speeches to exemplify good speaking practice. It was also the first book to offer author comments and critique. In this edition, we have expanded and updated this feature, gathering new sample speeches, examples, and topic suggestions that reflect contemporary interests and concerns. We have also specifically chosen to present speeches by speakers who represent the diversity of students in today's college classrooms. Students can use the Challenge of Effective Speaking CD-ROM to view the speeches, submit their own critique, and compare their critiques to the critiques of experts. In the text itself, students can study outlines and audience adaptation plans for the speeches, read transcripts of the speeches, and learn from the analyses of the speeches provided.

Greatly Expanded and Early Coverage of Speech Apprehension. Because today's students arrive on campus with little or no formal experience speaking in front of a group, many are unprepared to understand or cope with the anxiety associated with speaking in public. So in this edition we have increased the discussion of speaking apprehension. The text provides an overview of the research findings on the symptoms and causes of public speaking apprehension and presents strategies that can be used to effectively manage apprehension, including techniques for visualization, systematic desensitization, communication reorientation, and skills training.

Updated References Reflect Contemporary Scholarship. In addition to providing contemporary examples drawn from both student and professional speakers, the concepts are presented and discussed in light of recent research.

Electronic Learning. At the end of each chapter students are directed to specific learning aids that are specific to *The Challenge of Effective Speaking* and available to them on the companion CD-ROM or on the Challenge of Effective Speaking Web site. These activities include chapter concept quizzes, a digital glossary, Speech Preparation Activities, and InfoTrac College Edition exercises related to important concepts in each chapter.

Highlights of Changes in Sections and Chapters

The text has retained the basic organization of the previous edition with one exception: Audience Adaptation (Chapter 8 in the previous edition) has been moved to Chapter 5 because attention to audience needs is important throughout the preparation process. In addition, some material has been streamlined, and other material completely revised. To sum up the changes by section:

Part One, Orientation: This three-chapter introduction, giving students a solid base for making a first speech and listening to the speeches of their classmates, has been revised throughout.

Part Two, Principles: A more complete and cohesive approach to preparing speeches that are adapted to specific audiences has been provided. These eight chapters develop the six speech preparation Action Steps in such a way that by the end of Part Two students are well prepared to give their first major speech.

Part Three, Informative and Persuasive Speaking: This section has been revised throughout.

Part Four, Adapting to Other Occasions and Formats: Chapter 16, Increasing the Effectiveness of Problem-Solving Discussions has been completely revised.

Although the entire book has been updated and revised, the following chapters have been revised most extensively:

- **Chapter 1, Introduction to Public Speaking,** has a more complete section on critical and creative thinking.

- **Chapter 2, Overcoming Nervousness through Effective Speech Planning,** has been retitled and totally revised. The first section, Public Speaking Apprehension, has more complete sections on symptoms and causes, managing apprehension, and techniques for reducing apprehension. The second section, Developing an Effective Speech Plan, provides a preliminary explanation of the content of the six Action Steps. The third section, Preparing a Narrative/Personal Experience Speech, suggests an assignment for an ice-breaker speech that enables students to begin to put the Action Steps into practice.

- **Chapter 3, Effective Listening,** gives greater emphasis to the sections on Analyzing a Speech and Giving Postspeech Feedback.

- **Chapter 4, Determining a Speech Goal That Meets Audience Needs,** has been retitled to give greater emphasis to considering audience needs during the process of determining a speech goal. After Identifying Topics, Analyzing the Audience, and Considering the Setting, the final section, Writing a Speech Goal, focuses on using audience analysis information in the process. The student is asked to complete Speech Preparation Action Step Activities that lead the student through this stage of preparation.

- **Chapter 5, Adapting to Audiences** (Chapter 8 in the previous edition), has been moved to an earlier position to help students utilize audience information in all aspects of the speech preparation process. Students see how information from their audience analysis can be used to help them in developing adaptation during the remainder of the preparation process.

- **Chapter 6, Researching Information for Your Speech,** has been revised to include even more information and features using online resources as well as traditional ones to help students find sources for their speeches. Students are asked to find material by using different sources, with special emphasis on a hands-on approach to accessing information electronically through the school library's database and on the Internet.

- **Chapter 11, Practicing Delivery,** has a completely revised section on Rehearsal. The chapter also contains a new speech.

- **Chapter 12, Principles and Practices of Informative Speaking,** has two new speeches.

- **Chapter 13, Principles of Persuasive Speaking,** has a new speech.

- **Chapter 14, Practicing Persuasive Speaking Skills,** has a completely revised section on Reasoning with Audiences and also has a new speech.

- **Chapter 16, Increasing the Effectiveness of Problem-Solving Discussions,** has been completely revised to include Characteristics of Effective Problem-Solving Discussion and Member Responsibilities.

New Resources for Students

With this edition, we feel we have achieved the most outstanding array of supplements ever to assist in making this course as meaningful and effective as possible. All of these student resources are new to this edition. Please contact your local Wadsworth representative for an examination copy, contact our Academic Resource Center at 1-800-423-0563, or visit us at http://communication.wadsworth.com/

- **Challenge of Effective Speaking CD-ROM** featuring access to Speech Builder Express(™). The CD-ROM that accompanies each new student text features 12 sample student speeches (most of which are featured as models in the text) under Speech Interactive. All but one of the student speakers featured under Speech Interactive on the CD-ROM were recent students of ours and used this textbook and its featured Action Step Activities as their primary speech preparation guidance. The CD-ROM is also a gateway to four online resources that are integrated throughout the text. These include:
  1. Chapter-by-chapter learning aids including chapter outlines and self-tests at the Challenge of Effective Speaking Web site;
  2. Speech Builder Express, an online interactive version of the Action Step Activities. This program leads students through the process of organizing and outlining a speech. The outlines created in this program may be saved, printed, and/or submitted online to instructors;
  3. InfoTrac® College Edition (ICE), an online research database that students can use to complete InfoTrac assignments, that are integrated throughout the text, and to research speech topics;
  4. A tutorial and preview of Thomson Learning WebTutor.

- **InfoTrac College Edition.** A fully searchable, online database provides students with access to complete articles from more than 900 scholarly and popular periodicals, updated daily, and dating back four years. This database allows students to complete their speech research using contemporary articles from all the major media. A four-month subscription to InfoTrac College Edition is included in the purchase price of this new text, and exercises for using InfoTrac College Edition are integrated into each chapter of the new edition. Look for the InfoTrac College Edition logo to signal the InfoTrac College Edition feature.

- *InfoTrac College Edition Student Workbook for Communication 2.0,* written by Nancy Rost Goulden of Kansas State University, can be bundled with the text and features extensive individual and group activities that utilize InfoTrac College Edition. The workbook also includes guidelines for students on maximizing this resource.

- **WebTutor for WebCT or Blackboard.** WebTutor is a Web-based learning companion to this text. Features include presentation of chapter objectives and lessons; flashcards with audio, still images, and video; exercises that can be downloaded, completed, and returned to the instructor; discussion topics integrated within the chapter; online review questions and tutorials; links to real-world locations for timely information; real-time chat; calendar of syllabus information; email connections (using existing email accounts); and an announcement board. For a demonstration of this product please visit the Web site http://webtutor.thomsonlearning.com. This state-of-the-art class management and study tool is available bundled with the text, as a stand-alone, or via online subscription.

- **Student Workbook.** Written by John Matteson of Los Angeles City College, this study guide complements and expands students' understanding of the book. It includes an interactive summary of each chapter, all of the Speech Preparation Action Step Activities, multiple copies of speech evaluation forms included in the text, a research journal, and outlining activities and worksheets. This resource can be bundled with the text or sold separately.

- *A Guide to the Basic Course for ESL Students,* by Esther Yook of Mary Washington College. This saleable item can be bundled with the text and is designed to assist the nonnative speaker. It features Frequently Asked Questions (FAQs), helpful URLs, and strategies for accent management and overcoming speech apprehension.

- **Service Learning in Communication Studies: A Handbook,** by Rick Isaacson, San Francisco State University, Bruce Dorries, Radford University, and Kevin Brown, Montana State University. This handbook is an invaluable resource for students in the basic course that integrates or is planning to integrate a service learning component. The handbook provides guidelines for connecting service learning work with classroom concepts and advice for working effectively with agencies and organizations. It also provides model forms and reports and a directory of online resources.

New and Proven Resources for Teachers

- *Annotated Instructor's Edition,* written by Leonard Assante of Volunteer State Community College, couples the student text with extensive marginal annotations for the instructor to create an invaluable resource. Significantly enhanced for this new edition, this is a key resource for the first-time teacher, the adjunct, and the experienced. Marginal annotations include additional teaching strategies; class activities including short public speaking assignments; discussion topics; cross references; helpful URLs; and suggestions for strategic integration of our leading supplements program.

- *Instructor's Resource Manual,* by Leonard Assante, and Joshua Gregory of Pasadena City College, includes instructional strategies, sample syllabi, suggested grading criteria, chapter summaries, chapter-specific activities, possible answers to the InfoTrac College Edition activities included in the text, multiple speech evaluation checklists, and a test bank.

- **Multimedia Presentation and Lecture Tool,** by Linda Loomis Steck of Indiana University–South Bend, is text-specific software designed to work with the PowerPoint presentation program and is available on a cross-platform CD-ROM. All of the student speeches featured on Challenge of Effective Speaking CD-ROM and selected professional speeches are embedded into this outstanding presentation tool. If you have a computer and LCD display, you do not need a television and VCR to show the sample speeches in class.

- **ExamView.** Create, deliver, and customize tests and study guides (both print and online) in minutes with this easy-to-use assessment and tutorial system. ExamView offers both a Quick Test Wizard and an Online Test Wizard that guide you step-by-step through the process of creating tests, while the unique "WYSIWYG" capability allows you to see the test you are creating on the screen exactly as it will print or display online. You can build tests of up to 250 questions using up to 12 question types. Using ExamView's complete word-processing capabilities, you can enter an unlimited number of new questions or edit existing questions.

- *The Teaching Assistant's Guide to the Basic Course,* by Katherine G. Hendrix of The University of Memphis. This guidebook is designed for the new communication teacher or for those who want to refresh their approach. Based on leading communication teacher training programs, the guide covers general teaching and course management topics, as well as specific strategies for communication instruction, such as providing effective feedback on performance, managing sensitive class discussions, and conducting mock interviews. This guide is available free to adopters of the text and as a saleable item to other interested parties.

- **CNN Videos** help stimulate class discussions. The series of CNN videos, with video segments keyed to material in the text, is available to qualifying adopters. Ask your Wadsworth/Thomson Learning representative for more information. CNN Today: Public Speaking Volume I includes Clinton's "apology" speech, a speech from the Dali Lama, and Queen Elizabeth II's address on the death of Princess Diana.

- **Wadsworth Video Library** is a resource of more than thirty videos, including six volumes of "Student Speeches for Critique and Analysis." This series features sample narrative, self-introduction, informative, persuasive, impromptu, and invitational student speeches. Volume 4 includes all of the speeches featured on the Challenge of Effective Speaking CD-ROM.

How to Use InfoTrac College Edition

InfoTrac College Edition is a fully searchable online university library containing full-length articles from more than 600 well-known magazines, scholarly publications, professional association pamphlets, and encyclopedias.

To access InfoTrac College Edition, simply log on to www.infotrac-college.com/wadsworth. Enter your account ID number, which came with a copy of your text, and begin your search. If you did not receive a password, please contact your local Wadsworth representative or call our Academic Resource Center at 1-800-423-0563. You can use InfoTrac College Edition to search in three ways:

- **Subject Guide.** Subject Guide pages display every indexed topic in which the word you typed in the search box appears, as well as the number of references indexed under each topic. This lets you see exactly what matches your search before you view the citations and enables you to choose a single aspect or topic.

- **Key Words.** Entering one or more key words will give you the broadest range of citations. Literally any citation that includes your word or words in the title and/or abstract will appear. This is helpful if you have a very specific search word, but less helpful than the Subject Guide if your topic word is broad.

- **PowerTrac.** PowerTrac lets you create complex search expressions that combine different search methods, such as author and topic, or find articles from a particular publication and issue date.

Search Tips

1. Be as specific as possible with search words, so you get citations that are useful to you.

2. If you don't get a lot of matches, try different words. For instance, many articles use "public speaking" as the Subject Guide, but many other articles using "communication" as the subject might also be useful in speech preparation.

3. After you open up an article, use the Link feature to get a list of related articles and topics.

4. When your search results are too broad, use the Limit Search button. This button will enable you to limit the search, for instance, to within a specified range of dates, making your material more timely.

5. Please don't wait until the last minute to do your research with InfoTrac College Editon. As with any other library system, it takes time to get to know InfoTrac College Edition and the many ways it can help you do research.

Acknowledgments

Although we are responsible for what appears in this book, the content reflects the thoughts of a great many people. We gratefully acknowledge the students who contributed speeches and outlines to this edition. We also thank the many instructors who offered feedback and insights gained through their use of the 11th edition. And our special thanks goes to those who prepared detailed reviews of the previous edition as well as the final draft manuscript of this edition. Their names are listed inside the front cover of this book.

In addition, we appreciate the special assistance of Rolland Petrello of Moorpark College, Greg Poff of Solano College, and Gary Dreibelbis of Solano College in gathering sample speeches from their students, including Charone Frankel whose persuasive speech is featured in Chapter 14. Thanks also to Len Assante for creating a completely revised and updated *Annotated Instructor's Edition* and *Instructor's Resource Manual,* to Joshua Gregory of Pasadena City College for updating and revising the test bank, to Linda Loomis Steck who continues to work her PowerPoint magic and has created another outstanding Multimedia Presentation and Lecture Tool; to John Matteson of Los Angeles City College for revising the *Student Workbook,* to Nancy Goulden of Kansas State University for authoring the *InfoTrac College Edition Workbooks for Public Speaking and Communication;* and finally to Ken Sherwood who patiently worked with us on conceiving, creating, and testing Speech Builder Express.

We would also like to express our gratitude to Deirdre Anderson, executive editor; Cathy Linberg, project manager; and Mele Alusa, editorial assistant; as well as all of the other people at Wadsworth who were involved in this project; to Cecile Joyner of The Cooper Company who oversaw the production of this book; and to manuscript editor Kay Mikel.

The Challenge of Effective Speaking

CHAPTER 1

Introduction to Public Speaking

Joel Gordon

All the great speakers were bad speakers at first.
—Ralph Waldo Emerson, "Power," *The Conduct of Life,* 1860

Marquez was talking with Bill and Glenna about the movie they had seen. When Bill asked him what he thought of it, Marquez paused for a moment and then cited two reasons he thought the movie failed to portray characters realistically.

As Heather and Gavin were eating dinner, Heather tried to explain to Gavin why she was upset with the attention he was paying to Susan.

At the monthly meeting of the engineering department, Nancy Bauer, a purchasing clerk, presented a five-minute overview of how to fill out the new online requisition form all engineers would be using when ordering parts for newly designed machines.

Tom Simmons, candidate for Council, was invited to speak at the University Forum. When he was introduced, he presented his views on the role of government in education.

In each of the four situations presented above, one person is taking time to present his or her ideas to others. Read these short examples again. How is each situation similar? Different? You may have noticed that the first two situations seem like "conversations" whereas the last two seem more formal, more like **speeches**—oral presentations usually given without interruptions. Yet, if you look closer, you will notice that in each of the four situations one person has a clearly determined goal in mind—that goal is to get one or more other people to understand, believe, or act in a particular way. So, in this way at least, all four situations are similar.

Now you might be thinking, "But in the last two, Tom and Nancy knew that they were expected to speak to a group—they prepared ahead, and then gave a speech." OK. But isn't it likely that Heather tried to prepare ahead as well? She may have been thinking about Gavin's attentiveness to Susan for a long time. She probably spent time mulling over what she could say to Gavin, how she could say it, and when would be the best time to say it. Although this situation may seem less formal, Heather's remarks to Gavin draw on many skills normally associated with public speaking. Notice that Marquez even paused a moment to organize his thoughts before giving his opinion about the movie.

The point? This course focuses on developing your public speaking skills, but you will be able to draw on these skills across a variety of settings including work-related meetings, personal business transactions (such as negotiating to buy a new car), and personal relationships. In short, practicing public speaking skills will help you present your ideas more clearly and more persuasively in any setting.

In this chapter we begin our study by looking at the importance of public speaking skills for empowering people. By describing the communication process that occurs during a speech, we will see that effective speaking is an audience-centered activity. Then we will explore the challenges speakers face when communicating to

speeches oral presentations usually given without interruptions

diverse audience members, using critical thinking skills to guide their message development, and facing their ethical responsibilities. Finally you will see that effective speaking, thankfully, is a learned activity, one that this book is dedicated to helping you master.

Public Speaking Skills Empower Us

You may be taking this course because it is required, but we believe this may be the single most important course you take during your college career. Now that is a bold statement. Why do we say this? In this course you will develop your ability to clearly express your ideas and thoughts in front of other people. Good public speaking skills are empowering, putting you in a better position to advocate for your interests and to control what happens to you. Public speaking empowers in four ways.

First, mastering public speaking skills empowers you to communicate complex ideas and information in a way that all members of the audience can understand. Many of us have had the experience of understanding something but being unable to clearly explain it to others. Most of us have had an unfortunate experience with a teacher who "talked over our heads." The teacher understood the material but was unable to clearly express it to us. When we can clearly express our ideas, we are more likely to share them. When others understand our ideas, they learn from us.

Second, mastering public speaking skills empowers you to influence the attitudes and behavior of other people. We seem to be trying constantly to influence others. Have you ever tried to get a classmate to loan you her notes? Or tried to get an airline to change a reservation without changing the fee? Have you tried to get your boss to give you an extra shift at work? Or tried to get a professor to change a grade you received? When we thoughtfully articulate the reasons for our positions and requests, others are more likely to comply with our wishes. Public speaking skills equip us to fashion arguments that others may find compelling.

Third, mastering public speaking skills empowers you to achieve your career goals. For instance, recent studies show that for almost any job one of the most highly sought-after skills in new hires is oral communication skills.[1] So, whether you aspire to a career in business, industry, government, education, or almost any other field you can name, communication skills are likely to be a prerequisite to your success.

Effective speaking may be even more important once you have started work in your chosen career. Most jobs require people periodically to present oral reports, proposals, to respond to questions, and to train coworkers. Although you might be hired on the basis of your technical competency, your ability to earn promotions will depend on your ability to communicate what you know to others, including your boss, your clients, and your colleagues in other departments.

Fourth, public speaking skills empower you to participate in our democratic processes. Free speech is a hallmark of our democracy. The strategies and policies our government adopts are a direct result of the debate that occurs across the nation and in our executive, legislative, and judicial branches of government. When you are equipped with sound public speaking skills, you will have the confidence to speak out in town hall meetings and in other settings and voice your ideas on important public issues.

Our bold statement about the importance of what you will learn in this course is not made lightly. Whether you are informing, persuading, working within your career, or participating as a free citizen, speech-making skills will enable you to take control of your life.

The Public Speaking Process Is Audience Centered

More than two thousand years ago, Aristotle observed that "the audience is the end and object of the speech." That is, the eloquence of a speaker's words are irrelevant if the words are not understood or do not affect the people in the audience. As speakers, we prepare and deliver our speeches with the firm intention of achieving a specific goal. The audience of one or more other people have the freedom to accept or reject our goal. Thus, a speech is effective if the people in the audience listen to it, understand it, and act on their understanding in accordance with the speaker's goal.

To further understand why the public speaking process is audience centered, let's examine each of the elements of the communication process during a speech. This process involves a speaker, a message (the speech), a channel, an audience, a context, noise, and audience feedback.

Speaker

The **speaker** is the source or originator of the communication message. What a speaker discusses and the language used to express those ideas depend on the experiences that have formed that speaker's ideas, feelings, and mood. For instance, a woman from Mothers Against Drunk Driving (MADD) may be compelled to speak on behalf of the organization because her daughter was killed in a head-on crash involving a drunk driver. Likewise, a man may be motivated to speak out in support of a strike during contract negotiations because he has worked in nonunion settings.

speaker the source or originator of the communication message

Speech

A speech is a **message** presented to an audience through words, sound, and action that contains ideas and feelings selected and organized by the speaker but understood and interpreted by each individual member of the audience. The process the speaker uses to transform ideas and feelings into words, sounds, and actions that make sense to the speaker is called **encoding**. The process audience members use to transform speech messages back into ideas and feelings that make sense to the audience members is called **decoding**. When a speech is effective, the speech message the speaker encodes is similar to the speech message audience members decode. For example, in a speech on child poverty, you say, "Throughout the world, large numbers of children are starving." After listening to what you have said, a member of your audience may understand that "in all countries, vast numbers of young boys and girls are dying because they do not get enough food to sustain them."

message ideas and feelings presented to an audience through words, sound, and action symbols selected and organized by the speaker and interpreted by members of the audience

encoding the process the speaker uses to transform ideas and feelings into words, sounds, and actions

decoding the process the audience uses to transform messages back into ideas and feelings

You have been communicating for so long that you probably do not think consciously about either encoding or decoding processes. Nevertheless, these processes do occur. When your verbal and nonverbal messages are clear and meaningful and the members of your audience are able to share your intended meanings, then your speech will be effective.

Speech messages are usually complex and often lengthy, so they need to be carefully organized so audience members are able to follow the speaker's train of thought easily. Most of us are thankful when speakers carefully state a goal, enumerate the main points, and offer a conclusion that summarizes the message.

Because the processes of encoding and decoding messages are at the heart of public speaking and listening to speeches, the skills you will learn in this course are directed toward improving how you form speech messages.

Channel

channel   both the route traveled by the message and the means of transportation

The **channel** is both the route traveled by the message and the means of transportation. Spoken words are carried by sound waves; facial expressions, gestures, and movement are carried by light waves. In addition, public speaking may occur in person or be delivered over radio or television. Use of radio or television to broadcast a speech introduces different variables that the speaker must understand and adapt to.

Audience

audience   a specific group of people to whom the speech message is directed

The **audience** is a specific group of people to whom the speech message is directed. A central challenge that every speaker faces, then, is to understand the members of the audience and to fashion a speech message that is likely to be understood and accepted by each member. Because most audiences are composed of diverse members, speakers begin by understanding the characteristics of their audience. Then they must work hard to identify a goal that is appropriate to the makeup of a particular audience. Speakers are furthered challenged to choose examples, illustrations, and other information that audience members can identify with. Finally, speakers must be willing to adapt their own presentation style to the needs of their audience members.

Context

context   the interrelated conditions of communication

physical setting   the location, time of day, light, temperature, distance between communicators, and seating arrangements

The **context** is the setting in which a speech is presented that affects the expectations of the audience, the meaning audience members receive, and their subsequent behavior. One aspect of context is the **physical setting** for the speech—the location, time of day, light, temperature, distance between speaker and audience, and seating arrangements. For instance, a speech may be presented in a room where the speaker stands on a raised platform set at a distance from the audience. Or a speech may be presented in a room with no platform and no podium where the speaker is free to wander among audience members while speaking.

historical setting   previous communication episodes

A second aspect of context that affects the audience is the **historical setting**. The historical setting includes events that may have occurred prior to the speech that are relevant to the issue or the speaker, previous speeches given by the speaker with which audience members are familiar, or other encounters the audience members have had with the speaker. For example, a speech on police–community cooperation by the local president of the Fraternal Order of Police is likely to be received differently if there is a recent history of police corruption.

psychological setting   the manner in which people perceive both themselves and those with whom they communicate

A third aspect of context that affects communication is the **psychological setting**—the moods, feelings, attitudes, and beliefs of the speaker and individual audience members that affect how a speech message is sent or received. It is not only the historical context of slavery that can make speaking about racism difficult, it is also the strong feelings, beliefs, and attitudes speakers and audience members have about these issues.

cultural setting   the beliefs, values, attitudes, meanings, social hierarchies, religion, notions of time, and roles of a group of people

A final aspect of context that is important to public speaking is the **cultural setting**, the beliefs, values, attitudes, meanings, social hierarchies, religion, notions of time, and roles of a group of people.[2] Historically, public speaking practices in the United States have been rooted in Anglo European culture because most early American immigrants came from Western European countries. So, from political speech making to personal introductions, the behavior that has been expected, seen as effective, and taught in speech courses developed from our historical association with Europe in general and England in particular. Today, the U.S. population is more diverse, providing a mosaic of cultural backgrounds. Consequently, the expectations audience members have of speakers and that speakers have of audience members may differ. For example, cultural groups may differ in how and how much feedback is pro-

Although many people think of speeches as formal affairs, speech-making skills are relevant to many kinds of communication settings.

vided to speakers during the speech. Some cultural groups believe it is impolite for audience members to verbalize feedback during a speech, but other cultural groups expect audience members to offer verbal encouragement to speakers.

Noise

The audience's ability to interpret, understand, or respond to the message of a speech may be limited by **noise**—any stimulus that interferes with sending or understanding the speech message. Much of your success as a speaker depends on how you cope with external, internal, and semantic noises.

External noises are the sights, sounds, and other stimuli that draw people's attention away from listening to you. For instance, your audience's attention may be drawn away from your presentation because of a sudden siren whine or the momentary dimming of the lights.

Internal noises are random thoughts and feelings that interfere with meaning. Have you ever found yourself daydreaming during a speech? Perhaps you let your thoughts wander to the good time you had at a party the night before or to the argument you had with a friend that morning. If you have tuned out the speaker's words and tuned in a daydream or a past conversation, then you have created internal noise.

Semantic noises are unintended alternate meanings for the symbols decoded by audience members. Suppose you say in your speech that many companies are liberal, meaning generous, to immigrants. If audience members associate the word *liberal* with a political philosophy, they will probably miss your meaning. Meaning depends on personal experience, and others may at times decode a word or phrase differently from the way the speaker intended. When this happens, semantic noise is interfering with the attempt to communicate.

Feedback

As you speak, members of your audience provide you with **feedback**—verbal and nonverbal responses to the messages your audience is receiving. Feedback helps you assess whether your audience is paying attention, understands what you are saying, and/or agrees with your points. If the feedback indicates that your message was not received, was received incorrectly, or was misinterpreted, you can rephrase your message to help audience members understand what you meant.

Public speaking situations differ in the amount of feedback that speakers receive from the audience. A televised speech provides zero feedback, because the speaker is unable to gauge how the viewing audience perceives what is being said. A formal address given in person to a large audience provides the speaker with nonverbal feedback such as nodding, quizzical looks, and smiles. During an informal talk given to a small group, audience members may interact directly, asking the speaker to repeat information or asking questions to clarify what has been said.

Exhibit 1.1 illustrates the speech-making process between a speaker and one audience member. The speaker has a thought or a feeling that the person wants to share. The nature of that thought or feeling is created, shaped, and affected by the speaker's total field of experience, including such specific factors as values, attitudes, beliefs, knowledge, culture, gender, environment, experiences, occupation, and interests. To communicate, the speaker selects words and actions, organizes them into a coherent speech message, and transmits the message via appropriate channels, usually sound (speech) and light (nonverbal behavior).

The speech message that is transmitted may or may not be distorted by noise. Individual audience members receive the speech message, but how each interprets it depends on the individual's unique total field of experience. On interpreting the message, audience members may send verbal and nonverbal reactions or feedback mes-

noise any stimulus that gets in the way of sharing meaning

external noises the sights, sounds, and other stimuli that draw people's attention away from the intended meaning

internal noises the thoughts and feelings that interfere with meaning

semantic noises alternate meanings aroused by a speaker's symbols

feedback verbal and nonverbal responses to messages

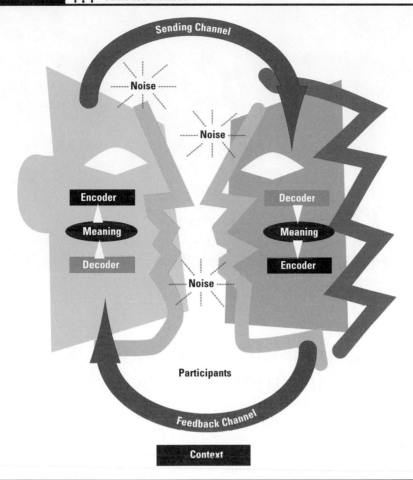

sages that enable the speaker to understand how the audience is receiving the speech. The physical, historical, psychological, and cultural context in which the speech occurs affects how speakers form messages, how audience members interpret them, and how feedback is sent and understood.

During a public address, this process is occurring between the speaker and each individual audience member. As a result, the communication process in public speaking settings is especially complex. While some people focus on the speaker's message, others may be distracted by noise, whether external (the hum of the air conditioning), internal (preoccupation with personal matters), or semantic (a reaction to the speaker's choice of words). Furthermore, all the participants bring their unique perspectives to the communication transaction. Less skillful speakers are oblivious to this complexity and are likely to be misunderstood. Skillful speakers carefully attend to the feedback they receive from individuals in the audience and quickly adapt their words and nonverbal behavior until they are confident that their listeners have received the message meanings they intended.

A good source of information about local demographics can be gleaned from the U.S. census data.

Alex Wong/Newsmakers

Public Speaking Challenges Us to Consider Audience Diversity

diversity differences between and among people that affect nearly every aspect of the communication process

Diversity—differences between and among people—affects nearly every aspect of the speech-making process. Audiences are diverse across a number of characteristics, and speakers must recognize this and tailor their speech messages so they will be effective with different audience members.

Lee Gardenswartz and Anita Rowe developed a category scheme for understanding diversity in work organizations.[3] Part of their scheme is useful for helping us think about audience diversity. First, according to Gardenswartz and Rowe, audience members have diverse personalities, which affect how they are likely to respond to speech messages. Second, audience members can differ from one another in age, race, gender, physical abilities, and ethnicity. These internal characteristics are difficult for the individual to change and affect how individuals think and communicate. Third, audience members can differ from each other in social and life experiences, such as marital and parental status, educational background, work experience, religion, income level, and personal and recreational habits. Therefore, audience members differ in their ability to understand or appreciate the information or arguments a speaker makes. To learn more about cultural differences in approaches to persuasion, see the InfoTrac College Edition exercise at the end of this chapter.

Effective public speaking is audience oriented, so you will want to adapt your message to your audience. This becomes a greater challenge when most of the people in the audience differ from you and others with whom your are familiar. Effective speakers learn about the diversity of their audience and prepare their messages with the mix in mind. Our goal is to help you effectively communicate with your audience, regardless of how diverse it is. In many places in this text, we will discuss strategies that will help you understand the diversity of your audience.

Public Speaking Challenges Us to Use Critical and Creative Thinking

Nichole: I've got to figure out a way to make this seem clearer.

Amy: I want to find the arguments that will convince my husband to take care of the kids while I finish my degree at night.

Manuel: Dawn's plan for raising the money just doesn't sound right to me, but I haven't been able to pinpoint what's wrong.

Each of these people is struggling with an issue that requires critical and creative thinking. **Critical thinking** is an analytical and evaluative process using logic or reasoning to present information in a way that is likely to provide understanding, change a belief, or uncover problems in another person's informative or persuasive message. For example, Nichole is looking for means of clarification; Amy is taking the initiative to provide a logical approach; and Manuel must be able to analyze what Dawn has said to uncover any potential weaknesses. **Creative thinking** is the ability to transcend traditional ideas and find new ideas, forms, methods, and interpretations. For instance, Nichole and Amy are evaluating, but they are also seeking something different.

Every day each of us faces problems that require us to think critically and creatively. In your study of public speaking, you will learn aspects of critical and creative thinking and how to apply them in your own speeches. As you prepare speeches, you will formulate goals, define concepts, ask questions, gather data, organize information, analyze information, put ideas together, and evaluate your own and others' arguments and information. All of these activities help to develop critical thinking. You will also be challenged to develop and express your ideas creatively so that you capture and hold the attention of others.

Throughout this book, you will learn specific skills that will help you improve your critical thinking, and you will have opportunities to test your critical thinking ability. In addition, you will learn methods for creatively expressing your ideas so that they are vivid and compelling to others.

> **critical thinking** an analytical and evaluative process using logic or reasoning to present information in a way that is likely to provide understanding, change a belief, or uncover problems in another person's informative or persuasive message
>
> **creative thinking** the ability to transcend traditional ideas and find new ideas, forms, methods, and interpretations

Public Speaking Challenges Us to Behave Ethically

Whether we look at the writings of ancient rhetorical scholars like Plato or Aristotle or modern rhetoricians like James McCrosky, we see that all students of public speaking stress the importance of ethical responsibility. Today as in times past we expect a speaker to hold to a standard of ethical behavior. So, regardless of whether the setting for your speeches is a classroom, a boardroom, the campaign trail, or the floor of a legislative body, you have an ethical responsibility to your listeners. In this section we will discuss the nature of ethical issues and offer guidelines for you to follow in your speaking.

Ethical issues, according to Richard Johannesen, a noted communication scholar in the field of ethics, focus "on degrees of rightness and wrongness in human behavior."[4] Although an ethical theory does not tell us what to do in any given situation, it does tell us what to consider in making our decisions. It directs our attention to the reasons that determine the rightness or wrongness of any act.

> **ethical issues** focus on degrees of rightness and wrongness in human behavior

A person cannot choose and act rationally without some explicit or implicit ethical system. Jimmie Carter has always been praised for his ethical standards.

What is considered ethical is to some extent a personal matter, yet we still expect society to uphold certain standards that can help us with our personal value judgments. As Carl Wellman, a noted philosopher, has pointed out, a person cannot choose and act rationally without some explicit or implicit ethical system.[5] Anyone discovered engaging in what a group believes to be immoral behavior is likely to be admonished by that society or group through social means. Families, schools, and religions all share the responsibility of helping individuals develop ethical standards that can be applied to specific situations. Your personal ethic is based on your belief in and acceptance of what is considered moral by the communities or groups with which you most closely identify. When you behave ethically, you voluntarily act in a manner that complies with expected behavior. Why do people internalize morals and develop a personal ethic? Because most of us regard ourselves as accountable for our conduct, and even, to some extent, for our attitudes and character, and blame ourselves when we fall short of these ideal principles.[6] When we communicate, we are constantly challenged with choices that have ethical implications.

To understand how ethical standards should guide our speech messages, we must recognize the ethical principles guiding our behavior. The following ethical guidelines are fundamental to responsible public speaking.

1. **Tell the truth.** Of all the guidelines, this one may be the most important. "An honest person is widely regarded as a moral person, and honesty is a central concept to ethics as the foundation for a moral life."[7] An audience that consents to listen to you is extending its trust to you and expects that you will be honest. If during your speech people believe you are lying to them, or if they later learn

that you have lied, they will reject you and your ideas. But telling the truth means more than avoiding deliberate, outright lies. If you are not sure whether information is true, don't use it until you have verified it.

2. **Keep your information in perspective.** Many people get so excited about their information that they exaggerate its importance. Although a little exaggeration might be accepted as a normal product of human nature, when the exaggeration is perceived as distortion, most people will consider it the same as lying. For instance, suppose you discover that capital punishment has lowered the murder rate in a few states, but in many other states the statistics are inconclusive. If, in your speech, you assert that statistics show that murder rates are lower in states with capital punishment, you would be distorting the evidence. It may be difficult to distinguish a clear line between mild exaggeration and gross distortion, but most people see any exaggeration as unethical.

3. **Resist personal attacks against those who oppose your ideas.** There seems to be almost universal agreement that name-calling and other irrelevant personal attacks are unethical and detrimental to a speaker's trustworthiness. Listeners recognize that such tactics do not enhance the speaker's argument and abuse the privileged status the speaker enjoys.

4. **Give the source for all derogatory information.** Where ideas originate is often as important as the ideas themselves, especially when a statement is damning. If you are going to discuss wrongdoing by individuals or organizations, or condemn an idea by relying on the words or ideas of others, provide the sources of your information and arguments. Moreover, since the mention of wrongdoing can bring a speaker to the edge of what is legally defined as slander, you should be aware of the legal as well as the ethical pitfalls of making damning statements without proof.

5. **Fully credit the sources of quotations and paraphrases.** When people are "under the gun," there is a temptation to use parts of other people's work without citation. But doing so, even in small amounts, is a form of plagiarism. **Plagiarism** means to steal and pass off the ideas and words of another as one's own or to use a created production without crediting the source. In addition to being unethical, plagiarism in many contexts is also illegal and can lead to lawsuits and monetary damages. Student speakers who plagiarize risk failing an assignment, the course, or being suspended from school. If you use the exact words of another person, you must indicate that you are quoting directly. For instance, if, in a speech, we used the definition of ethical issues given at the beginning of this section, we would say, "According to Richard Johannesen, in his book *Ethics in Human Communication*, ethical issues focus on, and we quote, "degrees of rightness and wrongness in human behavior.""

plagiarism to steal and pass off the ideas and words of another as one's own or to use a created production without crediting the source

Throughout this book, we will stress the importance of working with a number of different sources of information. Information that is general knowledge can be used without citing a source. In contrast, information that is derived from a single source should be credited. At various places in this text, we will discuss commonly accepted ethical principles for public speaking as they relate to specific parts of the speech preparation and presentation process. We will consider more specific ethical questions as we discuss topic selection, audience analysis, selection and use of supporting information, construction and use of visual aids, speech language, delivery, reasoning, use of emotional appeals, establishing credibility, and refutation.

Some of the ethical principles we will present are drawn from what is commonly accepted to be ethical behavior in the United States. Some principles come from what experts tell us will lead to trust and promote healthy relationships with our audience.

People aren't born knowing how to speak competently. Public speaking is a learned activity.

As we discuss ethics, we will note where standards differ across cultures and between men and women and how these difference lead to alternative ethics. A Reflect on Ethics box toward the end of each chapter will present a situation that challenges you to think about the ethical responsibilities of speakers.

Public Speaking Competence Is a Learned Activity

communication competence
the impression that communication behavior is appropriate and effective

Professor Brian Spitzberg defines **communication competence** as the perception that communication behavior is appropriate and effective.[8] Applying this definition to public speaking, you will be perceived as competent if your speeches are appropriate for the situation and effective in achieving their goals.

What should be of the greatest comfort to you is that you don't have to be born a great speaker. Public speaking competence can be learned.[9] Our goal is to help you understand what leads to effective speech making so that you can develop the specific skills you need to be successful. We recognize that no one learns all there is to know about a subject at once or on a first try. In this text, we use the learning principle of repetition applied to the study of the action steps of speech preparation. In Chapter 2 you will be introduced to the speech planning process and the action steps. Then, in Part Two, we will develop each of those action steps and expand them to cover preparation for all types of speeches. Finally, in Part Three, the action steps will be applied specifically to informative and persuasive speaking, and in Part Four we will address other formats and contexts. Each repetition of the steps will function as a new layer of information; by the time you have finished this text, you will have had numerous opportunities to practice using this process.

Bernice, who volunteers at the battered women's shelter, has been asked to speak this evening at a meeting of the local Kiwanis Club about the need for private donations. Although Bernice has a great deal of factual material at her disposal and has her speech pretty well prepared, she thinks her speech would have a lot more power if she could use some real experiences to make her speech more persuasive. As she thinks about various experiences she has heard about, she wonders whether it would be OK to use Angela's story. Angela, a middle-aged mother, has been staying at the shelter with her three children since she was released from the hospital. She is an excellent example of the heart-breaking situations that battered women face. Although Bernice knows that the stories of people at the shelter are confidential, she is reasonably sure that Angela would give her permission to tell her story. But Angela is at a doctor's appointment and will not be back at the shelter before Bernice is scheduled to speak. Bernice decides to include Angela's story in her speech.

1. Is it ethical for Bernice to discuss Angela's experience without first getting her permission?

2. Bernice is reasonably sure that Angela would give her permission. Does this make the decision to go ahead more ethical? Explain.

Summary

Public speaking is important to success in nearly every walk of life. Speeches—oral presentations that are usually given without interruption—occur at formal occasions where an audience has assembled expressly to listen, in less formal employment contexts, and during our informal daily conversations.

Public speaking is a kind of communication transaction that involves a speaker giving a prepared speech to an audience through both oral and visual symbols in a specific context. The audience, the speech's end and object, gives verbal and nonverbal feedback that tells the speaker whether the message of the speech was understood or whether some kind of noise interfered with understanding.

Public speaking challenges speakers to consider audience diversity—differences between and among people—which affects nearly every aspect of the communication process. An effective speaker is aware of, and adapts to, such differences.

Public speaking challenges us to use critical and creative thinking, an analytical and evaluative process using logic or reasoning to present information in a way that is likely to provide understanding, change a belief, or uncover problems in another person's informative or persuasive message.

In addition, public speaking challenges us to behave ethically. Ethics focuses on degrees of rightness and wrongness in human behavior. Although an ethical theory does not tell us what to do in any given situation, it does tell us what to consider in making our decisions. It directs our attention to the reasons that determine the rightness or wrongness of any act. To understand how our ethical standards influence our communication, we must recognize the ethical principles guiding our behavior. Ethical public speaking guidelines include telling the truth, keeping information in perspective, resisting personal attacks against those who oppose your ideas, giving the source for all damning information, and fully crediting sources of quotations or paraphrases to avoid being guilty of plagiarism (passing off the words or ideas of another as one's own).

Public speaking competence is learned. During this course, you have the opportunity to learn how to develop public speaking competence—the knowledge of what makes for good public speaking and the skill to put that knowledge into practice.

CHALLENGE ONLINE

Use your Challenge of Effective Speaking CD-ROM for quick access to the electronic study resources that accompany this text. Included on your CD-ROM is access to the Challenge of Effective Speaking Web site featuring Speech Builder Express at the Wadsworth Communication Café, InfoTrac College Edition, and a demo of WebTutor for *The Challenge of Effective Speaking*. The Web site offers chapter-by-chapter access to the Speech Preparation Action Step Activities, InfoTrac College Edition exercises, a digital glossary of key terms, Web links, Speech Preparation Forms, Speech Evaluation Checklists, and quizzes. Review the key terms and complete the InfoTrac College Edition exercises on the book's Web site:
http://www.wadsworth.com/product/0534563856

InfoTrac College Edition Exercise

Diversity has a significant influence on how we communicate with others. This is especially important for businesses. Open InfoTrac College Edition. In the Subject Guide, type "intercultural communication" and then click on "Search." Then under "Intercultural communication," click on "view periodicals." Scroll down to the article titled "Cross Cultural Awareness" by Lee Gardenswartz and Anita Rowe. Open the article and scroll to the section entitled "Role of Culture," March 2001. Look for suggestions for communicating with employees of diverse cultures. Then read the whole article for additional suggestions on dealing with diversity issues.

Key Terms

audience *(6)*	decoding *(5)*	message *(5)*
channel *(6)*	diversity *(10)*	noise *(8)*
communication competence *(14)*	encoding *(5)*	physical setting *(6)*
	ethical issues *(11)*	plagiarism *(13)*
context *(6)*	external noise *(8)*	psychological setting *(6)*
creative thinking *(11)*	feedback *(8)*	semantic noise *(8)*
critical thinking *(11)*	historical setting *(6)*	speaker *(5)*
cultural setting *(6)*	internal noise *(8)*	speeches *(3)*

Challenge of Effective Speaking CD-ROM

Your Challenge of Effective Speaking CD-ROM features links to InfoTrac College Edition and the Challenge of Effective Speaking Web Site on the Wadsworth Communication Café. Also included on this CD-ROM is Speech Interactive. Using this CD-ROM along with your textbook, you can not only read, but watch, listen to, critique, and analyze the student speeches featured in the text. Improve your own speech performance by learning from the speakers featured on the CD-ROM.

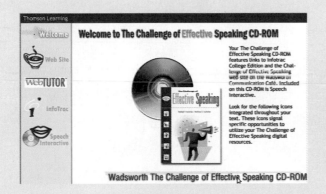

2 Overcoming Nervousness through Effective Speech Planning

Joel Gordon

Courage is resistance to fear, mastery of fear, not absence of fear.
—Mark Twain, *Pudd'nhead Wilson*, 1894

As Professor Montrose finished his introductory lecture, he announced that during the next two class periods everyone would present a short personal experience speech. "I'd like you to speak for two to four minutes. The goals of the assignment are to have you use the speech planning process and to learn how to use narratives effectively so that you will have this experience to draw on when using personal experiences in longer speeches later in the term." Garth's first reaction was anxiety. But as Professor Montrose explained that everyone experiences some apprehension, he also promised to give students help in coping with their fear. He then previewed how the speech planning process they were to learn would equip them to be successful. Garth felt his stomach begin to relax. "Maybe this won't be so bad," he thought. "Yeah, I think I can do this."

You may have been given such an assignment already, and, like Garth, you may be feeling uneasy about speaking in front of the class. Rest assured, you are not alone. Fear of speaking in public is so widespread that polls of American adults consistently find it to be among the top three fears. It is natural to feel nervous about speaking in front of people you don't know well. Some professional speakers also suffer serious prespeech jitters. After you have read this chapter, we hope that you, like Garth, will be more confident that you can overcome your anxiety and become an effective speaker.

In the first part of this chapter, we examine the concept of speech apprehension and discuss strategies that can help you overcome it. In the second part of this chapter, we preview the action steps of effective speech preparation. When you follow these steps, you will be able to cope with and often overcome speech nervousness. Finally, we explain how to apply the speech plan action steps to preparation of your first speech assignment.

Public Speaking Apprehension

People have feared speaking in public probably since they first began doing it. Those of us who teach others to speak have been concerned with helping students overcome their fears almost as long. **Public speaking apprehension**, a type of communication anxiety, is the level of fear a person experiences when anticipating or actually speaking to an audience. Almost all of us have some level of public speaking apprehension, but about 15 percent of the U.S. population experiences high levels of apprehension.[1] Today, we benefit from the results of a significant amount of research on public speaking apprehension and methods for helping us overcome it.

public speaking apprehension
the level of fear a person experiences when anticipating or actually speaking to an audience

Symptoms and Causes

The signs of public speaking apprehension vary from individual to individual, and symptoms ranging from mild to debilitating include physical, emotional, and cognitive reactions. Physical signs may be stomach upset (or butterflies), flushed skin, sweating, shaking, light-headedness, rapid or heavy heartbeats, and verbal disfluencies including stuttering and vocalized pauses ("like," "you know," "ah," "um," and so forth). Emotional symptoms include feeling anxious, worried, or upset. Symptoms can also include specific negative cognitions or thought patterns. For example, a highly apprehensive person might dwell on thoughts such as "I'm going to make a fool of myself" or "I just know that I'll blow it."

The level of public speaking apprehension we feel varies over the course of speaking. Researchers have identified three phases of reaction that speakers proceed through: anticipation reaction, confrontation reaction, and adaptation reaction.[2] **Anticipation reaction** is the level of anxiety you experience prior to giving the speech, including the nervousness you feel while preparing and waiting to speak. Your **confrontation reaction** is the surge in your anxiety level that you feel as you begin to speak. This level begins to fall about a minute or so into your speech and will level off at your prespeaking level about five minutes into your presentation. Your **adaptation reaction** is the gradual decline of your anxiety level that begins about one minute into the presentation and results in your anxiety level declining to its prespeaking level in about five minutes. Exhibit 2.1 depicts this cycle. Researchers have found that most speakers experience moderate levels of both anticipation and confrontation reactions.[3]

The causes of pubic speaking apprehension are still being studied, but several sources have been suggested. These include apprehension because of biologically based temperament, previous experiences, and level of skills.

anticipation reaction the level of anxiety you experience prior to giving the speech, including the nervousness you feel while preparing and waiting to speak

confrontation reaction the surge in your anxiety level that you feel as you begin to speak

adaptation reaction the gradual decline of your anxiety level that begins about one minute into the presentation and results in your anxiety level declining to its prespeaking level in about five minutes

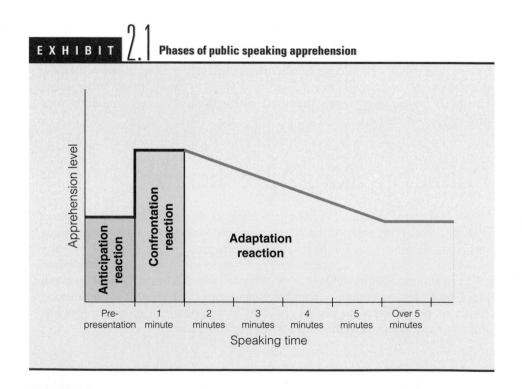

EXHIBIT 2.1 Phases of public speaking apprehension

First, recent research has found that some public speaking apprehension may be inborn. This "communibiological" explanation proposes that public speaking apprehension stems from your temperament, which is neurobiological in origin. Two aspects of inherited temperament, extroversion/introversion and neuroticism, blend together to create public speaking apprehension.[4] People who are more extroverted experience lower levels of public speaking apprehension than do people who are introverted. Extroverted people generally are more sociable, lively, active, assertive, dominant, and adventuresome than are introverted people. Public speaking apprehension is also related to the temperamental characteristic labeled *neuroticism*. People who are temperamentally neurotic experience greater levels of general anxiety, depression, guilt feelings, shyness, mood swings, and irrational thoughts than do those whose temperaments are more stable. According to the communibiological theory, public speaking apprehension is likely to be higher for people who are both more introverted and more neurotic. If you are temperamentally predisposed to high public speaking apprehension, does this mean that you are doomed to be ineffective in your speaking efforts? Of course not, but it does suggest that you will be "working against the grain" and may need special help in learning how to control some of these problematic aspects of your temperament.[5]

Second, your level of public speaking apprehension may be a result of the reinforcement you received from your previous speaking efforts.[6] From reading aloud during second grade, to giving an oral report in science class, to accepting a sports award at a banquet, you have probably had many "public speaking" experiences. How well you performed in past situations is likely to affect how apprehensive you are about speaking in public now. If your second grade teacher humiliated you when you read aloud, or if you flubbed that science report, or had friends laugh at your acceptance speech, you will probably be more apprehensive about speaking in public than if you had been praised for earlier efforts. The public speaking apprehension you feel because of your past experiences, while uncomfortable, does not have to handicap your future performances. Some strategies you can use as you prepare to speak that will help you to reduce your apprehension and be more effective will be discussed in the next section.

A third cause of public speaking apprehension comes from having underdeveloped speaking skills. This "skill deficit" theory was the earliest explanation for apprehension and continues to receive attention by researchers. It suggests that many of us become apprehensive because we don't understand or cannot do the basic tasks associated with effective speech making. These tasks include identifying our speaking goals, analyzing audiences and adapting to them, selecting ideas and putting them in order, choosing appropriate words to express our ideas, and using our body and voice in a way that enables others to easily listen to us.[7] The less skillful we are, the more anxious we feel. People experiencing high public speaking apprehension because they lack the skills necessary to be effective can be helped by studying and learning to apply public speaking skills.

There are many ways to measure public speaking apprehension. One measure widely used by researchers is presented in Exhibit 2.2. Complete the six questions to assess your current level of public speaking apprehension.

Managing Your Apprehension

Many of us believe we would be better off if we could be totally free from nervousness and apprehension. But based on years of study, Professor Gerald Phillips has concluded that nervousness is not necessarily negative. He noted that "learning proceeds best when the organism is in a state of tension."[8] In fact, it helps to be a little nervous

EXHIBIT 2.2 How do you feel about public speaking?

Personal Report of Public Speaking Apprehension

These statements give you a chance to express how you feel about speaking in public. Please indicate in the space provided the degree to which each statement applies to you by marking whether you: 1 = Strongly Agree; 2 = Agree; 3 = Are Undecided; 4 = Disagree; or 5 = Strongly Disagree.

_____ **1.** I have no fear of giving a speech.

_____ **2.** Certain parts of my body feel very tense and rigid while giving a speech.

_____ **3.** I feel relaxed while giving a speech.

_____ **4.** My thoughts become confused and jumbled when I am giving a speech.

_____ **5.** I face the prospect of giving a speech with confidence.

_____ **6.** While giving a speech, I get so nervous I forget the facts I really know.

_____ **TOTAL**

Scoring: Begin by reversing the numbers you assigned to statements 2, 4, and 6 (1=5, 2=4, 3=3, 4=2, 5=1). Then add all six numbers.

Interpreting: If your total is more than 24, you may experience a high level of public speaking apprehension. People who are highly apprehensive will benefit most from applying the techniques designed to reduce anxiety.

Source: Adapted from the PRCA-24, subscale Public Speaking. See Virginia P. Richmond and James C. McCroskey, *Communication Apprehension, Avoidance, and Effectiveness* (Scottsdale, AZ: Gorsuch Scarisbrick, 1998).

to do your best. If you are lackadaisical about giving a speech, you probably will not do a good job.[9]

Because at least some tension is constructive, the goal is not to eliminate nervousness but to learn how to cope with it. According to Phillips, studies that followed groups of students taking speaking courses found that, while nearly all students still experienced tension, almost all of them had learned to cope with the nervousness. Phillips concludes that "apparently they had learned to manage the tension; they no longer saw it as an impairment, and they went ahead with what they had to do."[10] So how does this apply to you?

1. **Recognize that despite your apprehension you can make it through your speech.** Very few people are so afflicted by public speaking apprehension that they are unable to function. You may not enjoy the "flutters" you experience, but you can still deliver an effective speech. In the years we have been teaching (quite a few), we have heard thousands of student speeches and presentations. In all of that time, only two students were so frightened that they were unable to give the speech. We have seen speakers forget some of what they planned to say, and some have strayed from their planned speech, but they all finished speaking. Moreover, we have had students who reported being scared stiff who actually gave excellent speeches.

2. **Realize that listeners may not perceive that you are anxious or nervous.** Some people's apprehension increases because they mistakenly think the audience will detect their fear. But the fact is that audience members are seldom aware of how nervous a person is. For instance, a classic study found that even speech instructors greatly underrate the amount of stage fright they believe a person has.[11]

Joel Gordon

Although most speakers confess to nervousness at the prospect of giving an important speech, the goal is not to eliminate nervousness, but to learn how to cope with it.

3. **Understand that preparation can help you cope with apprehension.** This entire textbook is devoted to helping you become prepared for your speeches so that you will have more confidence in your ability to be effective when you speak. As you work on the speech preparation action steps we recommend, you will find yourself paying less attention to your apprehension as you become engrossed in the challenges of communicating with your particular audience. Moreover, by becoming prepared for a speech, you will reduce the anxiety you can expect to have if you are "winging it." A study by Kathleen Ellis reinforces previous research findings that students who believe they are competent speakers experience less public speaking apprehension than those who do not.[12]

4. **Take comfort in the knowledge that students who take courses in public speaking reduce their apprehension.** If you seriously prepare and give your speeches, you will gain skill and will see improvement in your performance. From these experiences you will gain confidence and worry less. Research on the impact of basic courses on communication apprehension has shown that experience in a public speaking course can reduce students' communication apprehension scores.[13]

Techniques for Reducing Apprehension

Because there are multiple causes of public speaking apprehension, a variety of techniques are used to help people reduce their anxiety. Some techniques are targeted at reducing apprehension that results from worrisome thoughts and irrational beliefs. Other techniques are aimed at reducing the physical symptoms of anxiety. Yet others focus on helping people overcome the skill deficiencies that lead to stress. In this section we review four approaches to reducing public speaking apprehension that have been effective with some speakers.

communication orientation motivation (COM) techniques
techniques designed to reduce anxiety by helping the speaker adopt a "communication" rather than a "performance" orientation toward the speech

performance orientation
views public speaking as a situation demanding special delivery techniques in order to impress an audience aesthetically

communication orientation
views a speech as just an opportunity to talk with a number of people about a topic that is important to the speaker and to the audience

1. **Communication orientation motivation (COM) techniques** are designed to reduce anxiety by helping the speaker adopt a "communication" rather than a "performance" orientation toward the speech.[14] According to Michael Motley, public speaking anxiety is increased for people who hold a **performance orientation**. These people view public speaking as a situation demanding special delivery techniques in order to impress an audience "aesthetically."[15] Individuals with a performance orientation view audience members as hypercritical judges who will be unforgiving about even minor mistakes. In contrast, people who approach public speaking from a **communication orientation** view a speech as just an opportunity to talk with a number of people about a topic that is important to the speaker and to the audience. Speakers with a communication orientation are focused on getting their message across to the audience, not the audience's real or imagined reaction to them as a speaker.

So one technique for reducing public speaking apprehension is for performance-oriented individuals to develop a basic understanding of public speaking apprehension, to understand how their performance orientation adds to their apprehension, and to consciously work to adopt a communication orientation. This change comes about when performance-oriented individuals recognize that public speaking is very much like casual conversations that they succeed with every day. Further, audience members are not focused on judging the eloquence of the speaker but rather are concerned with understanding the content of the speech. COM techniques focus on providing speakers with information that helps them adopt a communication rather than a performance orientation.

visualization techniques
reduces apprehension by helping speakers develop a mental picture of them giving a masterful speech

2. **Visualization techniques** reduce apprehension by helping speakers develop a mental picture of themselves giving a masterful speech. Like COM techniques, visualization helps speakers overcome cognitive causes of apprehension. Joe Ayres and Theodore S. Hopf, two scholars who have conducted extensive research on visualization, have found that if people can visualize themselves going through an entire process they will have a much better chance of succeeding when they are in the situation.[16]

Visualization has been used as a major means of improving sports skills. One example is a study of players trying to improve their foul-shooting percentages. Players were divided into three groups. One group never practiced, another group practiced, and a third group visualized practicing. As we would expect, those who practiced improved far more than those who didn't. What seems amazing is that those who only visualized practicing improved almost as much as those who practiced.[17] Imagine what happens when you visualize and practice as well!

By visualizing speech making, not only do people seem to lower their general apprehension, but they also report fewer negative thoughts when they actually speak.[18] Visualization activities are a part of effective speech preparation. A visualization activity you can use as you prepare your speeches is provided on the Challenge of Effective Speaking Web site is at the end of this chapter. The InfoTrac College Edition exercise at the end of this chapter will help you access more information on this topic.

systematic desensitization a technique in which people first learn procedures for relaxation, then learn to apply these to the anxiety they feel when they visualize participating in a series of anxiety producing communication situations, so that they can remain relaxed when they encounter anxiety-producing situations in real life

3. **Systematic desensitization** is a technique in which people first learn procedures for relaxation, then learn to apply these to the anxiety they feel when they visualize participating in a series of anxiety-producing communication situations, so that they can remain relaxed when they encounter anxiety-producing situations in real life.[19] This technique is designed to help people overcome the physical symptoms of public speaking apprehension. Since relaxing is easier said than done, these programs focus on teaching you deep muscle relaxation procedures.

© Jeff Greenberg/PhotoEdit, Inc.

If people can visualize themselves going through an entire process, they will have a much better chance of succeeding when they are in the situation.

The process involves consciously tensing and then relaxing muscle groups to learn to recognize the difference between the two states. Then, while in a relaxed state, you imagine yourself in successively more stressful situations. For example, researching a speech topic in the library, practicing the speech out loud to a roommate, and finally giving a speech. The ultimate goal of systematic desensitization is to transfer the calm feelings you attain while visualizing to the actual speaking event. Calmness on command—and it works.

4. **Public speaking skills training** is systematically teaching the skills associated with the processes involved in preparing and delivering an effective public speech with the intention of improving speaking competence as a means of reducing public speaking apprehension. Skills training is based on the assumption that some of our anxiety about speaking in public is due to our realization that we do not know how to be successful, that we lack the knowledge and behaviors to be effective. Therefore, if we learn the processes and behaviors associated with effective speech making, then we will be less anxious.[20] Public speaking skills include those associated with the processes of goal analysis, audience and situation analysis, organization, delivery, and self-evaluation.[21]

public speaking skills training systematically teaching the skills associated with the processes involved in preparing and delivering an effective speech with the intention of improving speaking competence as a means of reducing public speaking apprehension

All four of these techniques for reducing public speaking apprehension have been successful in helping people reduce their anxiety. Researchers are just beginning to conduct studies to identify which techniques are most appropriate for a particular person. A study conducted by Karen Kangas Dwyer suggests that the most effective program for combating apprehension is one that uses a variety of techniques but individualizes them by presenting them in an order that corresponds to the order in which the individual experiences apprehension.[22] So, for example, if your immediate reaction when facing a speaking situation is to think worrisome thoughts ("I don't know what I'm suppose to do," "I'm going to make a fool of myself"), which then lead you to feel nervous, you would be best served by first undergoing skills training or COM techniques. A person who immediately feels the physical sensations (nausea, rapid heart beat, and so forth) when thinking about the event would benefit from first learning systematic desensitization techniques before working with visualization or receiving skills training. If you want to reduce your public speaking apprehension, you will want to use all four techniques—but use them in an order that matches the order in which you experience apprehension.

Reducing your public speaking apprehension draws on all four techniques. Public speaking skills training will enable you to feel less anxious, and by understanding and applying speech-making processes and skills you will also become more effective. As you read this textbook and work through the speech preparation activities, you will be developing the skills you need to be effective in speech making. At the heart of this is what we call the "speech plan."

Developing an Effective Speech Plan

Whether you are an account agent selling an advertising campaign to Procter and Gamble, a coach trying to motivate your team in its game with your arch rival, or a student giving a speech in class, to have the greatest chance for success you need to have a **speech plan**—a strategy for achieving your speech goal. An effective speech plan for most speeches is based on the answers to these six questions:

speech plan   a strategy for achieving your speech goal

1. How can I develop a speech goal that is adapted to my audience?
2. How can I best adapt my speech to my audience?
3. Where can I find the kind of information that I need to achieve this goal?
4. How can I organize and outline this information in a way that is most likely to help me achieve my goal?
5. How can I create visual aids that will dramatize my information?
6. What can I focus on in practicing the wording and the delivery of my speech?

In Part Two of this book, we will answer these questions more fully. For now, we want to provide the most basic answers that will help you in your total speech preparation process.

Speech Goal That Meets Audience Needs

speech goal   what you want your listeners to know, believe, or do

Your **speech goal** (or speech purpose) is a statement of what you want your audience to know, believe, or do. To arrive at such a goal, you begin by selecting a topic. Regardless of whether you are a renowned speaker or are preparing your very first speech, the advice for determining what to speak about is the same: select a topic that you know something about and that is important to you.

Because your speech will be given to a particular audience in a particular setting, before you get very far in your planning, think about your specific audience. To help you decide the aspect of the topic you will speak on and the needs of your audience, make a preliminary audience analysis based on the gender, culture, average age, education level, occupation, income level, and group affiliation of your audience members. As you study these factors, you can assess the kinds of material the audience is likely to respond to.

You also need to consider your setting, including the size of the audience, when the speech will be given, where the speech will be given, the equipment necessary to give the speech, the time limit for the speech, and the specific assignment. If you will be speaking in the same classroom all term, determine any peculiarities of the room that you need to take into consideration. Most important for this first speech are the size of the audience and your time limit.

Once you have a topic and have analyzed the audience and setting, you are ready to phrase your speech goal. Every speech has a general and a specific goal that the speaker intends to achieve. For most of your in-class speeches, your general goal is likely to be determined by the assignment. You will probably be giving either an informative speech, where you want your audience to understand information, or a persuasive speech, where you want your audience to believe something or act in a particular way. For an icebreaker speech, your goal is likely to be to have the audience enjoy your personal experience.

Your specific goal articulates exactly what you want your audience to understand, believe, or do. For instance, for an informative speech, Glen, a member of the basketball team, might phrase his goal as "I want my audience to understand how to shoot a jump shot." Ling, a student who was born in China, might phrase her goal as "I want the audience to have an appreciation of Chinese culture."

Audience Adaptation

Once you have a clear speech goal, you begin the task of determining how you will adapt that speech to your specific audience. **Adaptation** means relating to audience interests and needs verbally, visually, and vocally. An effective speaker considers audience needs at all stages of the preparation process.

adaptation relating to audience interests and needs verbally, visually, and vocally

It is important to consider the audience's level of interest in your goal, their ability to understand the content of the speech, and their attitude toward you and your topic. Especially for a first speech, the easiest way to adapt to your audience is to think of ways to speak directly to them by using personal pronouns and asking rhetorical questions. For instance, you might begin your speech by saying, "I'm sure we've all had experiences that we'd just as soon forget . . . " or asking "Do you remember what it was like when you . . . ?"

If you believe your audience has very little interest in your speech, you will need to take some time early in the speech to help them see why the topic is important to them. For instance, if Ling is talking with an audience that she believes has very little interest in understanding Chinese culture, she will have to motivate the audience to recognize why they need to know something about Chinese culture. She might ask, "Did you know that because of the number of Chinese who are immigrating to the United States more Americans are coming into contact with Chinese people, and understanding how Chinese culture differs from American culture is becoming more important to all of us?"

Not only will you need to adapt your speech by providing motivation where it is low, but if you believe your audience's knowledge of the topic is low, you will need to be especially careful in giving them the basic information they need to understand your speech. For instance, if Chala believes her audience is not familiar with basic heart functioning, she will want to make sure she briefly describes this process.

Later in the text, we will discuss other ways of personalizing information. As you gain skill, you will find that you are able to talk about your information in ways that tell audiences that you are thinking about them as you are speaking.

Speech Material

For most speeches, you will want to include factual information from research sources that you access manually and electronically, or information that you acquire by interviewing experts. Regardless of the speech, you also will want to use some of your own humorous, exciting, or interesting experiences. When you select a topic you already know something about, you are in a better position to evaluate the information you glean from sources. You also will have experiences to draw from to make the speech more meaningful. For instance, Chala, who rides on the local volunteer Life Squad, will be able to give a better speech on CPR than a person with no practical experience who has learned about CPR from reading and interviewing others. Why? Because in the course of her volunteer work, Chala has actually used this skill and will have real examples to draw from. She will also be in a position to evaluate whether the sources that she reads are presenting accurate up-to-date information. Likewise, Ling, an international student from China, will be able to bring her firsthand knowledge of Chinese culture to a speech to her class on Chinese manners. Her experience may enable her to describe things in a way that someone who had not experienced both Chinese and American culture would be unable to do.

For your major class assignments, you may draw material from your own knowledge and experiences, observations, interviews, surveys, and research.

Organization

Any well-organized speech has a beginning, a middle, and an end. Because it is difficult to work on an introduction until the content of a speech is determined, it often works best to start organizing the body of the speech before considering the introduction or the conclusion. Throughout the process, work in outline form. Although your inclination may be to sit down and "write out" the speech as it comes to mind, as you read through the following chapters, you will see how speeches are likely to be better organized and better developed when you work in an outline mode.

Begin by wording the main points carefully, following an organizational pattern that clearly communicates the material. Two basic organizational patterns are chronological and topical order. In later chapters, we will consider several types of organization that you may want to use in your informative and persuasive speeches. Chronological means following an order that moves from first to last. Chala, who is planning to speak on CPR, will organize her speech on the steps (what is done first, second, and third) involved in administrating CPR. In some circumstances, you may find that your speech is best presented topically. Topical presentation means following an order of headings. For instance, Ling might want to compare greeting practices, decision-making processes, and dinner manners of Chinese to those of Americans. First she may talk about greeting practices in each culture, then talk about decision-making processes, and conclude by describing simple dinner manners in each culture.

After you have outlined the body of the speech, you can outline your introduction and conclusion. At the least, your introduction should both get attention and lead into the body of the speech. Because there are never any guarantees that your audience is ready to pay full attention to the speech, find a way to start the speech that focuses

© Spencer Grant/PhotoEdit, Inc.

Visual aids clarify, emphasize, and often dramatize.

attention on your topic. Your conclusion should remind the audience of what you have said and hit home in such a way that the audience will remember your words.

When you think you are done, go back over the outline to make sure all of the parts are relevant to your goal. It is important to outline each speech on paper to test the logic and clarity of your proposed organization. A complete outline includes key parts of the introduction, the main points, major subpoints of the body and key support, section transitions, and key parts of the conclusion, plus a list of sources.

Although some experienced speakers are able to speak effectively from a mental outline, most of us need to see on paper what we are planning to do. If the parts of the speech flow logically from one to the next, then the audience should be able to follow your speech.

Selecting and Using Visual Aids

Even for a very short speech you may decide to create a visual aid that will help clarify, emphasize, or dramatize the verbal information. Audiences are likely to understand and retain information better when they have received that information through more than one sense. By using objects, models, charts, pictorial representations, projections, and computer graphics in creative ways, effective speakers are able to maximize the effect of their high-quality information. Visual aids can be especially valuable in informative speeches.

Practicing Speech Wording and Delivery

Ideas are communicated to the audience through verbal and nonverbal means. In your practice sessions, choose the wording of main points and supporting materials carefully. If you have not practiced various ways of phrasing your key ideas, you run the risk of missing a major opportunity for communicating your ideas effectively. In practice sessions, work on clarity, vividness, emphasis, and appropriateness of language.

Although a speech is comprised of words, your effectiveness is largely a matter of how well you use your voice and gestures in delivering your speech. Present the speech enthusiastically, with vocal variety and emphasis, using good eye contact (look at members of the audience while you are speaking). Later, we will spend considerable time discussing how to achieve these goals.

Very few people can present speeches effectively without considerable practice. The goal of practice is to give you confidence that you can talk comfortably with your audience and accomplish your speech goal within the time limit. Never try to memorize the speech. Memorized speeches make it difficult for you to adapt to the feedback you get from your audience and can add to your anxiety (fear of forgetting). Instead, practice to become familiar with your main points and the supporting material for them, to become comfortable transitioning from one point to another, and to become aware of where you might benefit from short notes. Throughout this text, we emphasize extemporaneous speaking—giving a speech that is researched, outlined, and practiced until the ideas of the speech are firmly in mind, but varying the wording from practice to practice and in the actual delivery. By keeping your mind on the main points of the sequence, you will be able to lengthen or shorten the story by including or deleting details of the experience. We will consider detailed information about methods of practice in Chapter 11.

Exhibit 2.3 summarizes the six action steps of an effective speech plan in outline form. These steps will be discussed in detail in the eight chapters that make up Part Two of this book. Each of these action steps is associated with specific speech preparation activities, which will help you understand the processes and skills necessary for effective speaking.

Preparing a Narrative/Personal Experience Speech

Your professor is likely to assign a short, ungraded first speech to help you "get your feet wet." This speech is designed to give you a chance to talk with your class with little or no pressure. For this first speech, we recommend a **narrative** (a tale, an account, or a personal experience) that you can present in two to four minutes. Let's look at how to apply the action steps to prepare such a speech using what Eric Wais did to prepare for his speech, "The Funeral," as an example.

narrative a tale, an account, or a personal experience

The first step is to determine a speech goal that meets audience needs. For his personal experience speech assignment, Eric considered several experiences he thought the class would enjoy hearing about. For his topic, he finally chose "The Funeral," a story of the funeral of Dan, one of Eric's best friends.

Eric thought his class could relate to his experience because many people find themselves in situations where mistakes occur when people don't really know those they are talking about.

He also knew that the speech would be for an audience of about fifteen classmates, that the assignment was a narrative/personal experience speech, and that his time limit was about three minutes.

Since Eric's assignment was a personal experience speech, his general goal was to have the audience enjoy his experience. Specifically, Eric wanted the audience to identify with his laughter at what appeared to be a total lack of understanding.

The second step is to develop a strategy for audience adaptation. Eric used personal pronouns and other means of creating common ground in telling his personal experience. He also tried to be as specific as possible in relating the details so that the audience would have a clear and vivid mental picture of the events.

The third step is to gather the kind of information you need to achieve this goal. For his personal experience narrative, Eric needed only to reconstruct the details of his funeral experience.

Determine a Speech Goal

I. Determine a speech goal that meets audience needs. (Chapter 4)

    A. Select a topic from a subject area you know something about and that is important to you.

    B. Analyze your audience.

    C. Consider your setting.

    D. Articulate your goal by determining the response that meets audience needs.

Develop a Strategy for Audience Adaptation

II. Develop a strategy for audience adaptation. (Chapter 5)

    A. Speak directly to members of the audience.

    B. Relate material to audience interests.

    C. Adjust content to appropriate level given audience level of understanding.

    D. Enhance your credibility with the audience.

    E. Adjust to your audience's attitude toward your topic.

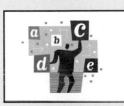

Gather Information

III. Gather information. (Chapter 6)

    A. Survey manual and electronic sources of information and evaluate the quality of information found.

    B. Observe and interview sources of information.

    C. On note cards record information that is relevant to your specific speech goal.

Organize and Develop Your Material

IV. Organize and develop your material in a way that is best suited to your audience. (Chapters 7 and 8)

    A. Write a thesis statement that indicates the specifics of the speech goal.

    B. Outline main points as complete sentences.

    C. Order the main points following an organizational pattern that meets audience needs.

    D. Add supporting information.

    E. Create section transitions to serve as guidelines.

    F. Create an introduction that gets attention, sets the tone, creates goodwill, builds your credibility, and leads into the body of the speech.

    G. Create a conclusion that both summarizes the material and leaves the speech on a high note.

    H. Review and complete speech outline.

Create Visual Aids

V. Create visual aids to clarify, emphasize, and dramatize verbal information. (Chapter 9)

Practice Speech Wording and Delivery

VI. Practice speech wording and delivery. (Chapters 10 and 11)

    A. Practice until the wording is clear, vivid, emphatic, and appropriate.

    B. Practice until the delivery is enthusiastic, vocally expressive, fluent, spontaneous, and direct.

    C. Continue practicing until you can deliver your speech extemporaneously within the time limit.

The fourth step is to organize and develop your material in a way that is best suited to your audience. Since a personal experience is like a story, there isn't likely to be a need for a typical outline of an introduction, main points, and a conclusion. Eric began his speech with a description of his friend. The body of his speech was the recounting of the funeral experience. And his conclusion was the "punch line" to his personal experience.

If you are called upon to give a narrative/personal experience speech, build your speech around the following elements:

- *A narrative usually has a point to it, a climax to which the details build up.* Think carefully about the point of your story.

- *A narrative is developed with supporting details that give background to and embellish the story so that the point has maximum effect.* Try to select and develop details that heighten the impact.

- *A narrative often includes dialogue.* A story is more enjoyable to an audience when the story unfolds through dialogue.

- *A narrative often is humorous.* Most narratives have elements of humor. If what happened can be made funny, the humor will hold attention and help establish a bond between speaker and audience.

Step five is creating visual aids for your speech. Visual aids are less likely to be used in a short narrative speech like Eric's.

The sixth step is to focus on practicing the language and the delivery of your speech. In a narrative, make sure you are being as specific as possible in relating the details so that the audience will have a clear and vivid mental picture of the events. Eric used clear and vivid language to tell his story. He also practiced his speech several times until he was comfortable with his ability to tell the story.

SPEECH assignment

Preparing a Narrative/Personal Experience Speech

Prepare a two- to four-minute personal experience (narrative) speech. Think about experiences you have had that were humorous, suspenseful, or dramatic, and select one that you think your audience would enjoy hearing about.

The sample speech that follows is an example of a student speech that was given to meet this assignment. You can watch, listen to, and evaluate this sample speech under Speech Interactive on your Challenge of Effective Speaking CD-ROM. Click on the Speech Interactive icon to launch the video and audio of this speech.

The Funeral

About two years ago, my friend Dan moved to Minneapolis and about two months later he died in a motorcycle accident. It wasn't anybody's fault—he skidded on a patch of oil. But he left a lot of friends here and everyone took the news really hard. Dan was just so full of life—he really was a great guy to be around, always telling jokes, singing songs, his bands. He was a great guy to hang out with. He had "King of Saturday Night" tattooed across his back in giant letters. And that's how we all really liked to think of him. He was the guy you always wanted to spend your Saturday nights with, because he knew how to have a great time.

So it was hard on all of us when we found out. The funeral was very difficult. We all showed up. It was really rough—it was really hard seeing him in the casket like that so quiet and so unlike we remembered him. They had taken out all of his piercings and they had covered up all of his tattoos for his family. But, uh, you know, it was still the Dan we all knew. It was just really hard to see him like that.

The crowd at church was actually a pretty funny group. The first couple of rows in church were all Dan's family, all middle-aged, middle-class white people in their suits and ties. And then the rest of the church was just a crazy assortment of people—blue hair, tattoos, and whatever anyone could come up with for nice funeral clothing, which in a lot of cases was just a clean T-shirt and a pair of jeans. That's all some people could do. And no one really minded. The service was really emotional, and, uh, it was really hard on all of us. Everyone was taking it really hard. And for a lot of us that wasn't really normal—we weren't really used to going through that with each other.

Um, but toward the end of the service, the Priest stood up to give his eulogy. We were all crying and trying not to cry. He stood up and said, "I know Dan was a musician. And I think if Dan was here today, he'd want to sing us a song." And like I said we were all kind of busy with our own thoughts. We knew that this guy had never met Dan and didn't know him. But we were willing to put up with—we were willing to go along with it. But he paused, and he took out a sheet of paper and he said, "I think Dan would sing this song in particular for his friends and family. 'Did you ever know that you're my hero. You're everything I wish I could be?" And he just said it so matter of factly that as soon as I heard it, I started laughing. I couldn't stop myself. And I felt awful about it, but I couldn't stop. And he just kept reading this song. The idea of Dan sitting on his motorcycle with tattoos and a cigarette hanging out of the corner of his mouth or standing up with one of his bands and singing this Bette Midler song was just so absurd to me that I just couldn't help just laughing out loud. And as the Priest kept reading the lyrics to this awful song, I looked around and everyone in the back of the church was just screaming laughing—falling out of their seats laughing, rolling in the aisles. And the Priest had no idea what was so funny. And the family certainly didn't think anything was funny about it. But, I think we all knew that it was the way Dan would have wanted it—if he was there he would have been laughing right along with us. It was one big last joke for him and it's really my last memory of Dan, and I can't think of a better way to say good-bye. ■

Eric Wais[23]

Summary

All speakers feel nervous as they approach their first speech. Public speaking apprehension has been studied for a long time. Symptoms include physical, emotional, and cognitive reactions, which vary from person to person. The level of apprehension varies over the course of speaking. The level of anxiety experienced prior to speaking is called the anticipation reaction. The surge in anxiety experienced at the beginning of a speech is called the confrontation reaction. The gradual decline of this is called the adaptation reaction. Since at least some tension is constructive, our goal is not to get rid of nervousness but to learn how to cope with it. Because nearly everyone who speaks in public experiences some nervousness, we need to be aware of several realities. Despite nervousness, you can make it through your speech; moreover, listeners are not nearly as likely to recognize your fear as you might think. In addition, the more experience you get in speaking and the better prepared you are, the better you will cope with nervousness. In fact, experienced speakers learn to channel their nervousness in ways that help them to do their best.

Public speaking apprehension is to be expected, and you can use four techniques to minimize it. Communication orientation motivation (COM) techniques help speakers switch from a performance orientation ("everyone is watching me to find

Paul is scheduled to give his first speech—one in which he is supposed to talk about a personal experience he has had. The more Paul realizes that his nervousness is being heightened by the personal nature of the topic, because he thinks his experiences are really ordinary and will bore the class. Suddenly he remembers his high school buddy, James. Now James was a wow—and man, did he have the stories. So Paul thinks, "Hey, I'll just pretend that the "dead rat incident" happened to me. After all, no one knows it didn't. So, Paul develops his speech around this experience that James had. It's a great story, he delivers it well, and he receives an "A" on the assignment.

Is it ethical for Paul to relate the experience as his? Explain.

my mistakes") to a communication orientation ("I have some really important and useful information I want to talk with audience members about"). Visualization is a technique that helps reduce apprehension by having speakers picture themselves being successful. Systematic desensitization teaches speakers deep relaxation techniques to use during visualization and in actual speech performances. Public speaking skills training teaches the processes and skills associated with speaking effectiveness so that apprehension due to unfamiliarity with effective speaking techniques is reduced. All four techniques have been found to reduce public speaking apprehension; however, speakers improve more when the technique used first is one that matches the immediate cause of their anxiety.

Effective speech planning reduces public speaking apprehension and increases speaking effectiveness. An effective speech plan is the product of six action steps. First, the speaker must develop a goal based on his or her own interest and expertise and an analysis of the audience. Second, the speaker must adapt the material to the audience. Third, the speaker must gather and evaluate information useful in reaching the speech goal. Fourth, the speaker must organize and develop supporting material. Fifth, the speaker may create visual aids to clarify, emphasize, and dramatize verbal information. Sixth, the speaker will practice wording until ideas are preasented clearly, vividly, emphatically, and appropriately, and the speaker will practice speech delivery until the delivery is enthusiastic, vocally expressive, fluent, spontaneous, and direct.

A good opening assignment is a narrative/personal experience speech that is ungraded. A narrative is a speech that has a point to it, a climax to which the details build up. It is developed with supporting details that give background to and embellish the story so that the point has maximum effect. A narrative often includes dialogue and is usually humorous.

Use your Challenge of Effective Speaking CD-ROM for quick access to the electronic study resources that accompany this text. Included on your CD-ROM is access to the Challenge of Effective Speaking Web site featuring Speech Builder Express at the Wadsworth Communication Café, InfoTrac College Edition, and a demo of WebTutor for *The Challenge of Effective Speaking*. The Web site offers chapter-by-chapter access to the Speech Preparation Action Step Activities, InfoTrac College Edition exercises, a digital glossary of key terms, Web links, Speech Preparation Forms, Speech Evaluation Checklists and quizzes. Review the key terms and complete the InfoTrac College Edition exercises on the book's Web site:
http://www.wadsworth.com/product/0534563856

InfoTrac College Edition Exercise

Visualization has been recognized as a means of improving performance in many areas, most specifically in athletics. Using InfoTrac College Edition, click on Subject Guide and type the word "visualization." Click on "search." Then under "Visualization (mental images)" click on "view Periodical references," where more than fifty articles are listed. Scroll down to and open the article "Visualization: The Mental Road to Accomplishment" by Dennis Best, August 1999, and look specifically for suggested procedures for using visualization in athletics that you can apply to speech making.

Key Terms

adaptation *(27)*

adaptation reaction *(20)*

anticipation reaction *(20)*

communication
  orientation *(24)*

communication orientation
  motivation techniques
  (COM) *(24)*

confrontation reaction *(20)*

narrative *(30)*

performance
  orientation *(24)*

public speaking
  apprehension *(19)*

public speaking
  skills training *(25)*

speech goal *(26)*

speech plan *(26)*

systematic
  desensitization *(24)*

visualization
  techniques *(24)*

Speech Interactive for Challenge

Using your Challenge of Effective Speaking CD-ROM, click on Speech Interactive and then click on Eric to view Eric presenting his speech on "The Funeral," which was discussed in this chapter. What are Eric's strengths as a speaker? If you were giving the speech, what might you do differently to make it even better?

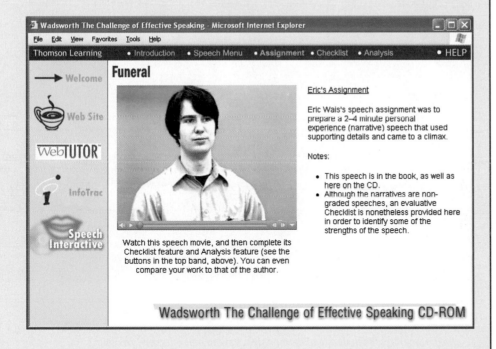

Funeral

Watch this speech movie, and then complete its Checklist feature and Analysis feature (see the buttons in the top band, above). You can even compare your work to that of the author.

Eric's Assignment

Eric Wais's speech assignment was to prepare a 2–4 minute personal experience (narrative) speech that used supporting details and came to a climax.

Notes:

- This speech is in the book, as well as here on the CD.
- Although the narratives are non-graded speeches, an evaluative Checklist is nonetheless provided here in order to identify some of the strengths of the speech.

Wadsworth The Challenge of Effective Speaking CD-ROM

3 Effective Listening

Tom McCarthy/corbisstockmarket.com

A good listener tries to understand thoroughly what the other person is saying.

—Kenneth A. Wells, *Guide to Good Leadership*

When Professor Norton finished her point on means of evaluating social legislation, she said, "Let me remind you that the primary criterion is the value to the general public at large, not the profit people can make from exploiting the legislation."

As Ben, Shawna, and Tim were walking from the class, Ben said, "I was glad to hear that Norton recognized the importance of making profit from social legislation."

"That wasn't her point," said Shawna. "She said that the emphasis is on the value to the general public."

"I'm sure she emphasized profitability," responded Ben. "Tim, what do you think she said?"

"Man, I don't even know what you're talking about. I was thinking about my math test this afternoon."

D oes this conversation sound familiar to you? Have you had times when you'd swear that you heard right when you didn't? If your answer is "Not me," then we congratulate you, for this example illustrates three of the most common listening problems: missing what was said, hearing it but misunderstanding, and not listening or not remembering what was said.

In Chapter 2 we previewed the speech planning process speakers should use when preparing speeches, and we discussed how to overcome nervousness or anxiety. In this chapter, we switch our emphasis from speaking to listening, the other role you play in public speaking settings. **Listening**, "the process of receiving, attending to, and evaluating and assigning meaning to aural and visual stimuli,"[1] is an important skill for you to hone. First, we listen far more than we speak. In most professional settings, from 41 percent to 60 percent or more of our communication time is spent listening.[2] For example, if you are scheduled for five speeches in this course, everyone in a class of fifteen will speak five times but will hear seventy other speeches! Second, many of us do not listen efficiently. For instance, after a ten-minute oral presentation, the average listener hears, comprehends, and retains only about 50 percent of the message. After forty-eight hours, most listeners can remember only about 25 percent of what they heard.[3] Third, many people suspend their own critical thinking skills when they listen. Yet in a democracy it is critical for listeners to use their abilities to process and test the truth and accuracy of the information they hear and the arguments speakers advance.

In this chapter, we consider the nature and importance of attending to speeches, understanding and retaining speech information, critically analyzing speech messages, and giving postspeech feedback. In other chapters, we will address the importance of the speaker's getting and keeping audience members' attention so that they can be more effective listeners.

listening the process of receiving, attending to, and assigning meaning to aural and visual stimuli

Which of these people are listening attentively? Which aren't? How can you tell?

Attending to the Speech

attending   paying attention to what the speaker is saying regardless of extraneous interferences

Attending is paying attention to what the speaker is saying regardless of extraneous interferences. Poor listeners have difficulty exercising control over what they attend to, often letting their mind drift to thoughts totally unassociated with the speech. Remember Tim's response to the question of which interpretation was more on target? "I don't even know what you're talking about. I was thinking about my math test this afternoon." Consider your own experiences listening to speeches, such as your professors' class lectures. Do you sometimes daydream about something else? Can a speaker's mannerisms, such as throat clearing or pacing, sometimes distract you from what is being said?

Some speeches are relatively uninterrupted, one-way communications that do not give us the option of interjecting comments. It is easier to let your attention drift during these speech events. Four techniques can help you maintain attention when listening to speeches (or to classroom lectures).

1. **Get physically and mentally ready to listen.** Suppose that a few minutes after class begins your professor says, "In the next two minutes, I'm going to cover some material that is especially important—in fact, I can guarantee that it will be on the test." What can you do to increase your attention? You can respond physically by sitting upright in your chair, leaning slightly forward, and stopping any random physical movement. You can also look directly at the professor: by making eye contact you increase the amount of information you get.[4] You can respond mentally by directing all of your attention to what the professor is saying, attempting to block out the miscellaneous thoughts constantly passing through your mind.

2. **Hear the speaker out regardless of your thoughts or feelings.** Far too often, we let a person's mannerisms and words "turn us off." For instance, we may become annoyed when a speaker mutters, stammers, or talks in a monotone. Likewise, we may let a speaker's language or ideas turn us off. If you find yourself upset by a

speaker's ideas on gay rights, welfare fraud, political correctness, or any controversial topic, instead of tuning out or getting ready to fight, work that much harder to listen objectively so that you can understand the speaker's position before you respond.

3. **Adjust to the listening goals of the situation.** When you are listening to a speaker for pleasure, you can afford to listen without much intensity. Unfortunately, many people approach all speech situations as if they were listening to pass time. But in public forums as well as in class, your goal is to understand and retain information or to listen critically to be able to evaluate what speakers say and how they say it. Later in this chapter we consider guidelines for adjusting your listening to meet the demands of these goals.

4. **Identify the benefits of attending to the speaker's words.** At times we do this almost automatically, especially when the speaker makes a point of stating the benefits. For instance, when your professor says, "Pay attention to this explanation—I'll tell you right now, it will be the basis for one of the major test questions," it is almost guaranteed to boost your listening efficiency. But you can provide your own motivation. As you listen, ask yourself how you might use the specific information in the near future. For instance, you may be able to use the information in a discussion with your friends, or to help you solve problems, or to understand how to profit. Identifying benefits may motivate you to apply each of the three previous behaviors even more regularly.

Understanding and Retaining Speech Information

The second aspect of listening to speeches is to understand and retain what the speaker is saying. **Understanding** is the ability to decode a message by correctly assigning a meaning to it. **Retaining** is using techniques that will help you identify

understanding   the ability to decode a message by correctly assigning a meaning to it

retaining   storing information in memory and using techniques that will help you identify and recall that information

Note taking is an important method for improving your memory of what you have heard in a speech.

passive listening making no conscious effort to remember what is being said

active listening specific behaviors that turn a speech into a kind of dialogue

and recall information that you have stored. Both understanding and retaining are facilitated by the use of active listening behaviors. **Passive listening** occurs when a person makes no conscious effort to remember what has been said. In contrast, **active listening** occurs when a person consciously tries to understand and remember what a speaker is saying. Active listing includes comprehending the organization of ideas, asking questions, silently paraphrasing, attending to nonverbal cues, and taking notes. To help you both understand better and retain more, let's consider these five active listening behaviors.

1. **Determine the speaker's organization.** Determining the organization helps you establish a framework for understanding and remembering the information.[5] In any extended message, the speaker is likely to have an overall organizational pattern for the information that includes a goal, key ideas (or main points) to develop the goal, and details to explain or support the main points. Effective listeners mentally outline the organization so that when the speech is over they can cite the goal, main points, and some of the key details.

   For instance, during a PTA meeting, Gloria Minton, a teacher, is speaking on the topic of student harassment. As she talks, she mentions information related to why students harass others. Then she explains what can be done in schools to deter such harassment. Finally, she encourages parents to take four specific actions at home to help their children with difficult peer relationships. In her talk, she includes information related to each of these points that she has gained from her experiences at the school and information that she has learned in workshops. When Gloria finishes speaking, her listeners should understand that Gloria's *goal* is to educate parents about peer harassment so that they can partner with teachers to reduce it. Furthermore, they should remember that her *main points* presented the causes of peer harassment, what can be done at school, and what can be done at home to alleviate it. Finally, they will be able to recall some of the *detail* that she used to explain or support each point.

   Although effective speakers organize their speeches so that it is easy to identify their goal, key points, and details, many times we, as listeners, must work to be sure that we have a grasp of the organization. As you take notes, first ask "What am I supposed to know/do because I listened to this?" (goal); second ask "What are the categories of information?" or "Why should I do/think this?" (main points); and third ask, "What's the support?" (details).

2. **Asking yourself questions.** Asking yourself questions, as we have seen, helps you identify key aspects of the speech. Asking yourself questions also helps you to determine whether enough information was presented. For instance, if a person says, "Swimming is an activity that provides exercise for almost every muscle," active listeners might inwardly question "How?" and then pay attention to the supporting material offered or request it if the speaker does not supply it.

3. **Silently paraphrase key information.** Silent paraphrases help listeners understand material. A **paraphrase** is not just a repetition; rather, it is a statement in your own words of the meaning you have assigned to a message. After you have listened to a message, you should be able to summarize your understanding. For example, after a speaker has explained the relationship between ingredients and amounts in recipes and the way a mixture is achieved, you can say to yourself, "In other words, how the mixture is put together may be more important than the ingredients used." If you cannot paraphrase a message, either the message was not well encoded or you were not listening carefully enough.

paraphrase a statement in your own words of the meaning you have assigned to a message

EXHIBIT 3.1 | **Listening competence assignment**

Listening Test

Have a friend assume the role of a fellow worker on your first day in an office job. Ask your friend to read the following information to you once, at a normal rate of speech, as you take notes. Then give yourself the test that follows without referring to your notes. Then repeat the quiz, but use your notes this time. How much does your score improve? Compare your notes to the sample notes found in Exhibit 3.2. Resist the temptation to read this item to yourself; try not to. You will miss both the enjoyment and the value of the exercise if you do.

****

"Since you are new to the job, I'd like to fill you in on a few details. The boss probably told you that typing and distribution of mail are your most important duties. Well, they may be, but let me tell you, answering the phone is going to take most of your time. Now about the typing. Goodwin will give the most, but much of what he gives you may have nothing to do with the department—I'd be careful about spending all my time doing his private work. Mason doesn't give much, but you'd better get it right—she's really a stickler. I've always asked to have tests at least two days in advance. Paulson is always dropping stuff on the desk at the last minute.

"The mail situation sounds tricky, but you'll get used to it. Mail comes twice a day—at 10 A.M. and at 2 P.M. You've got to take the mail that's been left on the desk to Charles Hall for pickup. If you really have some rush stuff, take it right to the campus post office in Harper Hall. It's a little longer walk, but for really rush stuff, it's better. When you pick up at McDaniel Hall, sort it. You'll have to make sure that only mail for the people up here gets delivered here. If there is any that doesn't belong here, bundle it back up and mark it for return to the campus post office.

"Now, about your breaks. You get ten minutes in the morning, forty minutes at noon, and fifteen minutes in the afternoon. If you're smart, you'll leave before the 10:30 classes let out. That's usually a pretty crush time. Three of the teachers are supposed to have office hours then, and if they don't keep them, the students will be on your back. If you take your lunch at 11:45, you'll be back before the main crew goes.

"Oh, one more thing. You are supposed to call Jeno at 8:15 every morning to wake him. If you forget, he gets very upset. Well, good luck."

****

With Notes	Without Notes		
_____	_____	**1.**	What are your main jobs, according to the boss?
_____	_____	**2.**	Who gives the most work?
_____	_____	**3.**	What's the problem with Goodwin's request to do work?
_____	_____	**4.**	What is Paulson's problem with work?
_____	_____	**5.**	How often does mail come?
_____	_____	**6.**	Where are you to take outgoing mail that's been left on the desk?
_____	_____	**7.**	Where is the post office?
_____	_____	**8.**	Where are you to take the mail that does not belong here?
_____	_____	**9.**	How many minutes do you get for your morning break?
_____	_____	**10.**	How many breaks do you get each day?
_____	_____	**11.**	What is the best time to get back from lunch?
_____	_____	**12.**	Who are you supposed to give a wake-up call?

Answers: 1. Typing/distributing mail. **2.** Goodwin. **3.** Not work-related. **4.** Dropping stuff at the last minute. **5.** Twice a day. **6.** Charles Hall. **7.** Harper Hall. **8.** Campus post office in Harper Hall. **9.** ten, **10.** three. **11.** Before the main crew goes. **12.** Jeno.

4. **Attend to nonverbal cues.** You can interpret messages more accurately by also observing the nonverbal behaviors accompanying the words. Regardless of the topic, pay attention to the speaker's tone of voice, facial expression, and gestures. For instance, the director of parking might tell a freshman that he stands a good chance of getting a parking sticker for the garage, but the sound of the person's voice may suggest that the chances are not really that good.

5. **Take good notes.** Although note taking might be inappropriate in casual interpersonal encounters, it is an important method for improving your memory of what you have heard in a speech. Not only does note taking provide a written record that you can go back to, but by taking notes you also take a more active role in the listening process.[6] In short, when you are listening to complex information, take notes.

What constitutes good notes varies by situation. For a short speech, good notes may consist of a brief list of main points, key ideas, or governing points plus a few of the most significant details. Or good notes may be a short summary of the entire concept presented in the complete speech (a type of paraphrase). For a lengthy and rather detailed presentation (like a class lecture), good notes will be an outline that summarizes the overall goal, the main ideas of the message, and key material used to develop each main point. Outlining creates a structure for the information you want to retain and helps you distinguish among main points, subpoints, and illustrative material. Good notes are not necessarily long; in fact, many speeches can be reduced to short notes in outline form.

Ideally, a listener will produce notes that are very similar to the outline notes the speaker used. You can test your ability to attend, understand, and retain what you hear by taking the listening test described in the listening competence assignment in Exhibit 3.1.

EXHIBIT 3.2 **Sample notes for listening test**

Duties
  Typing and distribution of mail most important
  Answering phone takes most time
Typing
  Goodwin gives most
    Question spending time on his private work
Mason does not give much
    Get it right—she's really a stickler
Ask for tests 2 days in advance
    Or get stuck by Paulson at last minute
Mail
  10 and 2
  Take the mail on the desk to Charles Hall
  Take rush stuff to the campus post office in Harper Hall
  Sort mail you pick up at McDaniel Hall—bundle what doesn't belong and mark it for return to the
    campus post office
Breaks
  10 minutes morning—take before 10:30
  40 minutes noon—take at 11:45
  15 minutes afternoon
Extra
  Call Jeno 8:15

Analyzing a Speech

Critical analysis, the means of analyzing and evaluating a speech, is based on well-established criteria. Charles Larson, a noted communication author, lays the foundation for these criteria when he says that listeners should systematically judge the speech message to determine how relevant, how truthful, and how applicable the information or arguments are. Second, listeners should be aware of how a speech message is affecting them.[7] When you analyze a speech, use these seven criteria.

critical analysis the means of analyzing and evaluating a speech

1. **Credibility of the speaker.** Does the speaker seem to have expertise in the subject area? Does the speaker seem trustworthy and sincere? Does the speaker make a good impression? How enthusiastic and forceful is the speaker?

2. **Quality of information sources.** Does the speaker reveal the sources for the information provided? What do you know or what does the speaker tell you about the quality of these sources? Are they respected? Can they be trusted?

3. **Quality of developmental information.** Does the speaker use illustrations, examples, and narratives that are typical, or do the illustrations, examples, and narratives come from unusual or extreme cases? Do the examples, illustrations, and narratives relate specifically to the points they are designed to clarify?

4. **Quality of statistical information.** Who compiled the statistics? For what purpose were they compiled? Was the sample truly random? Or was it a convenience sample?

5. **Organization of the information.** Do the items of information or arguments presented support the speaker's goal? Are the main ideas or arguments easy to identify? Are the main ideas presented in a meaningful order?

6. **Use of emotion.** Does the speaker use emotionally charged words or images? What does the speaker want us to feel? Does the speaker attempt to use emotion to supplement and motivate by use of good information? Or does the speaker attempt to get me to feel a particular way without sound information or with emotional language alone?

7. **Validity of conclusions.** Are the conclusions drawn by the speaker clearly supported with the information that has been provided?

Since each of the seven criteria for critical listening is important for speakers to meet successfully, you will read more about each in later chapters during discussions of specific speaking skills. Mastery of these criteria will not only enable you to better evaluate speeches you hear, mastery will also prepare you to deliver more effective speeches.

Determining Speech Effectiveness

The ultimate test of a speech's effectiveness is how well it accomplished its goal. Yet this measure of effectiveness can be difficult to determine. For example, if a speaker tries to convince union members to support a particular candidate for county commissioner, how will we know how many of the people actually voted for that candidate and how that speech affected their decisions? In this and many other situations, there is no objective way to measure the audience's degree of understanding or conviction.

Because overall effectiveness is so complex, most critics base their evaluation on how well the speaker has met specific speech-making criteria. This approach is built on the assumption that if a speech uses valid information, is well organized, well worded, and well delivered, then it is more likely to achieve its goal.

© Billy E. Barnes/PhotoEdit/PictureQuest

When critiquing classmates' speeches, begin with positive comments, since people are likely to continue behaviors for which they have been praised.

primary criteria   the most important elements for consideration in a particular type of speech

general criteria   those skills that are required for all speeches

The Speech Evaluation Checklist contains questions that can be adapted to evaluate any speech. Checklists like this one are useful when you are asked to provide feedback for a classmate or when you need to critique a speech in another setting. Although a general checklist like this is useful, a better approach is to tailor the checklist to the type of speech. For instance, to evaluate an informative demonstration speech effectively, you would want to comment on the visual aids used in the demonstration and how well the demonstration followed a sequential order. The evaluation of a persuasive speech of conviction should consider the reasons given and the evidence in support of those reasons.

For each type of speech that you study in this text, we will present a specific checklist. The questions on the checklist will help you assess the speaker's effectiveness for that type of speech. The customized critique sheets will include the **primary criteria** or specific skills your instructor is expecting speakers to demonstrate on a particular speech, as well as **general criteria**, skills that speakers will attempt to meet in all speeches. For instance, in your first major speech assignment (see Chapter 11), the primary criteria on the checklist include how well organized the speech is and how well it is delivered.

For each speech on a given day you may be asked to use the critique checklist to record your observations. When that day's group has finished speaking, your instructor may direct you to share your observations aloud.

Giving Constructive Postspeech Feedback

While it is important for you to know how to analyze a speech critically and to determine its effectiveness, it is also useful for you to know how to use that information to give postspeech feedback to other speakers in your class. One goal of postspeech feedback is to praise efforts at meeting the primary criteria. The better we are at empha-

SPEECH EVALUATION checklist

Check items that were accomplished effectively.

Content

_____ **1.** Was the goal of the speech clear?

_____ **2.** Did the speaker have high-quality information?

_____ **3.** Did the speaker use a variety of kinds of developmental material?

_____ **4.** Were visual aids appropriate and well used?

_____ **5.** Did the speaker establish common ground and adapt the content to the audience's interests, knowledge, and attitudes?

Organization

_____ **6.** Did the introduction gain attention and goodwill, set the tone, build credibility, and lead into the speech?

_____ **7.** Were the main points complete sentences that were clear, parallel, and meaningful?

_____ **8.** Did transitions lead smoothly from one point to another?

_____ **9.** Did the conclusion tie the speech together?

Language

_____ **10.** Was the language clear?

_____ **11.** Was the language vivid?

_____ **12.** Was the language emphatic?

_____ **13.** Was the language appropriate?

Delivery

_____ **14.** Did the speaker sound enthusiastic?

_____ **15.** Did the speaker show sufficient vocal expressiveness?

_____ **16.** Was the presentation spontaneous?

_____ **17.** Was the presentation fluent?

_____ **18.** Did the speaker look at the audience?

_____ **19.** Were the pronunciation and articulation acceptable?

_____ **20.** Did the speaker have good posture?

_____ **21.** Did the speaker have sufficient poise?

Based on these criteria, evaluate the speech as (check one):

_____ excellent, _____ good, _____ satisfactory, _____ fair, _____ poor.

sizing successful efforts, the more likely students who are speaking next are likely to try to emulate those efforts. A second goal of postspeech feedback is to show ways that students could have done even better on primary criteria. We should operate under the assumption that all students were trying to use skills in an effective manner. But regardless of how well students might have done with various skills, they are likely to be able to do even better. Thus the postspeech feedback can give specific examples of how students could have done even better. Although this kind of feedback is useful to those who have spoken, it is especially useful for those who will be speaking next time.

Notice, we always begin with positive feedback because people are likely to continue doing things they are praised for. Be sure to make your comments as specific as you can. Instead of saying, "Mary sounded very enthusiastic," you might say "Mary's delivery was particularly good; she did an excellent job in varying pitch and emphasizing key words."

After everyone has had a chance to share examples of what was well done, it is equally important to offer suggestions for what the speakers might have done to make their speeches even better. Notice we don't say what was bad. But regardless of how good a speech is, it can always be made better. Even an "A" speech can be improved. As with positive feedback, it is useful to phrase advice for improvement

EXHIBIT 3.3 Effective and ineffective listening behaviors

	Effective Listening Behavior	Ineffective Listening Behavior
Attending to the Speech	Physically positions self to attend and mentally focuses on what is being said	Fidgets in chair, looks out the window, and lets mind wander
	Attends even to emotionally difficult material	Visibly negative reaction to emotionally difficult material
	Adjusts listening behavior to the specific requirements of the situation	Listens the same way regardless of type of material
Understanding/ Retaining Speech Information	Assigns appropriate meaning to what is said	Hears what is said but is unable either to understand or to assign different meaning to the words
	Consciously listens to identify goals, main points, and supporting information	Listens to individual bits of information without regard for structure
	Takes good notes	Relies on memory alone
	Asks questions to get information	Seldom or never asks questions
	Paraphrases to solidify understanding	Seldom or never paraphrases
	Seeks out subtle meanings based on nonverbal cues	Ignores nonverbal cues
Critically Analyzing Speeches	Uses criteria to assess speaker credibility, use of emotion, organization of information, quality of information sources, quality of specific supporting information, validity of reasons and evidence	Relies on how he or she reacts to the speech in general
Providing Feedback by Critiquing Speeches of Others	Analyzes on the basis of specific criteria relevant to the type of speech given	Gives overall evaluation without mentioning specifics
	Gives useful, specific positive feedback	Gives generalized comments without mentioning specifics
	Suggests one or two ways to improve	Focuses on negative aspects without showing what could have been done better

As they were returning from the rally at the University Field House for candidates for the two congressional districts that surround the university, Nikita asked Lance what he thought of the speech given by Steve Chabot, the Republican candidate for office in the first district.

"Chabot, he's just like any Republican, he's going to make sure that big business is all right."

"I didn't hear him talking about big business. I thought he was talking about the importance of limiting the amount of federal government intrusion in state matters."

"Sure, that's what he said, but we know what he really meant."

"I asked you what you thought of the speech. What ideas did he present that turned you off?"

"Listen, you don't really have to listen to any Republican speaking. Everyone knows that Republicans are for big business and only Democrats are going to watch out for people like us."

1. Is Lance's failure to listen critically an ethical issue? If so, why?

2. If Lance really had been listening critically, what should he be discussing with Nikita?

very specifically. Although you might start by saying, "I think the speakers could have done even better with sectional transitions," you will want to continue with statements such as, "I particularly liked the way Jack said, 'Now that we've seen one way to test whether a diamond is real, let's consider a second way.' I would like to have heard more of those kinds of statements in the speeches." This specific, constructive phrasing shows speakers how they can do even better in their next speeches.

Exhibit 3.3 summarizes effective and ineffective listening behavior related to attending to what is said, understanding/retaining information, critically analyzing what is heard, and providing feedback to speakers.

Summary

Listening is the process of receiving, attending to, assigning meaning to, and evaluating aural and visual stimuli. Effective listening in public speaking settings is an active process that requires the skills of attending, understanding/retaining, and critical analysis. Reasons for studying listening include becoming better speakers, becoming better speech critics, and, as a bonus, learning more about many topics.

Attending (hearing) effectiveness is sharpened by getting ready to listen, hearing the speaker out regardless of your thoughts or feelings, and adjusting attention to the listening goals of different situations.

Determining the speaker's organization, taking good notes, asking rhetorical questions, silently paraphrasing, and paying attention to nonverbal cues enhance understanding and retention.

Critical analysis is the process of determining how truthful, authentic, or believeable you judge both a speaker and the speaker's information to be. Critical analysis requires assessing the speaker's credibility, quality of sources, type and organization of information, use of emotion, and validity of conclusions. In public speaking classes, listeners are encouraged to provide effective postspeech feedback by critiquing the speeches of others. Effectiveness of a speech is based on how well it accomplishes its goal, which includes how well the speaker meets specific criteria.

Effective postspeech feedback includes citing specific strengths of speeches and dealing with weaknesses of speeches in ways that show how speakers can improve.

CHALLENGE ONLINE

Use your Challenge of Effective Speaking CD-ROM for quick access to the electronic study resources that accompany this text. Included on your CD-ROM is access to the *Challenge of Effective Speaking* Web site, featuring Speech Builder Express at the Wadsworth Communication Café, InfoTrac College Edition, and a demo of WebTutor for *The Challenge of Effective Speaking*. The Web site offers chapter-by-chapter access to the Speech Preparation Action Step Activities, InfoTrac College Edition exercises, a digital glossary of key terms, Web links, Speech Preparation Forms, Speech Evaluation Checklists, and quizzes. Review the key terms and complete the InfoTrac College Edition exercise on the book's Web site:
http://www.wadsworth.com/product/0534563856

InfoTrac College Edition Exercise

Using the key words "listening skills" in the Subject Guide, search for the article "Is Anyone Listening (listening skills in the corporate setting)," by Jennifer J. Salopek. Although 80 percent of a group of businesspeople indicated that listening is important, this article points out that they also rated the skill as most lacking in business employees (Salopek, *Training and Development*, September 1999). How does the article answer the question "Why don't we listen better?" What suggestions for improving listening mentioned in the article do you find most beneficial?

Key Terms

active listening *(42)*   **listening** *(39)*   **primary criteria** *(46)*

attending *(40)*   **paraphrase** *(42)*   **retaining** *(41)*

critical analysis *(45)*   **passive listening** *(42)*   **understanding** *(41)*

general criteria *(46)*

Challenge of Effective Speaking Web Site

Use your Challenge of Effective Speaking CD-ROM to access the book's Web Site and try out the activity for Listening Critically.

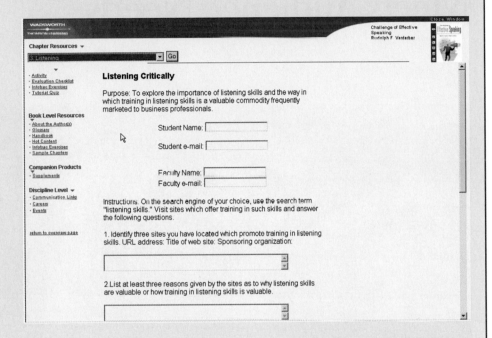

4 Determining a Speech Goal That Meets Audience Needs

© Jeff Greenberg/PhotoEdit, Inc.

The secret of success is constancy to purpose.
—Benjamin Disraeli, June 24, 1870

Donna Montez is a marine biologist. She knows that her audience wants to hear her talk about marine biology, but she doesn't know what aspect of the topic she should focus on.

Dan Wong has been invited to speak to an assembly at his old inner-city high school. He thinks he may have a lot to say to these students coming up behind him, but most of all, he wants them to understand the qualities a person needs to do well in college.

Ayanna Cartland is taking a public speaking class. Her first speech is scheduled for two weeks from tomorrow. As of today, she doesn't have the foggiest idea what she is going to talk about.

ACTION STEP 1

Determine a speech goal that meets audience needs.

A. Select a topic from a subject area you know something about and that is important to you.
B. Analyze your audience.
C. Consider your setting.
D. Articulate your goal by determining the response that meets audience needs.

D o any of these situations seem familiar to you? These are examples of where we might stand regarding the clarity of our goal when we start preparing for an assigned speech. Although you may be as far along as Donna or Dan in knowing what you want to achieve in your speech, in this chapter we will assume that for your classroom speech your situation is more like Ayanna's.

In preparing any speech, the first action step is to determine a specific speech goal that is adapted to your audience and setting. In this chapter, we consider the four major activities that comprise the action step: identifying topics from areas of expertise, analyzing audience, analyzing setting, and writing a speech goal that meets audience needs. Although each issue in the process is discussed separately, they do overlap and are sometimes accomplished in a different order.

Identifying Topics

In real-life settings, people are invited to give speeches because of their expertise in a particular subject area. But even when an organization requests a speech in that area, selecting the topic is often in the hands of the speaker. What is the difference between subject and topic? A **subject** is a broad area of expertise, such as the stock market, cognitive psychology, baseball, or the Middle East. A **topic** is a more specific aspect of a subject. Thus, an authority on the subject of the stock market might be qualified to speak on such diverse topics as how the New York Stock Exchange operates, what it takes to bring a stock to public market, investment strategies, or bull versus bear markets.

The goal of this section is to help you identify subject areas in which you have an interest and knowledge and then to identify and select potential specific topics from those subject areas.

subject a broad area of knowledge, such as the stock market, cognitive psychology, baseball, or the Middle East

topic some specific aspect of a subject

Listing Subjects

When you are asked (or required) to give a speech, use the same criteria for listing subjects as those used by professional speakers. Start by listing subject areas that (1) are important to you and that (2) you know something about. Then consider topics within those areas. Just as Bill Gates draws many of his topics from the subjects of computers and computer programming, Gloria Steinem draws from the subject of feminism, and Jesse Jackson draws from the subject of social and political issues, you should draw your topics from subjects that you know something about and that are important to you.

Subjects that meet these criteria probably include such things as your vocation (major, prospective profession, or current job), your hobbies or leisure activities, and special interests (social, economic, educational, or political concerns). Thus, if retailing is your actual or prospective vocation, tennis is your favorite activity, and problems of illiteracy, substance abuse, and toxic and nontoxic waste are your special concerns, then these are subject areas from which you could draw topics.

Let's consider Ayanna, whom you met at the beginning of this chapter. In high school Ayanna loved dramatics and was on the debate team. She thinks she might like to be a lawyer or a politician, and her tentative major is history. As Ayanna begins to think about subject areas, she selects history (her college major), dramatics (a hobby), and welfare reform (a personal concern or issue).

At this point, it is tempting to think, "Why not just talk on a subject I know an audience wants to hear about?" The reason for avoiding this temptation is that an audience chooses to listen to a speaker because of perceived expertise or insight on a particular subject. Even professional speakers who believe they can talk about anything find it very easy to get in "over their heads."

Exhibit 4.1 contains subjects that students in two classes at the University of Cincinnati listed under major or vocational interest, hobby or activity, and issue or concern.

Brainstorming for Potential Topics

brainstorming an uncritical, nonevaluative process of generating associated ideas

Recall that a topic is a specific aspect of a subject, thus one can list an unlimited number of topics from one subject. To generate a list of specific topics from the subject areas you have identified, use a form of **brainstorming**—an uncritical, nonevaluative process of generating associated ideas. Under the subject of tennis, for example, you might list players, equipment, oversize rackets, balls, shoes, serves, drop shots, volleys, forehands, backhands, lobs, net play, two-handed backhand stroke, Wimbledon, U.S. Open, grass, clay, concrete, scoring, and rules. Notice that some of the items in this list seem to be categories, and other items seem to be specific items. As you go through this process, don't worry about whether there is any order to your items. The goal of brainstorming is to amass lots of ideas. When you start with a subject area of expertise and interest, you often can list twenty, thirty, or even more related topics.

To brainstorm for potential topics, follow the three steps in Speech Preparation Activity 1.1. Brainstorming allows you to take advantage of this basic commonsense principle: Just as it is easier to select a correct answer to a multiple-choice question than to think of the answer to the same question without the choices, so too it is easier to select a topic from a list than to come up with a topic out of the blue.

Even if you are quite sure that you know what you want to talk about for your first speech, it is still a good idea to complete Activity 1.1. Not only will this provide

Major or Vocational Interest	Hobby or Activity	Issue or Concern
communication	soccer	crime
disc jockey	weightlifting	governmental ethics
marketing	music	environment
public relations	travel	media impact on society
elementary teaching	photography	censorship
sales	mountain biking	same-sex marriage
reporting	hiking	taxes
hotel management	volleyball	presidential politics
motherhood	tennis	cloning
fashion design	genealogy	global warming
law	backpacking	child abuse
human resources	horseback riding	road rage
computer programming	sailing	illiteracy
nurse	swimming	effects of smoking
doctor	magic	women's rights
politics	gambling	abortion

alternate choices that may prove to be more suitable than what you had planned, but it will also provide you with options for later speech assignments as well. The Student Response for Activity 1.1 provides a sample of what a student who completed this exercise came up with. Use it as a guide for your own work.

SPEECH PREPARATION **ACTION STEP** 1

Activity 1.1
Brainstorming for Topics

The goal of this practice is to help you identify prospective topics for speeches.

1. Divide a sheet of paper into three columns. Label column 1 with your major or vocation, such as Acting; label column 2 with a hobby or an activity, such as Rock Climbing; and label column 3 with a concern or an issue, such as Racial Profiling.

2. Working on one column at a time, brainstorm a list of at least twenty related topics for major/vocation, hobby/activity, and concern/issue.

3. Check *three* topics in each column that attract you or that may be appropriate for your classroom audience.

Activity 1.1
Brainstorming for Topics

Major/Vocation	Hobby/Activity	Concern/Issue
Geology	**Lacrosse**	**Environment**
faults	history	habitat destruction
folds	rules	rain forests
volcanoes	equipment	extinctions
earthquakes	helmet	jaguars
fluvial systems	pads	air pollution
gems	Crosse	water pollution
diamond tests	skills	fertilizers
fossils	ball	oil wells
Hopper crystals	field	industrialization
Morrison formation	players	overpopulation
geophysics	midfield	Washington salmon
archeology	goalie	littering
soil	strategy	lakes
oil	break-away	rivers
drilling	attack	ozone layer
hydrology	scoring	fires
rock collecting	shooting	birds
caves	conditioning	swamps
minerology	penalties	forests
sediments	coach	atomic waste

Analyzing the Audience

audience analysis the study of the specific audience for a speech

Speeches are given to a particular audience, so early in your preparation process you need to analyze your prospective audience. **Audience analysis** is the study of the specific audience for your speech. Audience analysis includes gathering essential audience demographic data that can help you select a topic within a subject of your interest and that is appropriate for your specific audience. The results of your audience analysis will also help you develop strategies for effective **audience adaptation**—the active process of developing a strategy for tailoring the material to your specific speech audience.

audience adaptation the active process of developing a strategy for tailoring the material to your specific speech audience

Kinds of Audience Data Needed

The first step of audience analysis is to gather essential audience demographic data to determine in what ways a majority of audience members are alike and different. The specific categories in which you need accurate data are education, age, gender, income, occupation, race, ethnicity, religion, geographic uniqueness, and language.

Joel Gordon

Effective speakers can use audience age as a particularly good predictor of their interests, knowledge, and attitudes.

Education. What percentage of your audience have a high school, college, or postcollege education?

Age. What is the age range of your audience, and what is the average age?

Gender. What percentage of your audience is male? Female?

Income. What percentage of your audience is high, middle, or low income?

Occupation. Does the majority of your audience share a single occupation, such as nursing, banking, drill-press operating, teaching, or sales, or do audience members come from diverse occupational groups?

Race. Are most members of your audience of the same race or a mixture of races?

Ethnicity. Are most members of the audience the same ethnicity or a mixture of ethnicities?

Religion. Are most members of your audience of the same religion or a mixture of religions?

Geographic Uniqueness. Are audience members from the same state, city, or neighborhood?

Language. Do most members of the audience speak English as a first language or do most members speak English as a second language (ESL)?

Ways of Gathering Audience Data

Now that we have considered the kinds of audience data you need, let's consider three ways to gather that information.

1. **You can gather data through observation.** If you are familiar with members of your audience (as you are with members of your classroom audience), you can get much of the significant data about them from personal observation. For instance, from being in class for even a couple of sessions, you will have a good idea of class members' approximate age, the ratio of men to women, and their

racial makeup. As you listen to them talk, you will learn more about their interest in, knowledge of, and attitudes about many issues.

2. **You can gather data by questioning the person who scheduled your speech.** When you are invited to speak, ask your contact person to supply as much of the data listed previously as possible. Even if the information is not as specific as you would like, it will still be useful. Be especially sure to ask for the kind of data that will be likely to be most important for your topic. For instance, you may be speaking on a topic for which audience education level is especially important.

3. **You can make intelligent guesses about audience demographics.** If you cannot get information in any other way, you will have to make informed guesses based on such indirect information as the general makeup of the people who live in a specific community or the kinds of people who are likely to attend a speech on your topic.

Using Data for Audience Adaptation

Once you have gathered data, the next step is to use these data to help you adapt your speech to your audience. As we said earlier, audience adaptation is the active process of developing a strategy for tailoring the material to your specific speech audience. The point is that the audience is both the end and the object of your speech. Regardless of the nature of your speech, it is given for the benefit of an audience. For instance, in your history class your evaluation of your professor's teaching includes whether you believe your professor is able to talk about history in ways that *spark your interest* in the historical events and is able to talk in ways that *help you understand* these events. To do so, your professor must apply his or her knowledge of you as a class.

Likewise, regardless of the topic you select, your fellow students are expecting you to talk about that topic in ways that will spark their interest and increase their understanding. In the next chapter we will discuss audience adaptation more completely. For now it's important that you think about your audience in determining your speech goal.

Speech Preparation Activity 1.2 gives you instructions for completing your audience analysis. Student Response Activity 1.2 on page 60 provides an example of what a completed survey might look like.

SPEECH PREPARATION **ACTION STEP** 1

Activity 1.2
Analyzing Your Audience

The goal of this activity is to help you understand your speech audience.

1. Copy or duplicate the audience analysis checklist.

2. Fill in the checklist.

3. Write a paragraph describing your audience. Be sure to discuss how similar and different audience members are from one another.

4. Save the results. You will use the data from this checklist throughout the preparation process.

1. The audience education level is ___ high school ___ college ___ postcollege.

2. The age range is from ___ to ___. The average age is about ___.

3. The audience is approximately ___ percent male and ___ percent female.

4. My estimate of the income level of the audience is ___ below average ___ average ___ above average.

5. The audience is basically ___ of the same occupation/major ___ different occupations/majors.

6. The audience is basically ___ the same race ___ a mixture of races.

7. The audience is basically ___ the same ethnicity ___ a mixture of ethnicities.

8. The audience is basically ___ the same religion ___ a mixture of religions.

9. The audience is basically from ___ the same state ___ the same city ___ the same neighborhood ___ from different areas.

10. The audience is mostly ___ English as first language ___ English as second language (ESL).

Description of audience:

Considering the Setting

The location for your speech, or the **setting**, also provides you with guidelines for both meeting audience expectations and determining the tone of the speech. Because your class meets regularly at the same time under the same conditions, your consideration of setting is not much of a challenge. For speeches under other conditions, however, you will need to spend some time considering the setting. Let's review the questions about the setting that are most important to answer.

setting the location for a speech

1. **How large will the audience be?** If you are anticipating a small audience (perhaps up to fifty people or so), you will be close enough to all of them to talk in a normal voice and to move about. In contrast, if you anticipate a large audience, you will probably need a microphone, and you will be less likely to be able to move about.

2. **When will the speech be given?** A speech given early in the morning requires a different approach from one given right after lunch or in the evening. If a speech is scheduled after a meal, for instance, the audience may be lethargic, mellow, or even on the verge of sleep. As a result, it helps to insert more "attention getters" (examples, illustrations, and stories) to counter potential lapses of attention.

3. **Where in the program does the speech occur?** If you are the only speaker or the featured speaker, you have an obvious advantage—you are the focal point of audience attention. In the classroom, however, and at some rallies, hearings, and other events, there are many speeches, and your place on the schedule may affect how you are received. For example, if you go first, you may need to "warm up" the listeners and be prepared to meet the distraction of a few audience members strolling in late. If you speak last, you must counter the tendency of the audience to be weary from listening to several speeches.

Activity 1.2
Audience Analysis

1. The audience education level is ___ high school _X_ college ___ postcollege.

2. The age range is from _19_ to _24_. The average age is about _20_.

3. The audience is approximately _65_ percent male and _35_ percent female.

4. My estimate of the income level of the audience is ___ below average _X_ average ___ above average.

5. The audience is basically ___ of the same occupation/major ___ different occupations/major.

6. The audience is basically _X_ the same race (2 African American, 1 Asian American) ___ a mixture of races.

7. The audience is basically ___ the same ethnicity _X_ a mixture of ethnicities.

8. The audience is basically _X_ the same religion ___ a mixture of religions.

9. The audience is basically from ___ the same state ___ the same city ___ the same neighborhood _X_ from different areas

10. The audience is mostly _X_ English as first language ___ English as second language (ESL)

Description of audience: From these data I conclude that although audience members are different in many ways, the fact that all are students at UC and that most are around twenty years old suggests that we are alike in key ways. Although there are more men than women in the class, the difference is not that great. I will have to keep both men's and women's interests in mind.

Joel Gordon

If you were speaking to an audience of this size, what changes would you have to make in your presentation?

4. **What is the time limit for the speech?** The time limit for classroom speeches is usually quite short, so you will want to make sure you are not choosing a topic that is too broad and packing too much information into your speech. "Two Major Causes of Environmental Degradation" can be presented in five minutes, but "A History of the Human Impact on the Environment" cannot. Problems with time limits are not peculiar to classroom speeches. Any speech setting includes actual or implied time limits. For example, a Sunday sermon may be limited to twenty or thirty minutes.

5. **What are the expectations for the speech?** Every occasion provides some special expectations. At an Episcopalian Sunday service, for example, the congregation expects the minister's sermon to have a religious theme. For classroom speeches, one of the major expectations is meeting the assignment. Whether the speech assignment is defined by purpose (to inform or to persuade), by type (expository or demonstration), or by subject (book analysis or current event), your goal should reflect the nature of that assignment.

6. **Where will the speech be given?** Because classrooms vary in size, lighting, seating arrangements, and the like, consider the factors that may affect your presentation. In a long, narrow room, you may need to speak louder than usual to reach the back row. In a darkened room, make sure the lights are on and that the blinds or shades are open to bring in as much light as possible.

   Venues outside of school settings offer even greater variations in conditions. Ask for specific information about seating capacity, shape, number of rows, nature of lighting, existence of a speaking stage or platform, distance between speaker and first row, and so on, before you speak. If possible, visit the place and see it for yourself.

Tom Bean/AllStock/Picture Quest

Because where your speech is given is so important, you may want to visit the location sometime before you speak.

Activity 1.3
Analyzing the Setting

The goal of this activity is to help you understand your speech setting. Complete the following checklist:

1. What type of speech is expected? _____

2. When will the speech be given? _____

3. Where will the speech be given? _____

4. How large will the audience be? _____

5. Where in the program does the speech occur? _____

6. What is the time limit for the speech? _____

7. What is the layout of the room? _____

8. What equipment is available for use during the speech? _____

Most important aspects of setting (and why):

Activity 1.3
Analyzing the Setting

1. What type of speech is expected? ___informative or persuasive___

2. When will the speech be given? ___9:30 Tuesday___

3. Where will the speech be given? ___614 Dyer___

4. How large will the audience be? ___13–15 people___

5. Where in the program does the speech occur? ___I will try to go first___

6. What is the time limit for the speech? ___4–6 minutes___

7. What is the layout of the room? ___Square: five rows, about five seats in a row___

8. What equipment is available for use during the speech? ___overhead and chalkboard___

Most important aspects of setting (and why): Time is certainly important, three to five minutes is not really very long. Also I want to make sure that I am one of the first speakers.

7. **What equipment is necessary to give the speech?** For some speeches, you may need a microphone, a chalkboard, an overhead or slide projector and screen, or a hookup for your laptop computer. In most instances, speakers have some kind of speaking stand, but it is wise not to count on it. If the person who has invited you to speak has any control over the setting, be sure to explain what you need—but always have alternative plans in case what you have asked for is unavailable. It is frustrating to plan a computer PowerPoint presentation, for example, and then discover that there is no place to plug in the computer!

By completing Speech Preparation Step Activity 1.3 you will have the information on your setting that you will want to take into consideration as you determine your speech goal. The Student Response for Activity 1.3 provides an example of a student's completed analysis.

Writing a Speech Goal

Once you have chosen your topic, continue the preparation process by identifying the general speech goal you hope to achieve and then writing a specific speech goal that meets audience needs. For instance, if you have selected the topic of illiteracy for your speech, you still need to determine the goals you want to achieve through your speech.

Understanding General and Specific Speech Goals

The **general goal** is the overall intent of your speech. Most speeches can be classified as having one of these three goals: to entertain, to inform, or to persuade. Effective speeches may include material that is entertaining, informative, and persuasive, but one overriding general goal is likely to predominate. Consider the following examples.

general goal the intent of your speech

Jay Leno's opening monologue on the *Tonight Show* is intended to entertain, even though it may include material that is perceived as informative or persuasive. Likewise, when President Bush addressed Congress and the American people two days after the World Trade Center attack, his purpose was to inform Congress and the people about what the U.S. government intended to do even though at one point he urged Americans to return to their normal lives.

Some public speakers give speeches solely for the purpose of entertaining, but in this text we focus attention on informative and persuasive speeches—the kinds of speeches most adults give as part of their job or community activities.

E X H I B I T 4.2 Specific informative and persuasive speech goals

Informative Goals

I would like my audience to understand the major techniques graphologists use to analyze handwriting.

I would like my audience to be able to identify the three basic forms of mystery stories.

Persuasive Goals

I would like my audience to believe that drug testing by business and industry should be prohibited.

I would like my audience to join Amnesty International.

The **specific goal**, or specific purpose, of a speech is a single statement that identifies the exact response the speaker wants from the audience. For a speech on the topic "Evaluating Diamonds," the goal could be stated as "I would like the audience to understand the four major criteria for evaluating a diamond." For a speech on "Supporting the United Way," the goal could be stated as "I would like the audience to donate money to the United Way." In the first example, the goal is informative: the speaker wants the audience to understand the criteria. In the second example, the goal is persuasive: the speaker wants to convince the audience to donate money. Exhibit 4.2 on page 63 provides additional examples of specific informative and persuasive goals that clearly state how each speaker wants the audience to react to a specific topic.

Phrasing Speech Goals

At this stage of preparation you have selected a prospective topic, analyzed your audience, and considered your setting. Now you are ready to begin considering your speech goal. During this course, the general goals of your speeches are likely to be dictated to you by the assignment. But in other settings you will have to decide whether your speech goal should be to entertain, to inform, or to persuade. In deciding on a general goal, you will have to balance your desires against the needs of your audience and the setting for your speech.

Regardless of the general goal you choose, you will need to phrase the specific goal of your speech carefully. The following guidelines can help you craft a well-worded specific goal. To illustrate each of these steps, we will follow Julia's progress as she refines her general goal of giving a speech on the topic of illiteracy.

1.   **Write a first draft of your speech goal using a complete sentence that specifies the type of response you want from the audience.** For example, suppose Julia begins her first draft on the topic of illiteracy this way:

     I want my audience to understand illiteracy.

     Julia's draft is a complete sentence, and it specifies the response she wants from the audience: *to understand* illiteracy. As phrased, we see that Julia is planning to give an informative speech.

2.   **Revise the infinitive (and the infinitive phrase) until it indicates the specific audience reaction desired.** If you regard your goal as providing an explanation, then your intent is primarily informative, and the infinitive that expresses your desired audience reaction should take the form "to understand" or "to appreciate." If, however, you see the goal of your speech as changing a belief or giving a call to action, then your intent is persuasive and will be reflected by the use of such infinitives as "to believe" or "to change," or "to do."

     If Julia wanted to persuade her audience, her specific goal might be worded like this:

     I want my audience to believe that illiteracy is a major problem.

3.   **Make sure the goal statement contains only one idea.** Suppose Julia had written,

     I would like the audience to understand the problem of illiteracy in the workplace and to prove how it is detrimental to both industry and the individual.

     This statement is not effective because it includes two distinct ideas. Either one would be a good goal, but trying to accomplish both in one speech would confuse the audience. Julia needs to decide whether she wants to focus her talk on aspects of the problem, in which case her goal statement might be,

     I would like the audience to understand illiteracy.

or whether she wants to focus on how harmful illiteracy is, in which case her goal statement would be,

I would like to convince the audience that illiteracy is detrimental to the individual and to industry.

4. **Revise your first draft until the infinitive phrase articulates the complete response you want from your audience.** Julia's draft, "I want my audience to understand illiteracy," is a good start, but the infinitive phrase "to understand illiteracy" is vague. Exactly *what* about illiteracy is it that Julia wants her audience to understand? At first she might think, "I want my audience to understand what illiteracy means." But after a few seconds of reflection she realizes that her audience is composed of college students, and most of them already understand the definition of illiteracy. So, just defining illiteracy will not meet audience needs. As Julia works with the wording, she amends it to read,

I would like the audience to understand three aspects of the problem of illiteracy.

This draft is an improvement in at least two ways. First, from an audience standpoint she reasons that her audience may be well aware of what illiteracy is but not very aware of aspects of the problem of illiteracy. So she thinks this goal will provide more of the kinds of information that her audience needs to know. Second, the goal is expanded to focus on "three aspects," so she has made her goal more specific.

Now the question becomes, is the phrase "understand three aspects of illiteracy" specific enough? As Julia thinks of her audience again, she considers how she can align the goal statement even more with her audience's needs. As Julia thinks about it, she sees that what she really wants to communicate is how illiteracy hurts people who are trying to perform in the workplace. With this in mind, she revises the goal by writing,

I would like the audience to understand three aspects of the problem of illiteracy in the workplace.

Now she has limited the goal not only in number of aspects but also by situation. Moreover, she has a goal that she believes will be considered meaningful to her classmates. That is, she believes this college-age audience is likely to see the importance of a speech on this topic. Moreover, she believes she will be able to talk about the topic in ways that hold their interest and further their understanding.

5. **Write at least one different version of the goal statement.** The clearer your specific goal, the more purposeful and effective your speech is likely to be. Even if Julia likes her goal as written, she should write at least one additional version. The second version may prove to be an even clearer statement. For instance, on a second try, she might write,

I would like the audience to understand three major effects of the problem of illiteracy in the workplace.

Changing "three aspects" to "three major effects" gives the goal a different emphasis. She may decide she likes that emphasis better.

To analyze a speaker's goal, complete the InfoTrac College Edition exercise at the end of this chapter.

By completing Speech Preparation Activity 1.4, you will develop a well-written specific goal statement for your speech. Student Response Activity 1.4 provides an example of this activity completed by a student in this course.

Exhibit 4.3 gives several examples of the relationship among subject, topic, general goal, and specific goal.

Activity 1.4
Writing Speech Goals

The goal of this activity is to develop an effective specific speech goal.

1. Write a first draft of your speech goal using a complete sentence that specifies the type of response you want from the audience:

2. Review what you have written. Underline the infinitive phrase. Does the infinitive phrase express precisely the specific audience reaction desired? If not, revise the infinitive phrase:

3. Review what you have written. If the statement contains more than one idea, revise the sentence so that the goal contains only one idea:

4. Review what you have written. Does the statement clearly express the complete response you want from your audience? If not, revise the infinitive phrase until it has this clarity:

5. Write at least one different version of this goal statement:

Now, select the version you plan to use for your speech, and write it here:
Specific goal:

Summary

The first step of effective speech preparation is to determine your speech goal. You begin by selecting a subject that you know something about and are interested in, such as a job, a hobby, or a contemporary issue of concern to you. To arrive at a specific topic, brainstorm a list of related words under each subject heading. When you have brainstormed at least twenty topics, check off the specific topic under each heading that is most meaningful to you.

The next step is to analyze the audience to decide how to shape and direct your speech. Audience analysis is the study of your audience's knowledge, interests, and attitudes. Gather specific data about your audience to determine how its members are

Activity 1.4
Writing Speech Goals

1. Write a first draft of your speech goal using a complete sentence that specifies the type of response you want from the audience:

   I would like my audience to learn the skills necessary to play the game of lacrosse.

2. Revise the infinitive (and the infinitive phrase) until it indicates the specific audience reaction desired:

   to learn how to catch, throw, and cradle a lacrosse ball

3. Make sure that the goal contains only one idea:

   it does

4. Revise your first draft until the infinitive phrase articulates the complete response you want from your audience:

   I would like my audience to recognize the three skills of catching, throwing, and cradling the ball that are necessary to play the game of lacrosse.

5. Write at least one different version of the goal:

   I want my audience to be able to execute the three skills of catching, throwing, and cradling the ball that are necessary to play the game of lacrosse.

Now, select the version you plan to use for your speech.

Specific goal: I want my audience to be able to execute the three skills of catching, throwing, and cradling the ball that are necessary to play the game of lacrosse.

EXHIBIT 4.3 Relationship among subject, topic, general goal, and specific goal

Subject Area: Career counseling
Topic: Networking
General Speech Goal: Informative
Specific Goal: I want the audience to understand the procedure for networking in career development.

Subject Area: Finance
Topic: Debt
General Speech Goal: Informative
Specific Goal: I would like the audience to understand two major factors that are increasing the problem of personal debt in the United States.

Subject Area: National Collegiate Athletic Association (NCAA)
Topic: Sanctions
General Speech Goal: Persuasive
Specific Goal: I would like the audience to believe that sanctions are an ineffective means of punishing colleges that violate NCAA rules.

alike and how they differ. Use this information to predict audience interest in your topic, level of understanding of your topic, and attitude toward you and your topic.

The third step is to consider the setting of the speech, which will affect your overall speech plan. Analyzing the setting includes considering the type of speech, time of day, location, size of audience, place in program, time limit, layout of room, and available equipment.

The final step is to write and test your speech goal. The general goal of a speech is to entertain, to inform, or to persuade. To refine this general goal, write a complete sentence that specifies the exact response you want from the audience. Writing a specific speech goal involves the following five-step procedure: (1) Write a first draft of your speech goal that includes the infinitive phrase that articulates the response you want from your audience. (2) Revise your first draft until you have written a complete sentence that specifies the nature of the audience response. (3) Make sure that the goal contains only one idea. (4) Revise the infinitive or infinitive phrase until it indicates the specific audience reaction desired. (5) Write at least one different version of the goal and compare them before deciding on one.

REFLECT ON ethics

Although Glen and Adam were taking the same speech course, they were in different sections. One evening when Adam was talking with Glen about his trouble finding a topic, Glen mentioned that he was planning to speak about affirmative action. Since the number of different speech goals from this topic seemed unlimited, Glen didn't see any harm in showing Adam his bibliography, so he brought it up on his computer screen.

As Adam was looking at it, Glen went down the hall to get a book he had lent to a friend earlier that morning. While Glen was away, Adam decided to take a look at what else Glen had in the file. He was soon excited to see that Glen had a complete outline on the goal "I want the class to understand the steps in designing a home page." Figuring he could save himself some time, Adam printed the outline—he justified his action on the basis that it represented a good start that would give him ideas. As time ran short, Adam decided to just use Glen's outline for his own speech.

Later in the week Glen's instructor happened to be talking to Adam's about speeches she had heard that week. When she mentioned that Glen had given a really interesting speech on home pages, Adam's teacher said, "That's interesting, I got a good one just this morning. Now what did you say the goal of the speech you heard was?" When the goals turned out to be the same, Glen's instructor went back to her office to get the outline that she would be returning the next day. As the two instructors went over the outlines, they saw that the two speeches were exactly the same. The next day, they left messages for both Adam and Glen to meet with them and the department head that day.

1. What is the ethical issue at stake?

2. Was there anything about Glen's behavior that was unethical? Anything about Adam's?

3. What should be the penalty, if any, for Glen? For Adam?

CHALLENGE ONLINE

Use your Challenge of Effective Speaking CD-ROM for quick access to the electronic study resources that accompany this text. Included in your CD-ROM is access to the Challenge of Effective Speaking Web site featuring Speech Builder Express at the Wadsworth Communication Café, InfoTrac College Edition, and a demo of WebTutor for *The Challenge of Effective Speaking*. The Web site offers chapter-by-chapter access to the Speech Preparation Action Step Activities, InfoTrac College Edition exercises, a digital glossary of key terms, Web links, Speech Preparation Forms, Speech Evaluation Checklists, and quizzes. Review the key terms and complete the InfoTrac College Edition exercise on the book's Web site:

http://www.wadsworth.com/product/0534563856

InfoTrac College Edition Exercise

Open InfoTrac College Edition and click on PowerTrac. Select Journal Name (jn) from the index (or) scroll down to Journal Name (jn). Type in "Vital Speeches" and search for "How to Downsize: Doing It with Dignity," December 1, 2001, by John A. Challenger. Read the first few paragraphs in order to determine Challenger's goal. Was the goal clearly stated in the introduction? Was it implied but clear? Was it unclear? Consider how this analysis can help you clarify your own speech goal.

Key Terms

audience adaptation *(56)*   **general goal** *(63)*   **subject** *(53)*

audience analysis *(56)*   **setting** *(59)*   **topic** *(53)*

brainstorming *(54)*   **specific goal** *(64)*

Bob Daemmrich/Stock, Boston

*You persuade a man only insofar as you can talk his language by speech, gesture, tonality,
order, image, attitude, idea,* identifying *your ways with his.*
—Kenneth Burke, *A Rhetoric of Motives,* 1950

Jeremy has asked his friend Gloria to listen to one of his speech rehearsals. As he finished the final sentence of the speech, "So, violence does affect people in several ways—it not only desensitizes them to violence, it also contributes to making them behave more aggressively," he asked Gloria, "So, what do you think?"

"You're giving the speech to your classmates, right?"

"Yeah."

"And they're mostly mass media majors?"

"Uh huh."

"Well, you have a lot of good material, but I didn't hear anything that showed that you had members of the class in mind."

Develop a strategy for audience adaptation.

A. Speak directly to members of the audience.

B. Relate material to audience interests.

C. Adjust content to appropriate level given audience level of understanding.

D. Enhance your credibility with the audience.

E. Adjust to your audience's attitude toward your topic.

---

audience adaptation developing a strategy for tailoring the material to your specific speech audience

Gloria saw that Jeremy had forgotten something that has been recognized as long as speeches have been given: an effective speech is geared to the specific audience. In this chapter we focus our attention specifically on audience adaptation. **Audience adaptation** means developing a specific strategy for tailoring the material to your specific speech audience. We begin by explaining how to use the audience analysis you performed in Action Step 1 to predict your audience's reaction to your speech goal. Second, we explain methods for adapting speeches to specific audiences to increase the likelihood that the audience will understand and accept the message. Third, we describe how you can develop a written strategy for adapting your speech to your specific audience. And fourth we consider means of adapting the same speech to different audiences.

Determining Initial Disposition of Audience

Before you can develop a strategy for adapting your speech to your specific audience, you need to understand what information, feelings, and attitudes your audience has about you and your speech goal. In this section we will show how to use data from your audience analysis (see Speech Preparation Activity 1.2), to predict an audience's initial disposition and how you might survey audience members to test your predictions.

Using Audience Data to Predict Initial Reactions

The first step of audience adaptation is to use the data you have collected to predict audience reactions to your speech. Consider the audience's potential interest in your speech goal, the audience's knowledge level on your topic, the audience's attitude

AP/Wide World Photos

Even though Jay Leno is a professional entertainer, he still needs to consider his audience when he plans his opening monologue.

toward your credibility, and the audience's attitude toward your topic. These predictions form a basis for the development of your speech strategy.

Once you have predicted your audience's interest, knowledge level, and attitude toward you and your goal, compare these to your own. You may find that you share quite a bit with your audience, in which case adapting your material will be less challenging. On the other hand, you may discover areas where you are different from your audience. In these areas you will need to work to create common ground so the audience will accept your ideas. Let's look at how each of these factors may influence your speech strategy.

1. **Audience interest.** The first challenge is to predict how interested the audience is likely to be in your speech goal. For instance, suppose that one student is planning to talk about rock and roll music and another student is planning to talk about classical music. Because of the nature of a typical classroom audience, we might predict that a traditional college-age class is likely to show more immediate interest in rock and roll than in classical music. This does not mean that the speech on classical music is doomed. All it means is that the one speaking on classical music should recognize that initial interest of the audience in this topic might be low. So, this person will want to develop an introduction to the speech that will spark interest and work to maintain that interest throughout the speech.

2. **Audience understanding.** The second challenge is to predict whether most members of the audience have sufficient background to understand your information. For instance, in our example of the two speeches on music, both speakers have potential problems they must consider. The rock and roll speaker must recognize that the audience may already know quite a lot about traditional rock and roll. This audience has the background to understand the speech but will be bored with a speech on the basics. This audience will be looking for more depth in the speech. The classical music speaker must recognize that because the audience is likely to know less about classical music he or she will have to cover the

basics, define terms carefully, and relate the material to audience experience. We will consider how this is done later in the chapter.

3. **Audience attitude toward you as speaker.** The third challenge is to predict your audience's attitude toward you. Your success in informing or persuading an audience is likely to depend on whether members perceive you as a *credible* source of information: that is, whether that audience perceives you as expert, trustworthy, and personable.

   Expertise includes your qualifications or capability, or what is referred to as your "track record." Why should your audience accept you as an authority on your topic? If your audience will not automatically recognize your knowledge and expertise, then you will have to adapt to this challenge by building your credibility during the speech.

   Being trustworthy refers to both your character (honesty, dependability, moral strength) and your apparent motives (reasons for giving a speech on this topic). Why should your audience see you as trustworthy? Again, if your audience has no reason to view you as having character and proper motives, then you will need to demonstrate your trustworthiness during the speech.

   Being personable refers to a person's likability, a judgment that is often based on first impressions. Why should your audience like you? If you have had previous experiences with most audience members, you will be able to judge this. Perhaps your previous experiences have led you to believe that others find you charming. But if you are not sure of how personable others will perceive you, you will want to adapt in ways that will cause audience members to like you. Because perception of personality weighs so heavily in determining a person's credibility, we will take this up in more detail in Chapter 11.

4. **Audience attitude toward your speech goal.** Your final challenge is to predict your audience's initial attitude toward your speech goal. What information from your audience analysis suggests that your audience will have a favorable attitude toward listening to a speech on your topic? For instance, an audience dominated by skilled workers is likely to look at minimum wage proposals differently from an audience filled with business executives; many men will look at women's rights proposals differently from most women; an audience composed of naturalized citizens is likely to view immigration reform differently from an audience who has not immigrated.

The more data you have about your audience and the more experience you have in analyzing audiences, the better are your chances of accurately judging audience attitudes. Use Speech Preparation Activity 2.1 on page 74 to help you develop a set of predictions upon which your audience adaptation plans can be built. Student Response for Activity 2.1 on page 75 shows an example of this activity completed by a student in this course.

Surveying Students to Test Predictions

At times, you may find that you are not confident making predictions of your audience's initial disposition toward your speech goal based only on your audience analysis. In these cases it may be worthwhile to survey your audience to test or to validate your predictions. A **survey**, often in the form of a questionnaire, is a means of gathering information directly from people. Surveys may be conducted orally or in writing. Whatever your topic, you can obtain useful information through a survey. Four kinds of questions are most likely to be used in a survey: two-sided, multiple-choice, scaled, and open-ended.

survey gathering information directly from people

Activity 2.1
Predictions

Based on the information from your audience analysis in Activity 1.2, complete the following predictions.

Speech goal:

1. Most audience members' interest in this topic is likely to be ___ high ___ moderate ___ low. Why?

2. Most audience members' understanding of the topic will be ___ great ___ moderate ___ little. Why?

3. Most audience members' attitudes toward me as speaker are likely to be ___ positive ___ neutral ___ negative. Why?

4. Most audience members' attitudes toward my topic will be ___ positive ___ neutral ___ negative. Why?

---

two-sided questions questions that call for a yes/no or true/false response

Two-sided questions call for a yes/no or true/false response. These questions are used most frequently to get easily sorted answers. For a survey on audience attitudes about television violence, you might consider a two-sided phrasing such as this:

> Do you believe prime time television programming contains too much violence? ❒ Yes ❒ No

Although two-sided questions do not offer people the opportunity to express their degree of agreement or disagreement, you do get a snapshot of audience opinion, and two-sided questions are easy to ask orally.

Multiple-choice questions give respondents several alternative answers. For a survey of television viewing habits, you might ask this kind of multiple-choice question:

> For the following question, check the choice that is most accurate.
> I watch television
> _____ 0 to 5 hours a week
> _____ 5 to 10 hours a week
> _____ 10 to 15 hours a week
> _____ 15 to 20 hours a week
> _____ more than 20 hours a week

multiple-choice questions respondents choose from a number of alternative answers

scaled questions questions that allow for a range of responses

Scaled questions allow a range of responses to a statement. Scaled responses are particularly good for measuring the strength of a person's attitude toward a subject. Here is an example of a scaled question:

> Circle the answer that best represents your opinion:
> I believe prime time television programming contains too much violence.
> Strongly agree / Agree somewhat / Don't know / Disagree somewhat / Strongly disagree

Activity 2.1
Predictions

Based on the information from your audience analysis Activity 1.2, complete the following predictions.
Speech goal: I would like the audience to understand the three ways to tell if a diamond is real.

1. Most audience members' interest in this topic is likely to be ___ high _X_ moderate ___ low. Why? Although chances of purchasing (or receiving) a diamond ring in the future are likely to be high, this is not a topic that is likely to be highly relevant to the class now.

3. Most audience members' understanding of the topic will be ___ great ___ moderate _X_ little. Why? To talk about this topic, I have to use a lot of technical terms. Moreover, none of the members of class is majoring in mineralogy.

4. Most audience members' attitudes toward me as speaker are likely to be ___ positive _X_ neutral ___ negative. Why? This is the first major speech and none of the members of class really know me.

5. Most audience members' attitudes toward my goal will be ___ positive _X_ neutral ___ negative. Why? Again, mineralogy is hardly likely to be a topic of conversation with class members.

Open-ended questions encourage people to share their opinions without directing them to answer in a predetermined manner. These questions produce the richest information, but because of the wide variety of responses they produce, open-ended questions are the most difficult to process. For your survey on television violence, you might ask this open-ended question:

> If you were to write a letter to the FCC about whether there is too much violence on prime time television, what would you say?

After you give the survey, you can use the results to help you adapt to the audience.

open-ended questions ask for opinions without directing respondents to answer in a predetermined manner

Guidelines for Effective Adaptation

Now that you have predicted how your audience will perceive you and your speech goal initially, you can plan how to adapt your speech to overcome potential problems and build on initial areas of strength. In this section we look at specifics for adapting a speech given initial interest, level of understanding, and attitude toward you and your speech goal. We begin with the easiest means of audience adaptation, speaking directly to members of the audience.

Speaking Directly to Members of the Audience

Speeches are given to audiences that come to hear the speech; audiences have expectations that speakers recognize their presence. The first and in many ways the most important sign that speakers are aware of their audiences' presence is for those speakers to talk directly to the audience.

Reactions such as applause, laughter, head nodding, and smiles are all signs that the audience is relating well to what you are saying.

Direct adaptation is easy, yet speakers resist it. Sometimes speakers simply fail to understand their audience. More often, speakers just aren't really thinking about the specific audience when they prepare their outline and practice the speech, or when they are actually presenting the speech. Let's look at several specific means of direct audience adaptation.

Use Personal Pronouns

personal pronouns words that refer directly to members of the audience

An important way of letting an audience know that you are talking with *them* is to use **personal pronouns**—words that refer directly to members of the audience. By talking in terms of *you, us, we,* and *our,* you give listeners verbal signs that you are talking with them. In Jeremy's speech to his classroom audience on the effects of television violence, for example, instead of saying,

> When people think about violence on TV, they often wonder how it affects viewers.

Jeremy could say,

> When you think about violence on TV, you may wonder how it affects viewers.

The use of just these two personal pronouns in the sentence may not seem like much, but it can mean the difference between audience attention and audience indifference to you and your speech.

Ask Rhetorical Questions

rhetorical questions questions phrased to stimulate a mental response rather than an actual spoken response on the part of the audience

A second easy way of speaking directly to the audience is to ask **rhetorical questions**—questions phrased to stimulate a mental response rather than an actual spoken response on the part of the audience. Although public speaking is not a direct conversation with your audience, you can create the impression of conversation by asking rhetorical questions. For instance, to increase the sense of audience participation in the speech, instead of saying,

> When you think about violence on TV, you may wonder how it affects viewers.

Jeremy might say,

When you watch a particularly violent TV program, have you ever asked yourself, I wonder whether watching such violent programs has any negative effects on viewers?

Rhetorical questions generate audience participation; once the audience participates, it becomes more involved in the content. Rhetorical questions must be sincere to be effective, so practice them until you can ask these questions naturally and sincerely.

Share Common Experiences

Audience adaptation is based on a conscious awareness of the audience, their feelings and their behaviors. A third way of showing audiences that you are thinking about them specifically is to share common experiences in the speech. Talking about common experiences allows your audience to identify with you. Suppose you are talking to a group of Scouts or former Scouts; you might drive home the point that important tasks require hours of hard work by saying,

> Remember the hours you put in working on your first merit badge? Remember wondering whether you'd ever get the darned thing finished? And do you remember how good it felt to know that the time you put in really paid off?

In this case, the members of the audience are led to think, "Yes, I remember—I worked hard because I had a specific goal in mind." In addition to relating the common experience, also notice how this example incorporates personal pronouns and rhetorical questions to heighten the sense of shared experience. When members of an audience identify with you as a speaker, they will pay more attention to what you say. You want your listeners to identify with the common experience so that they will think about it with you.

Personalize Information

A fourth way of speaking directly to the audience is to **personalize** information by using specific audience references. Rather than using information in the form they found it, effective speakers look for ways to adapt information by relating it to the audience's frame of reference. Suppose Devon is giving a speech on how the Japanese economy affects U.S. markets to the student chapter of the American Marketing Association at a university in California. He begins by helping listeners understand geographic data about Japan. He could just cite the following statistics from the 2001 *World Almanac:*[1]

personalize relate it to audience references

> Japan is small and densely populated. The nation's 126 million people live in a land area of 146,000 square miles, giving them a population density of 867 persons per square mile.

Although this would provide the necessary information, it does not show that Devon has an audience of people in college in California, a large state in the United States, in mind. Let's see how Devon could state the same information in a way that would be both more interesting and more meaningful to his specific audience.

> Japan is a small, densely populated nation. Its population is 126 million—less than half that of the United States. Yet the Japanese are crowded into a land area of only 146,000 square miles—roughly the same size as California. Just think of the implications of having half the population of the United States living here in California, where 30 million now live. In fact, Japan packs 867 persons into every square mile of land, whereas in the United States we average about 74 persons per square mile. Overall, then, Japan is about 12 times as crowded as the United States.

This revision adapts the information by developing a comparison of the unknown, Japan, with the familiar, the United States and the audience's home state of California. Even though most Americans do not have the total land area of the United States on the tip of their tongue, they do know that the United States covers a great deal of territory. Likewise, a California audience would have a sense of the size of their home state compared to the rest of the nation. If Devon were speaking to an audience from another part of the country, he could adapt his comparison to a different state. Such detailed comparisons enable the audience to visualize just how small and crowded Japan is.

Reworking information so that it creates common ground takes time, but the effort pays big dividends. Listeners are always going to be asking, "What does this have to do with me?" Unless you present your information in a way that answers that question, your speeches are not going to be as effective as they should be.

Now that we have considered ways of speaking directly to the audience, let's consider specifics of creating interest, increasing understanding, and developing a positive attitude toward you and your speech goal.

Creating and Maintaining Audience Interest

Listeners' interest depends on whether they believe information has a personal impact (that it speaks to the question, "What does this have to do with me?"). Let's consider three tactics that help you adapt your material so that you build and maintain audience interest.

Demonstrating Timeliness of Topic

timely relating to now

Listeners are more likely to be interested in information they perceive as **timely**—they want to know how they can use the information now. Even for topics that seem timely, you will still want to call audience attention to the fact. For instance, in Rhonda's speech about Rohypnol, she works to increase audience interest by saying,

> Perhaps you've never heard of the drug Rohypnol. But far too many people our age, and especially women, have become aware of it too late and with tragic consequences. For Rohypnol, or "roofies" as it's called on the street, has become known as the "date rape drug."

No matter what your topic, you can create a way of showing its timeliness.

Showing Proximity of Information

proximity a relationship to personal space

Listeners are more likely to be interested in information that has **proximity**—a relationship to their personal space. Psychologically, we pay more attention to information that affects our "territory" than to information we perceive as remote. You've heard speakers say something like, "Let me bring this closer to home by showing you . . . ." Statements like these work because information becomes important to people when they perceive it as affecting "their own backyard." If, for instance, you were giving a speech on the EPA's difficulties with its environmental cleanup campaigns, you would want to focus on examples in your audience's own community. If you don't have that kind of information, take time to find it. For instance, for the EPA topic, a telephone call to the local or regional EPA office, or even to the local newspaper, will get the information you need to make the connection.

Emphasizing Seriousness of Topic

serious having physical, economic, or psychological impact

Listeners are more likely to be interested in information that is **serious**—that has a physical, economic, or psychological impact on them. To build or maintain interest during a speech on toxic waste, you could show serious physical impact by saying, "Toxic waste affects your health"; you could show serious economic impact by saying, "Toxic waste cleanup and disposal are expensive—they raise our taxes"; or you could show serious psychological impact by saying, "Toxic waste erodes the quality of our life and the lives of our children."

Think of how dramatically your classroom attention picks up when the professor reveals that a particular piece of information is going to "be on the test." The potential serious economic impact (not paying attention can cost us a lowered grade) is often enough to jolt us to attention. Most of us don't put our attention into high gear unless we see the seriousness of information.

Adapting to Audience Level of Understanding

If your listeners do not have the necessary background to understand the information you will present in your speech, you will need to orient them. If your audience does have sufficient background, you will need to present the information in a way that challenges them and adds to their understanding.

Orienting Listeners

Because your listeners are likely to stop paying attention if they get lost during your speech, a good rule of thumb is to err on the side of expecting too little knowledge rather than expecting too much. So, if there is any reason to believe that some audience members may not have the necessary background knowledge, take time to quickly review basic facts. For instance, for a speech about changes in political and economic conditions in Eastern Europe, you can be reasonably sure that everyone in your audience is aware of the breakup of the Soviet Union and Yugoslavia, but many may not remember the specific new countries that have been created. So before launching into the changing conditions in these countries, remind your listeners by listing the new nations you are going to be talking about.

Some of your listeners may be well versed on your topic. A good way to present basic information without offending people by appearing to talk down to them is to acknowledge that you are reviewing information the audience may already know. By saying "As you will remember," "As you know," or "As we all learned in our high school courses," your orientation will be accepted as a reminder and not a as put-down. For instance, for the speech on changes in political and economic conditions in Eastern Europe, you might say, "As you will recall, what was the old Soviet Union now consists of the following separate states." If listeners already know the information, they will see your statements as reminders; if they do not know it, they are getting the information in a way that doesn't call attention to their information gaps—they can act as if they do in fact remember.

The amount of orientation you can give depends on how much time is available. When you don't have time to give a complete background, determine where a lack of information will impinge on your ability to get through to your audience and fill in the crucial information that closes those gaps.

Presenting New Information

Even when the audience has the necessary background information, we still need to work on ways of presenting new information that adds to their understanding. Speakers can use such devices as *defining, describing, exemplifying,* and *comparing* to help clarify complex information that may be confusing or difficult for some audience members. A speaker must keep in mind that an audience is made up of individuals, and an effective speaker anticipates the different comprehension styles of those individuals. As you plan your speech, ask yourself these questions.

1. **Have I defined all key terms carefully?** For instance, if your speech goal is "I want my audience to understand four major problems faced by those who are functionally illiterate," in the opening of your speech you might present a definition:

By "functionally illiterate," I mean a person who has trouble accomplishing transactions involving reading and writing in which that person wishes to engage.

2. **Have I supported every generalization with at least one specific example?** For instance, suppose you made the statement,

> Large numbers of Americans who are functionally illiterate cannot read well enough to understand simple directions.

You could then use the example,

> For instance, a person who is functionally illiterate might not be able to read or understand a label that says "Take three times a day after eating."

3. **Have I compared and/or contrasted new information to information my audience already understands?** If you want to give the audience a sense of what it feels like to be functionally illiterate, you might compare the problems of functional illiterates to problems your audience may have experienced, such as dealing with a foreign language. Perhaps you have had a personal experience that you could use to make such a comparison.

> Many of us have taken a foreign language in school. As a result, we figure that we can visit a place where that language is spoken and "get along." Right? But as we enter a "foreign" territory, we often discover that even road signs can be difficult to comprehend when we're under even a little pressure. For instance, when I was fortunate enough to visit Montreal last summer, I saw a sign that said the place I was looking for was "à droite." Now I took French in school, and I thought I could handle simple directions, yet for just a minute I found myself puzzling whether "à droite" was "to the right" or "to the left." Just imagine what it must be like if you had to puzzle for a while for many such "simple" ideas or directions, and then run the risk that you were making a major mistake.

4. **Have I used more than one means of development for significant points I want the audience to remember?** This final bit of advice is based on a sound psychological principle: The more different kinds of explanations a speaker gives, the more listeners will understand. Let's go back to a significant statement made in the speech on functional illiteracy:

> Large numbers of Americans who are functionally illiterate cannot read well enough to understand simple directions.

To this statement we added an example:

> For instance, a person who is functionally illiterate might not be able to read or understand a label that says "Take three times a day after eating."

The example makes the statement more meaningful. Now let's see how we can build that statement even further:

> A significant number of Americans are functionally illiterate. That is, large numbers of Americans—about 20 percent of the adult population, or around 35 million people—have serious difficulties with common reading tasks. They cannot read well enough to understand simple cooking instructions, directions on how to work an appliance, or rules on how to play a game. For instance, a person who is functionally illiterate might not be able to read or understand a label that says "Take three times a day after eating."

The first statement, "A significant number of Americans are functionally illiterate," consists of eight words that are likely to be uttered in slightly less than five seconds! A listener who coughs, drops her pencil, or happens to remember an appointment she has during those five seconds will miss the entire sentence. The first expansion with an example adds twenty-five words. Now it is likely that more people will get the point. But the fully developed point contains eighty-five words and much more information. Now, even in the face of some distractions, it is likely that most listeners will have heard and registered the information, and even those who knew about the problem of functional illiteracy are likely to have acquired additional information.

In short speeches, you cannot fully develop every point. What you can do is to identify two or three of your highest priority points and discuss them fully, using two or three different kinds of development.

Building Speaker Credibility

If your audience has a positive attitude toward you as a speaker, then you need only try to maintain that attitude. If, however, your audience has no opinion or for some reason has a negative attitude toward you, then you will want to adapt your speech so that you build your **credibility** with the audience—the level of trust that an audience has or will have in you. As you recall from the discussion earlier in this chapter, your credibility is based primarily on the listener's perception of your knowledge/expertise on the particular subject and your trustworthiness and personality.

credibility the level of trust that an audience has or will have in the speaker

Knowledge and Expertise

One way of building credibility is to build the audience's perception of your **knowledge and expertise**, which includes your qualifications or capability, or what is referred to as your "track record."

knowledge and expertise qualifications or capability—a track record

The first step in building a perception of knowledge and expertise is to go into the speaking situation fully prepared. Audiences have an almost instinctive knowledge of when a speaker is "winging it," and most audiences lose respect for a speaker who hasn't thought enough of them or the situation to have a well-prepared message.

The next step is to demonstrate your command of the material with high-quality examples, illustrations, and personal experiences. Recall how much more favorably you perceive professors who have an inexhaustible supply of supporting information as opposed to those professors who present, and seem to have, only the barest minimum of facts.

The third step is to discuss your direct involvement with the topic. By demonstrating your personal involvement, your audience becomes aware of how your personal experiences have provided you with a practical understanding of the issues. For example, Sasha, who is speaking on toxic waste, will increase his credibility by sharing his personal experience of petitioning his local government for increased local environmental controls.

Trustworthiness

A second tactic for building credibility is to increase audience members' perception of your **trustworthiness,** which refers to both your character and your apparent motives for speaking. The more your listeners see you as one of them, the easier it will be for you to establish your trustworthiness; the more your listeners see you as different, the more difficult it will be. Whether people should be or not, we are more distrustful of those we see as different. Thus, women are generally more trusting of other women than of men; African Americans are more trusting of other African Americans than of European Americans or Asian Americans; Christians are more trusting of other Christians than of Jews or Muslims. Part of building your credibility, then, depends on your ability to bridge gaps between you and members of your audience.

trustworthiness both character and apparent motives for speaking

First, listeners will make value judgments of your character based on their assessment of your moral and ethical traits. What are your character strengths? Are you an

Joel Gordon

The audience's perception of your trustworthiness results from their assessment of your character and your apparent motives for presenting the information.

honest, industrious, dependable, morally strong person? As you plan your speech, ask yourself what you can do in the speech to demonstrate these moral and ethical traits. For instance, how can you convince your audience that you have presented your information honestly? One method is to cite your information sources so audience members can check the truthfulness of what you have said. A second method is to present all sides of an issue accurately—even those you do not favor.

Listeners will also consider your apparent motives. If listeners believe your purpose in speaking will benefit you, but may harm them, they will doubt your motives. It is important to establish what benefit listeners will gain early in your speech. Then, throughout the speech, you can reemphasize your sincere interest in their well-being. For a speech on toxic waste, for example, Sasha could explain how a local dumpsite affects the community. As he presents documented facts and figures showing the extent of danger to individuals, his audience is likely to form the belief that he has a sincere interest in the well-being of the community.

Personableness

personableness the impression you make on your audience based on such traits as enthusiasm, friendliness, warmth, and a ready smile

A third way of building credibility is to build audience perception of you as a person. A **personable** speaker is viewed by audience members as being enthusiastic, friendly, warm, and with a ready smile.

Because your audience members' perceptions of your personableness are likely to be based on their first impressions of you, how you dress, groom, and carry yourself is important. The old compliment "He/she cleans up real good" is worth remembering. It is surprising how much an appropriately professional dress and demeanor will increase audience perception of personality.

In addition, audiences react favorably to a speaker who acts friendly. A smile and a pleasant tone of voice go a long way in showing a warmth that will increase your listeners' comfort with you and your ideas.

We will discuss three additional features of personableness—enthusiasm, eye contact, and vocal expressiveness—in Chapter 11.

Adapting to Initial Audience Attitude toward Your Speech Goal

Although adapting to listeners' attitudes toward your speech goal is especially important for persuasive speeches, it can be important for informative speeches as well. An audience member's **attitude** is a predisposition for or against people, places, or things, usually expressed as an opinion. For a speech on refinishing wood furniture, for example, your listeners may hold the opinion "Refinishing furniture is too hard."

When the audience's initial attitude toward your speech goal is supportive, you will have less need to worry about accommodating their attitude. If, however, you think your listeners are neutral or unsupportive, then you will have to adapt your material to accommodate their attitudes. For example, if the majority of your audience views refinishing furniture as too hard, you will need to counter this initial attitude if you expect them to listen and learn from your speech. In Chapter 13, Principles of Persuasive Speaking, we explain in depth a variety of tactics for changing listeners' attitudes when the goal of the speech is to persuade.

attitude a predisposition for or against people, places, or things, that is usually expressed as an opinion

Forming a Specific Plan of Adaptation

Now that you have used your audience analysis and perhaps additional surveys to make predictions about your audience members' initial reaction to your speech goal and you have been introduced to the tactics you can use to adapt your material, you are ready to draw up a specific plan for adapting your speech to your specific audience. Your adaptation plan should answer the following questions.

1. **How will I speak directly to the audience?** Write how you will use personal pronouns, rhetorical questions, common experiences, hypothetical situations, and personalizing information.

2. **How will I build and maintain interest in my speech goal?** Write how you will use personal experiences, stories, examples, illustrations, comparisons, and contrasts.

3. **How will I adapt my material to this audience's current knowledge level?** Write how you will orient your listeners if they have insufficient background to understand your speech or how you plan to further enhance the knowledge base of your audience.

4. **How will I build and maintain credibility?** Write what you will do to demonstrate your knowledge/expertise, trustworthiness, and personability.

5. **How will I adapt my material to my audience's initial attitude toward my speech goal?** Write what you will do to maintain or build audience support for your speech goal.

When you listen to speeches in class or in public, evaluate whether the speakers have tailored their speeches to the audience as effectively as they could have.

When you have completed Speech Preparation Activity 2.2 on page 84, you will have a set of actions you can institute as you practice your speech that will help adapt your material to this audience. The Student Response for Activity 2.2 provides an example of this activity completed by a student in this course.

Activity 2.2
Adapting to the Audience

The goal of this activity is to develop specific strategies for adapting your speech to your audience.

1. Write the specific speech goal:

2. Review your results from Speech Preparation Activity 1.2 in Chapter 4.

3. Working with these data, write an audience adaptation strategy in which you include specifics about how you will adapt to that audience. Consider the following questions:

   A. How will you speak directly to the audience?

   B. How will you build and maintain interest in your speech goal?

   C. How will you adapt your material so that it is appropriate to your audience members' current level of knowledge?

   D. How will you build and maintain your credibility?

   E. How will you adapt your material to your audience's initial attitude toward your speech goal?

Activity 2.2
Adapting to the Audience

1. *Speech goal:* I would like the audience to understand the three ways to tell if a diamond is real.

2. *Results from Speech Preparation Activity 2.1:* Audience interest, moderate; audience understanding, little; audience attitude toward me as speaker, neutral; audience attitude toward goal, neutral.

3. *Audience adaptation strategy:*

   A. How will you speak directly to the audience? I will ask appropriate rhetorical questions and use personal pronouns.

   B. How will you build and maintain interest in your speech goal? Because interest might vary, I will try to stimulate interest in the introduction by asking two questions: one to men and the other to women. Then throughout the speech I will use specific examples.

   C. How will you adapt your material so that it is appropriate to your audience members' current level of knowledge? Not only will I use specific examples, but for each of the three tests I will use visual aids and actually show the class how the tests are done.

   D. How will you build and maintain your credibility? The audience is likely to be skeptical of my expertise at the beginning, so I will describe my knowledge and training in geology.

   E. How will you adapt your material to your audience's initial attitude toward your speech goal? Again, audience attitude may vary at the beginning, but throughout the speech I will give examples and other information to help the class understand why knowledge of this information will be useful.

Adapting Your Speech to Different Audiences

So far we've been looking at adapting to your classroom audience—one that you are familiar with. Now let's change the situation. Suppose you were asked to give your speech, with the same goal, to two totally different audiences. Let's look at how Lana Jackson dealt with this situation.

Audience Factors Known and in Speaker's Favor

Lana Jackson, the manager of all clerical staff at her company, is to present a talk informing the staff about the latest software package scheduled to be installed on all computers at the company. Because Lana is the manager, she knows her audience well. For example, she knows that the audience will be about twenty-five Cincinnatians: 60 percent women and 40 percent men, 80 percent of whom are white, and the rest African American. They will be from Judeo-Christian religious backgrounds and vary in age from nineteen to forty. All will be high school graduates, over half will have associate degrees, and another 10 percent will be pursuing bachelor's degrees.

Based on that information, her analysis could include the following predictions:

1. Audience interest is likely to be high because their job performance depends on becoming proficient with the new program in a short period of time.

2. Because of their familiarity with the company, the types of computers, and the previous package, audience preparation for understanding the information is likely to be high.

E X H I B I T 5.1 **Favorable factors**

Speaking Directly: Throughout the speech I will use personal pronouns and ask appropriate rhetorical questions. Whenever possible, I will try to personalize information.

Interest: Because interest is likely to be high, I will place my emphasis on maintaining that interest. The staff are familiar with word processing packages, so I can focus on several of the features that will enable them to produce better copy more easily. I will also use visual material to show my listeners what I am talking about.

Understanding: The staff understand computer packages, so I will use comparisons of the key features of the new package to operations they are familiar with. Where possible I will share common experiences and personalize information. I will use overhead projections to help clarify difficult ideas.

Attitude toward Speaker: Audience attitude toward me may be skeptical. Because I am "management," they may be a little cynical about my intentions. I will have to stress that what is good for the company is also good for them. They may also wonder about my expertise with the new package. So I will tell them about the week of intensive training I attended. I will have to be especially careful to present information smoothly and accurately.

Initial Attitude toward Speech Goal: Although their attitude toward the speech goal is likely to be favorable, I will still attempt to feature improvements so that they will understand why they need to spend their time and energy learning the new system. I will show them that the improvements are significant.

3. Although my credibility with my employees may be OK, I will need to demonstrate my expertise with the new package.

4. The initial attitude of the audience about changing programs may vary, but members can be convinced to embrace the change if they are provided with evidence that the new package will enable them to accomplish their goals more easily.

Based on these predictions, Lana might write the strategy shown in Exhibit 5.1 on page 85.

Audience Factors Inferred and Less Favorable

Lana Jackson has also been asked to talk about the new computer software package to a monthly breakfast roundtable of the local Chamber of Commerce. Because members of the Chamber want to be "up to date," they thought it would be worthwhile to have a speech on this topic so that their members could learn about the latest software package for this application.

If the only information Lana has about the audience is that they are all members of the local Chamber who have chosen to attend a speech on this new software package, she can still perform a basic audience analysis to help her adapt her material.

Because it is an adult organization, Lana can infer that the audience will be comprised of both males and females of mixed race, religion, and nationality, with a mixed educational background, whose ages range from about twenty-five upward. Moreover, she can infer that many have homes and families and, because they are members of a local Chamber of Commerce, that they have a geographic bond and an interest in business issues. Further, she can assume many own their businesses or are executives in corporations.

Even though her data are inferred, Lana can still make predictions about interests, understanding, and attitude. Based on that information, her analysis might include the following predictions:

1. The audience's interests are likely to vary, because they probably have no immediate need for information about computer packages other than some natural curiosity. Still, they wouldn't come if they didn't have some interest.

2. Because their background knowledge ranges widely, it is likely that for most members the level of understanding of the specifics of this software package is relatively low.

3. My initial credibility is likely to be neutral because they won't know that much about me.

4. The audience's attitude about new software packages is likely to range from favorable to neutral or even slightly negative. Some will be very positive about what the new software can do for them, most may be indifferent, and a few will see the new package as a waste of money.

Based on these predictions, Lana might develop the adaptation strategy shown in Exhibit 5.2.

Summary

Audience adaptation is the process of tailoring your speech material to your specific audience. This process begins by examining your audience analysis and using it to predict the audience members' initial level of knowledge about, interest in, and atti-

EXHIBIT 5.2 Unfavorable factors

Speaking Directly: Throughout the speech I will use personal pronouns and ask appropriate rhetorical questions. Whenever possible, I will try to personalize information.

Interest: Because interest levels will vary, I will have to begin the speech with an anecdote or a personal experience about "changing software" that will capture initial interest. Very early in the speech I will also try to focus on the ease with which the new package enables people to complete the tasks. I will stress aspects of the software package that would be useful immediately to a variety of business settings and would have a real impact on them. And, of course, I will develop visual aids to reinforce key points.

Understanding: Because I do not know the number of the audience members who have used the previous version of this software, early in the speech I will ask how many have any experience with this package. Then, based on the percentage that answers "yes," I will adjust the background information I give before I get into the meat of the speech. If need be, I will use generic language, and I may need to define all terms carefully. I must also take into account the needs of people from different types of businesses. I will need a variety of examples, illustrations, and anecdotes that relate to different applications. And, of course, wherever possible, I will try to personalize information. I will also give them a simple example that demonstrates the ease of using this software.

Attitude toward Speaker: Because they know little about me, I will have to demonstrate my expertise and assure them that my intentions are to help them learn more about this software package. Moreover, since they may perceive themselves as being different from me, I'm going to have to demonstrate my trustworthiness. I will be sure to dress professionally. I will be especially careful with the way I present information so that they will see me as reliable. I will also try to keep the speech light and somewhat humorous.

Initial Attitude toward Speech Goal: Because their attitudes are also likely to vary, I will use examples and illustrations of "average business users" who have found this computer package helpful.

tude toward you and your speech goal. Based on your predictions, you can develop a strategy that adapts your material to audience needs.

A first stage of audience adaptation is to determine how you might speak directly to the audience. Speakers can increase audiences' perception that the speaker recognizes the audience by using personal pronouns, rhetorical questions, and personalizing information.

Tactics for increasing audience interest in your speech goal include stressing the timeliness of the topic, the way in which the issue is close or proximate to the audience, and the seriousness of the topic for the audience.

Tactics for adapting to your audiences' initial level of knowledge include supplying sufficient background information, defining unfamiliar terms, supplying sufficiently challenging information, and using well-developed examples and comparisons.

Tactics for maintaining or enhancing your credibility with the audience include being fully prepared, emphasizing sincere interest in the audience members' well-being, dressing and grooming well, presenting yourself appropriately, and being personable.

Audience attitudes toward the speech goal can be classified as no opinion, in favor, or opposed. If the audience has no opinion, is in favor, or is only slightly opposed to your topic, efforts to create and build attention and relate to level of understanding will also work to improve attitude. If the audience is opposed to your topic or goal, you'll need to work to change their opinion.

"Kendra, I heard you telling Jim about the speech you're giving tomorrow. You think it's a winner, huh?"

"You got that right, Omar. I'm going to have Bardston eating out of the palm of my hand."

"You sound confident."

"This time I have reason to be. See, Professor Bardston's been talking about the importance of audience adaptation. These last two weeks that's all we've heard—adaptation, adaptation."

"What does she mean?"

"Talking about something in a way that really relates to people personally."

"OK—so how are you going to do that?"

"Well, you see, I'm giving this speech on abortion. Now here's the kick. Bardston let it slip that she's a supporter of Right to Life. So what I'm going to do is give this informative speech on the Right to Life movement. But I'm going to discuss the major beliefs of the movement in a way that'll get her to think I'm a supporter. I'm going to mention aspects of the movement that I know she'll like."

"But I've heard you talk about how you're pro choice."

"I am—all the way. But by keeping the information positive, she'll think I'm a supporter. It isn't as if I'm going to be telling any lies or anything."

1. In a speech is it ethical to adapt in a way that resonates with your "audience" but isn't in keeping with what you really believe?

2. Could Kendra have achieved her goal by using different methods? How?

Effective speakers meet the challenge of audience adaptation by completing a written strategy that specifies the actions they will take. Effective speakers also use adaptation tactics to develop unique speeches with a common speech goal tailored to the specific needs of different audiences.

CHALLENGE ONLINE

Use your Challenge of Effective Speaking CD-ROM for quick access to the electronic study resources that accompany this text. Included on your CD-ROM is access to the *Challenge of Effective Speaking* Web site featuring Speech Builder Express at Wadsworth Communication Café, InfoTrac College Edition, and a demo of WebTutor for *The Challenge of Effective Speaking*. The Web site offers chapter-by-chapter access to the Speech Preparation Action Step Activities, InfoTrac College Edition exercises, a digital glossary of key terms, Web links, Speech Preparation Forms, Speech Evaluation Checklists, and quizzes. Review the key terms and complete the InfoTrac College Edition exercise on the book's Web site at
http://www.wadsworth.com/product/0534563856

InfoTrac College Edition

How important is credibility or trustworthiness to a communicator? Using InfoTrac College Edition, enter "truthfulness and falsehood" in the Subject Guide. Click on "Periodical References" and scroll down to the article, "The Truth about Credibility," *Public Management*, June 2001. List the key elements the author considers. Then, to see the importance of trustworthiness in real life, scroll to the article "A Historian Who Lies about His Own Past (Joseph Ellis)," by Stephen Goode, July 23, 2001. Why did Joseph Ellis's behavior receive such a negative response? Based on what you've learned from these two articles, what do you need to do in your speeches to build credibility?

Key Terms

attitude *(83)*

audience adaptation *(71)*

credibility *(81)*

knowledge and expertise *(81)*

multiple-choice questions *(74)*

open-ended questions *(75)*

personableness *(82)*

personalize *(77)*

personal pronouns *(76)*

proximity *(78)*

rhetorical questions *(76)*

scaled questions *(74)*

serious *(78)*

survey *(73)*

timely *(78)*

trustworthiness *(81)*

two-sided questions *(74)*

6 Researching Information for Your Speech

David Young-Wolff/PhotoEdit, Inc.

An empty bag cannot stand upright.
—Benjamin Franklin, *Poor Richard's Almanac,* 1740

Jeremy was panicked. He was scheduled to give his first speech on the effects of television violence on children in a week, but he hadn't begun to do any research. When he was in high school, he remembered discussing the subject of media violence in a class, and he was really taken with the subject. Just a couple of months ago he had read an article in a magazine at the doctor's office, but he couldn't remember the issue of the magazine the article was in. He knew he'd better get to the library, but he wasn't sure how to find information once he got there.

Gather information.

A. Survey manual and electronic sources of information and evaluate the quality of the information found.

B. Observe and interview sources of information.

C. On note cards record information that is relevant to your specific speech goal.

D oes Jeremy's experience sound familiar? You may believe your topic is important and you may be really interested in it, but you may not be sure how to go about finding the information you need. Libraries—especially those at large universities—can seem intimidating. So can the Internet. In this chapter we explain how to gather and evaluate information you can use to reach your speech goal.

Finding Information: Traditional and Electronic Sources

Where should you look for the best material available on your topic? It depends on your topic and the kind of information you want. For instance, consider Jeremy's concerns as he prepares for a speech on the effects of media violence on children.

Richard Hamilton Smith/CORBIS

Careful observation is an often-overlooked research strategy. In addition to facts, observation can provide the kinds of specific details that make your topic come alive for an audience.

Where he looks for information may well differ from where Erin would look if she were planning to talk about how to spike a volleyball, or where Rhonda would look if she were planning to talk about the dangers of designer drugs like Rohypnol and Ecstasy. In the next section we will describe various approaches to finding information using Jeremy, Erin, and Rhonda as examples.

An effective research strategy begins by considering the speaker's knowledge and experiences; then moves to identifying information from print sources such as books, periodicals, magazines, and other specialized sources. These print resources can be located manually through card catalogues or periodical indexes or through electronic resource databases such as InfoTrac College Edition. Using an effective research strategy, you will also examine Internet Web sites and Web pages to determine what high-quality information may be available online. Finally, interviewing experts provides yet another resource.

Using Personal Knowledge, Experience, and Observation

If you have chosen to speak on a topic you know something about, you may already have some material that you can use in your speech. For instance, athletes have special knowledge about their sport, entrepreneurs about starting up their own business, cancer survivors about health systems, marine biologists about marine reserves, musicians about music and instruments, and camp counselors about camping. For many of your speeches, then, you are likely to already have information that may be usable in your speech—especially examples drawn from personal experiences. Your firsthand knowledge will contribute to the development of an imaginative and original speech.

If Erin, a member of the varsity volleyball team, plans to give her first speech on "How to Spike a Volleyball," we would expect her to draw a great deal of her material from her own experience and the experiences of her teammates. Discussing such personal volleyball experiences is likely to be especially important in helping her gain interest and/or adapt her information to audience needs. This does not mean that Erin should not consult other sources (we'll consider additional choices for her in other sections). For any speech, we expect a person to consult several sources of information.

For many topics, your personal knowledge from experience can be supplemented with careful observation. If, for instance, you are planning to talk about how a small claims court works or how churches are helping the homeless find shelter, food, job training, and hope, you can learn more about these subjects by attending court sessions or visiting a church's outreach center. Observation adds a personal dimension to your speeches that can make them more informative as well as more interesting. Focus your attention on specific behaviors and take notes of your observations. This will provide a record of specifics that you can use in your speech.

Locating Printed Resources

Much of the material you will need for your speech will come from information that is in books, periodicals, and magazines that can be located through card catalogues or printed indexes or via electronic databases.

In the past the only way to find information was to go to the library's card catalogue, which lists all books, or go to indexes and periodical catalogues, which list magazines and journals in various categories. Today books and periodicals can also be found through computerized searches of these same sources. In this section we provide an overview of electronic searching, but library methods and procedures change frequently. Please heed the following advice: Ask a librarian for help. You pay their salary and they are delighted to answer your questions. They will also be able to refer you to one of the many workshops and learning programs that are sponsored by college and university libraries.

Books

If your topic has been around for more than six months, there are likely to be books written about it. So a good starting place is to locate several books. Most libraries have transferred records of their book holdings to a computerized online catalogue system. Whether you choose to thumb through a card catalogue or conduct a computerized search, you will be able to find books by title, author, or subject. Although you may occasionally know the title or author of a book you want, you are more likely to be looking for books using a subject label, such as "violence mass media."

In addition to being able to search for specific author, title, and subject, most online catalogues now also include search capabilities that allow you to enter "key words." You are likely to find this feature most useful for your topic searches. Even with this user-friendly system, you may find that you need to exercise some creativity in discovering the best key word(s) to use in the search.

For instance, if Jeremy is looking for books on the subject "violence in mass media," a few minutes of creative thinking will provide several key word phrases that would bring a variety of "hits." Each hit (or item found) aids Jeremy in his search. Notice the difference in hits Jeremy found using each of the following key words:

media violence (95)

violence in mass media (57)

violence television (88)

The information about one book Jeremy located under "media violence" is shown in Exhibit 6.1.

Although some of the information on the card may seem to be irrelevant, you certainly want the *location* (for instance, the University of Cincinnati has several college libraries and one all-university library on campus), the *call number*, and the

EXHIBIT 6.1 Library card

Author:	Marker, Martin & Petley, Julian (Eds.)
Title:	Ill Effects: The Media/Violence Debate
Pub Info:	London; New York: Routledge, 2001
Description:	ix, 229 p.:ill.; 24cm
Note	Includes bibliographical references and Index
Subject:	Violence in Mass Media
OCLC#:	45172651
ISBN:	0415225124
LCCN:	00045952

Location	Call No.	Status
1) Langsam stacks	P96 V5 I55 2001	Available

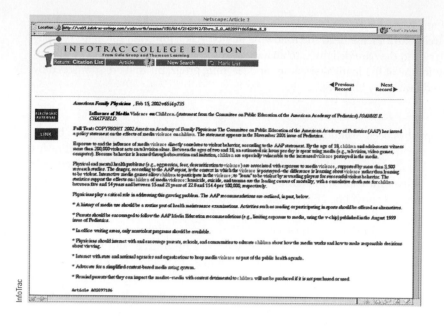

book's availability. The other bit of useful information is under "Note." In this case that heading tells us that the book includes bibliographical references and an index.

In addition to providing a great deal of useful information, finding a book on your topic often leads you to additional sources. For instance, Jeremy might find several excellent additional sources from the *Ill Effects* bibliography of references alone.

Using a manual or electronic card catalogue database is a quick way to find appropriate books, but it is not the only way. If you have the call number for one book on a topic, you can then go to the section of the library in which books using that general call number are housed (in this case P96 V5 I55 2001) and find other books on the subject. You can then thumb through them quickly to check their usefulness.

Periodicals

periodicals magazines and journals that appear at fixed periods

Magazines and journals that appear at fixed periods are called **periodicals**. *Magazines* are periodicals published primarily for commercial reasons. The content of magazines is under the direction and control of the editorial staff, who may or may not be content experts. *Journals* are periodicals published by learned societies primarily for informational and educational purposes. The content of journals is under the control of the editorial staff, who are content experts. Articles in many journals undergo a process of review by other experts so that the information presented in the article is believed to be true by experts other than the authors. Information from magazines or periodicals published weekly, biweekly, or monthly may be more current than information you find in books. A periodical may be your best source when your topic is "in the news," when the topic is so limited in scope that it is unlikely to provide enough material for a book, or when you are looking for a very specific aspect of the topic.

Many libraries no longer keep hard copies of periodical indexes, so to find information that is in journals or magazines you will need to look for the electronic indexes that your college or university subscribes to. Here you will find sources for popular magazines such as *Time* and *Newsweek* as well as for academic journals such as *Communication Quarterly* and *Journal of Psychology*.

InfoTrac College Edition is the electronic index that came with each new copy of this textbook. *InfoTrac College Edition* gives you access to articles in more than seven hundred popular magazines and academic journals. You can use InfoTrac College Edition at home, in your college dormitory, or wherever you have Internet access.

InfoTrac University Library is an expanded version of *Infotrac College Edition*. It is available online through most college and university libraries and provides access to several hundred additional popular magazines and academic journals.

Periodical Abstract, another electronic database available online in most college and university libraries, provides access to articles in more than one thousand popular magazines and academic journals. Offerings of these online catalogues are likely to vary from place to place, so it is wise to check with a librarian to see which of these and other catalogues you have access to at your university library.

To find articles on your topic, begin by typing in the subject heading that you are researching. A search of the index database will result in a list of articles related to your subject. You can then choose to read or print the individual articles or use the list of citations to locate the printed copies of original articles in your library's periodicals section. For instance, Rhonda has identified "Ecstasy" as a topic under the heading of "designer drugs" on her brainstorming list. Rhonda had written her tentative speech goal as, "I want my audience to understand the dangers of the drug Ecstasy." Working from her computer at home, Rhonda opens up *InfoTrac College Edition,* types in "ecstasy," and finds fifty-two citations including these:

> Ecstasy abuse: The danger of getting high without flying. Frederick V. Malmstrom, *Flying Safety,* March 2002
>
> Survey finds rise in Ecstasy use among teens. *Alcoholism & Drug Abuse Weekly,* Feb 25, 2002
>
> Club drugs more agony than Ecstasy for young patients. Susan Landers, *American Medical News,* August 13, 2001

All three of these articles are available for downloading to her home computer. At The University of Cincinnati college library, Rhonda could open the extended InfoTrac University Library or Periodical Abstracts index and find lists of articles that include some of these same articles and some different ones. Become familiar with the online indexes available at your library.

Unfortunately, not all articles listed in indexes can be downloaded. For those that can't, check your library's journal and magazine index to see whether the library has printed copies of the journal articles you want. Then you can manually access these.

Now let's turn to other sources that your library is likely to have on its reference shelves.

Newspapers

Newspaper articles are excellent sources of facts about and interpretations of both contemporary and historical issues. Your library probably holds both an index of your nearest major daily newspaper and the *New York Times* index.

Three electronic newspaper indexes that are most useful if they are available to you are (1) *National Newspaper Index,* which indexes five major newspapers—*New York Times, Wall Street Journal, Christian Science Monitor, Washington Post,* and *Los Angeles Times;* (2) *Newsbank,* which not only indexes but also gives you the text of articles from more than 450 U.S. and Canadian newspapers; and (3) InfoTrac College Edition's *National Newspaper Index.*

United States Government Publications

Some government publications are especially useful for locating primary sources. The *Federal Register* is the official daily publication of the rules, proposed rules, and notices of federal agencies, as well as executive orders and other presidential documents. The *Monthly Catalog of United States Government Publications* covers publications of all branches of the federal government. It has semiannual and annual cumulative indexes by title, author/agency, and subject. *GPO Access* is a service of the U.S.

Government Printing Office that provides free electronic access to many important information products produced by the federal government including the *Federal Register*, the *Congressional Record*, and *Statistical Abstracts of the USA*. *GPO Access* can be found at http://www.access.gpo.gov/su_docs/index.html.

Encyclopedias

Most libraries have a recent edition of *Encyclopaedia Britannica*, *Encyclopedia Americana*, and *World Book Encyclopedia*. An encyclopedia can be an excellent starting point for research. Your library is also likely to have a wide variety of specialized encyclopedias to choose from in such areas as religion, philosophy, and science. For instance, your library may have the *African American Encyclopedia*, *Latino Encyclopedia*, *Asian American Encyclopedia*, *Encyclopedia of Computer Science*, *Encyclopedia of Women*, and *Encyclopedia of Women in American Politics*, as well as many more.

Many libraries now have *Encyclopaedia Britannica* online. If yours does, you will be able to access it just as you did the periodical sources.

Statistical Sources

Statistical sources present numerical information on a wide variety of subjects. When you need facts about demography, continents, heads of state, weather, or similar subjects, refer to one of the many single-volume sources that report such data. Two of the most popular statistical sources are *The Statistical Abstract of the United States* (now available online), which provides reference material and numerical information on various aspects of American life, and *The World Almanac and Book of Facts*. You'll find many other almanacs in the same section of reference material where you find these two sources.

Biographical Sources

When you need an account of a person's life, from a thumbnail sketch to a reasonably complete essay, you can turn to one of the many biographical sources. In addition to full-length books and encyclopedia entries, consult such books as *Who's Who in America* and *International Who's Who*. Your library is also likely to carry *Contemporary Black Biography*, *Dictionary of Hispanic Biography*, *Native American Women*, *Who's Who of American Women*, *Who's Who Among Asian Americans*, and many more.

Books of Quotations

A good quotation can be especially provocative as well as informative, so you might also want access to books of quotations. You most likely have heard of *Bartlett's Familiar Quotations*, which has quotations from historical as well as contemporary figures. But your library may also have the *International Thesaurus of Quotations*, *Harper Book of American Quotations*, *My Soul Looks Back, 'Less I Forget: A Collection of Quotations by People of Color*, the *New Quotable Woman*, and the *Oxford Dictionary of Quotations*.

Skimming

Because you are likely to uncover far more articles and books than you can use, you will want to skim sources to determine whether or not to read them in full. **Skimming** is a method of rapidly going through a work to determine what is covered and how. You can skim quickly by reading the first sentence in each paragraph.

If you are evaluating a magazine article, spend a minute or two finding out whether it really presents information on the exact area of the topic you are exploring

skimming a method of rapidly going through a work to determine what is covered and how

David Young-Wolff/PhotoEdit, Inc.

Library research is essential for many speech topics, but merely the fact that something is in print doesn't make it good supporting material. The information you uncover needs to be evaluated for its trustworthiness and relevance to your topic and specific purpose.

and whether it contains any documented statistics, examples, or quotable opinions. (We'll examine the kind of information to look for in the next section.) If you are evaluating a book, read the table of contents carefully, look at the index, and skim pertinent chapters, asking the same questions as you would for a magazine article.

Skimming helps you decide which sources should be read in full, which should be read in part, and which should be abandoned. Minutes spent in such evaluation will save hours of reading.

If you are compiling a periodical bibliography on a computer, you will discover that the services your library subscribes to are likely to include short abstracts for each article that can be viewed on the computer screen. A look at these abstracts will help you determine which sources you want to read in their entirety. Once you have the sources in hand, however, you'll still want to follow a skimming procedure.

Locating Internet Resources

In addition to printed resources, you will want to browse resources located on the **Internet**, an international electronic collection of thousands of smaller networks. The

Internet an international electronic network of networks

World Wide Web (WWW) is one network that houses information on a broad range of topics. Today, you have access to the Internet either through your college or university library or its computer labs, or through your own personal computer. Public libraries also often provide Internet access. You can find traditional print resources through the Internet, but you can also access databases and bulletin boards, scholarly and professional electronic discussion groups, Web sites, and Web pages authored by individuals or groups.

Most Internet service providers have a search feature that will help you locate sites. To use this feature, type in a key word for your search. If you want to be more effective, find out which computer symbols help limit and focus your search. For example, if Jeremy uses AltaVista and puts quotation marks around the words "media violence," he will only get hits in which these two words appear together. If he does not use quotation marks, he will get hits in which either word appears—which gives him a lot of information that is not useful for his speech. Just as there are different types of print resources, so too there are several types of electronic sources.

Newsgroups

A *newsgroup* or *bulletin board* is "an electronic gathering place for people with similar interests."[1] To communicate in a newsgroup, a user posts a message (called an *article*) about some topic that is appropriate for the site. Other users read these articles and, when so disposed, respond. The result is a kind of ongoing discussion in which users (ten, fifty, or maybe even hundreds) may participate. The Internet offers literally thousands of newsgroup opportunities.[2] Today many college classes require students to share their ideas and opinions about course-related topics in class-specific newsgroups.

Internet Chat

Besides joining newsgroups, you can also interact online with people through "chat." Chat is an online interactive message exchange between two or more people. In newsgroups people post articles and responses, but in a chat room typed responses appear instantly on all participants' computer screens. Thus chat approximates face-to-face conversation in that feedback is relatively instantaneous.

In most chat rooms the conversation is focused on a particular subject area, for example, music, travel, current events, or almost any other topic you can think of. Look for a chat room that is discussing your topic.[3] On most servers, locating a chat room is relatively easy. If you enter "chat (and) wine," for instance, the search results are likely to give you many choices.

Keep in mind that in a chat room everything that is typed appears on everyone's screen. Most people use nicknames rather than their real names, so you can be whoever you want—and so can everyone else. You really have no idea whether a person you are talking with is male or female, young or old, rich or poor. There is no way to ensure that conversational partners are really who they are representing themselves to be.

Hosted Web Sites

Many commercial and nonprofit organizations host Web sites that provide information on the organization and on issues of interest to the organization and its members. For example the Sierra Club Web site at http://sierraclub.org/ provides updates on a variety of environmental issues.

Personal Web Pages

Personal Web pages are created and maintained by individuals. Information that is posted supports specific causes or points of view.

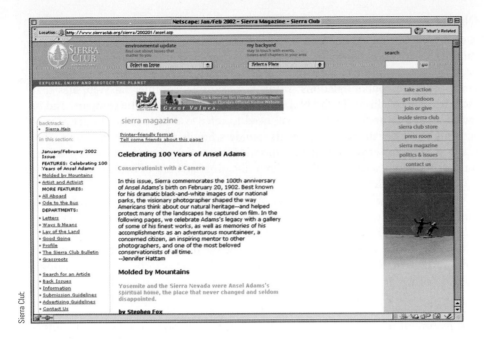

Evaluating Online Resources

The Internet contains information from a wide variety of sources. Some information is posted by authoritative sources, and other information is self-published. Unlike a library where the quality of the collection is overseen by professional librarians, there is no quality control to ensure that information on the Internet is accurate or up to date.

For instance, as the authors of *Researching Online* mention, "While the universality of the Internet can be good in that it allows previously marginalized voices to be heard, it also adds a new layer of difficulty for researchers."[4] What does this mean? Editors of academic articles and books "have always made it a relative certainty that any source in a college library meets a basic standard of reliability and relevance." They go on to say, "Since the Internet lacks those gatekeepers, you're just as likely to encounter uninformed drivel there as you are to find a unique resource that's unavailable in any other form."[5] With this in mind, it's important for you to critically evaluate the information and authorship of the material you find on the Internet. Three criteria to evaluate online sources have been suggested by research librarians.

Authority

The first test of an online resource is the expertise of its author and the reputation of the sponsoring organization. A Web site that doesn't mention the source for the information presented should be disregarded. A first filter of quality is the type of URL. Those ending in gov (governmental), edu (educational), and org are noncommercial sites with institutional publishers. Next check the qualifications of the source or the author. If an author is listed, you can check to see whether the author has a home page that lists professional qualifications. Use a search engine and search by author's name to see whether the author has projects that show expertise, or check the Library of Congress to see whether the author has published in the field.[6]

From some sites you will find information that is anonymous or credited to someone whose background is not clear. In these cases your ability to trust the information depends on evaluating the qualifications of the sponsoring organization. If you do not know whether you can trust the sources, then do not use the information.

Objectivity

A second test for online resources is how impartially the information is presented. Be cautious of Web documents created under the sponsorship of business, government, or public interest groups. These documents are likely to have biases or may be presenting a good "public relations" front. For example, commercial Web sites may include corporate histories and biographical essays that present the company and its founders in a favorable light. You will need to refer to other sources to get a more accurate picture of the company and its founders. Similarly, although the Sierra Club is a well-respected environmental organization, the articles found on its Web site are unlikely to present a balanced discussion of the pros and cons of drilling in the Arctic National Wildlife Refuge.

To evaluate the potential biases of a Web site with which you are unfamiliar, look for the purpose of the Web site. Most home pages contain a purpose or mission statement that can help you understand why the site was created. Armed with this information you are in a better position to recognize the biases that may be contained in the information. Remember, at some level all Web pages can be seen as "infomercials," so always be concerned with who created this information and why.[7]

Currency

One reason for using online sources is that they can provide more up-to-date information than traditional sources.[8] But just because a source is found online does not mean that the information is timely. To determine how up-to-date the information is, you will need to find out when the item was produced, when it was posted (put on the site), and when it was revised.[9] This information should be provided at the end of the page. For example, when we were researching how to determine whether a Web page was current, we found the article cited as note 9. At the end of that article was the following statement: "Created by Esther Grassian, UCLA College Library, 6/95. © Regents of the University of California updated Sept. 6, 2000." From this we knew that the information was originally created in 1995, so it was pretty ancient by Internet standards. But we also saw that the article had been updated in the fall of 2000. Because of the update, we felt that the material in the article could be trusted to reflect current thinking on this topic.

In some cases knowing when a page was last updated is crucial to evaluating the usefulness of the information. For example, suppose Donita is giving a speech on current U.S. policy in the Middle East. She will want to be very careful to examine when entries were created and last updated. Entries created before September 11, 2001, the date of the attack on the World Trade Center, that have not been updated will likely reflect information that is not current.

Even some recent publications use old information. With statistics, especially, you want to know when the data were collected. If, for instance, you are talking about the number of women in Congress, you don't want to be using data more than two years old. Congressional elections occur every two years, and even data from a recent publication could be wrong. Ask, "Is the resource regularly updated? Are dates given?"

Interviewing

interviewing *skillfully asking and answering questions*

Like media reporters, you may get some of the best information for your speech from **interviewing**—skillfully asking and answering questions. How relevant interviewing is to getting information for your speech will of course depend on your topic. To be effective, you'll want to select the best person to interview and have a list of good questions to ask.

When you need to know how people feel about a particular political, economic, or social issue, you can conduct an interview to get their opinions.

Selecting the Best Person

Somewhere on campus or in the larger community are people who have expertise in the topic area of your speech and who can provide you with information. A few telephone calls will usually lead you to the person who would be best to talk with about your topic. For instance, for a speech on "The Effects of Media Violence on Viewers," Jeremy could interview a professor of mass communication or sociology who studies violence in the media. When you have decided whom you should interview, make an appointment—you cannot walk into an office and expect the prospective interviewee to drop everything just to talk to you. Be forthright in your reasons for scheduling the interview. Whether your interview is for a class speech or for a different audience, say so.

Before interviewing the expert, make sure you have done other research on the topic. Interviewees are more likely to talk with you if you appear to be informed; moreover, familiarity with what has been written on the subject will enable you to ask better questions.

If you are trying to get an interview with someone on campus, you might proceed as follows:

> Hello, my name is _____. I am taking a college course in fundamentals of speech, and I'm preparing a speech on the effects of mass media violence on viewers. I understand that you are an expert on this subject. If possible, I'd like to make an appointment to talk with you. Would you be available to talk with me for fifteen or twenty minutes during the next few days?

At the end of the conversation, thank the person, repeat the date and time of the interview, and confirm the office location. If you make the appointment more than a few days ahead, it is usually wise to call the day before the interview to confirm the appointment.

Writing Good Questions

The heart of an effective interviewing plan is a list of good questions. They are likely to be a mix of open-ended and closed questions, both primary and follow-up, phrased to be neutral rather than leading.

primary questions questions the interviewer plans ahead of time that serve as the main points for the interview outline

follow-up questions questions designed to pursue the answers given to primary questions

Primary questions are those main-point questions the interviewer plans ahead of time. **Follow-up questions** are designed to pursue the answers given to primary questions. Although some follow-ups are planned ahead by anticipating possible answers, more often than not they are composed as the interview goes along. Some ("And then?" "Is there more?") encourage further comments, others ("What does 'frequently' mean?" "What were you thinking at the time?") probe, still others ("How did it feel to get the prize?" "Were you worried when you didn't find her?") plumb the feelings of the interviewee. All are designed to motivate a person to enlarge on an answer.

open-ended questions broad-based questions that ask the interviewee to provide whatever information he or she wishes

Open-ended questions ask the interviewee to provide whatever information he or she wishes ("What kinds of people are likely to be most affected by television violence?" "What are some kinds of behaviors that viewers exhibit as a result of viewing violence?" "What research studies would you recommend?"). Through open-ended questions, the interviewer finds out about the person's perspectives, values, and goals, but they do take time to answer.[10]

closed questions narrowly focused questions ranging from those that require yes or no to short answers

Closed questions range from those that require a simple yes or no ("Are young children affected by TV violence more than older children?") to those that require only a short answer ("What behavior seems to be most affected by television violence?"). By asking closed questions, interviewers can control the interview and obtain large amounts of information in a short time. On the other hand, the closed question seldom enables the interviewer to know why a person gave a certain response, nor is the closed question likely to yield much voluntary information.[11]

leading questions questions phrased in a way that suggests the interviewer has a preferred answer

neutral questions questions phrased without direction from the interviewer

For the most part, questions should be phrased neutrally. **Leading questions** are phrased in a way that suggests the interviewer has a preferred answer, for example, "Television violence has a major effect on children's behavior, doesn't it?" **Neutral questions** are phrased without direction from the interviewer, as in "Do you believe television violence has a major effect on children's behavior?"

The content of your questions will depend on what information you seek. In general you should not waste your expert's time by asking questions whose answers are easily obtained through print or electronic sources. Try to formulate a list that stays on the subject so that you can get the information you need without taking up too much time.

How many questions you plan to ask depends on how much time you have for the interview. Keep in mind that you never know how a person will respond. Some people are so talkative and informative that in response to your first question they answer every question you were planning to ask in great detail; other people will answer each question with just a few words.

Early in the interview, plan to ask some questions that can be answered easily and that will show your respect for the person you are interviewing. In an interview with a professor, you might start with background questions such as "How did you get interested in doing research on the effects of media violence?" The goal is to get the interviewee to feel at ease and to talk freely.

The body of the interview includes the major questions you have prepared. You may not ask all the questions you planned to, but don't end the interview until you have the important information you intended to get. Your questions should be designed to illicit the information necessary to achieve your goal.

Exhibit 6.2 shows some of the questions you might ask to get information on the effects of television violence on viewers.

EXHIBIT 6.2 **Sample questions**

Background Information

How did you get interested in doing research on the effects of media violence?

Findings

Does your research show negative effects of television violence on viewers?

Are heavy viewers more likely to show negative effects than light viewers?

Have you found evidence that shows major effects on aggressiveness? Desensitization?

Have you found evidence that shows effects on civility?

How is violence on TV changing?

How are these changes likely to impact heavy viewers?

Action

Are effects great enough to warrant limiting viewing of violent programming for children?

Do you have any recommendations that you would offer the viewing public?

Conducting the Interview

The following guidelines provide a framework for ensuring an effective interview.

1. **Be courteous during the interview.** Start by thanking the person for taking the time to talk to you. Throughout the interview, respect what the person says regardless of what you may think of the answers.

2. **Listen carefully.** In addition to listening to what is said, also pay attention to how it is said. A person's tone of voice, facial expression, and gestures often communicate as much or more than what the person says. If you don't understand, take time to ask questions. If you are not sure you understand, tell the person what you think he or she meant, such as "If I understand you correctly, you're saying that older and younger children react differently to television violence."

SPEECH PREPARATION   **ACTION STEP** 3

Activity 3.1
Identifying Potential Sources

The goal of this exercise is to help you compile a list of potential sources for your speech.

Speech goal:

For the topic you selected for your speech, fill in the following information:

1. Identify a person, an event, or a process you could observe to broaden your personal knowledge base.

2. Working with paper or electronic versions of your library's card catalogue and periodical indexes (including InfoTrac College Edition), find and list specific print resources that appear to provide information for your speech.

3. Using a search engine, identify online resources that may be sources of information for your speech.

4. Identify a person you could interview for additional information for this speech.

Activity 3.1
Identifying Potential Sources

Speech goal: I would like the audience to understand three tests that can be used to tell if a diamond is real.

For the topic you selected for your speech, fill in the following information:

1. Identify a person, an event, or a process you could observe to broaden your personal knowledge base: An event I could observe is a geology teacher explaining to a freshman-level class how to identify rocks and minerals.

2. Working with paper or electronic versions of your library's card catalogue and periodical indexes (including InfoTrac College Edition), find and list specific print resources that appear to provide information for your speech: *Fundamentals of Geology, Earth Structure, Earth System History, Principles of Sedimentology and Stratigraphy, The Solid Earth, Manual of Mineralogy.*

3. Using a search engine, identify any online resources that may be sources of information for your speech: http://www.mcli.dist.maricopa.edu/aaim/linear/Lo.html

4. Identify a person you could interview for additional information for this speech: I could interview my mineralogy teacher, John Farver.

---

3. **Keep the interview moving.** Although some people will get so involved that they will not be concerned with the amount of time spent, most people will have other important business to attend to.

4. **Make sure your nonverbal reactions are in keeping with the tone you want to communicate.** Maintain good eye contact with the person. Nod to show understanding. And smile occasionally to maintain the friendliness of the interview.

Processing the Interview

It's likely that your interview notes were taken in an outline or shorthand form, and they may be difficult to translate later. As soon as possible after the interview, sit down with your notes and make individual note cards of the information you want to use in the speech. If at any point you are not sure whether you have accurately transcribed what the person said, take a minute to telephone the person to double check. You do not want to risk your credibility by misquoting an expert.

Speech Preparation Activity 3.1 on the previous page asks you to identify potential sources you can peruse to find information for your speech. The Student Response for Activity 3.1 provides an example of a student's completed list.

What Information to Look For

Whatever the source, your task will be to look for factual statements, which are presented as examples and illustrations, expert opinions, and various kinds of material to elaborate on your main points.

Factual Statements

Factual statements are statements that can be verified. "A recent study confirmed that preschoolers watch an average of 28 hours of television a week," "The Gateway Solo laptop comes with a CD-ROM drive," and "Johannes Gutenberg invented printing from movable type in the 1400s" are all statements of fact that can be verified. One way to verify whether the information is factual is to check it against material from another source on the same subject.

Be especially skeptical of "facts" that are asserted on the Internet. Because anyone can say virtually anything online, you need to be especially vigilant. Never use any information that is not carefully documented unless you have corroborating sources.

Factual information is often presented in the form of examples and statistics.

Examples

Examples are specific instances that illustrate or explain a general factual statement. When an example is more fully developed, it is called an *illustration*. One or two short examples like these from Susan Paddock in her speech on preventing violence can be used as evidence for a generalization.

> Television is increasing the amount of violence it shows; The XFL—the football league created by the World Wrestling Federation that debuted a month ago—is promoting higher levels of violence in hopes of getting young boys and men to watch.[12]

Examples are useful because they provide concrete instances that make a general statement more meaningful to the audience.

Although most of the examples you find will be real, you may also find hypothetical examples you can use. Hypothetical examples use the facts we have to consider issues that have not actually happened. They develop the idea "What if . . . ?" In the following excerpt, John Ahladas presents hypothetical examples of what it will be like in the year A.D. 2039 if global warming continues at its present rate:

> In New York, workers are building levees to hold back the rising tidal waters of the Hudson River, now lined with palm trees. In Louisiana, 100,000 acres of wetland are steadily being claimed by the sea. In Kansas, farmers learn to live with drought as a way of life and struggle to eke out an existence in the increasingly dry and dusty heartland. . . . And reports arrive from Siberia of bumper crops of corn and wheat from a longer and warmer growing season.[13]

Now let us consider guidelines for selecting and using examples. First, the examples should clarify general facts. Look at the following general facts and supporting examples.

General Fact: Electronics is one of the few areas in which products are significantly cheaper today than they were in the 1980s.

Supporting Example: Cellular phones cost less than they did then.

Even though the support statement is a type of example, it is not a very good one. Listeners do not have a clear picture. "Cost less" is not specific; nor does it exemplify the assertion of being "significantly cheaper."

Look at the difference in the following supporting example.

General Fact: Electronics is one of the few areas in which products are significantly cheaper today than they were in the 1980s.

Supporting Example: In the mid-1980s, Motorola sold cellular phones for $5,000 each; now a person can buy a Motorola cellular phone for under $150.

©Jon Feingersh/corbisstockmarket.com

Use statistics from only the most reliable sources, and double-check any startling statistics with another source.

Second, the examples you choose should be representative and should not be misleading. The cellular phone example that is so vivid would be misleading, and thus unethical, if in fact cellular phones were the only electronics product whose prices had declined dramatically over the same period. Any misuse of data is unethical, especially if the user knows better.

So, as you gather examples to use in your speeches, be sure they are clear and representative. Because good examples can give a clear, vivid picture in a relatively few words, it's a good idea to follow this rule of thumb in preparing your speeches: Never let a general fact stand without at least one example.

Statistics

statistics   numerical facts

Statistics are numerical facts: "Only six out of every ten local citizens voted in the last election." "The cost of living rose 2.5 percent last year." "This year, African Americans, Asian Americans, and Hispanic Americans will represent more than 32 percent of the population of the United States." Such statistical statements enable you to pack a great deal of information into a small package. Statistics can provide impressive support for a point, but when they are poorly used in the speech, they may be boring and, in some instances, downright deceiving. Following are some general guidelines on using statistics effectively.

1. **Record only statistics whose reliability you can verify.** Take statistics from only the most reliable sources and double-check any startling statistics with another source to guard against the use of faulty statistics. For example, it is important to double-check statistics that you find in such sources as paid advertisements or publications distributed by special interest groups. Be especially wary if your source does not itself provide documentation of the statistics it reports.

2. **Record only recent statistics so your audience will not be misled.** For example, suppose you come across the statistic that only 2 of 100 members (or 2 percent) of the U.S. Senate are women. If you used that statistic in a speech, you would be

misleading your audience, because it is way out of date. If you want to make a point about the number of women in the Senate, find the most recent statistics. Check for both the year and/or the range of years to which the statistics apply.

3. **Look for statistics that are used comparatively.** By themselves, statistics are hard to interpret, but when used comparatively, they convey useful information. The statistic that more than two thousand people died last year from flu is not very meaningful unless we know how this compares to previous years. Notice how Jerry Yelverton uses comparative statistics in the following example:

> In all, nuclear energy accounted for about 20 percent of all electricity generated in the United States last year. If you think back a few years to our last big energy crisis, you'll see how oil and nuclear have swapped places. At that time, we generated about 20 percent of our electricity with oil and 3 percent with nuclear power. Today, oil only accounts for about 3 percent of our electricity generation.[14]

> In a speech on chemical waste, Donald Baeder pointed out that whereas in the past chemicals were measured in parts per million, today they are measured in parts per billion or even parts per trillion. Had he stopped at that point the audience would have had little sense of the immensity of the figures. Notice how he goes on to use comparisons to put the meaning of the statistics in perspective:

> One part per billion is the equivalent of one drop—one drop!—of vermouth in two 36,000 gallon tanks of gin and that would be a very dry martini even by San Francisco standards! One part per trillion is the equivalent of one drop in two thousand tank cars.[15]

4. **Do not overuse statistics.** Although statistics may be an excellent way to present a great deal of material quickly, be careful not to overuse them. A few pertinent numbers are far more effective than a battery of statistics. When you need to present a lot of statistical information, prepare a visual aid, such as a chart, to help your audience understand them.

Although statistics add important information, statistics must always be used ethically. The old statement "Figures don't lie, but liars figure" is worth keeping in mind as you evaluate the statistics (figures) you are considering for your speech. To maintain an appropriate ethic, you must take into account several variables: When were the statistics true? Do they still provide an accurate picture? Exactly what do the statistics cover? Are they representative of the group you wish to apply them to? How were the statistics calculated? If the statistic is based on only a sample, how was that sample selected? Is the statistic an average? A median point? The most common response? A percentage? How does the method by which the statistic is reported affect what you can conclude?

When well used, and well presented, statistics can be most illuminating. Consider this picture of global demographic data presented by William Franklin, President of Franklin International, Ltd.

> I recently saw some demographic information which may help to bring perspective to your opportunities and responsibilities, some perspective on your place or role in the world.
>
> If we shrink the world's 5.7 billion population to a village of 100 people . . . with all existing human ratios remaining the same, here is the resulting profile.
>
> Of those 100 people, 57 are Asian, 21 European, 14 from North and South America, and 8 from Africa
>
> 51 female, 49 male
>
> 80 live in sub-standard housing
>
> 70 cannot read

Half suffer from malnutrition

75 have never made a phone call

Less than one is on the Internet

Half the entire village's wealth would be in the hands of 6 people

Only one of the hundred has a college education

You are in a very elite group of only 1% who have a college education.[16]

Expert Opinions

expert opinions interpretations and judgments made by authorities in a particular subject area

Expert opinions are interpretations and judgments made by authorities in a particular subject area. "Watching 28 hours of television a week is far too much for young children," "Having a CD-ROM port on your computer is a necessity," and "The invention of printing from movable type was for all intents and purposes the start of mass communication" are all opinions based on the factual statements cited previously. Whether they are expert opinions or not depends on who made the statements.

How do you tell if a source is an expert? First, the expert must be a master of the specific subject. Second, the expert is recognized by others in his or her field as having expertise. For instance, a history professor may qualify as an expert in his or her field of study of Ancient Greece but not qualify as an expert in Incan history. Third, experts have engaged in long-term study of a subject.

When you use expert opinions in your speech, be sure to identify them as opinions and indicate to your audience the level of confidence that should be attached to them. For instance, an informative speaker may say, "The temperatures throughout the 1990s were much higher than average. Paul Jorgenson, a space biologist, believes these higher than average temperatures represent the first stages of the greenhouse effect, but the significance of these temperatures is not completely accepted as fact."

Although opinions cannot entirely take the place of documented facts, expert opinion can be used to interpret and give weight to facts that you have discovered.

Elaborations: Anecdotes, Narratives, Comparisons and Contrasts, and Quotations

Factual information and expert opinions can be elaborated upon through anecdotes and narratives, comparisons and contrasts, or quotable explanations and opinions. In addition to providing information, these forms are chosen to adapt the factual material or expert opinion to a particular audience.

Anecdotes and Narratives

anecdotes brief, often amusing stories

narratives tales, accounts, personal experiences, or lengthier stories

Anecdotes are brief, often amusing stories; **narratives** are tales, accounts, personal experiences, or lengthier stories. Each presents material in story form. Because holding audience interest is important in a speech and because audience attention is likely to be captured by a story, anecdotes and narratives are worth looking for, creating, and using. In a five-minute speech, you have little time to tell a detailed story, so one or two anecdotes or a very short narrative would be preferable.

The key to using stories is to make sure that the point of the story states or reinforces the point you are making in your speech. In this speech John Howard made a point about failure to follow guidelines:

The knight was returning to the castle after a long, hard day. His face was bruised and badly swollen. His armor was dented. The plume on his helmet was broken, and his steed was limping. He was a sad sight.

The lord of the castle ran out and asked, "What hath befallen you, Sir Timothy?"

"Oh, Sire," he said, "I have been laboring all day in your service, bloodying and pillaging your enemies to the West."

"You've been doing what?" gasped the astonished nobleman. "I haven't any enemies to the West!"

"Oh!" said Timothy. "Well, I think you do now."[17]

There is a moral to this little story. Enthusiasm is not enough; you need to have a sense of direction.

Good stories and narrative may be humorous, sentimental, suspenseful, or dramatic. Your choice should reflect the emotional tone you want to convey to your audience.

Comparisons and Contrasts

One of the best ways to give meaning to new ideas is through comparison and contrast. **Comparisons** illuminate a point by showing its similarities to something else. Although you can easily create comparisons, you should still keep your eye open for creative comparisons developed by the authors of the books and articles you have found.

comparisons illuminate a point by showing similarities

Comparisons may be literal or figurative. Literal comparisons show similarities between real things:

> The walk from the lighthouse back up the hill to the parking lot is equal to walking up the stairs of a thirty-story building.

Figurative comparisons express one thing in terms normally denoting another:

> I always envisioned myself as a four-door sedan. I didn't know she was looking for a sports car!

Comparisons not only make ideas clearer but also more vivid. Notice how Stephen Trachtenberg, in a speech to the Newington High School Scholars' Breakfast, used a figurative comparison to demonstrate the importance of being willing to take risks even in the face of danger. Although the speech was given years ago, the point is timeless:

> The eagle flying high always risks being shot at by some hare-brained human with a rifle. But eagles and young eagles like you still prefer the view from that risky height to what is available flying with the turkeys far, far below.[18]

Whereas comparisons suggest similarities, **contrasts** highlight differences. Notice how the following humorous contrast dramatizes the difference between "participation" and "commitment."

contrasts highlight differences

> If this morning you had bacon and eggs for breakfast, I think it illustrates the difference. The eggs represented "participation" on the part of the chicken. The bacon represented "total commitment" on the part of the pig![19]

Quotations

When you find an explanation, an opinion, or a brief anecdote that seems to be exactly what you are looking for, you may quote it directly in your speech. Because audiences want to listen to your ideas and arguments, they do not want to hear a string of long quotations. Nevertheless, a well-selected quotation might be perfect in one or two key places.

Quotations can both explain and vivify. Look for quotations that make a point in a particularly clear or vivid way. For example, in his speech "Enduring Values for a Secular Age," Hans Becherer, Executive Officer at Deere & Company, used this Henry Ford quote to show the importance of enthusiasm to progress:

> Enthusiasm is at the heart of all progress. With it, there is accomplishment. Without it, there are only alibis.[20]

Frequently, historical or literary quotations can reinforce a point vividly. Cynthia Opheim, Chair of the Department of Political Science at Southwest Texas State University, in her speech "Making Democracy Work" quoted Mark Twain on the frustration of witnessing legislative decision making when she said:

> There are two things you should never watch being made: sausage and legislation.[21]

To take advantage of such opportunities, you need access to one or more of the many books of quotations mentioned earlier in this chapter. Most books of quotations are organized by topic, which helps in finding a particularly appropriate quote to use in your speech.

When you use a direct quotation, keep in mind that it is necessary to credit the person who formulated it. Using any quotation or close paraphrase without crediting its source is plagiarism.

Recording Information and Citing Written and Electronic Sources

Whether the research materials you find are factual statements or opinions, you need to record the data accurately and keep a careful account of your sources so that they can be cited appropriately.

Recording Information on Note Cards

It is important to record information so that you can provide the information and its source in a speech or report the documentation to anyone who might question the information's accuracy. How should you record information you plan to use? Because you can never be sure of the final order in which it is used, it is best to record information on note cards.

In the note card method, each factual statement or expert opinion, along with source documentation, is recorded on a separate 4-by-6-inch or larger index card. Although it may seem easier to record all material from one source on a single sheet of paper (or to photocopy source material), sorting and arranging material is much easier when each item is recorded separately. On each card, indicate the topic of the recorded information, the information, and the publication data necessary for a complete bibliographic citation. Any part of the information that is quoted directly should be enclosed in quotation marks.

Publication data differ depending on whether the information is from a book, a periodical or newspaper, an interview, observation, personal experience, or a Web site.

For books, include names of authors, title of the book, the place of publication and the publisher, the date of publication, and the page or pages from which the information is taken.

EXHIBIT 6.3 **Example of a note card with information recorded**

Topic: Ebola

Heading: Resurfacing of the disease

"After lying dormant for three years, the Ebola virus has resurfaced—this time in Uganda, where 31 people have died from the deadly disease."

Henry Wasswa, "Ebola outbreak in northern Uganda claims 31 lives in past two weeks," *Naples Daily News,* October 16, 2000, p. 11A.

For a periodical or newspaper, include the name of the author (if given), the title of the article, the name of the publication, the date, and the page number from which the information is taken.

For online sources, include the author (if known), the page title, the URL for the Web page, the date the page was last updated, and the date that you accessed the site.

For interviews, include the person interviewed, his or her title, and the location and date of the interview.

For observations, record the title of the process and/or person observed, the place where the observation occurred, and the date of the observation.

Specifics and samples for preparing source citations (including interviews) for inclusion in the complete outline are shown in Chapter 8. In all cases, list source information in enough detail so that the information can be found later if needed. Exhibit 6.3 illustrates correct note card form.

SPEECH PREPARATION   **ACTION STEP** 3

Activity 3.2
Preparing Note Cards

The goal of this activity is to review the source material you identified in Activity 3.1 and record specific items of information that you might wish to use in your speech. The number of note cards you have will vary by topic and type of speech.

1. Read all print and electronic sources. As you come upon an item (example, illustration, statistic, anecdote, narrative, comparison/contrast, quotation, definition, or description) that you think would be useful in your speech, record the item on a note card using the form detailed in Exhibit 6.3.

2. Visit the Web sites and Web pages. Evaluate the quality of the Web site or page using the criteria discussed in this chapter. Read the relevant content, and as you locate items of information, record each on a note card using proper form.

3. If you observe the person, event, or process you identified in Activity 3.1, take notes. Review your notes after the observation and record items of information from your notes onto note cards using the proper form.

4. If you interview someone, take thorough notes or tape record the interview. Be sure to specify exact quotations. Then review your interview notes/recording and transfer specific items of information you might want to use onto note cards using proper form.

Activity 3.2
Preparing Note Cards

Speech goal: I would like the audience to understand three tests that can be used to tell if a diamond is real.

Card 1

Topic: Testing Diamonds

Heading: streak test

"A streak test is conventionally tested by scraping the sample across a piece of englazed tile or porcelain and then examining the color of the mark made."

Carla W. Montgomery, *Fundamentals of Geology,* 3d ed. (Dubuque, IA: Wm. C. Brown, 1997), p. 22.

Card 2

Topic: Testing Diamonds

Heading: streak test

Malachite leaves a green streak mark; Hematite leaves a reddish-brown streak mark.

Cornelius Klein, *Manual of Mineralogy,* 2d ed. (New York: John Wiley & Sons, (1993).

Card 3

Topic: Testing Diamonds

A new pocket-sized diamond and gemstone identification device may be available to jewelers soon.

John Gallagher, Diamond Detector Measures Density, *National Jeweler,* June 16, 2001, v45 p. 14.

Card 4

Topic: Testing Diamonds

Hardness tests of minerals are among the easiest tests to perform.

The Hardness of Minerals and Rocks. Dr. William S. Cordua, University of Wisconsin (Home page). http://www.rockhounds.com/rockshop/hardness1.html

As your stack of information note cards grows, you can sort the material, placing each item under the heading to which it is related. For instance, for a speech on Ebola, the deadly disease that has broken out in Africa, you might have note cards related to causes, symptoms, and means of transmission. The card in Exhibit 6.3 would be indexed under the heading "Deadliness of Disease."

The number of sources that you will need depends in part on the type of speech you are giving. For a narrative/personal experience, you will be the main, if not the only, source. For informative reports and persuasive speeches, however, speakers ordinarily use several sources. For a five-minute speech on Ebola in which you plan to talk about causes, symptoms, and means of transmission, you should probably have two or more note cards under each heading. Moreover, the note cards should come from at least three different sources. Avoid using only one source for your information because this often leads to plagiarism; furthermore, basing your speech on one or two sources suggests that you have not done sufficient research. Selecting and using information from several sources enables you to develop an original approach to your topic and ensures a broader research base for the information you present.

Speech Preparation Activity 3.2 on page 111 directs you in preparing note cards with information that you can use in your speech. The Student Response for Activity 3.2 gives an example of this activity completed by a student in this course.

Citing Sources in Speeches

In your speeches, as in any communication in which you use ideas that are not your own, you need to acknowledge your sources. Specifically mentioning your sources not only helps the audience evaluate the content but also adds to your credibility. In addition, citing sources will give concrete evidence of the depth of your research. Failure to cite sources, especially when you are presenting information that is meant to substantiate a controversial point, is unethical.

In a written report, ideas taken from other sources are credited in footnotes; in a speech, these notations must be included in your statement of the material. Although you do not want to clutter your speech with long bibliographical citations, be sure to mention the sources of your most important information. Exhibit 6.4 gives several examples of appropriate source citations.

Summary

Effective speaking requires high-quality information. You need to know where to look for information, what kind of information to look for, how to record it, and how to cite your sources in your speeches.

To find material, begin by exploring your own knowledge and work outward through observation, written and electronic sources, and interviewing. Look for material in books, periodicals, encyclopedias, statistical sources, biographical sources, newspapers, government publications, electronic databases, and on the Internet. Skim materials to evaluate sources quickly and determine whether or not to read them in full.

EXHIBIT 6.4 Appropriate speech source citations

"According to an article about Japanese workers in last week's *Time* magazine . . ."

"In the latest Gallup poll cited in the February 10 issue of *Newsweek* . . ."

"But to get a complete picture we have to look at the statistics. According to the 2000 *Statistical Abstract*, the level of production for the European Economic Community rose from . . ."

"In a speech on business ethics delivered to the Public Relations Society of America last November, Preston Townly, CEO of the Conference Board, said . . ."

"According to Gloria Hollister, Women's Basketball Coach, whom I interviewed last week . . ."

"From a survey that I took Tuesday of your opinions . . ."

"According to statistics included on the U.S. Department of Justice Drug Enforcement Administration Web site report on Rohypnol . . ."

"Dan, I was wondering whether you'd listen to the speech I'm giving in class tomorrow. It will only take about five minutes."

"Sure." Tom and Dan found an empty classroom and Tom went through his speech.

"What did you think?"

"Sounded pretty good to me. I could follow the speech—I knew what you wanted to do. But I was wondering about that section where you had the statistics. You didn't give any source."

"Well, the fact is I can't remember the source."

"You remember the statistics that specifically but you don't remember the source?"

"Well, I don't remember the statistics all that well, but I think I've got them about right."

"Well, you can check it can't you?"

"Check it? Where? That would take me hours. And after all I told you I think I have them about right."

"But Tom, the accuracy of the statistics seems pretty important to what you said."

"Listen, trust me on this—no one is going to say anything about it. You've already said that my goal was clear, my main points were clear, and I sounded as if I know what I'm talking about. I really think that's all Goodwin is interested in."

"Well, whatever you say, Tom. I just thought I'd ask."

"No problem, thanks for listening. I thought I had it in pretty good shape, but I wanted someone to hear my last practice."

"Well, good luck!"

1. What do you think of Tom's assessment of his use of statistics that "No one is going to say anything about it"?

2. Does Tom have any further ethical obligation? If so, what is it?

Two major types of supporting material for speeches are factual statements and expert opinions. Factual statements report verifiable occurrences. Expert opinions are interpretations of facts made by qualified authorities. Although you will use some of your material as you find it, you may want to present the information in a different form. Depending on your topic and speech goal, you may use facts and opinions orally in the form of examples, illustrations, statistics, anecdotes, narratives, comparisons, contrasts, and quotations.

A good method for recording material that you may want to use in your speech is to write each item of information, along with its bibliographical documentation, on a separate note card. As your stack of information grows, sort the material under common headings. During the speech, cite the sources for your information. You'll want to include a complete list of sources for the speech on your completed outline.

CHALLENGE ONLINE

Use your Challenge of Effective Speaking CD-ROM for quick access to the electronic study resources that accompany this text. Included on your CD-ROM is access to the Challenge of Effective Speaking Web site featuring Speech Builder Express at Wadsworth Communication Café, InfoTrac College Edition, and a demo of WebTutor for *The Challenge of Effective Speaking*. The Web site offers a chapter-by-chapter access to the Speech Preparation Action Step Activities, InfoTrac College Edition exercises, a digital glossary of key terms, Web links, Speech Preparation Forms, Speech Evaluation Checklists, and quizzes. Review the key terms and complete the InfoTrac College Edition exercise on the book's Web site at:
http://www.wadsworth.com/product/0534563856

InfoTrac College Edition Exercise

Use InfoTrac College Edition to find information on the subject you have selected for your speech. Enter your speech subject in the search bar and then press Enter. Look for articles that include information that seems relevant to your speech. Whether you download the article or make note cards, make sure you have the necessary data to cite the source of information if you use it in your speech.

Key Terms

anecdotes *(108)*	**factual statements** *(105)*	**neutral questions** *(102)*
closed questions *(102)*	**follow-up questions** *(102)*	**open-ended questions** *(102)*
comparisons *(109)*	**Internet** *(97)*	**periodicals** *(94)*
contrasts *(109)*	**interviewing** *(100)*	**primary questions** *(102)*
examples *(105)*	**leading questions** *(102)*	**skimming** *(96)*
expert opinions *(108)*	**narratives** *(108)*	**statistics** *(106)*

Organizing and Outlining the Speech Body

Peter Chapman Photography

Every discourse like a living creature, should be put together that it has its own body and lacks neither head nor feet, middle nor extremities, all composed in such a way that suit both each other and the whole.

—Plato, *Phaedrus*

"Troy, that was a terrific speech that Mareka gave on how we can recycle paper on campus.
I didn't realize the efforts other universities are making to help the environment. I
haven't heard so many good stories in a long time."

"You're right, Brett, the stories were interesting, but, you know, I had a hard
time following the talk. What did you make of it?"

"Well, she was talking about ways that we can help save the environment—but,
you're right, I can't seem to remember anything but that one point about recycling.
Let's see, what were the other key points?"

ACTION STEP 4

Organize and develop your material in a way that is best suited to your audience.

A. Write a thesis statement that indicates the specifics of the speech goal.

B. Outline main points as complete sentences that are clear, parallel, and meaningful.

C. Order the main points following an organizational pattern that meets audience needs.

D. Add supporting information.

E. Create section transitions to serve as guidelines.

Troy and Brett's experience is not that unusual, for even some well-known
speakers give speeches that aren't as clearly organized as they could be. Yet a
speech that is well organized is far more likely to achieve its goal than one that
is not. In this chapter and in Chapter 8 we consider the fourth action step: Organize
and develop your material in a way that is best suited to your audience. This chapter
focuses on writing a thesis statement that indicates the specifics of the speech goal,
outlining main points, ordering the main points, adding supporting information, and
creating section transitions; Chapter 8 focuses on adding the introduction, conclusion, and other necessary elements to complete the speech outline. The value of
working with an outline is that you can test the logic, development, and overall
strength of the structure of your speech before you prepare the wording or begin
practicing its delivery.

Writing a Thesis Statement

Once you have a tentative speech goal and have drawn together information for your
speech, begin framing the structure of the speech by writing a **thesis statement**, a
sentence that outlines the elements of the specific goal statement. The clearer your
thesis statement is at this stage of preparation, the easier it is to select, state, and begin
to build your main points.

The more specifically you have written your speech goal, the easier it is to write a
thesis statement. Let's first look at Erin's experience. Here is Erin's speech goal: "I
want to inform the audience of the three steps for executing an effective volleyball
spike." Because Erin is a member of the women's varsity volleyball team, she already
knows her subject matter well enough to write her thesis statement: "The three steps
for executing an effective volleyball spike are to have a good approach, a powerful
swing, and a good follow-through."

Often, however, you will have collected a variety of information related to your
specific speech goal. Then you have to make a decision about what information is the

thesis statement a sentence
that outlines the specific elements
of the speech supporting the goal
statement

most valuable for achieving your goal. Let's consider an example to illustrate how you might proceed to select the points you want to talk about now that you have found most of the information you will use in your speech.

Emming wanted to give a speech on choosing a credit card, and he wrote this specific goal: "I would like the audience to understand the major criteria for choosing a credit card." Emming already had a few ideas about what he might focus on in the speech, but it wasn't until he completed most of his research that he really had enough information to write down seven specific ideas of what might be the key criteria for finding a suitable credit card:

> interest rate
>
> convenience
>
> discounts
>
> annual fee
>
> rebates
>
> institutional reputation
>
> frequent flyer points

List several potential idea for your main points, then you can begin to evaluate them and select two to five that are most relevant for your thesis statement. For instance, Emming noticed that several of his sources discussed both interest rate and annual fee. Moreover, nearly every source mentioned at least one inducement, such as rebates. Emming crossed out those criteria (topics) that did not have as much support and combined individual inducements under a single heading. Now his list looked like this:

> interest rate
>
> ~~convenience~~
>
> discounts ⟍
>
> annual fee
>
> rebates ——————————⟶ perks
>
> ~~institutional reputation~~
>
> frequent flyer points ⟋

Now Emming was able to write his tentative thesis statement using this structure: "Three criteria that will enable the audience to find the most suitable credit card are level of real interest rate, annual fee, and advertised inducements (perks)."

Speech Preparation Activity 4.1 asks you to develop a well-written thesis statement for your speech. Student Response Activity 4.1A on page 120 gives an example of this activity completed by a student in this course. Student Response Activity 4.1B, also on page 120, puts Emming's work in student response form.

Outlining Main Points

main points complete-sentence representations of the ideas you have used in your thesis statement

Once you've determined a thesis statement, you can begin outlining the main points that will make up the body of your speech. **Main points** are complete-sentence representations of the ideas you have specified in your thesis statement. Think of your main points as the key building blocks of a speech—the ideas you want your audience to remember if they remember nothing else.

Activity 4.1
Writing Thesis Statements

The goal of this activity is to develop a well-worded thesis statement for your speech.

1. Write the specific goal you developed from Speech Preparation Activity 1.4:

2. Does your speech goal list a specific number of ideas?

3. If yes, list the ideas and move to item 6:

4. If no, based on your research, identify and list the specific ideas your audience must learn about if you are to reach your speech goal:

5. Review this list and identify items that can be grouped together under a larger category. Then select the two to five items that your research suggests are most important for this audience to understand:

6. After identifying the specific ideas that must be communicated to your audience in order to reach your goal, write a thesis statement that incorporates these ideas:

Write Main Points as Complete Sentences

It is important to write main points as complete sentences because only sentences can fully express the relationships associated with the key elements of the thesis statement.

Let's consider Emming's speech in which his thesis statement is written as follows: "Three criteria you can use to find a suitable credit card are level of real interest rate, annual fee, and advertised perks."

Suppose he wrote his first draft of main points as follows:

I. Level of interest rate
II. Annual fee
III. Advertised perks

Think of yourself as an audience member who hears only these words. Would you really understand what they meant? Not likely, because these words alone do not capture the meanings expressed in the thesis statement. These elements only make sense insofar as they are criteria used for selecting a credit card.

So, as his first attempt at complete-sentence main points, Emming might write the following:

I. Examining the interest rate is one criterion you can use to find a credit card that is suitable for where you are in life.

II. Another criterion you can use to make sure you find a credit card that is suitable for where you are in life is to examine the annual fee.

III. Finding a credit card can also depend on weighing the advertised perks, which is the third criterion you will want to use to be sure that it is suitable for where you are in life.

Now he has complete sentences. But do these wordings achieve his goal? No. Notice that we referred to this rendering as "a first draft of the main points." Occasionally,

Activitiy 4.1 A
Writing Thesis Statements

1. Write the specific goal you developed from Speech Activity 1.4.
   Specific Goal: I want my audience to understand three skills necessary to learn to play the game of lacrosse.

2. Does your speech goal list a specific number of ideas? Yes

3. If yes, list the items and move to item 6: catching, cradling, throwing

4. If no, based on your research, identify and list the specific ideas your audience must learn about if you are to reach your speech goal:

5. Review this list and identify items that can be grouped together under a larger category. Then select the 2 to 5 items that your research suggest are the most important for this audience to understand:

6. After identifying the specific ideas that must be communicated to your audience in order to reach your goal, write a thesis statement that incorporates these ideas:

   Three skills necessary to learn to play the game of lacrosse are catching, throwing, and cradling the ball.

Activitiy 4.1 B
Writing Thesis Statements

1. Write the specific goal you developed from Speech Preparation Activity 1.4:
   Specific Goal: I want the audience to be able to find the credit card that is most suitable for them.

2. Does your speech goal list a specific number of ideas? No

3. If yes, list the items and move to item 6:

4. If no, based on your research, identify and list the specific ideas your audience must learn about if you are to reach your speech goal: interest rate, convenience, discounts, annual fee, rebates, institutional reputation, frequent flyer points

5. Review this list and identify items that can be grouped together under a larger category. Then select the two to five items that your research suggests are most important for this audience to understand: real interest rate, convenience, annual fee, advertised perks (combination of discounts, rebates, and frequent flyer points)

6. After identifying the specific ideas that must be communicated to your audience in order to reach your goal, write a thesis statement that incorporates these ideas: Three criteria you can use to find a suitable credit card are level of real interest rate, annual fee, and advertised perks.

your first draft will actually become the wording you want to use. More often, how-ever, you will find that your initial wording can be improved.

Revise Main Points

To help you improve the wording of your main points, ask yourself the following questions:

- Are main points clear?
- Are main points parallel in structure?
- Are main points meaningful?
- Are main points limited to a maximum of five?

To see how you can use these questions to refine your speech plan, let's consider Emming's main points more carefully. Emming has made a pretty good start. His three main points are complete sentences that capture the essence of the thesis state-ment. Now let's see how Emming might use the four questions to assure himself that he has achieved the best wording for his points.

1. **Are the main points clear?** Main points are **clear** when their wording is likely to call up the same images in the minds of most audience members. Emming has drafted his third main point as follows:

   III. Finding a suitable credit card can also depend on weighing the advertised perks, which is the third criterion you will want to use to be sure that it is suitable for where you are in life.

   As he reviews the wording of this point, he notices that it is repetitive ("suitable . . . suitable"), too general ("where you are in life"), and wordy ("which is the third criterion that you will want to use to be sure that it is suitable").

   Emming could eliminate several of the problems by cutting all the words before "weighing the advertised perks," cutting "which," and changing the rest of the sentence to "is the third criterion for finding a suitable credit card." After these changes, Emming would then have a main point written as follows:

   III. Weighing the advertised perks is the third criterion for finding a suitable credit card.

2. **Are the main points parallel in structure?** Main points are **parallel** when their wording follows the same structural pattern, often using the same introductory words. Parallel structure helps the audience recognize main points by recalling a pattern in the wording.

   Emming notices that each of his main points begins with different wording. He now decides to begin each main point with the words "One (a second, a third) criterion for finding a suitable credit card":

   I. One criterion for finding a suitable credit card is to examine the interest rate.

   II. A second criterion for finding a suitable credit card is to examine the annual fee.

   III. A third criterion for finding a suitable credit card is to weigh the perks.

   Parallelism can be achieved in many other ways. A second way is to start each sentence with an active verb. To take a different example, suppose Kenneth wants his audience to understand the steps involved in antiquing a table. He might write the following first draft of his main points:

> **clarity of main points** when main point wording is likely to call up the same images in the minds of all audience members

> **parallel structure of main points** when main point wording follows the same structural pattern, often using the same introductory words

I. Clean the table thoroughly.

II. The base coat can be painted over the old surface.

III. A stiff brush, sponge, or piece of textured material can be used to apply the antique finish.

IV. Then you will want to apply two coats of shellac to harden the finish.

After further consideration, Kenneth might revise his main points to make them parallel in structure. Note the parallel active verbs (italicized) used in his final draft:

I. *Clean* the table thoroughly.

II. *Paint* the base coat over the old surface.

III. *Apply* the antique finish with a stiff brush.

IV. *Harden* the surface with two coats of shellac.

Notice how the similarity of structure clarifies and strengthens the message. The audience can immediately identify the key steps in the process.

meaningful main points when main points are informative

3. **Are the main points meaningful?** Main points are **meaningful** when they are informative. If the main points are not really meaningful, even if the audience remembers them, what is remembered may not be useful.

For instance, let's go back to Emming's first main point. Suppose he had written it as follows:

I. Thinking about the interest is one thing.

If he really decided to word his first point this way, and if his audience remembered it, what would they know? This phrasing just isn't very meaningful. Obviously, the following is a much better choice:

I. One criterion for finding a suitable credit card is to examine the interest rate.

Now here is a classic example of total failure to achieve the goal of meaningful main points.

Specific Goal: I want the audience to understand the characteristics of three different bears.
Thesis Statement: Black bears, grizzly bears, and polar bears all have different characteristics.

I. There are facts about the American black bear.

II. There are facts about grizzly bears.

III. There are facts about polar bears.

Obviously, remembering these main points does nothing for the audience. In a case like this, the speaker should recognize that the tentative main points are meaningless. To correct the problem, the speaker may need to reconsider the thesis statement. For example, this thesis statement is likely to lead the speaker to a much better statement of main points: **Thesis Statement:** Black bears, grizzly bears, and polar bears differ in size, eating habits, and aggressiveness.

4. **Are main points limited to a maximum of five?** Although we stated that the thesis statement should suggest two to five main ideas, as you begin to phrase prospective main points, you may find your initial list has grown to six, seven, or even ten points that seem to be main ideas. A list that long is usually a clue that some points can be grouped. If you have more than five, rework your thesis statement to limit the number of main points by grouping similar points under a

single heading, or determine whether some points are subpoints that can be included under main points.

Suppose you were giving a speech on shooting an effective foul shot. You may think that the following eight points are really essential:

I. Face the basket before shooting.
II. Hold your shoulders parallel to the foul line.
III. Spread your feet comfortably, with your knees bent.
IV. Put your foot that is opposite to your shooting arm slightly forward.
V. Hold the ball in your shooting hand, with your elbow bent.
VI. Concentrate on a spot just over the rim.
VII. Straighten your knees as you shoot the ball.
VIII. Follow through after the ball is released.

Now notice how you can make the steps even more meaningful by grouping them under three headings:

I. First, square yourself to the basket.
   A. Face the basket before shooting.
   B. Hold your shoulders parallel to the foul line.
II. Second, have proper balance.
   A. Spread your feet comfortably, with your knees bent.
   B. Put your foot that is opposite to your shooting arm slightly forward.
III. Third, deliver the ball smoothly.
   A. Hold the ball in your shooting hand, with your elbow bent.
   B. Concentrate on a spot just over the rim.
   C. Straighten your knees as you shoot the ball.
   D. Follow through after the ball is released.

Notice that this organization actually results in more items (eleven versus eight). Yet it is easier to remember two to four items under each of three subheadings than it is to remember eight separate items.

Ordering Main Points

A speech can be organized in many different ways. Although your thesis statement will suggest the type of organization you will be using, there are times when you may decide to revise the thesis statement (or even the goal) to evolve a more appropriate organization. Your objective in ordering your main points is to find or to create a structure that will help the audience make sense of the material and so achieve your speech goal. The three basic methods for organizing main points beginning speakers should master are topic and time for informative speeches and logical reasons for persuasive speeches.

Topic Order

Topic order organizes the main points of the speech by categories or divisions of a subject. This is the most common way of ordering main points. When choosing which topic to discuss first, second, or last, a speaker may order topics from general to specific, least important to most important, or in some other logical sequence.

topic order organizing the main points of the speech by categories or divisions of a subject

A time order is appropriate when you are showing others how to do or make something or how something works.

However you choose to order the topics, you should have some rationale because the order in which you discuss topics can affect how well they are remembered.

If topics vary in weight and importance—to the audience or to the goal of the speech—how you order them may influence your audience's understanding or acceptance of them. For example, audiences will often perceive the last point as the most important. In the example that follows, the topics vary in weight. They are presented in the order that the speaker believes is most suitable for the audience and speech goal, with the most important point at the end.

> **Specific Goal:** I want the audience to understand three proven methods for ridding our bodies of harmful toxins.
>
> **Thesis Statement:** Three proven methods for ridding our bodies of harmful toxins are reducing animal foods, hydrating, and eating natural whole foods.

    I. One proven method for ridding our bodies of harmful toxins is reducing our intake of animal products.

    II. A second proven method for ridding our bodies of harmful toxins is eating more natural whole foods.

    III. A third proven method for ridding our bodies of harmful toxins is keeping well hydrated.

Emming's speech on the three criteria that will enable the audience to find the credit card that is most suitable is another example of a speech using topic order. Recall that Emming chose to discuss interest rates as his first main point because his research suggested that it was the most important criterion.

Time Order

Time order organizes main points by a chronological sequence or steps in a process. It focuses on what comes first, second, third, and so on. When you select a time order of main points, the audience understands that there is a temporal relationship among

time order organizing the main points of the speech by a sequence of ideas or events, focusing on what comes first, second, third, and so on

the main points. Time order is appropriate when you are explaining how to do something, how to make something, how something works, or how something happened.

Kenneth's speech on the steps in antiquing a table is an example of time order. Notice how the order of main points is as important for audiences to remember as the ideas of the main points.

> **Specific Goal:** I want the audience to understand the four steps involved in developing a personal network.
>
> **Thesis Statement:** The four steps involved in developing a personal network are to analyze your current networking potential, to position yourself in places for opportunity, to advertise yourself, and to follow up on contacts.

> I. First, analyze your current networking potential.
> II. Second, position yourself in places for opportunity.
> III. Third, advertise yourself.
> IV. Fourth, follow up on contacts.

Although the use of "first," "second," and so forth is not a requirement when using a time order, their inclusion serves as markers that help audience members understand that the sequence is important.

Logical Reasons Order

Logical reasons order organizes main points of a persuasive speech by the reasons that support the goal. Like topic order, speakers using logical reasoning may order the main point reasons according to their weight of importance. Like time order, there are situations in which reason main points build on one another and so are presented in a specific sequence. Using logical reasons order enables the speaker to emphasize why the audience should believe something or behave in a particular way. Unlike the two other arrangements of main points, the logical reasons order is most appropriate

logical reasons order organizing the main points of a persuasive speech by the reasons that support the speech goal

©Steve Dunwell/Getty Images/The Image Bank

The time and thought that you put into creating a meaningful organization for your speech will pay off in audience understanding.

for a persuasive speech. Let's look at the way Tyreece chose to order his main points in a speech on the United Way.

> **Specific Goal:** I want the audience to donate money to the United Way.
> **Thesis Statement:** Donating to the United Way is appropriate because your one donation covers many charities, you can stipulate which specific charities you wish to support, and a high percentage of your donation goes to charities.

> I. When you donate to the United Way, your one donation covers many charities.
> II. When you donate to the United Way, you can stipulate which charities you wish to support.
> III. When you donate to the United Way, you know that a high percentage of your donation will go directly to the charities you've selected.

Notice how Tyreece built his argument by ordering the reasons from the broadest to the most specific. In Chapter 13, Principles of Persuasive Speaking, we consider advanced methods for organization.

In summary, then, to organize the body of your speech, follow these three steps:

1. Turn your speech goal into a thesis statement that forecasts main points.

2. State main points in complete sentences that are clear, parallel, meaningful, and limited to a maximum of five in number.

3. Organize the main points in the pattern best suited to your material and the needs of your specific audience.

At this point, you have the structure for your complete outline: a speech goal, a thesis statement, and an outline of the main points of the speech.

Exhibit 7.1 shows what Emming's outline would look like at this stage of preparation. Notice that his specific speech goal is written at the top of the page. His thesis statement comes right after the goal because later it is likely to become part of his introduction.

Use Speech Preparation Activity 4.2 to develop well-written main points for your speech. The Student Response for Activity 4.2 on page 129 gives an example completed by a student in this course.

EXHIBIT 7.1 | **Goal, thesis statement, and main points**

Specific Goal: I would like the audience to understand the major criteria for finding a suitable credit card.

Thesis Statement: Three criteria that will enable the audience to find the credit card that is most suitable for them are level of real interest rate, annual fee, and advertised perks.

I. One criterion for finding a suitable credit card is to examine the interest rate.

II. A second criterion for finding a suitable credit card is to examine the annual fee.

III. A third criterion for finding a suitable credit card is to weigh the perks.

Activity 4.2
Determining the Main Points of Your Speech

The goal of this activity is to help you develop your main points.

1. Write your thesis statement:

2. Underline the two to five specific ideas identified in your thesis statement that you want to communicate to your audience to achieve your goal.

3. For each underlined item, write one sentence that summarizes what you want your audience to know about that idea.

4. Review the main points as a group.

    A. Are main points clear?

       If not, consider why and revise:

    B. Are the main points parallel in structure?

       If not, consider why and revise:

    C. Are the main points meaningful?

       If not, consider why and revise:

5. Decide how to order these main points. Write the main point statements in an order that will aid audience members in understanding your thesis and help you reach your goal.

6. Identify the type of order you have used:

Selecting and Outlining Supporting Material

The main points are the basic structure or skeleton of your speech. Whether your audience understands, believes, or appreciates what you have to say usually depends on how well those main points are developed. In your outline include the basic supporting material, the material that begins to put the "meat on the bones" of your main points. Once you have covered all the aspects of audience adaptation, you will fill out the speech during speech practice periods. For a four- to six-minute speech, you should be able to read the total outline in no more than two minutes or so. The final three minutes or so includes material that builds the speech. For instance, your outline will not include quotations, comparisons, sets of statistics, and so forth. These kinds of material are added as you work with your speech during your practice sessions. Think of the outline of the body of your speech as the main points and the first level of supporting material.

List Supporting Material

Begin by writing down a main point. Then, under that main point, using your research note cards, list the key elements of information you have found that you believe are related to that main point. Don't worry if ideas are out of order or don't seem to relate to each other. Your goal at this point is to see what you have to work with. For example, Emming might write this support for the first main point of his speech:

I. One criterion for finding a suitable credit card is to examine the interest rate.

Most credit cards carry an average of 18 percent.

Some cards carry an average of as much as 21 percent.

Some cards offer a grace period.

Department store rates are often higher than bank rates.

Average rates are much higher than ordinary interest rates.

Variable rate means that the rate will change from month to month.

Fixed rate means that the rate will stay the same.

Many companies quote very low rates (6 percent to 8 percent) for specific periods.

Identify and Organize Subpoints

Once you have listed the items of information that make the point, look for relationships between and among ideas. As you analyze, you may draw lines connecting information that fits together logically, you may cross out information that seems irrelevant or doesn't really fit, and you may combine similar ideas using different language. For instance, Exhibit 7.2 on page 130 depicts Emming's analysis of the information listed under his first main point.

In most cases, similar items that you have linked can be grouped under broader headings. For instance, Emming has four statements related to specific percentages and two statements related to types of interest rate. For the four statements related to specific percentages, he might create the following heading:

Interest rates are the percentage that a company charges you to carry a balance on your card past the due date.

Then, under that heading, he can list the relevant items:

Most credit cards carry an average of 18 percent.

Some cards carry an average of as much as 21 percent.

Many companies quote very low rates (6 percent to 8 percent) for specific periods.

For the two statements related to types of interest rates, he might create the following heading:

Interest rates can be variable or fixed.

Then, under that heading, he can list the two types:

Variable rate means that the rate will change from month to month.

Fixed rate means that the rate will stay the same.

Activity 4.2
Determining the Main Points of Your Speech

1. Write your thesis statement: The three tests you can use to determine whether a "diamond" is real are the <u>acid test</u>, the <u>streak test</u>, and the <u>hardness test</u>.

2. Underline the two to five specific ideas identified in your thesis statement that you want to communicate to your audience to achieve your goal.

3. For each underlined item, write one sentence that summarizes what you want your audience to know about that idea.

   One way to identify a diamond is by using the <u>acid test</u>.

   You can also identify a diamond by using the <u>streak test</u>.

   You can also identify a diamond by using the <u>hardness test</u>.

4. Review the main points as a group.
   A. Are main points clear? No. Purpose of test is to identify whether the "diamond" is *real* by using a test. The following revision puts emphasis in the right place.
      Revision:
      One way to identify whether a diamond is real is by using the acid test.
      You can also identify whether a diamond is real by using the streak test.
      You can also identify that a diamond is real by using the hardness test.
   B. Are the main points parallel in structure? No. They need to start the same way.
      Revision:
      One way to determine whether a diamond is real is to use the acid test.
      A second way to determine whether a diamond is real is to use the hardness test.
      A third way to determine whether a diamond is real is to use the streak test.
   C. Are the main points meaningful? Yes

5. Decide how to order these main points. Write the main point statements in an order that will aid audience members in understanding your thesis and help you reach your goal.
   One way to determine whether a diamond is real is to use the acid test.
   A second way to determine whether a diamond is real is to use the streak test.
   A third way to determine whether a diamond is real is to use the hardness test.

6. Identify the type of order you have used: Topic

You are also likely to have listed information that you decide not to include in the outline:

> Department store rates are often higher than bank rates.
>
> Some cards offer a grace period.

Emming decided to cut the department store point because his emphasis was not on who was offering the rates but on what percentages were being charged. Likewise, he thought that the grace period point wasn't directly related to either of the main ideas he wanted to emphasize.

EXHIBIT 7.2 **Editing of Material Supporting Main Point**

I. One criterion for finding a suitable credit card is to examine the interest rate.

Most credit cards carry an average of 18 percent.

Some cards carry an average of as much as 21 percent.

~~Some cards offer a grace period.~~

~~Department store rates are often higher than bank rates.~~

Average rates are much higher than ordinary interest rates.

Variable rate means that the rate will change from month to month.

Fixed rate means that the rate will stay the same.

Many companies quote very low rates (6 percent to 8 percent) for specific periods.

Sometimes you'll find you have stated the same point two different ways:

Most credit cards carry an average of 18 percent.

Average rates are much higher than ordinary interest rates.

Emming might combine the two to read as follows:

Most credit cards carry an average of 18 percent, which is much higher than ordinary interest rates.

A main point will be supported by two or more subpoints, and each subpoint may have two or more specific information items that relate to it. When you outline, you need to follow a consistent form. The form we suggest is to designate main points with Roman numerals, major subpoints with capital letters, and supporting points with regular (Arabic) numbers.

The items of information listed for Emming's first main point might be grouped and subordinated as follows:

I. One criterion for finding a suitable credit card is to examine the interest rate.

  A. Interest rates are the percentages a company charges you to carry a balance on your card past the due date.

   1. Most credit cards carry an average of 18 percent, which is much higher than ordinary interest rates.

   2. Some cards carry an average of as much as 21 percent.

   3. Many companies quote very low rates (6 percent to 8 percent) for specific periods.

  B. Interest rates can be variable or fixed.

   1. A variable rate means that the rate will change from month to month.

   2. A fixed rate means that the rate will stay the same.

The outline identifies the basic subpoints of a speech, but it does not include all the development. For instance, in this speech, Emming might further develop his points by using personal experiences, examples, illustrations, anecdotes, statistics, quotations, and other forms of supporting material.

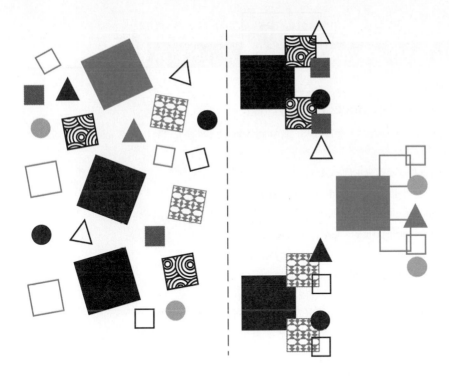

Subordination creates order.

Developing Section Transitions

Once you have outlined your main points and supporting material, consider how you will move smoothly from one main point to another. **Transitions** are words, phrases, or sentences that show the relationship between or bridge two ideas. Transitions act like tour guides, leading the audience from point to point through the speech.

Section transitions bridge major parts of the speech and occur between the introduction and body, between main points within the body, and between the body and the conclusion. Section transitions are important for two reasons. First, they help the audience to follow the organization of ideas in the speech. If every member of the audience were able to pay complete attention to every word, then perhaps section transitions would not be as important. But audience members' attention is likely to wander during a speech, and members can find themselves lost when they refocus. Section transitions give them a chance to reorient their thinking. Second, section transitions help people retain main point ideas. Because most section transitions involve either summarizing or previewing a main point, they repeat the main idea. Although audience members might remember something said once, their retention will increase if the idea is repeated. Section transitions should be preplanned and included in your outline. Other transitions should be spontaneous. We will discuss these in Chapter 10.

Now let's look at an example of section transitions. In his speech on antiquing tables, Kenneth knew he would need to move smoothly from his introduction to his main points, so he planned to use the following transition when he completed his introductory statements:

Antiquing a table is a process that has four steps. Now let's consider the first one.

transitions words, phrases, or sentences that show a relationship between or bridge other words, phrases, or sentences

section transitions complete sentences that link major sections of a speech

Activity 4.3
Outlining the Speech Body

The goal of this exercise is to help you get started on the outline for the body of your first speech. Using complete sentences, write the following:

1. The speech goal you developed in Activity 1.4 in Chapter 3.

2. The thesis statement you developed in Activity 4.1.

3. A transition to the first main point.

4. The first main point you developed in Activity 4.2.

5. The outline of the support for your first main point.

6. A transition from your first main point to your second.

7. The second main point you developed in Activity 4.2.

8. A transition from your second main point to your third.

9. Other points and transition statements.

Use the outline form shown in Student Response for Activity 4.3. The words Introduction, Conclusion, and Sources are put in just to help you understand the requirements for the final outline. For a sample of a completed outline, see pages 152–153 in Chapter 8.

When his listeners hear this transition, they are signaled to mentally prepare to listen to and remember the first main point. When he finishes his first main point, he will use another similar section transition:

> Now that we see what is involved in cleaning the table, we can move on to the second step.

This transition not only repeats the substance of the first step but also signals that he will be moving on to a different step.

In your speech outlines, section transitions are written in parentheses at the junctures in the speech where they occur. Complete the outline for the body of your speech by doing Speech Preparation Activity 4.3. Student Response for Activity 4.3 shows the progress of Emming's outline. It now contains the specific goal, the thesis statement, the three main points, and the tentative development of his first main point.

Summary

A speech that is well organized is likely to achieve its goal. Speech organization begins by writing a thesis statement based on your specific speech goal. The thesis statement identifies the key ideas you will present in the speech.

These ideas become the main points of your speech outline. Main points should be written in complete sentences and checked to make sure that they are clear, parallel in structure, meaningful, and limited in number to five or less.

Activity 4.3
Emming's Outline

Goal, thesis statement, body of the speech (complete development of one main point and subpoints), and transitions.

Specific Goal: I would like the audience to understand the major criteria for finding a suitable credit card.

Thesis Statement: Three criteria that will enable the audience to find the credit card that is most suitable for them are level of real interest rate, annual fee, and advertised perks.

Introduction

    (Let's consider the first criterion)

Body

I. One criterion for finding a suitable credit card is to examine the interest rate.

    A. Interest rates are the percentages that a company charges you to carry a balance on your card past the due date.

        1. Most credit cards carry an average of 18 percent.

        2. Some cards carry an average of as much as 21 percent.

        3. Many companies quote very low rates (6 percent to 8 percent) for specific periods.

    B. Interest rates can be variable or fixed.

        1. Variable rate means that the rate will change from month to month.

        2. Fixed rate means that the rate will stay the same.

    (Now that we've considered interest rates, let's look at the next criterion)

II. A second criterion for finding a suitable credit card is to examine the annual fee.

    (After considering interest rates and annual fee, you can consider the final criterion.)

III. A third criterion for finding a suitable credit card is to weigh the perks.

Conclusion

Sources

The order in which you present your main points depends on the type of speech you are giving and on the specific nature of the material you want to present. The three simplest organizational patterns are topic, time, and logical reasons order. You will want to choose an organizational pattern that best helps your audience understand and remember your main points.

The next step in organizing your speech is to choose and order material that you will use to explain each main point. To begin this process, create lists of the information you have that relates to each of your main points. Then review each list, grouping similar information under larger headings and identifying the information that is most important for helping the audience understand and remember the main point.

Carson had done a variety of computer searches for his speech on cloning and had come up with more than seven major articles, but time was getting short. He had had three tests the week prior to his assigned speech, and even though he had taken the time to get an excellent list of sources, the speech itself was due the next morning.

As Carson thought about his problem, it occurred to him that one magazine article he had read really "said it all." In fact, as far as he could see, most of the key ideas he had noticed in scanning the other articles were included in this one source. Suddenly a "plan" for his speech organization hit him. He would use the organization of this article for his speech and adopt the thesis statement from the article as his own. He would list the other articles in his bibliography. Moreover, since the article actually referenced three of the sources his search had uncovered, his bibliography really did reflect what he had found and what was in the speech.

Carson took the three key paragraphs from the article and quickly outlined them for his speech. He used a story related in the article as his introduction and wrote a short summary of the three main points for the conclusion. "Great," he thought, "in just about fifteen minutes I've created a great speech for tomorrow." He even had time to read through the three paragraphs about four times before he went to bed—he knew he was in great shape for the speech.

1. Was Carson's method of organizing his speech ethical? Explain.

2. How should material from a key article be used?

These subpoints should be written in complete sentences and entered on your outline below the main point to which they belong.

Sectional transitions bridge major parts of the speech and occur between the introduction and the body, between main points within the body, and between the body and the conclusion. Sectional conclusions should be preplanned and placed in the outline as parenthetical statements where they are to occur.

CHALLENGE ONLINE

Use your Challenge of Effective Speaking CD-ROM for quick access to the electronic study resources that accompany this text. Included on your CD-ROM is access to the Challenge of Effective Speaking Web site featuring Speech Builder Express at the Wadsworth Communication Café, InfoTrac College Edition, and a demo of WebTutor for *The Challenge of Effective Speaking*. The Web site offers chapter-by-chapter access to the Speech Preparation Action Step Activities, InfoTrac College Edition exercises, a digital glossary of key terms, Web links, Speech Preparation Forms, Speech Evaluation Checklists, and quizzes. Review the key terms and complete the InfoTrac College Edition exercise on the book's Web site at
http://www.wadsworth.com/product/0534563856

InfoTrac College Edition Exercise

Use PowerTrac to search Vital Speeches for the speech titled "How to Downsize" by John A. Challenger, in *Vital Speeches,* Dec. 1, 2001. Read through the speech and identify Challenger's goal and main points. Then answer these questions.

1. Was the goal clearly stated in the introduction?
2. Were main points previewed in the speech introduction?
3. During the speech, were there transition statements leading into main points?
4. Were all main points clearly stated as complete sentences?
5. Had you been advising Challenger, what suggestions would you have given him for sharpening the organization and/or wording main points?

Key Terms

clarity of main points *(121)*

logical reasons order *(125)*

main points *(118)*

meaningful main
  points *(122)*

parallel structure of main
  points *(121)*

section transitions *(131)*

thesis statement *(117)*

timc order *(124)*

topic order *(123)*

transitions *(131)*

Challenge of Effective Speaking Web Site

You can complete Activities 4.1, 4.2, and 4.3 online using your CD-ROM to access Speech Builder Express at the Challenge of Effective Speaking Web site at the Wadsworth Communication Café. If you have completed and stored other activities, you will notice that the work from these activities has automatically been incorporated into the new activity. Once you have completed an activity, you can print it out and save it for use in later activities.

8 Organizing the Introduction and the Conclusion and Completing the Outline

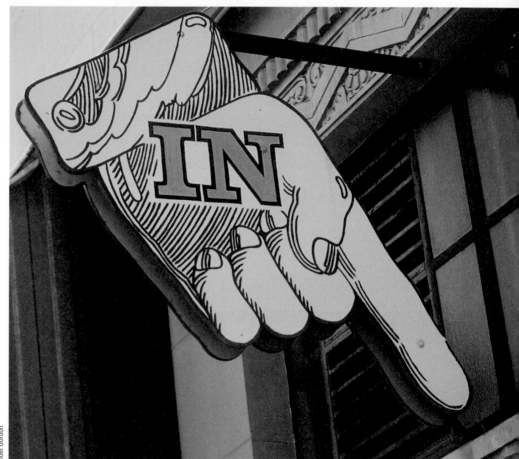

Joel Gordon

To lose our fluency of speech, has nowhere a worse effect than at the commencement . . .
that pilot is surely one of the worst who runs his vessel aground as it is leaving the harbor.
—Quintilian, *Institutes of Oratory,* IV, 1, 61

Margot has asked Donna to listen to her rehearse her speech. As she stood in front of the classroom where she was practicing, she began, "Today I want to tell you some things about diamonds. There are several criteria you can use in evaluating a diamond."

"Whoa, Margot." Donna said. "That's your introduction?"

"Yes," Margot replied. "People know what diamonds are, why shouldn't I just get on with the speech?"

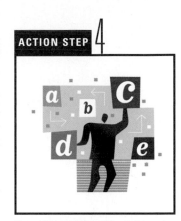

ACTION STEP 4

Organize and develop your material in a way that is best suited to your audience.

F. Create an introduction that gets attention, sets the tone, creates goodwill, builds your credibility, and leads into the body of the speech.

G. Create a conclusion that both summarizes the material and leaves the speech on a high note.

H. Review and complete the speech outline.

Margot's question sounds reasonable—most people know what diamonds are. But this doesn't mean that everyone in the audience is ready to listen to a speech about evaluating diamonds. People might think the topic is boring, irrelevant to them, or for some other reason not worth their time. For most speeches, how well you start the speech may determine whether most members of the audience even listen, and how well you start and finish your speech can play a major role in the speech's overall success.

In the previous chapter, we described the first few tasks involved with organizing your speech. These resulted in a complete sentence outline of the body. In this chapter we describe how to complete the organizational process by creating an introduction that both gets attention and leads into the body of your speech, by creating a conclusion that both summarizes the material and leaves the speech on a high note, by writing a title, and by completing a list of sources used to develop the speech.

Creating the Introduction

At this stage of preparation, the body of the speech is sufficiently well developed that you can concentrate on how to begin your speech. Although your introduction may be only a few sentences, it is especially important. If you are not able to motivate members of the audience to pay attention to the speech opening, you may have a difficult time capturing their attention during the main part of your speech. As Quintilian, the great Roman rhetorician, reminds us with his comparison of speech making to captaining a ship, "that pilot is surely one of the worst who runs his vessel aground as it is leaving the harbor." Effective speakers understand and rise to the challenge of beginning their speeches creatively.

Goals of the Introduction

Unlike Margot's "Today I want to tell you," all good introductions serve to (1) get attention, (2) set the tone for a speech, (3) create a bond of goodwill between speaker and audience, (4) establish your credibility, and (5) lead into the content of a speech.

Getting Attention

An audience's physical presence does not guarantee that people will actually listen to your speech. Your first goal, then, is to create an opening that will win your listeners' attention by arousing their interest and motivating them to continue listening. Even if

An effective speech introduction will not only get attention and lead into the body of the speech but will also build goodwill and set the tone for the speech.

you are giving a speech to an audience that has chosen to attend your speech because they have a real need to hear what you will be saying, it is still useful to start with an attention-getter. Later in this chapter, we discuss several types of attention-getting devices you can use.

Setting a Tone

The introductory remarks should reflect the emotional tone that is appropriate for the topic. A humorous opening will signal a lighthearted tone; a serious opening signals a more thoughtful or somber tone. A speaker who starts with a rib-tickling ribald story is putting the audience in a lighthearted, devil-may-care mood; if that speaker then says, "Now let's turn to the subject of abortion (or nuclear war or drug abuse)," the audience will be confused, and the speech may be doomed.

Creating a Bond of Goodwill

In your first few words, you often establish how an audience will feel about you as a person. If you are enthusiastic, warm, and friendly and give a sense that what you're going to talk about is in the audience's best interest, it will make them feel more comfortable with spending time listening to you.

Establishing Your Credibility

Regardless of your topic or goal, your audience is going to wonder why they should pay attention to what you have to say. Although credibility is built and maintained throughout the speech, your introduction should include something about your qualifications for speaking on this topic. For instance, when Erin starts her speech on the volleyball spike, her audience is likely to accept her authority if she mentions that she is a member of the women's varsity volleyball team. In the introduction to his speech about violence in the media, Jeremy might say that he has had an interest in the effects of television violence since high school and has read widely on the subject. If your credibility comes from the research you have done on the topic, then you will build that credibility as the speech goes along and members hear what you have learned.

Leading into Content

Audiences want to know what the speech is going to be about, so it is useful to forecast your organization in the introduction. If you have a well-written speech goal and thesis statement, then you have the material necessary to meet this goal. For instance, in a speech on campaigning, just before you actually state your first main point, you might draw from your specific goal and say, "In this speech, I'll explain the four stages of a political campaign." A clear forecast of the main points is appropriate unless you have some special reason for not revealing the organization; such a forecast is almost always called for in an informative speech.

In many cases, you will find that you can accomplish these five goals in a few sentences. In some cases, you may need to continue establishing an appropriate tone, developing goodwill, and building your credibility as the speech moves along.

Types of Introductions

There is no "one best way" to introduce your speech. In fact, the ways to begin a speech are limited only by your imagination. To find the most effective opening, try two or three different introductions in practice and select the one that seems best suited to your purpose and meets the needs of your audience and setting.

Because you will be giving short speeches this term, we will highlight specific types of openings that are appropriate for short speeches. In longer speeches, you will have more leeway in developing introductions using startling statements, rhetorical questions, stories, personal references, quotations, and suspense.

Startling Statement

One excellent way to grab your listeners' attention and focus on the topic quickly is to open with a startling statement that will override the competing thoughts that are flitting through your listeners' minds. The following example illustrates the attention-getting effect of a startling statement:

> If I pointed a pistol at you, you would be justifiably scared. But at least you would know the danger to your life. Yet every day we let people fire away at us with messages that are dangerous to our pocketbooks and our minds, and we seldom say a word. I'm talking about television advertisers.
>
> Today I want to look at our choices in how we can go about letting our feelings about advertising be heard.

In just seventy-six words—about thirty seconds—this introduction grabs attention and leads into the speech.

Rhetorical Question

Asking a **rhetorical question**—a question seeking a mental rather than a vocal response—is another appropriate opening for a short speech. Notice how a student began her speech on counterfeiting with three short questions:

> What would you do with this ten-dollar bill if I gave it to you? Take your friend to a movie? Treat yourself to a pizza and drinks? Well, if you did either of these things, you could get in big trouble—this bill is counterfeit!
>
> Today I want to share with you the extent of counterfeiting of American money worldwide and what our government is doing to curb it.

Again, a short opening, just seventy words—less than thirty seconds—gets attention and leads into the speech.

Now let's consider a longer opening that shows the potential for using rhetorical questions in a major speech. Notice how Wendy Liebermann, President of WSL

rhetorical question a question seeking a mental rather than a vocal response

Strategic Retail, gets the attention of her audience—members of the Non-Prescription Drug Manufacturers Association—and leads into her speech with a series of short questions:

> Have you wondered of late what's going on with consumers? Why they are so full of contradictions when it comes to spending money? Why will they buy a $500 leather jacket at full price but wait for a $50 sweater to go on sale? Will buy a top-of-the-line sport utility vehicle then go to Costco to buy new tires? Will eagerly pay $3.50 for a cup of coffee but think $1.29 is too expensive for a hamburger? Will spend $2.00 for a strawberry-smelling bath soap but wait for a coupon to buy a $0.99 twin pack of toilet soap?
>
> The economy is booming. Unemployment is at a 25-year low. Real income has increased. Why isn't everyone out spending like they did in the 1980s—shopping everywhere, buying everything? Why are so many companies struggling? What is this paradox? Is there a paradox?
>
> Well, that's what we are going to talk about today. This apparent consumer paradox: what it is; what it means and how to make sense out of it. Because if we don't understand it and respond to it, there's a very good chance we won't attract the consumers we want, and a very, very good chance we won't build long-term profitable sales, and a very, very, very good chance we won't all be sitting here this time next year.[1]

This 221-word opening (well under two minutes) would work for a ten- to fifteen-minute speech or longer. Notice that the series of questions in the first paragraph touches the behavior of many of us and even introduces some light humor. Right away the speaker is not only getting attention but gaining goodwill. In addition, the lighthearted approach sets the tone for her speech. The second series of questions starts to really get the audience to think with her. Both series set up the subject matter of the speech. The third paragraph then tells the audience exactly what she will be looking at in reference to these questions.

So, we can see that rhetorical question openings can be adapted to speeches of any length.

Story

If you have a good story that gets an audience's attention and is really related to the goal of the speech, you probably have an excellent candidate for your opening. Because many good stories take time to tell, they are generally more appropriate for longer speeches. However, you will occasionally find or think of a story that is just right for your speech, as this one was on balancing stakeholder interests:

> A tightrope walker announced that he was going to walk across Niagara Falls. To everyone's amazement, he made it safely across, and everybody cheered. "Who believes I can ride a bicycle across?" And they all said, "Don't do it, you'll fall!" But he got on his bicycle and made it safely across. "Who believes I can push a full wheelbarrow across?" Well, by this time the crowd had seen enough to make real believers of them, and they all shouted, "We do! We do!" At that he said, "OK . . . Who wants to be the first to get in?"
>
> Well, that's how many investors feel about companies who have adopted the philosophy that balancing the interests of all stakeholders is the true route to maximum value. They go from skeptics to believers, but are very reluctant to get in that wheelbarrow.
>
> What I would like to do this afternoon is share with you Eastman's philosophy of stakeholder balance, give you some specific examples of how we're putting this philosophy into practice, and then I'll give you some results.[2]

Most people understand the need to get attention. What better way than to tell a good story? But the goal of telling a story to open the speech is not just to get attention; it is to get attention on the subject matter of the speech. Notice that Deavenport's opening story focuses on the issue of balance—then notice that his speech is about "stakeholder balance" as his organization's philosophy.

So, if a person has heard a really funny story that relates to the subject of dogs, and if the speech is about dogs, then telling that funny story may really help the speaker focus audience attention on the speech. But if the speech is about the economy, the audience is going to laugh at the dog story and then mentally drift when they discover that the speech is about something else. So, if you have a relevant story, use it in your speech—but if it does not relate to your topic, don't use it.

Personal Reference

Although any good opening should engage the audience, the personal reference to audience experience is directed solely to that end. In addition to getting attention, a personal reference can be especially effective at engaging listeners as active participants in a speech. A personal reference opening like this one on exercise may be suitable for a speech of any length:

> Say, were you panting when you got to the top of those four flights of stairs this morning? I'll bet there were a few of you who vowed you're never going to take a class on the top floor of this building again. But did you ever stop to think that maybe the problem isn't that this class is on the top floor? It just might be that you are not getting enough exercise.
>
> Today I want to talk with you about how you can build an exercise program that will get you and keep you in shape, yet will only cost you three hours a week, and not one red cent!

This 112-word opening can be presented in less than a minute; you can build the personal reference into an opening for a major speech. Let's see how Dana Mead, Chairman and Chief Executive Officer of Tenneco, used a personal reference in the opening to his speech to the Executives' Club of Chicago:

> Thank you and good afternoon. It's great to be back in Chicago, the city of new beginnings. In 1893, Chicago hosted the world's fair—the Columbian Exposition—commemorating one of the world's greatest beginnings, the 400th anniversary of Columbus' voyage to America. (Actually, it took 401 years before Chicago completed the exhibition—but it was so grand no one was nitpicking!)
>
> The fair had a real second purpose—to demonstrate to the world what progress Chicago had made since the fire of 1871—and of course it succeeded in truly impressing the world.
>
> Chicago continues to impress the world. As one of the global economy's industrial titans, your hosting of the Transatlantic Business Dialogue, in my recent experience, was the catalyst for the impressive progress which that meeting produced. So, when I talk about the new American economy, my remarks should be familiar—you are already part of it.[3]

Although this personal reference was only the first part of Mead's speech introduction, it gives you a good idea of the kinds of information you can use to relate to your audience.

Quotation

A particularly vivid or thought-provoking quotation makes an excellent introduction to a speech of any length. You will need to use your imagination to relate the quotation to your topic so that it yields maximum benefits. For instance, in the beginning of her introduction, notice how Suzanne Morse, Director of the Pew Partnership for Civic Change, uses a quotation to get the attention of her audience:

> A few years ago one of America's foremost philosophers, Yogi Berra, remarked to his wife on a trip to the Baseball Hall of Fame in Cooperstown, New York, "We are completely lost but we are making good time." I am afraid Yogi's observation may be true for more than just his navigational skills. For Americans, our direction on the important social issues of the day finds us lost but still driving.
>
> As we think about strategies for change needed for America's third century, we must go in new directions.[4]

As the introduction progresses, he introduces the topic of his speech, liberty versus power.

In the following excerpt from her speech to the annual meeting of the American Medical Association, AMA President Nancy Dickey exemplifies the way a clever speaker can use a quotation in the opening to serve as the theme for the entire speech:

> A wise person once said, "Always have your bags packed, you never know where life's journey is going to take you." I couldn't agree more. In fact, as you can see, I have my bag with me tonight [she holds up her standard medical bag for the audience to see]. I've chosen to bring that traditional black bag that physicians have carried with them for generations. And I'm here to tell you—my bag is packed and ready to go as I prepare for this year-long journey of my AMA presidency.
>
> Of course, having your bag packed isn't really about having a change of clothes ready. It's about being prepared to take advantage of the opportunities that come your way in life. And I am prepared. . . .
>
> I've also packed some more tangible items in my bag tonight. Symbolic items, really, which represent my presidential priorities for the year ahead. And tonight I want to share these items and priorities with you—and ask for your help in making them a reality during the next 12 months.[5]

If you were a physician in her audience, I think you would be intrigued by what she had to say about her priorities for the year.

Suspense

If you can start your speech in a way that gets the audience to ask, "What is she leading up to?" you may well get them hooked for the entire speech. The suspense opening is especially valuable when the topic is one that the audience might not ordinarily be willing to listen to if the speech were opened less dramatically. Consider the attention-getting value of this introduction:

> It costs the United States more than $116 billion per year. It has cost the loss of more jobs than a recession. It accounts for nearly 100,000 deaths a year. I'm not talking about cocaine abuse—the problem is alcoholism. Today I want to show you how we can avoid this inhumane killer by abstaining from it.

Notice that by putting the problem, "alcoholism," at the end the speaker encourages the audience to try to anticipate the answer. And since the audience may well be thinking "narcotics," the revelation that the answer is alcoholism is likely to be that much more effective.

Selecting and Outlining an Introduction

Because the introduction is critical in establishing your relationship with your audience, it's worth investing the time to compare different openings. Try working on two or three different introductions; then pick the one you believe will work best for your specific audience and speech goal.

For instance, Emming created the following three introductions for his speech on evaluating credit cards:

> Have you seen the number of agencies that have showered the campus with credit card applications? Sounds good, doesn't it? Take just a few minutes to fill out a statement, and you'll be in control of your economic destiny. But wait a minute. The road down consumer credit lane is not as smooth as the companies would have you believe. Today I'm going to share with you the criteria gained from my reading and personal experience that you'll want to consider for selecting a credit card. (86 words)

> Each of these pieces of plastic I hold in my hand is a credit card. They look about the same, don't they? They're not. Before you travel into credit card land, you had better consider what you're getting into. Today I'm going to share with you the criteria gained from my reading and personal experience that you'll want to consider for selecting a credit card. (64 words)

Banks and credit unions are willing to shower us with incentives in order to get us to sign up for our own credit card. But we'd be wise to look before we leap. P. T. Barnum said, "There's a sucker born every minute." Today I'm going to share with you the criteria that you'll want to consider for selecting a credit card so that you won't end up being one of those "suckers." (72 words)

Which one do you prefer?

Each of these possibilities is an appropriate length. An introduction should be between 5 percent and 10 percent of the speech. Thus, for a five-minute speech (approximately 750–800 words), an introduction of 40 to 75 words is appropriate; for a thirty-minute speech, an introduction of two to four minutes is appropriate.

Whether or not your speech introduction meets all five of the goals directly, it should be long enough to put listeners in a frame of mind that will encourage them to hear you out, without being so long that it leaves too little time to develop the substance of your speech. Of course, the shorter the speech, the shorter the introduction.

The introduction will not make your speech an instant success, but it can get an audience to look at and listen to you and to choose to focus on your topic. That is about as much as a speaker can ask of an audience during the first minute or two of a speech.

By completing Speech Preparation Activity 4.4, you will develop three choices for your speech introduction. The Student Response for Activity 4.4 on page 144 provides an example completed by a student in this course.

Creating the Conclusion

Shakespeare said, "All's well that ends well," and nothing could be truer of an effective speech. Too many speakers either end their speeches abruptly and leave the audience hanging or ramble on aimlessly, unsure how to stop talking. A weak conclusion—or no conclusion at all—can destroy the impact of an otherwise effective speech. Even the best conclusion cannot save a poor speech, but a strong conclusion can heighten the impact of a good speech.

SPEECH PREPARATION **ACTION STEP** 4

Activity 4.4
Writing Speech Introductions

The goal of this activity is to create choices for how you will begin your speech.

1. For the speech body you outlined in Chapter 7 (Activity 4.3), write three different introductions. Use a startling statement, rhetorical question, story, personal reference, quotation, or suspense opening that you believe meets the goals of effective introductions and is appropriate for your speech goal and audience.

2. Which do you believe is the best? Why?

3. Write that introduction in outline form.

Activity 4.4
Writing Speech Introductions

1. For the speech body you outlined earlier, write three separate introductions that you believe would be appropriate for your speech and present them aloud.

Specific Goal: I would like the audience to understand the three ways to tell if a diamond is real.

(1) As Dr. Verderber mentioned earlier in the course, we are in the age group where buying or receiving diamonds might be on our minds. I would like to tell you how you can know for sure if your diamond is real.

(2) Men, have you ever wondered if you would know if the diamond that the jeweler is trying to sell you is real? Ladies, have you ever wondered how you would be able to tell if your engagement ring is fake? Today, I am going to share some information that can help you answer these questions.

(3) Calcite, quartz, cubic zirconia, diamond. How can you tell these minerals apart? They are all colorless and can sometimes look alike. Let me tell you three ways that you can tell if you are holding a diamond.

2. Which do you believe is the best? I believe the second one is the best.

Why? Because the rhetorical questions are likely to motivate the audience to listen, and it leads into the body of the speech.

3. Write that introduction in outline form:

I. Men, have you ever wondered if you would know if the diamond that the jeweler is trying to sell you is real?

II. Ladies, have you ever wondered how you would be able to tell if your engagement ring is fake?

III. Today, I am going to share some information that can help you answer these questions.

Goals of the Conclusion

The conclusion of a speech has two major goals. The first is to review the key ideas in the speech so that the audience remembers what you have said; the second is to leave the audience members with a vivid impression so that they will understand the importance of what you have said or be persuaded by your arguments. Even though the conclusion will be a relatively short part of the speech—seldom more than 5 percent (thirty-five to forty words for a five-minute speech)—it is important that your conclusion be carefully planned.

Types of Conclusions

Just as there is no one best way to introduce your speech, so there is no one best way to end it. You will want to experiment with the following four types of conclusions and choose the one that you believe will work best with your audience.

Summary

By far the most common way to end a speech is to summarize the main points. Thus, a short appropriate ending for a speech on the warning signs of cancer would be, "So

The conclusion offers you one last chance to hit home with your point. Supplementing a summary with a quote or a short anecdote is often a good way of emphasizing what you want the audience to get from the speech.

remember, if you experience a sudden weight loss, lack of energy, or blood in your urine or bowels, then you should see a doctor immediately." Such an ending restates the main points the speaker wants the audience to remember.

Summaries can be used for both informative and persuasive speeches. Although a summary achieves the first goal of an effective conclusion, a speaker will need to develop additional material designed to achieve the second goal: leaving the audience with a vivid impression. A story, an appeal to action, or an emotional conclusion are three ways to supplement or replace the summary.

Story

Storylike or anecdotal material that reinforces the message of the speech works just as well for the conclusion as for the introduction. In his speech on banking, Edward Crutchfield ends with a personal experience showing that bankers must be ready to meet competition coming from any direction:

> I played a little football once for Davidson—a small college about 20 miles north of Charlotte. One particularly memorable game for me was one in which I was blindsided on an off-tackle trap. Even though that was 17 years ago, I can still recall the sound of cracking bones ringing in my ears. Well, 17 years and 3 operations later my back is fine. But, I learned something important about competition that day. Don't always assume that your competition is straight in front of you. It's easy enough to be blindsided by a competitor who comes at you from a very different direction.[6]

Storylike conclusions will work for either informative or persuasive speeches.

Appeal to Action

The appeal to action is a common way to end a persuasive speech. The **appeal** describes the behavior that you want your listeners to follow after they have heard your arguments. Notice how Richard Harwood concludes his speech on what the audience can do now to take personal responsibility for their actions with a strong appeal to action:

> Today we have a choice, a choice to stand up on the rock and declare our intentions, a choice about which story we will tell about this community, this nation, and how we will move forward.

appeal describes the behavior that you want your listeners to follow after they have heard the arguments

When you stand up on the rock, if you so choose, do not stand there alone. Reach out your hand and grab someone who has not yet made it up there, and pull them up with you so that they too can see that their destiny is not that far off. And as you stand there together, make this simple and profound declaration of intention: Our souls, too, will rise and fly. [7]

By their nature, appeals are most relevant for persuasive speeches, especially when the goal is to motivate an audience to act.

Emotional Impact

Some conclusions are designed to drive home the most important points with real emotional impact. Consider the following example, in which Richard Lamm, of the Center for Public Policy and Contemporary Issues, ends his speech on unexamined assumptions with a powerful emotional appeal for unity.

Diverse people must unify or they have conflicts. Melting pots that don't melt become pressure cookers. A country is not a rooming house where we just live while we make our living. What is the social glue that holds diverse people together? Beware of "pyrrhic victories." Listen to John Gardner: "If a community is lucky, and fewer and fewer are, it will have a shared history and tradition. It will have its 'story,' its legends and heroes and will retell those stories often. It will have symbols of group identity—a name, a flag, a location, songs and stories in common—which it will use to heighten its merciless sense of belonging. To maintain the sense of belonging and the dedication and commitment so essential to community life, members need inspiring reminders of shared goals and values."[8]

Like the appeal, the emotional conclusion is likely to be used for a persuasive speech where the goal is to reinforce belief, change belief, or motivate an audience to act.

Selecting and Outlining a Conclusion

To determine how you will conclude your speech, create two or three conclusions, then choose the one that you believe will best reinforce your speech goal with your audience.

For his short speech on evaluating credit cards, Emming created the following three variations of summaries for consideration. Which do you like best?

Having a credit card gives you power—but only if you make a good choice. If you decide to apply for a credit card, you'll now be able to make an evaluation based upon sound criteria: interest rates, annual fee, and perks.

So don't play Russian roulette when choosing a card, instead examine interest rates, annual fee, and perks. That way you'll know that the odds are in your favor.

Now you see the importance of making sure that you have examined interest rates, annual fee, and perks before you select a credit card. And you can rest with the knowledge that the card you selected is the best one for you.

Because this first speech is relatively short, Emming decided to end his speech with just a couple of sentences. For speeches that are no longer than five minutes, a one- to two-sentence conclusion is often appropriate. You're likely to need as much of your time as possible to do a good job of presenting the main points. But as speech assignments get longer, you'll want to consider supplementing the summary to give the conclusion more impact. Refer to the InfoTrac College Edition exercise at the end of this chapter.

By completing Speech Preparation Activity 4.5, you will develop choices for your speech conclusion. The Student Response for Activity 4.5 gives an example completed by a student in this course.

Activity 4.5
Creating Speech Conclusions

The goal of this activity is to help you create choices for how you will conclude your speech.

1. For the speech body you outlined in Activity 4.3, write three different conclusions (summary, story, appeal to action, or emotional impact) that review important points you want the audience to remember and leave the audience with vivid imagery or an emotional appeal.

2. Which do you believe is the best? Why?

3. Write that conclusion in outline form.

Completing the Outline

At this point you have a draft outline of your speech. To complete the outline, you will want to compile a list of the source material you will be drawing from in the speech, create a title (if required), and review your draft to make sure that the outline conforms to a logical structure.

Activity 4.5
Creating Speech Conclusions

1. For the speech body you outlined earlier, write three different conclusions (summary, story, appeal to action, or emotional impact) that review important points you want the audience to remember and leave the audience with vivid imagery or an emotional appeal.

Specific Goal: I would like the audience to understand the three ways to tell if a diamond is real.

(1) So, the next time you buy or receive a diamond, you will know how to do the acid, streak, and hardness tests to make sure the diamond is real.

(2) Before making your final diamond selection, make sure it can pass the acid test, streak test, and hardness test. Remember you want to make sure you're buying a diamond—not paste!

(3) You now know how to tell if your diamond is real. So, folks, if you discover that the gem you are considering effervesces in acid, has a streak that is not clear, or can be scratched, you will know that the person who tried to sell it to you is a crook!

2. Which do you believe is the best? The third one.

   Why? It restates the characteristics.

3. Write that conclusion in outline form.

Conclusion

    I. You now know how to tell if your diamond is real.

    II. If it effervesces, streaks, or scratches, the seller is a crook.

Listing Sources

Regardless of the type of speech or how long or how short it will be, you'll want to list your sources in the outline. The two standard methods of listing sources are to list sources alphabetically by author's last name or to list sources by content category, with items listed alphabetically by author within each category. For speeches with a short list, the first method is efficient. But for long speeches with a lengthy source list, it is helpful to group sources by content categories.

Although the specifics of listing sources differ depending on whether the source is a book, a periodical or newspaper, or an Internet source or Web site, certain common elements are essential to all: author, name of article, title of publication, date of publication, and page numbers. Exhibit 8.1 gives examples of proper citations for the various types of written sources.

EXHIBIT 8.1 | Citation form for sources

Book

Fuhrman, Joel, *Fasting and Eating for Health* (New York: Simon & Schuster, 1995).

Edited Book

Janzen, Rod, "Five Paradigms of Ethnic Relations," in Larry Samovar and Richard Porter, eds., *Intercultural Communication,* 9th ed. (Belmont, CA: Wadsworth, 2000), pp. 52–58.

Magazine

Quinn, Jane Bryant, "Should You Be Worried?" *Newsweek,* August 17, 1998, 40–42.

Academic Journal

Shedletsky, Leonard J. and Joan E. Aitken, "The Paradoxes of Online Academic Work," *Communication Education* 44 (July 2001): 206–217.

Newspaper

Gedda George, "Mexico's Fox Calls for New Security Pact in Americas," *The Cincinnati Enquirer,* September 8, 2001, A4.

Electronic Article

http://ballyfitness.com/ Dr. Paul Kennedy, "Muscle Soreness," May 12, 1998.

Electronic Site

http://www.lec.org/DrugSearch/Documents/Rohypnol.htm David Smith, Donald R. Wesson, and Sarah R. Calhoun, "Rohypnol (Flunitrazepam) Fact Sheet," October 1998.

Experience

Fegel's Jewelry, senior year of high school, 2000–2001.

Observation

Schoenling Brewery, April 22, 2001. Spent an hour on the floor observing the use of various machines in the total process and employees' responsibilities at each stage.

Interviews

Interview with Bruno Mueller, diamond cutter at Fegel's Jewelry, March 19, 2001.

SPEECH PREPARATION   **ACTION STEP** 4

Activity 4.6
Compiling a List of Sources

The goal of this activity is to help you record the list of sources you used in the speech.

1. Review your note cards, separating those whose information you have used in your speech from those you have not.

2. List the sources whose information was used in the speech by copying the bibliographic information recorded on the note card.

3. For short lists, organize your list alphabetically by the last name of the first author. Be sure to follow the form in Exhibit 8.1. If you did not record some of the bibliographic information on your note card, you will need to revisit the library or database to find it.

Speech Preparation Activity 4.6, helps you compile a list of sources used in your speech. The Student Response for Activity 4.6 provides an example completed by a student in this course.

STUDENT RESPONSE   **ACTION STEP** 4

Activity 4.6
Compiling a List of Sources

1. Review your note cards, separating those whose information you have used in your speech from those you have not.

2. List the sources whose information was used in the speech by copying the bibliographic information recorded on the note card.

3. For short lists, organize your list alphabetically by the last name of the first author. Be sure to follow the form in Exhibit 8.1. If you did not record some of the bibliographic information on your note card, you will need to revisit the library or database to find it.

Sources

Dixon, Dougal, *The Practical Geologist* (New York: Simon & Schuster, 1992).

Interview with John Farver, Professor of Geology, June 23, 2001.

Klein, Cornelius, *Manual of Mineralogy,* 2nd ed. (New York: John Wiley & Sons, 1993).

Montgomery, Carla W., *Fundamentals of Geology,* 3rd ed. (Dubuque, IA: Wm. C. Brown, 1997).

http://www.tradeshop.com/gems/tools.html John Miller, "Tools Used by Gemologists," June 2, 2000.

Writing a Title

In many classroom situations, speeches are not required to have titles. But in most speech situations outside the classroom, it helps to have a title that lets the audience know what to expect. A title is probably necessary when you will be formally introduced, when the speech is publicized, or when the speech will be published. A good title helps to attract an audience and builds interest in what you will say. Titles should be brief, descriptive of the content, and, if possible, creative. Most speakers don't settle on a title until the rest of the speech preparation is complete.

Three kinds of titles can be created: (1) a simple statement of subject—which is a shortened version of the speech goal; (2) a question; or (3) a creative title.

1. **Simple statement of subject.** This straightforward title captures the subject of the speech in a few words.

   Courage to Grow

   Selling Safety

   The Dignity of Work

   America's Destiny

2. **Question.** To spark greater interest, you can create a title by phrasing your speech goal as a question. A prospective listener may then be motivated to attend the speech to find out the answer.

   Do We Need a Department of Play?

   Are Farmers on the Way Out?

   What Is the Impact of Computers on Our Behavior?

   Are We Living in a Moral Stone Age?

3. **Creative title.** A more creative approach is to combine a familiar saying or metaphor with the simple statement of subject.

   Teaching Old Dogs New Tricks: The Need for Adult Computer Literacy

   Promises to Keep: Broadcasting and the Public Interest

   The Tangled Web: How Environmental Climate Has Changed

   Freeze or Freedom: On the Limits of Morals and the Worth of Politics

The simple statement of subject gives a clear idea of the topic but is not especially eye- or ear-catching. Questions and creative titles capture interest but may not give a clear idea of content unless they include subtitles.

Once you are comfortable with your goal, you can begin thinking about a title. When you are trying to be creative, you may find a title right away or not until the last minute.

Reviewing the Outline

Now that you have developed a complete draft of your outline, you will want to review it to make sure you have an outline that will be most useful to you as you move into the adaptation and rehearsal phase of speech planning. The following questions can help you as you review and, if necessary, revise.

1. **Have I used a standard set of symbols to indicate structure?** Main points are indicated by Roman numerals, major subdivisions by capital letters, minor subheadings by Arabic numerals, and further subdivisions by lowercase letters.

2. **Have I written all main points and major subpoints as complete sentences?** Complete sentences help you to see (1) whether each main point actually develops your speech goal and (2) whether the wording makes your intended point. Unless the key ideas are written out in full, it will be difficult to follow the next guidelines.

3. **Do main points and major subpoints each contain a single idea?** This guideline ensures that the development of each part of the speech will be relevant to the point. Thus, rather than

   I. The park is beautiful and easy to get to.

   divide the sentence so that both parts are separate:

   I. The park is beautiful.
   II. The park is easy to get to.

This two-point example sorts out distinct ideas so that the speaker can line up supporting material with confidence that the audience will see and understand its relationship to the main points.

4. **Does each major subpoint relate to or support its major point?** This principle, called subordination, ensures that you don't wander off point and confuse your audience. For example:

   I. Proper equipment is necessary for successful play.
      A. Good gym shoes are needed for maneuverability.
      B. Padded gloves will help protect your hands.
      C. A lively ball provides sufficient bounce.
      D. And a good attitude doesn't hurt.

Notice that the main point deals with equipment. A, B, and C (shoes, gloves, and ball) all relate to the main point. But D, attitude, is not equipment and should appear somewhere else, if at all.

5. **Does the outline include no more than one-third the total number of words anticipated in the speech?** An outline is only a skeleton of the speech—not a complete manuscript with letters and numbers attached. The outline should be short enough to allow you to experiment with different methods of development during practice periods and to adapt to audience reaction during the speech itself. An easy way to judge whether your outline is about the right length is to estimate the number of words you are likely to be able to speak during the actual speech and compare this to the number of words in the outline. (Count only the words in the outline minus speech goal, thesis statement, headings, and list of sources.) Approximate figures are all you need. To compute the approximate maximum words for your outline, start by assuming a speaking rate of 160 words per minute. (Last term, the speaking rate for the majority of speakers in my class was 140 to 180 words per minute.) Thus, using the average of 160 words per minute, a three- to five-minute speech would contain roughly 480 to 800 words, and the outline should be 160 to 300 words. An eight- to ten-minute speech, roughly 1,280 to 1,600 words, should have an outline of approximately 426 to 533 words.

The sample outline in Exhibit 8.2 illustrates the principles in practice. The commentary in the margin relates each part of the outline to the guidelines we have discussed.

EXHIBIT 8.2 **Sample complete outline**

Analysis

Write your specific goal at the top of the page. Refer to the goal to test whether everything in the outline is relevant.

Specific Goal: I would like the audience to understand the major criteria for finding a suitable credit card.

The heading Introduction *sets the section apart as a separate unit. The introduction attempts to (1) get attention, (2) set a tone, (3) gain goodwill, (4) establish credibility, and (5) lead into the body.*

Introduction

I. How many of you have been hounded by credit card vendors outside the Student Union?

II. They make a credit card sound like the answer to all of your dreams, don't they?

III. Today I want to share with you three criteria you need to consider carefully before deciding on a particular credit card.

The thesis statement states the elements that are suggested in the specific goal. In the speech, the thesis serves as a forecast of the main points.

Thesis Statement: Three criteria that will enable audience members to find the credit card that is most suitable for them are level of real interest rate, annual fee, and advertised perks.

The heading Body *sets this section apart as a separate unit. In this example, main point I begins a topical pattern of main points. It is stated as a complete, meaningful sentence.*

Body

I. One criterion for finding a suitable credit card is to examine the interest rate.

The two major subdivisions designated by A and B indicate the equal weight of these points. The second-level subdivisions— designated by 1, 2, and 3 for the major subpoint A, and 1 and 2 for the major subpoint B—give the necessary information for understanding the subpoints. The number of major and second-level subpoints is at the discretion of the speaker. After the first two levels of subordination, words and phrases may be used in place of complete sentences in further subdivisions.

A. Interest rates are the percentages that a company charges you to carry a balance on your card past the due date.

    1. Most credit cards carry an average of 18 percent, which is much higher than ordinary interest rates.

    2. Some cards carry an average of as much as 21 percent.

    3. Many companies quote very low rates (6 percent to 8 percent) for specific periods.

B. Interest rates can be variable or fixed.

    1. A variable rate means that the rate will change from month to month.

    2. A fixed rate means that the rate will stay the same.

This transition reminds listeners of the first main point and forecasts the second.

(Now that we have considered rates, let's look at the next criterion.)

II. A second criterion for finding a suitable credit card is to examine the annual fee.
  A. The annual fee is the cost the company charges you for extending you credit.
  B. The charges vary widely.
    1. Some cards advertise no annual fee.
    2. Most companies charge fees that average around 25 dollars.

(After you have considered interest and fees, you can weigh the benefits that the company promises you.)

III. A third criterion for finding a suitable credit card is to weigh the perks.
  A. Perks are extras that you get for using a particular card.
    1. Some companies promise rebates.
    2. Some companies promise frequent flyer miles.
    3. Some companies promise discounts on "a wide variety of items."
  B. Perks don't outweigh other criteria.

Conclusion

  I. So, getting the credit card that's right for you may be the answer to your dreams.
  II. But only if you exercise care in examining interest rates, annual fee, and perks.

Sources

"Congratulations, Grads—You're Bankrupt: Marketing Blitz Buries Kids in Plastic Debt," *Business Week,* May 21, 2001, p. 48.

Lloyd, Nancy, "Charge Card Smarts," *Family Circle,* February 1998, pp. 32–33.

Orman, Suze, "Minding Your Money," *Self,* February 1998, p. 98.

Rose, Sarah, "Prepping for College Credit," *Money,* September 1998, pp. 156–157.

Speer, Tibbett L., "College Come-ons," *American Demographics,* March 1998, pp. 40–45.

Main point II, continuing the topical pattern, is a complete, meaningful statement paralleling the wording of main point I. Furthermore, notice that each main point considers only one major idea.

This transition summarizes the first two criteria and forecasts the third.

Main point III, continuing the topical pattern, is a complete, meaningful statement paralleling the wording of main points I and II.

Throughout the outline, notice that main points and subpoints are factual statements. The speaker adds examples, experiences, and other developmental material during practice sessions.

The heading Conclusion *sets this section apart as a separate unit.*
The content of the conclusion is intended to summarize the main ideas and leave the speech on a high note.

A list of sources should always be a part of the speech outline. The sources should show where the factual material of the speech came from. The list of sources is not a total of all sources available—only those that were used, directly or indirectly.

Each of the sources is shown in proper form.

Activity 4.7
Completing the Speech Outline

The goal of this activity is to write and review a complete sentence outline of the speech using material developed in previous activities.

Relevant activities are shown in parentheses; use these activities to help you complete an outline for your speech.

Outline

Specific Goal: (Activity 1.4)

Introduction (Activity 4.4)

Thesis Statement (Activity 4.1)

Body (Activities 4.2 and 4.3)

   I.

(Transition)

   II.

(Transition)

   III.

Conclusion (Activity 4.5)

Sources (Activity 4.6)

By completing Speech Preparation Activity 4.7, you will have your complete outline prepared. Student Response for Activity 4.7 gives an example completed by a student in this course.

Summary

The organization process is completed by creating an introduction and a conclusion, by listing the sources you used in the speech, by writing a title (if required), and by reviewing the draft outline.

An effective speech introduction motivates us to listen, sets the tone for the speech, creates goodwill, establishes credibility, and leads into the body of the speech. Types of speech introductions include startling statements, rhetorical questions, stories, personal references, quotations, and suspense.

A well-designed speech conclusion summarizes the main points and leaves the audience with vivid images or emotional appeals. Types of conclusions include summaries, stories, appeals to action, and emotional impacts.

Although most classroom speeches may not require a title, in most speech situations outside the classroom it helps to have an informative and appealing title. Three kinds of titles are the simple statement of subject, the question, and the creative title.

The list of sources is compiled from the bibliographic information recorded on research note cards. Short lists are alphabetized by authors' last names. Longer source lists group sources by content category before alphabetizing.

Activity 4.7
Sample Complete Outline

Speech Goal: I want my audience to know how to have a successful job interview.

Introduction

I. What does it take to land you a good job after college?

II. In addition to a strong résumé, getting a job offer is likely to depend upon how well you perform during an interview.

Thesis Statement: How well you are able to do in the interview is likely to depend on how knowledgeable you are about the company, whether you can make a good first impression, and how effectively you communicate with the interviewer.

Body

I. The first factor is being knowledgeable about the company.

   A. Research the company beforehand so that you are well informed about its business and the current issues it confronts.

   B. Use the information you find to help you anticipate the kinds of questions you might be asked.

(Once you are knowledgeable about the company, it is time to think about how you will prepare for the interview.)

II. The second factor is to make a good initial impression.

   A. Dress appropriately.

   B. Arrive a few minutes early.

   C. Show interest in the job and the company.

(Not only must you begin positively, but you also need to answer questions well.)

III. The third factor is to communicate effectively throughout the interview.

   A. Listen carefully to the questions.

   B. Be willing to elaborate on your answers to questions by giving specific examples.

   C. Be willing to engage the interviewer in discussion about the company and the position.

Conclusion

I. The better your interview goes, the more likely you are to get the job.

II. How successful you are is likely to depend on whether you do your homework about the company, make a good first impression, and work to communicate effectively during the interview.

Sources

Plack, Harry J. Stand out from the rest. *Baltimore Business Journal,* August 3, 2001, p. 26

Tittle, David. Tittle's Top 10: Job interviewing in a downturn. *Washington Businesss Journal,* Sept 28, 2001, p. 35.

Job interview and employment interview technique. http://www.careercity.com/content/interview

Best Employment Interviewing Tips—Interview questions and questions to ask the employer http://www.careercc.com/interv3.shtml

As Marna and Gloria were eating lunch together, Marna happened to ask Gloria, "How are you doing in Woodward's speech class?"

"Not bad," Gloria replied. "I'm working on this speech about product development. I think it will be really informative, but I'm having a little trouble with the opening. I just can't seem to get a good idea for getting started."

"Why not start with a story—that always worked for me in class."

"Thanks, Marna, I'll think on it."

The next day, when Marna ran into Gloria again, she asked, "How's that introduction going?"

"Great. I've prepared a great story about Mary Kay—you know, the cosmetics woman? I'm going to tell about how she was terrible in school and no one thought she'd amount to anything. But she loved dabbling with cosmetics so much that she decided to start her own business—and the rest is history."

"That's a great story. I really like that part about being terrible in school. Was she really that bad?"

"I don't know—the material I read didn't really focus on that part of her life. But I thought that angle would get people listening right away. I did it that way because you suggested starting with a story."

"Yes, but . . ."

"Listen, she did start the business. So what if the story isn't quite right? It makes the point I want to make: If people are creative and have a strong work ethic, they can make it big."

1. What are the ethical issues here?
2. Is anyone really hurt by Gloria's opening the speech with the story?
3. What are the speaker's ethical responsibilities?

The complete draft outline should be reviewed as revised to make sure that you have used a standard set of symbols, used complete sentences for main points and major subdivisions, limited each point to a single idea, related minor points to major points, and made sure the outline length is no more than one-third the number of words of the final speech.

CHALLENGE ONLINE

Use your Challenge of Effective Speaking CD-ROM for quick access to the electronic study resources that accompany this text. Included on your CD-ROM is access to the Challenge of Effective Speaking Web site featuring Speech Builder Express at Wadsworth Communication Café, InfoTrac College Edition, and a demo of WebTutor for *The Challenge of Effective Speaking*. The Web site offers chapter-by-chapter access to the Speech Preparation Action Step Activities, InfoTrac College Edition exercises, a digital glossary of key terms, Web links, Speech Preparation Forms, Speech Evaluation Checklists, and quizzes. Review the key terms and complete the InfoTrac College Edition exercises on the book's Web site at
http://www.wadsworth.com/product/0534563856

InfoTrac College Edition Exercise

Use PowerTrac to search Vital Speeches for the speech titled "The Music in Your Soul: A Celebration of Life" by Francis J. McLain (November 1, 2001). Read the speech and identify the introduction, main points, and conclusion. Then answer these questions:

1. Of the goals of introductions listed in this chapter, which did she meet best?
2. Of the goals of conclusions listed in this chapter, which did she meet best?
3. On the criteria of speech organization, what grade would you give this speech? Why?

Key Terms

appeal *(145)*   **rhetorical question** *(139)*

Challenge of Effective Speaking CD-ROM

Use your Challenge of Effective Speaking CD-ROM to access Speech Builder Express at the Wadsworth Communication Café. Complete Speech Plan Action Step Activities 4.4, 4.5, and 4.6 before completing 4.7. If you have used Speech Builder Express to complete all Speech Plan Action Step Activities and have saved your work, the Speech Builder Express will automatically use the information you stored to provide a complete draft of your outline. Then you can review and revise the outline by completing Speech Plan Action Step Activity 4.7.

9 Creating and Using Visual Aids

A picture is worth a thousand words.

"How's it going with the speech, Jeremy?"

"I'm frustrated."

"Why's that?"

"Well, we're supposed to think about using visual aids with this speech. But I can't think of what I could depict that would be useful."

"What's your topic?"

"Effects of media violence, but I don't see any sense in showing any act of violence."

"Right, but there are lots of other visuals you could show that would be helpful."

"Like what?"

"Well, I'll bet you're using some statistics about the amount of violence."

"Sure."

"Well, couldn't you show statistics while you talk about them?"

"But wouldn't showing statistics be just as boring as giving them?"

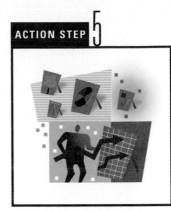

ACTION STEP 5

Create visual aids to clarify, emphasize, and dramatize verbal information.

Jeremy makes a good point. It is probable that just showing some statistics would be boring. But the question he needs to answer is what he could do to show the statistics in an interesting, meaningful way. In this chapter the focus is on developing a strategy for adapting to your audience visually. And although there are times when visual aids may not be necessary, having them will help capture your audience's attention and make your speech more interesting.

A **visual aid** is a form of speech development that allows the audience to see as well as hear information. You'll want to consider using visual aids because they enable you to adapt to an audience's level of knowledge by clarifying and dramatizing your verbal message. Visual aids also help audiences retain the information they hear. Research has shown that people are likely to remember features of visual aids even over long periods,[1] and people are likely to learn considerably more when ideas appeal to both eye and ear than when they appeal to the ear alone.[2] In our classes, students report that they enjoy the speeches more and remember more information during the round of speeches in which we require the use of visual aids than in any other round. In addition, when speakers use visual aids, they tend to be less anxious and have more confidence.[3]

In this chapter, we begin by describing the types of visual aids you might use, the methods for displaying visual aids, the criteria for making choices about which and how many visual aids to use, ways of designing visual aids to best adapt to your audience's needs, and guidelines for using them in your speech.

visual aid a form of speech development that enables the audience to see as well as to hear information

When deciding what type of visual aid would be most effective for your presentation, be sure to consider the setting and audience.

Types of Visual Aids

Before you can choose what visual aids you might want to use for a specific speech, you need to recognize the various types of visual aids that you can choose from. Visual aids range from those that are simple to use and readily available from some existing source, to those that require practice to use effectively and must be custom produced for your specific speech. In this section we describe the types of visual aids you can consider using as you prepare your speech.

Objects

Objects are three-dimensional representations of the idea that you are communicating. Objects make good visual aids if they are large enough to be seen by all audience members but small enough to be carried to the site of the speech. A volleyball or a braided rug are objects that would be appropriate for most classroom-sized audiences. A cell phone might be OK if the goal is simply to show a phone, but it might be too small if you want to demonstrate how to key in certain specialized functions.

On occasion, *you* can be an effective visual aid object. For instance, through descriptive gestures you can show the height of a tennis net; through your posture and movement you can show the motions involved in the butterfly swimming stroke; and through your own attire you can illustrate the native dress of a different country.

Models

When an object is too large to bring to the speech site or too small to be seen (like the cell phone), a three-dimensional model is appropriate. In a speech on the physics of bridge construction, a scale model of a suspension bridge would be an effective visual aid. Likewise, in a speech on genetic engineering, a model of the DNA double helix might help the audience to understand what happens during these microscopic procedures.

Still Photographs

If an exact reproduction of material is needed, enlarged still photographs are excellent visual aids. In a speech on "smart weapons," enlarged before and after photos of target sites would be effective in helping the audience understand the pinpoint accuracy of these weapons.

Slides

Like photographs, slides allow you to present an exact visual image to the audience. The advantage of slides over photographs is that the size of the image can be manipulated on site so that they are easy for all audience members to see. In addition, if more than one image is to be shown, slides eliminate the awkwardness associated with manually changing photographs. The remote-control device allows you to smoothly move from one image to the next and to talk about each image as long as you would like. One drawback to using slides, however, is that in most cases the room must be darkened for the slides to be viewed. In this situation, it is easy for the slides to become the focal point for the audience. Moreover, many novice speakers are tempted to look and talk to the slides rather than to the audience. In addition, to use slides you must bring a projector to class with you.

Film and Video Clips

You can use short clips from films and videos to demonstrate processes or to expose audiences to important people. But because effective clips generally run one to three minutes, for most classroom speeches they are ineffective and inappropriate because they dominate the speech and speaker. When clips are used in longer speeches, speakers must ensure that the equipment needed is available and operative. This means performing a dry run on site with the equipment prior to beginning the speech.

Simple Drawings

Simple drawings are easy to prepare. If you can use a compass, a straightedge, and a measure, you can draw well enough for most speech purposes. For instance, if you are

EXHIBIT 9.1 Sample drawing

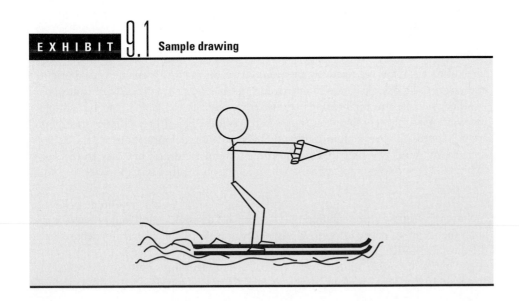

EXHIBIT 9.2 Sample map

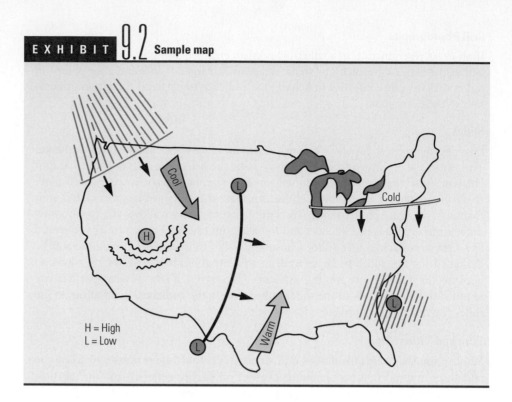

making the point that water skiers must hold their arms straight, with the back straight and knees bent slightly, a stick figure (see Exhibit 9.1 on page 161) will illustrate the point. Stick figures may not be as aesthetically pleasing as professional drawings or photographs, but to demonstrate a certain concept they can be quite effective. In fact, elaborate, detailed drawings may not be worth the time and effort, and actual photographs may be so detailed that they obscure the point you wish to make.

Prepare drawings so that they are easily seen by all audience members. Drawings should be prepared on poster board or foamcore so that they remain rigid and are easy to display.

Maps

Like drawings, maps are relatively easy to prepare. Simple maps enable you to orient audiences to landmarks (mountains, rivers, and lakes), states, cities, land routes, or weather systems. You might choose to use commercially available maps, but simple maps are relatively easy to prepare and can be customized so that audience members are not confused by visual information that is irrelevant to your purposes. Like drawings, maps should be prepared so that they remain rigid and are easy to display. Exhibit 9.2 is a good example of a map that focuses on weather systems.

Charts

chart graphic representation that presents information in an easily interpreted format

word chart a summary, list, or outline

A **chart** is a graphic representation that distills a lot of information and presents it to an audience in an easily interpreted visual format. Word charts and flow charts are the most common.

Word charts are used to preview, review, or highlight important ideas covered in a speech. In a speech on Islam, a speaker might make a word chart that lists the five

EXHIBIT 9.3 Word chart

Five Pillars of Islam

1. Shahadah—Witness to Faith
2. Salat—Prayer
3. Sawm—Fasting
4. Zakat—Almsgiving
5. Hajj—Pilgrimage

pillars of Islam, as shown in Exhibit 9.3. An outline of speech main points can become a word chart.

Flow charts use symbols and connecting lines to diagram the progressions through a complicated process. Organizational charts are a common type of flow chart that shows the flow of authority and chain of command in an organization. Exhibit 9.4 illustrates the organization of a student union board.

As with most visual aids, charts should be prepared ahead of time. One method for preparing charts allows you to add information to the chart as the speech progresses. To do this, prepare a series of charts on a large newsprint pad so that additional information is added on succeeding pages. Then mount the pad on an easel and as you are talking you can flip the pages to reveal more information as you discuss it.

Flow chart symbols and connecting lines used to diagram a complex system or procedure

Graphs

A **graph** is a diagram that presents numerical information. Bar graphs, line graphs, and pie graphs are the most common forms of graphs.

graph a diagram that compares information

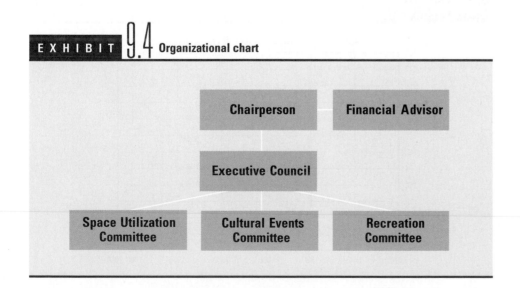

EXHIBIT 9.4 Organizational chart

Chairperson   Financial Advisor

Executive Council

Space Utilization Committee   Cultural Events Committee   Recreation Committee

EXHIBIT **9.5** Bar graph

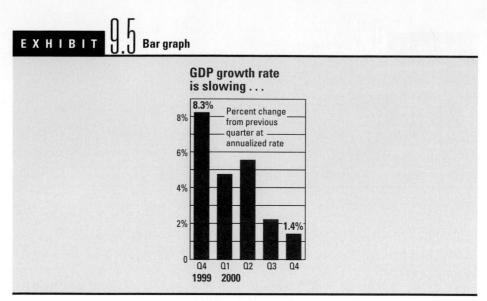

**GDP growth rate
is slowing . . .**

Percent change
from previous
quarter at
annualized rate

Source: U.S. News & World Report,
February 12, 2001, p. 22.

bar graph   chart with vertical or
horizontal bars to show relationships
between two or more variables at
the same time or at various times on
one or more dimensions

line graph   chart that indicates
changes in one or more variables
over time

Bar graphs are diagrams that compare information with vertical or horizontal
bars. These graphs can show relationships between two or more variables at the same
time or at various times on one or more dimensions. For instance, in a speech on
fluctuations of the economy, the bar graph in Exhibit 9.5 shows a sharp drop in the
GDP (gross domestic product) between the end of the fourth quarter in 1999 and the
fourth quarter in 2000.

Line graphs are diagrams that indicate changes in one or more variables over
time. In a speech on the population of the United States, for example, the line graph
in Exhibit 9.6 helps by showing the population increase, in millions, from 1810 to
2000.

EXHIBIT **9.6** Line graph

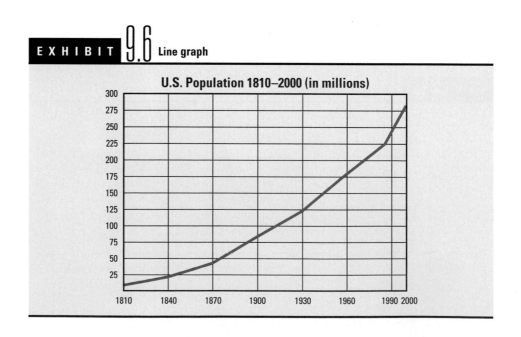

U.S. Population 1810–2000 (in millions)

EXHIBIT 9.7 Pie graph showing public opinion

Pie graph showing public opinion with segments: No effect 28%, Make worse 22%, Not sure 9%, Improve economy 41%

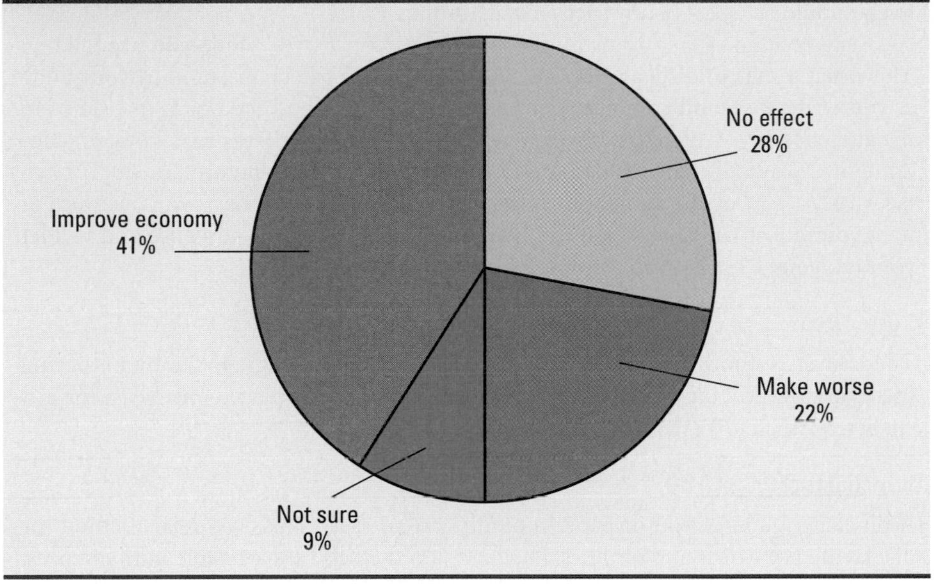

Source: Time, February 19, 2001, p. 30.

Pie graphs are diagrams that show the relationships among parts of a single unit. In a speech on the effect of tax cuts, a pie graph such as the one in Exhibit 9.7 could be used to show public opinion.

When choosing or preparing graphs, make sure that labels are large enough to be read easily by audience members.

pie graph chart that helps audiences to visualize the relationships among parts of a single unit

Methods for Displaying Visual Aids

Once you have decided on the types of visual aids you will use in your speech, you will need to choose the best method to display your visual aids. Methods for displaying visual aids vary in the type of prespeech preparation they require and the amount of specialized training a speaker needs to use them effectively. Some methods, such as chalkboarding, require little prespeech preparation. Other methods, such as computer-generated presentation aids, can require hours of prespeech preparation. Similarly, you don't need much practice to use a chart or handout effectively, but you may need a special tutorial to master setting up and using computer-generated presentational aids. The purpose of visual aids is to help audience members understand and retain information; speakers should choose methods that enable them to meet this goal effectively. Speakers can choose from the following methods.

Chalkboard

A chalkboard is appropriate to use for very short items of information that can be written in a few seconds. Because the chalkboard is a staple in every college classroom, it is tempting to rely on this method. Unfortunately, the chalkboard is easy to misuse and to overuse. Moreover, it is unlikely that the chalkboard would be your first choice for any major analysis of a process or procedure because of its limitations in displaying complex material. Nevertheless, being able to use a chalkboard effectively should be a part of any speaker's repertoire.

One common error in using the chalkboard is to write while you are talking. This often results in displays that are either illegible or partly obscured by your body as you write. A second common error is to end up talking to the board instead of to the audience. If you plan to draw or write on the board while you are talking, practice doing it. If you are right-handed, stand to the right of what you are drawing. Try to face at least part of the audience while you work. Although it may seem awkward at first, your effort will enable you to maintain contact with your audience and will let your audience see what you are doing while you are doing it.

Poster Boards

The easiest method to display drawings, charts, maps, and graphs is by preparing them on stiff cardboard or foamcore. Then the visual can be placed on an easel or in a chalk tray when it is referred to during the speech.

Flipcharts

A flipchart is a large pad of paper mounted on an easel. This a popular method for displaying key words and outlines. Flipcharts (and easels) are available in many sizes. For a presentation to four or five people, a small table-top version works well; for a larger audience, it is wise to use a larger size, such as thirty by forty inches.

In preparing flipcharts, leave several pages between each chart in the pad. If you discover a mistake or decide to revise a chart, you can tear out that sheet without disturbing the order. After you have finished all the charts, tear out all but one sheet between each chart. The one sheet serves as both a transition page and a cover sheet. Because you want your audience to focus on your words and not on visual material that is no longer being discussed, you can flip to the empty page while you are talking about material not covered by the charts. Also, the empty page between charts ensures that heavy lines or colors from the next chart will not show through.

Overhead Transparencies

An easy way to display drawings, charts, and graphs is to transfer them to an acetate film and project them onto a screen via an overhead projector. Overhead transparencies can be made by hand (traced or hand-lettered), by machine (copy machine, thermographic, color lift), or by computer. A major advantage of overheads is that you can make them rather easily and inexpensively. If you have access to a computer, you may have software (MicroSoft Word, Power Point, or PageMaker) that you can use.

Overheads work well in nearly any setting, and unlike other kinds of projections, they don't require dimming the lights in the room. Moreover, overheads can be useful for demonstrating a process because it is possible to write, trace, or draw on the transparency while you are talking. The size at which an overhead is projected can also be adjusted so that all audience members can see the image.

Handouts

At times it may be useful for each member of the audience to have a personal copy of the visual aid. In these situations, you can prepare a handout. On the plus side, you can prepare handouts (material printed or drawn on sheets of paper) quickly, and all the people in the audience can have their own professional quality material to refer to and take with them from the speech. On the minus side is the distraction of distribut-

If you have access to an LCD (liquid crystal display panel) that allows you to project your visual aid directly from your computer, make sure that the lighting in the room isn't so bright that it competes with your presentation.

ing handouts and the potential for losing audience members' attention when you want them to be looking at you. Before you decide to use handouts, carefully consider why a handout is superior to other methods. If you do decide on handouts, you may want to distribute them at the end of the speech.

Computer-Mediated Visual Aids

Today, in most professional settings speakers are expected to use computer-generated visual aids. Whereas overheads require only an overhead projector (standard in many college classrooms), computer-mediated visual aids require much more complicated machinery.

Still, you will want to become adept at using computer presentation software. With the right equipment, graphics can be displayed directly on to a screen or TV monitor as a computer "slide show," printed out and enlarged, photographed to make slides, or used to create overhead transparencies or handouts. Computer graphics are not so much a new type of visual aid as a new way of producing visual aids. They enable you to add a very polished look to your speech and can allow you to develop complex multimedia presentations.

While you are in school, you will want to experiment with one of the many computer graphics systems, such as Microsoft PowerPoint, Adobe Persuasion, or Lotus Freelance. Today, many colleges and universities offer courses to help you develop skills in using presentation software and have dedicated classrooms that house or are user-ready for advanced electronic equipment.

Additionally, through the Internet you can find, download, and store your own "library" of images. Most presentation graphics software allows you to insert virtually any image from your "library" into your presentation. If you have access to a computer scanner, you can also digitize a photograph from a book or magazine and transfer it to your computer library.

Preparing good presentations using computer graphics takes time and practice. Start simply, and over time you will become more adept at creating professional quality programs. Computer graphics can be fascinating, and many speakers overuse them as a result. Instead of having visual aids that emphasize and reinforce the speaker's ideas, the graphics become the show and the speaker becomes the projectionist.[4] It is important to use restraint when employing this media and focus on how the image enhances your speech.

Criteria for Choosing Visual Aids

Now that you understand the various types of visual aids and the methods you can use to display them, you have to decide what content needs to be depicted and the best way to do this. In this section, we focus on some of the key questions you need to answer to help you make visual aid choices.

1. **What are the most important ideas the audience needs to understand and remember?** These ideas are ones you may want to enhance with visual aids. Visual aids are likely to be remembered. So, you will want to make sure that what you present visually is what you want your audience to remember.

2. **Are some ideas complex or difficult to explain verbally but easy to understand visually?** The old saying "one picture is worth a thousand words" is true. At times we can help our audience by providing a visual explanation. Demonstrating the correct way to hold a golf club is much easier and clearer than simply describing the positioning of each hand and finger.

3. **How many visual aids should I consider?** Unless you are doing a slide show in which the total focus of the speech is on visual images, the number of visual aids you use should be limited. For the most part, you want the focus of the audience to be on you, the speaker. Use visual aids when their use will hold attention, exemplify an idea, or help the audience remember. For each of these goals, the more visual aids used, the less value they will contribute. For a five-minute speech, using three visual aids at crucial times will get attention, exemplify, and stimulate recall far better than using six or eight.

    There is another reason for keeping visual aids to a small number. A couple of really well-crafted visual aids may well maximize the power of your statements, whereas several poorly executed or poorly used visual aids may actually detract from the power of your words.

4. **How large is the audience?** The kinds of visual aids that will work for a small group of twenty or less differ from the kinds that will work for an audience of a hundred or more. For an audience of twenty or less, as in most of your classroom speeches, you can show relatively small objects and use relatively small models and everyone will be able to see. For larger audiences, you'll want projections that can be seen with ease from 100 or 200 feet away.

5. **Is necessary equipment readily available?** At times, you may be speaking in an environment that is not equipped for certain visual displays. At many colleges and universities, most rooms are equipped with only a chalkboard, an overhead projector, and electrical outlets. Anything else you want to use you will have to bring yourself or schedule through the appropriate university media office. Be prepared! In any situation in which you have scheduled equipment from an outside source, you need to prepare yourself for the possibility that the equipment may not arrive on time or may not work the way you thought it did. Call ahead, get to your speaking location early, and have an alternative visual aid to use, just in case.

6. **Is the time involved in making or getting the visual aid and/or equipment cost effective?** Visual aids are supplements. Their goal is to accent what you are doing verbally. If you believe that a particular visual aid will help you better achieve your goal, then the time spent is well worth it.

   You'll notice that most of the visual aids we've discussed can be obtained or prepared relatively easily. But because some procedures are "so easy," we find ourselves getting lost in making some of them. Visual aids definitely make a speech more interesting and engaging. However, I've found that the best advice is to "keep it simple."

Take a few minutes to consider your visual aid strategy, and use the following guidelines when choosing visual aids:

- Where would some kind of visual aid make the most sense? What kind of visual aid is most appropriate?
- Adapt your visuals to your situation, speech topic, and audience needs.
- Choose visual aids with which you are both comfortable and competent.
- Check out the audiovisual resources of the speaking site before you start preparing your visual aids.
- Be discriminate in the number of visual aids you use and the key points that they support.

SPEECH PREPARATION   **ACTION STEP** 5

Activity 5.1
Choosing and Preparing Visual Aids

The goal of this activity is to identify information whose visual presentation would increase audience interest, understanding, and retention.

1. Identify ideas you believe should be depicted with visual aids in order to create audience interest, facilitate understanding, or increase retention.

2. What type of visual aid will be most appropriate to develop for each of the ideas you have identified? List:

3. What method will you use to display each visual aid?

Activity 5.1
Choosing and Preparing Visual Aids

Speech Goal: I would like my audience to learn the skills necessary to play the game of lacrosse.

1. Identify ideas you believe should be depicted with visual aids to create audience interest, facilitate understanding, or increase retention.

   Catching, throwing and cradling.

2. What type of visual aid will be most appropriate to develop for each of the ideas you identified above?

   List: I will use a lacrosse stick and a ball.

3. What method will you use to display each visual aid?

   I will use myself to demonstrate catching, throwing, and cradling with the lacrosse stick and ball.

Speech Preparation Activity 5.1 on page 169 helps you choose and prepare visual aids. Student Response to Activity 5.1 provides an example of this activity completed by a student in this course.

Principles for Designing Visual Aids

However simple you may think your visual aids will be, you still have to carefully design them. The visual aids that you are most likely to design for a classroom presentation are charts, graphs, diagrams, and drawings written on poster board or flipcharts or projected on screens using overheads or slides.

In this section, we will discuss eight principles for designing effective visual aids. Then, we'll look at several examples that illustrate these principles.

1. **Use printing or type size that can be seen easily by your entire audience.** If you're designing a hand-drawn poster board, check your lettering for size by moving as far away from the visual aid you've created as the farthest person in your audience will be sitting. If you can read the lettering and see the details from that distance, then both are large enough; if not, draw another sample and check it for size.

   When you project a typeface from an overhead onto a screen, the lettering on the screen will be much larger than the lettering on the overhead itself. A good rule of thumb for overhead lettering is 36-point type for major headings, 24-point for subheadings, and 18-point for text. Exhibit 9.8 shows how these sizes look on paper. The 36-point type will project to about two to three inches on the screen, 24-point will project to about one to two inches, 18-point will project to one inch.

EXHIBIT 9.8 **Visual aid print sizes**

36 Major Headings

24 Subheads

18 Text material

2. **Use a typeface that is easy to read and pleasing to the eye.** Modern software packages, such as Microsoft Word, come with a variety of typefaces. Yet only a few of them will work well in projections. Exhibit 9.9 shows a sample of four standard typefaces in regular and boldface 18-point size. Most other typefaces are designed for special situations.

   Which of these typefaces seem easiest to read and most pleasing to your eye? Perhaps you'll decide that you'd like to use one typeface for the heading and another for the text. In general, you will not want to use more than two typefaces—headings in one, text in another. You want the typefaces to call attention to the material, not to themselves.

3. **Use upper- and lowercase type.** The combination of upper- and lowercase is easier to read. Some people think that printing in all capital letters creates emphasis. Although that may be true in some instances, ideas printed in all

EXHIBIT 9.9 **Type faces in 18-point regular and boldface**

Helvetica	Selecting Typefaces **Selecting Typefaces**
Times	Selecting Typefaces **Selecting Typefaces**
Frutiger	Selecting Typefaces **Selecting Typefaces**
Souvenir	Selecting Typefaces **Selecting Typefaces**

EXHIBIT 9.10 **All capitals versus upper- and lowercase letters**

CARAT—THE WEIGHT OF A DIAMOND

Carat—The Weight of a Diamond

capital letters are more difficult to read—even when the ideas are written in short phrases (see Exhibit 9.10).

4. **Try to limit the lines of type to six or less.** You don't want the audience to spend a long time reading your visual aid—you want them listening to you. Limit the total number of lines to six or fewer and write points as phrases rather than as complete sentences. The visual aid is a reinforcement and summary of what you say, not the exact words you say. You don't want the audience to have to spend more than six or eight seconds "getting" your visual aid.

5. **Include only items of information that you will emphasize in your speech.** We often get ideas for visual aids from other sources, and the tendency is to include all the material that was original. But for speech purposes, keep the aid as simple as possible. Include only the key information and eliminate anything that distracts or takes emphasis away from the point you want to make.

Because the tendency to clutter is likely to present a special problem on graphs, let's consider two graphs that show college enrollment by age of students (Exhibit 9.11), based on figures reported in the *Chronicle of Higher Education.* The graph on the left shows all eleven age categories mentioned; the graph on the right simplifies this information by combining age ranges with small percentages. The graph on the right is easier to read, and it also emphasizes the highest percentage classifications.

EXHIBIT 9.11 **Comparative graphs**

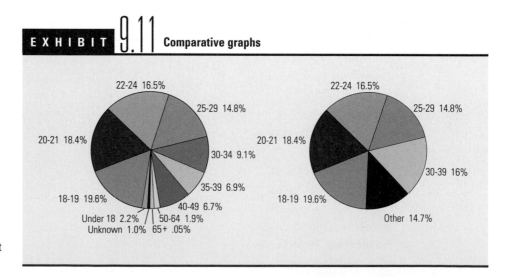

Source: Chronicle of Higher Education, Almanac Issue, August 1998, p. 18.

6. **Make sure information is laid out on the aid in a way that is aesthetically pleasing.** Layout involves leaving white space around the whole message, indenting subordinate ideas, and using different type sizes as well as different treatments, such as bolding and underlining.

7. **Add clip art where appropriate.** If you are working with computer graphics, consider adding clip art. Most computer graphics packages have a wide variety of clip art that you can import to your document. You can also buy relatively inexpensive software packages that contain thousands of clip art images. A relevant piece of clip art can make the image look both more professional and more dramatic. Be careful, though; clip art can be overdone. Don't let your message be overpowered by unnecessary pictures.

8. **Use color cautiously.** Although black and white will work well for most of your visual aids, you may want to experiment with using color. As with clip art or graphics, however, don't go overboard. Poorly used color can be a distraction, not an enhancement.

   With that said, here are some tips for using color in your visual aids:
   - Use color to show similarities and differences between ideas.
   - Use the same color background for each visual. Avoid dark backgrounds.
   - Use bright colors, such as red, to highlight the most important information.
   - Use black or blue for lettering, especially on flipcharts.
   - Avoid using yellow or orange for lettering; they can't be seen well from a distance.
   - Leave lots of white space around your lettering and clip art.
   - Use no more than four colors; two or three are even better.
   - If you want to get into more complex color usage, use a color wheel to select harmonizing colors.

EXHIBIT 9.12 A cluttered and cumbersome visual aid

I WANT YOU TO REMEMBER THE THREE R'S OF RECYCLING

Reduce the amount of waste people produce like overpacking or using material that won't recycle.

Reuse by relying on cloth towels rather than paper towels, earthenware dishes rather than paper or plastic plates, and glass bottles rather than aluminum cans.

Recycle by collecting recyclable products, sorting them appropriately, and getting them to the appropriate recycling agency.

EXHIBIT 9.13 A simple but effective visual aid

Remember the Three R's of Recycling

Reduce waste

Reuse
cloth towels
dishes
glass bottles

Recycle
collect
sort
deliver

- Always make a quick template before you prepare all your visual aids. Pretend you are your audience. Sit as far away as they will be sitting, and evaluate the colors you have chosen for their readability and appeal.

Now let's see if we can put all of these principles to work. Exhibit 9.12 contains a lot of important information that the speaker has presented, but notice how unpleasant this is to the eye. As you can see, this visual aid ignores all principles. However, with some thoughtful simplification, this speaker could produce the visual aid shown in Exhibit 9.13, which sharpens the focus by emphasizing the key words (reduce, reuse, recycle), highlighting the major details, and adding clip art for a professional touch.

Guidelines for Presenting Visual Aids

Many speakers think that once they have prepared good visual aids they will have no trouble using them in the speech. However, many speeches with good visual aids have become shambles because the speaker neglected to practice with them. As a general rule of thumb, you will want to make sure that you practice using visual aids in your rehearsals. During practice sessions, indicate on your notes exactly when you will use each visual aid (and when you will remove it). Work on statements for introducing the visual aids, and practice different ways of showing the visual aids until you are comfortable using them and satisfied that everyone in the audience will be able to see them. Here are several guidelines for using visual aids effectively in your speech.

1. **Plan carefully when to use visual aids.** As you practice your speech, indicate on your outline when and how you will use each visual aid. Avoid displaying visual aids before you begin talking about the specific information to which they relate, as they may distract your audience's attention from important information that precedes the visual. Likewise, if you find that a visual aid does not contribute directly to the audience's attention to, understanding of, or retention of information on your topic, then reconsider its use.

2. **Show visual aids only when talking about them.** Visual aids will draw audience attention. Use this basic rule of thumb: When the visual aid is no longer the focus of attention, remove it, turn it off, or get rid of it.

   If you use an overhead projector, it may come with a lid or cover on the light. If yours doesn't, then either turn the machine off or cover your transparency with a blank sheet of paper. If you are using an LCD and a computer, show your visual and then advance to a blank screen. You can insert blank pages in areas where you know you will need them.

   Often a single visual aid contains several bits of information. To keep audience attention where you want it, prepare the visual aid with cover-ups. Then, as you move from one portion of your speech to another, you can remove covers to expose the portion of the visual aid that you are then discussing.

Don't display visual aids when you're not referring to them.

3. **Talk about the visual aid while showing it.** Since you know what you want your audience to see in the visual aid, tell your audience what to look for: explain the various parts and interpret figures, symbols, and percentages.

   When you show your visual—for example, a transparency projected onto a screen in front of the class—use the following "turn-touch-talk" technique.

   When you display the visual, walk to the screen—that's where everyone will look anyway. Slightly turn to the visual and touch it—that is, point to it with your arm or a pointer (use carefully). Then, with your back to the screen and your body still at a slight forty-five degree angle to the group, talk to your audience about the visual.

   When you finish making your comments, return to the podium or your speaking position and turn off the projector or otherwise put the visual away.

4. **Display visual aids so that everyone in the audience can see them.** If you hold the visual aid, position it away from your body and point it toward the various parts of the audience. If you place your visual aid on a chalkboard or easel or mount it in some way, stand to one side and point with the arm nearest the visual aid. If it is necessary to roll or fold the visual aid, bring some transparent tape to mount it to the chalkboard or wall so that it does not roll or wrinkle.

5. **Talk to your audience, not to the visual aid.** You may need to look at the visual aid occasionally, but it is important to maintain eye contact with your audience as much as possible—in part so that you can gauge how they are reacting to your visual material. When speakers become too engrossed in their visual aids, looking at them instead of the audience, they tend to lose contact with the audience entirely.

6. **Avoid passing objects around the audience.** People look at, read, handle, and think about whatever they hold in their hands. While they are so occupied, they are not likely to be listening to you.

Karen is planning to give her speech on late term "partial birth" abortions. As she thinks about what she should do, she decides to go on the Web to see whether she can come up with any visual ideas. Along the way, she finds a picture of an aborted fetus. She downloads it on her computer and into her PowerPoint file. Later that day, she tells Paula what she has done, how she is planning to use the image, and asks her what she thinks of her plan.

"Hey," Paula replies. "That'll knock their socks off. Go for it."

As she rehearses her speech, she is still wondering whether using that visual aid is a good idea. But with Paula's apparent encouragement, she uses it in her speech.

During oral critiquing of the speeches, one classmate raises the question of the ethics of showing graphic pictures like aborted fetuses, mutilated bodies, and pornographic images in a speech.

1. Is the use of disquieting graphic images unethical?

2. What ethical arguments support the use of disquieting graphic images?

3. What arguments would hold the use of these images to be unethical?

4. What ethical principle will you follow in making decisions like this?

Summary

Visual aids enable audiences to see as well as hear information. They are useful when they help audience members understand or remember important information. The most common types of visual aids are objects, models, photographs, film and video clips, slides, simple drawings, graphs, maps, and computerized presentations. Speakers can use various methods to present visual aids, including chalkboards, poster boards, flipcharts, overhead transparencies, handouts, and computer graphics. Advancements in computer graphics give the speaker a wide range of flexibility in creating professional quality visual materials.

Before you start collecting or creating the visual aids you plan to use, consider these questions. What are the most important ideas in helping me achieve my speech goal? Are there ideas that are complex or difficult to explain verbally but would be easy for members to understand visually? How many visual aids should I consider? How large is the audience? Is necessary equipment readily available? Is the time involved in making or getting the visual aid and/or equipment cost effective?

Take time to design your visual aids with the following principles in mind. Use printing or a type size that can be seen easily by your entire audience. Use a typeface that is easy to read and pleasing to the eye. Use upper- and lowercase type. Try to limit the lines of type to six or less. Include only items of information that you will emphasize in your speech. Present information in short phrases rather than in complete sentences. Make sure information is laid out in a way that is aesthetically pleasing. Add clip art where appropriate. Use color cautiously.

When you plan to use visual aids in a speech, make sure that you practice using them in rehearsal. Keep the following suggestions in mind. Plan carefully when you will use each visual aid. Show visual aids only when talking about them. Talk about the visual aid while showing it. Display visual aids so that everyone in the audience can see them. Talk to your audience, not to the visual aid. Avoid passing objects around the audience.

CHALLENGE ONLINE

Use your Challenge of Effective Speaking CD-ROM for quick access to the electronic study resources that accompany this text. Included on your CD-ROM is access to the *Challenge of Effective Speaking* Web site featuring Speech Builder Express at Wadsworth Communication Café, InfoTrac College Edition, and a demo of WebTutor for *The Challenge of Effective Speaking*. The Web site offers chapter-by-chapter access to the Speech Preparation Action Step Activities, InfoTrac College Edition exercises, a digital glossary of key terms, Web links, Speech Preparation Forms, Speech Evaluation Checklists, and quizzes. Review the key terms and complete the InfoTrac College Edition exercise on the book's Web site at **http://www.wadsworth.com/product/0534563856**

InfoTrac College Edition Exercise

Using PowerTrac, enter the term "title" in the search box, and search for the article titled "Make Your Point with Effective A/V" by Maggie Weaver, in *Computers in Libraries,* April 1999. What suggestions offered here seem especially useful for you in using visual aids in a four- to seven-minute speech? Then look for any other articles that may provide additional tips for constructing and using visual aids.

Key Terms

bar graph *(164)*	**flow chart** *(163)*	**line graph** *(164)*	**visual aid** *(159)*
chart *(162)*	**graph** *(163)*	**pie graph** *(165)*	**word chart** *(162)*

Challenge of Effective Speaking Web Site

Use your Challenge of Effective Speaking CD-ROM to access the text's Web site and try out the activity for Using Visual Aids.

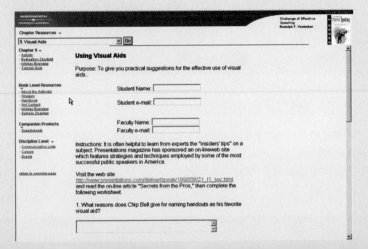

Practicing Speech Wording

Peter Holst/Getty Images

A speech reminds us that words, like children, have the power to make dance the dullest beanbag of a heart.
—Peggy Noonan, *What I Saw at the Revolution,* 1990

As Rhonda replayed the recording she had made of her first speech practice session, she listened carefully to the section on the effects of Rohypnol. She stopped the tape after she heard herself saying:

"Rohypnol leaves many bad effects on people. And a lot of these are really, really treacherous. I mean, you can be totally out of it for a long time."

"Yuck," thought Rhonda, "sounds so vague. I say, 'leaves bad effects,' but I don't specifically state any of the effects. And calling the effects 'really, really treacherous' isn't vivid or emphatic."

Practice speech wording and delivery.

A. Practice until the wording is clear, vivid, emphatic, and appropriate.

When you are ready to begin practicing your speech, the focus switches from the content of what you plan to say to how you plan to say it. Rhonda is working on the first challenge of presenting a speech—achieving clear, vivid, emphatic, and appropriate wording. The second challenge is achieving a fluent, enthusiastic, and expressive delivery. In this chapter we focus on wording; in Chapter 11 we focus on delivery.

Unlike written communication, where wording evolves through editing and finally appears on the printed page, wording in speech communication develops through oral practice. By carefully outlining your speech, you have produced a skeleton that includes anywhere from 20 percent to 40 percent of the words you will use in the speech. During the first practice, you will fill out the outline to speech length. Then, through several practice periods, you will work to improve the speech.

The goal of this chapter is to help you learn to use the kind of language that is instantly intelligible to the *ear*, so that the audience receives the same meaning the speaker intends. If a written sentence is unclear, the reader can reread it and puzzle out its meaning. If a speech sentence is unclear, the listener cannot go back. Thus, a speaker must focus on how to help the specific audience understand the meaning *as the speech is given.*

We begin our discussion by briefly explaining the complex relationship between language and meaning that makes language choices so important in speech making. Then, we describe specific tactics you can use to increase the clarity, vividness, emphasis, and appropriateness of the words you use.

Language and Meaning

On the surface, the relationship between language and meaning seems perfectly clear: You select a word to represent your meaning, and audience members will interpret your words and understand the meaning you wished to convey. In fact, the relationship between language and meaning is not so simple for three reasons.

First, we are not born knowing a language—we must learn it. Moreover, each generation within a language community learns the language anew. Much of our language we learn early in life from our families; we learn more in school and continue to learn more throughout our lives. But we do not all learn to use the same words in the same way.

Second, although each language has a system of syntax and grammar, each utterance is a creative act. When we speak, we use language to create new sentences that represent our meaning. Although on occasion we repeat other people's sentence constructions to represent what we are thinking or feeling, most of our talk is unique.

Third, even though two people may know the same word, they may interpret the meaning of the word differently. Words have two kinds of meaning: denotative and connotative. Thus, when Melissa tells Trish that her dog died, what Trish understands Melissa to mean depends on both word denotation and connotation.

Denotation

denotation the direct, explicit meaning a language community formally gives a word

The direct, explicit meaning a language community formally gives a word is its **denotation**. Word denotation is the meaning found in a dictionary. So denotatively, when Melissa said her dog died, she meant that her domesticated canine no longer demonstrates physical life. In some situations the denotative meaning of a word may not be clear. Why? First, dictionary definitions reflect current and past practice in the language community; and second, the dictionary uses words to define words. The end result is that words are defined differently in various dictionaries and may include multiple meanings that change over time.

context the position of a word in a sentence and its relationship to other words around it

Moreover, meaning may vary depending on the context in which the word is used. For example, the dictionary definition of *gay* includes both having or showing a merry, lively mood and homosexual. Thus, **context**, the position of a word in a sentence and its relationship to the other words around it, has an important effect on correctly interpreting which denotation of a word is meant. Not only will the other words, the syntax, and the grammar of a verbal message help us to understand the denotative meaning of certain words, but so will the situation in which they are spoken. Whether the comment "He's really gay" is understood to be a comment on someone's sexual orientation or on his merry mood may depend on the age of the speaker or the circumstances in which it is said.

Connotation

connotation the feelings or evaluations we associate with a word

The feelings or evaluations we associate with a word, its **connotation**, color the meaning we give it. Thus our perception of a word's connotation may be even more important than its denotation in how we interpret the meaning of the word.

C. K. Ogden and I. A. Richards were among the first scholars to consider the misunderstandings resulting from the failure of communicators to realize that their subjective reactions to words will be a product of their life experiences.[1] For instance, when Melissa tells Trisha that her dog died, Trisha's understanding of the message depends on the extent to which her feelings about pets and death—her connotations of the words—correspond to the feelings that Melissa has about pets and death. Melissa, who sees dogs as truly indispensable friends, may be intending to communicate her overwhelming grief, but Trisha, who has never had a pet and doesn't particularly care for pets in general or dogs in particular, may miss the emotional meaning of Melissa's statement.

Pablo Corral V/CORBIS

To differentiate among individuals in this picture, you would have to be precise, specific, and concrete in your description.

Being aware of and sensitive to word denotation and connotation are important. Regardless of what a speaker says, the only message meaning that counts is the message meaning that is understood by audience members.

Speaking Clearly

Speaking more clearly results from reducing ambiguity and confusion. Compare the clarity of the following two descriptions of the same incident:

> Some nut almost got me a while ago.

> An older man in a banged-up Honda Civic crashed the light at Calhoun and Clifton and came within inches of hitting me while I was waiting to turn left at the cross street.

You can reduce ambiguity and confusion by using specific, concrete, precise, and familiar words.

Use Specific, Concrete, Precise, and Familiar Language

Often, as we try to express our thoughts, the first words that come to mind are general, abstract, and imprecise. The ambiguity of these words makes the listener choose

General and abstract words invite different interpretations.

EXHIBIT 10.1 Level of specificity

Art
Painting
Oil painting
Impressionist oil painting
Renoir's *La Promenade*

from many possible images rather than picturing the single focused image we have in mind. The more listeners are called on to provide their own images, the more likely they are to see meanings different from what we intend.

specific words words that clarify meaning by narrowing what is understood from a general category to a particular group within that category

Specific words clarify meaning by narrowing what is understood from a general category to a particular item or group within that category. Thus saying "It's a Honda Civic" is more specific than saying "It's a car." If, for instance, Nevah says that Ruben is a "blue-collar worker," you might picture any number of occupations that fall within this broad category. If, instead, she is more specific and says he is a "construction worker," the number of possible images you can picture is reduced. Now you select your image from the subcategory of construction worker, and your meaning is likely to be closer to the one she intended. If she is even more specific, she may say "Ruben is a bulldozer operator. Now you "see" Ruben driving the dozer and you are clearer on Ruben's occupation.

In the preceding example, the continuum of specificity goes from blue-collar worker to construction worker to construction vehicle operator to bulldozer operator. Exhibit 10.1 provides another illustration of this continuum.

concrete words words that are likely to appeal to our senses or conjure up a picture

Concrete words are sense related. In effect we can see, hear, smell, taste, or touch concrete words. Thus, we can picture that "banged-up" Civic. Abstract ideas such as justice, equality, or fairness can be made concrete through examples or metaphors. As we move from general to specific, we also move from abstract to concrete. Consider the word *speak*. This is a general, abstract term. To make it more concrete, we can use words such as *mumble, whisper, bluster, drone, jeer,* or *rant*. Say these words aloud. Notice the different sound of your voice when you say *whisper* as opposed to *bluster, jeer,* or *rant*. Further, notice how each of these words conveys a different sense of how someone is speaking.

precise words words that most accurately or correctly capture the sense of what we are saying

Precise words are those that most accurately express meaning—they capture shades of difference. It is more precise to note that the Civic came "within inches of hitting me" than it is to say "some nut almost got me." Here is another example. In seeking the most precise way to describe Phillip's speech, we might say, "Phillip blustered. Well, to be more precise, he ranted." Notice that we are not moving from general to specific—both words are on roughly the same level of abstraction. Nor are we talking about abstract versus concrete; both words are concrete. Rather, we are now concerned with precision in meaning. *Blustering* means talking in a way that is loudly boastful; *ranting* means talking in a way that is angry and noisy. When you work to word your ideas precisely, choose the word that expresses your idea most accurately. So, depending on *how* the person was talking, *blustering* or *ranting* would be the more precise word. Let's try another one. "Susan laughed at my story; well, to be more precise, she chuckled." What is the difference between laughing and chuckling? A laugh is a loud show of mirth; a chuckle is a more gentle sound expressing suppressed mirth. Similar? Yes. But different—showing shades of meaning.

Although specific, concrete, and precise words enable us to reduce ambiguity and sharpen meaning through individual words, sometimes clarity is best achieved by adding a detail or an example. For instance, Linda says, "Rashad is very loyal." The meaning of "loyal" (faithful to an idea, person, company, and so on) is abstract, so to avoid ambiguity and confusion, Linda might add, "He never criticizes a friend behind her back." By following up her use of the abstract concept of loyalty with a concrete example, Linda makes it easier for her listeners to "ground" their idea of this personal quality in a concrete or "real" experience.

You'll know that you have improved when, instead of saying "The senator brought *several things* with her to the meeting," you say, "The senator brought *recent letters from her constituency* with her to the meeting"; instead of saying "He lives in a *really big house*," you say, "He lives in a *fourteen-room Tudor mansion*"; or instead of saying "I think Professor Morgan is a *fair grader*," you say, "Morgan *uses the same standards for grading all students*."

Familiar words are words that your specific audience will understand. When you use familiar words, understanding is assured. Some speakers think that to be effective they must impress their audience with their extensive vocabulary. As a result, instead of looking for common or simple words, they use words that appear pompous, affected, or stilted to the listener. Speaking precisely and specifically does not mean speaking obscurely. So when you have a choice, select the simplest, most familiar words that convey your specific meaning. The following story illustrates the problem with pretentious, unfamiliar words.

familiar words words that your specific audience will understand

> A plumber wrote to a government agency, saying that he found that hydrochloric acid quickly opened drain pipes but that he wasn't sure whether it was a good thing to use. A scientist at the agency replied, "The efficacy of hydrochloric acid is indisputable, but the corrosive residue is incompatible with metallic permanence."
> The plumber wrote back thanking him for the assurance that hydrochloric acid was all right. Disturbed by this turn of affairs, the scientist showed the letter to his boss, another scientist, who then wrote to the plumber: "We cannot assume responsibility for the production of toxic and noxious residue with hydrochloric acid and suggest you use an alternative procedure."
> The plumber wrote back that he agreed, hydrochloric acid worked fine. Greatly disturbed by this misunderstanding, the scientists took their problem to the top boss. She wrote to the plumber: "Don't use hydrochloric acid. It eats the hell out of pipes."

Use a more difficult word *only* when you believe that it is the very best word for a specific context. Suppose you wanted to use a more precise or specific word for *building*. Using the guideline of familiarity, you might select *house, apartment, high-rise,* or *skyscraper,* but you would avoid *edifice.* Each of the other choices is more precise or more specific, but *edifice* is neither more precise nor more specific, and in addition to

Elle Schuster/Getty Images

The larger your vocabulary, the more chance you have of communicating effectively. One way to enrich your vocabulary is through study of basic vocabulary books and books of synonyms.

being less well understood, it will be perceived as affected or stilted. Likewise, when given the choice, choose *clothing* instead of *apparel, bury* instead of *inter, avoid* instead of *eschew, predict* instead of *presage,* and *beauty* instead of *pulchritude.*

Develop Your Ability to Speak More Clearly

Being able to speak more clearly requires building your working vocabulary and brainstorming to generate word choices from your active vocabulary.

Vocabulary Building

A long-term strategy for improving your ability to word your speeches effectively is to increase your vocabulary. As a speaker, the larger your vocabulary, the more choices you have from which to select the word you want; as a listener, the larger your vocabulary, the more likely you are to understand the words used by others.

One way to increase your vocabulary is to study one of the many vocabulary building books on the shelves of most any book store, such as *Merriam Webster's*

Vocabulary Builder.[2] You might also study magazine features such as "Word Power," in *The Reader's Digest.* By completing this monthly quiz and learning the words with which you are not familiar, you could increase your vocabulary by as many as twenty words per month.

A second way to increase your vocabulary is to make note of words that people use in their conversations with you that you are not able to define precisely. For instance, suppose you hear, "I was inundated with phone calls today!" If you can't define *inundated,* write it down. Later, look it up in the dictionary and then say the sentence with a synonym, in this case *overwhelmed* or *flooded.* If you then say to yourself, "She was inundated—overwhelmed or flooded—with phone calls today," you are likely to remember that meaning and apply it the next time you hear the word. You can follow the same procedure when you read. Once you have learned new words, work consciously at using them in conversation so that they will come to mind when you want to use them during a speech.

Mental Brainstorming

Having a larger vocabulary won't help your speaking if you don't have a procedure for using it. One way to practice accessing choices from your memory is to brainstorm during practice sessions and later in conversation. **Brainstorming** is an uncritical, nonevaluative process of generating alternatives. Suppose you were practicing a speech on registration and said "Preregistration is awful." If you don't think *awful* is the right word, you might be able to quickly brainstorm the words *frustrating, demeaning, cumbersome,* and *annoying.* Then, in your next practice you might say, "Preregistration is overly cumbersome."

You will really know that you have made strides in improving specificity, precision, and concreteness when you find that you can form clear messages even under the pressure of presenting your speeches.

brainstorming   an uncritical, nonevaluative process of generating alternatives

Be Sensitive to Cultural Differences

Verbal communication rules and expectations about clarity of language vary from culture to culture. One major dimension that is used by theorists to explain similarities and differences in language and behavior is individualism and collectivism.[3] In general, in *individualistic cultures* individuals' goals are emphasized more than the group's goals because these cultures value uniqueness. Individualistic cultures include many nations of western Europe and the United States. In contrast, in *collectivistic cultures* group goals are emphasized more than individual goals as these cultures value harmony and solidarity. Collectivistic cultures are found in many nations in Asia, Africa, and South America.[4]

Individualistic cultures tend to use *low-context communication,* in which information is (1) embedded mainly in the messages transmitted and (2) presented directly. Collectivistic cultures tend to use *high-context communication,* in which (1) subtle communication cues carry meaning about how people are thinking and feeling and (2) messages are presented indirectly to avoid embarrassing the other person. Speakers from low-context cultures like the United States prize clear and direct messages that do not depend on an interpretation of the context to be understood. Their approach may be characterized by expressions such as "Say what you mean" and "Don't beat around the bush."[5] In contrast, speakers from high-context cultures like China form messages with language that is intentionally ambiguous

People from different cultures may encounter misunderstandings in their communication in public speaking resulting from their differing perspective.

and indirect but can be correctly interpreted by understanding not only the message but the context in which it is uttered.

What does this mean to you as a student of public speaking? When you are a member of a cultural group that operates differently from that of the majority of your audience members, you need to adapt your language so that it is clear and appropriate for your audience. If you are uncertain, ask someone from the same cultural group as the majority of your audience to listen during your rehearsals to the parts of your speech in which your wording is raising questions and to suggest ways in which your wording can be adapted to the audience. For speaking to low-context audiences, this may mean using more concrete examples so that your audience members will be more likely to get the meanings you intend. For high-context audiences, this may mean stating certain parts of your message indirectly and trusting that the context will enable them to understand your meaning.

Speaking Vividly

vividness full of life, vigorous, bright, and intense

Clear language helps the audience grasp the meaning, but vivid language paints meaning in living color. **Vividness** means full of life, vigorous, bright, and intense. Vivid language begins with vivid thought. You must have a striking mental picture before you can communicate one to your audience. If you can feel the bite of the wind and the sting of the nearly freezing rain, if you can hear the thick, juicy sirloin strip steaks sizzling on the grill, if you can feel the exhilaration as the jet climbs from takeoff, then you will be able to describe these sensations vividly. The more imaginatively you can think about your ideas, the more vividly you can state them.

The contrast between the following two sentences illustrates the value of vivid language.

A great deal of potential was seen in Helen Keller by Anne Sullivan. She worked hard on Helen until the potential that enabled Helen to help people such as herself all over the world was realized.

Anne Sullivan saw great potential in Helen Keller. "She loved her, disciplined her, played, prayed, pushed, and worked with her until the flickering candle that was her life became a beacon that helped light the pathway and lighten the burdens of people all over the world."[6]

The first passage describes what Sullivan did with and for Helen Keller. The second passage from Beverly Chiodo's speech on "Choose Wisely" vivifies the passage through active rather than passive voice, specific, active verbs that create mental pictures, and figurative language. Below we consider each of these methods for increasing vividness.

Use active rather than passive voice. Voice is the form of a transitive verb that tells whether the grammatical subject performs the action stated in the verb or is acted upon. Casting all your sentences in active voice lays a foundation for vivid speech. For instance "Burglars often steal jewelry," "Tom hit the ball," and "Marsha took the test" are all active voice because the grammatical subject (*burglars, Tom, Marsha*) performs the action. "Jewelry is often stolen by burglars," "The ball was hit by Tom," and "The test was taken by Marsha" are all passive voice; each interjects a form of the verb "to be" so that the grammatical subject is acted upon. Notice how much more lively the sentences in active voice are.

voice the form of a transitive verb that tells whether the grammatical subject performs the action stated in the verb or is acted upon

Use specific, active verbs that form sharp mental pictures. In the Helen Keller example, the general phrase "worked hard" in the first passage does not create a sharp mental picture of what Anne did. In contrast, Chiodo's phrasing, "disciplined her, played, prayed, pushed," uses specific verbs that each evoke a different image.

Use figurative language. Figurative language means using a word or words in an imaginative rather than a literal sense. The first passage—Anne's work "enabled Helen to help people such as herself"—states Helen's contribution literally. Chiodo's version—"the flickering candle that was her life became a beacon that helped light the pathway and lighten the burdens of people all over the world"—contains figurative language that uses words imaginatively. "The flickering candle" is a figurative expression of a life that contained potential; "her life became a beacon" is a figurative expression of a life that served as a role model.

figurative language using a word or words in an imaginative rather than a literal sense

There are many types of figurative language,[7] and two of the most common, similes and metaphors, work well in speeches.

Using Similes

Perhaps the easiest comparative figure to create is the **simile**, which is a direct comparison of dissimilar things. Similes usually contain the word *like* or *as*. Many common clichés are similes. To make a point about lack of speed, we may say, "He runs like a turtle" or "She's slow as molasses." Likewise, to dramatize a negative description, we may say, "He swims like a rock" or "She's built like a pencil." The problem with using clichés in speeches is that their familiarity often destroys the vividness they once possessed. Similes are vivid when the basis for the direct comparison is imaginative or different. Thus, "Trucks are like monstrous boxcars that eat

simile a direct comparison of dissimilar things

highways for breakfast"[8] is a vivid simile. Likewise, an elementary school teacher's description of being being back at school after a long absence as "like trying to hold 35 corks under water at the same time"[9] is a fresh, imaginative simile for the nature of a public school teacher's task after a long holiday.

Using Metaphors

metaphors like a simile, but instead of a direct comparison using *like* or *as,* build a direct identification between the objects being compared

A second common comparative figure of speech is the metaphor. **Metaphors** are much like similes, but instead of a direct comparison using *like* or *as*, metaphors build a direct identification between the objects being compared. Metaphors are such a common part of our language that we seldom think of them as special. We call problem cars "lemons"; we describe a baseball team's infield as a "sieve."

As you create metaphors for your speeches, avoid the trite or hackneyed. Note the creativity shown in the following examples:

> Human progress is a chain, and every generation forges a little piece of it.[10]

> It is imperative that we weave our fabric of the future with durable thread.[11]

In reply to the statement that TV is just a toaster with pictures:

> This particular toaster is not just browning bread. It is cooking our country's goose.[12]

And my personal favorite, describing New Orleans:

> I can attest to the fact that this fair city must surely be the one place on earth where sound travels faster than light. Here is a circus of curved mirrors and distorted images of lights and shadows, of leads and red herrings—where it daily becomes more difficult to separate fact from fiction.[13]

One downside of using similes and metaphors is that some of them are idioms that are difficult for second language listeners to understand. For instance, some audience members whose first language is not English may have difficulty understanding such common idioms as "he bought the farm" and "she really sent me on a wild goose chase." As you work to develop similes and metaphors, be sensitive to the problems that idioms might present to some members of your audience.

Speaking Emphatically

In your speech, you know that certain words and phrases are especially important. It's up to you to help your listeners recognize these by emphasizing them. In this section, we consider several verbal means of emphasis: placement and sequencing, proportion, repetition, and transition.

Emphasize through Placement and Sequencing

placement and sequencing
constructing a list of items in a way that the most important comes last

Placement and sequencing mean constructing a list of items in a way that the most important comes last. If a speaker says that the president is the chief of foreign relations, commander-in-chief of the armed forces, head of a political party, and head of the executive branch, there is a natural tendency for the audience to perceive the last role as the most important. Unfortunately, many speakers list items with no consideration of order. To take advantage of the natural tendency to look for the most important idea to come last, emphasize by building a sequence that moves from least important to most important.

Emphasize through Repetition

Repetition means saying the same words again. If you say, "An analysis of more than 5,000 hours of programming on cable and broadcast television found that violence went unpunished 73 percent of the time—that's 73 percent of violent TV behavior that goes unpunished," a listener will perceive the repetition as an indication that the point must be important and should be remembered. Repetition is widely used because it is easy to practice and quite effective.

If you want the audience to remember your exact word, then repeat it once or twice: "The number is 572638—that's 5, 7, 2, 6, 3, 8"; or "A ring-shaped coral island almost or completely surrounding a lagoon is called an atoll—the word is *atoll*."

If you want the audience to remember an idea but not necessarily the specific language, you might restate, rather than repeat, it. Whereas repetition is the exact use of the same words, **restatement** means echoing the same idea but in different words. Here are two examples:

> "The population is 975,439—that's roughly 1 million people,"

> "The test will be composed of about four essay questions; that is, all the questions on the test will require you to discuss material in some detail."

repetition saying the same words again

restatement echoing the same idea using different words

Emphasize through Transitions

Of the four methods of emphasis discussed here, transition is perhaps the most effective and yet the least used. **Transitions** are the words, phrases, and sentences that show relationships between and among ideas. You'll recall that in Chapter 7 we discussed one type of transition, *section transitions*, complete sentences placed between major sections of a speech to indicate shifts in meaning, degree of emphasis, and movement from one idea to another. Now we consider internal transitions.

Internal transitions are words and phrases that link parts of a sentence in ways that help audience members see the relationships of the ideas within the sentence: they summarize, clarify, forecast, and, in almost every instance, emphasize. In the following sentences, notice how internal transition words clarify and emphasize the relationships between ideas.

transitions words, phrases, and sentences that show relationships between and among ideas

internal transitions words and phrases that link parts of a sentence in ways that help people see the relationships of the parts

1. Miami gets a lot of rain. Phoenix does not.

   Miami gets a lot of rain, *but* Phoenix does not.

   (or)

   Although Miami gets a lot of rain, Phoenix does not.

2. You should consider donating money to United Way. It will make you feel better.

   You should consider donating money to United Way *because* it will make you feel better.

3. Buckeye Savings is in good financial shape. Buckeye pays high interest.

   Buckeye Savings is in good financial shape; *moreover*, it pays high interest.

The English language contains many words that show idea relationships. Exhibit 10.2 indicates many of the common transition words and phrases that are appropriate in a speech.[14]

Internal transitions can announce the importance of a particular word or idea. As the speaker, you know which ideas are most important, most difficult to under-

EXHIBIT 10.2 **Common transition words and phrases and their uses**

Transitions	Uses
■ also ■ and ■ likewise ■ again ■ in addition ■ moreover	■ Use these words to add material.
■ therefore ■ and so ■ so ■ finally ■ all in all ■ on the whole ■ in short	■ Use these expressions to add up consequences, to summarize, or to show results.
■ but ■ however ■ yet ■ on the other hand ■ still ■ although ■ while ■ no doubt	■ Use these expressions to indicate changes in direction, concessions, or a return to a previous position.
■ because ■ for	■ Use these words to indicate a reason for a statement.
■ then ■ since ■ as	■ Use these words to show causal or time relationships.
■ in other words ■ in fact ■ for example ■ that is ■ more specifically	■ Use these expressions to explain, exemplify, or limit.

stand, or most significant. If you emphasize these ideas with internal transitions, the audience will know how to react. For example, you might say any of the following:

Now I come to the most important idea in the speech.

If you don't remember anything else from this presentation, make sure you remember this.

But maybe I should say this again, because it is so important.

Pay particular attention to this idea.

These examples represent only a few of the possible expressions that interrupt the flow of ideas and interject keys, clues, and directions to stimulate audience memory or understanding.

Speaking Appropriately

During the last few years, we have seen a great controversy over "political correctness," especially on college campuses. Although many issues germane to the debate on political correctness go beyond the scope of this chapter, at the heart of this controversy is the question of what language behaviors are appropriate—and what language behaviors are inappropriate.

Speaking **appropriately** means using language that adapts to the needs, interests, knowledge, and attitudes of the listener and avoiding language that alienates audience members. Through appropriate language we communicate our respect and acceptance of those who differ from us. In this section, we discuss specific strategies that will help you craft appropriate verbal messages.

appropriateness using language that adapts to the needs, interests, knowledge, and attitudes of the listener and avoiding language that alienates

Formality of Language

Language should be appropriately formal for the situation. Your goal is to adapt your language to the specific audience to which you are speaking. Thus, we are likely to use more informal language when we are speaking to an audience of colleagues and more formal language when we are speaking with those we know less well or who have great power and authority.

Some people may think that adapting to an audience means speaking the way the speaker believes the members of the audience speak. Rather than being helpful, this is likely to be counterproductive. For instance, when an adult is giving a speech to young teenagers and tries to use teen slang or street talk, he or she may come off to the teens as a phony. Likewise, a black talking to a Hispanic audience, a Caucasian talking to a black audience, or a northerner talking to a southern audience will not improve adaptation by trying to adopt what he or she believes is the vocabulary, sentence structure, or dialect of the audience. Members of the audience will perceive this as condescending and question the speaker's motives.

Use Words Meaningful to the Language Community

A language community usually includes within it subgroups with unique cultures who develop their own idiosyncratic connotations for words. These groups may be based on similarities of age, race, sex, religion, ethnicity, career type, or political orientation. Hecht, Collier, and Ribeau point out that "Cultural groups define themselves in part through language, and members establish identity through language use."[15] Subgroups within a language community develop variations on the core language that enables them to share meanings that are unique to their subgroup cultural experiences. Thus when people from different subgroup cultures try to talk with one another, they may misunderstand each other because they have different associations for the same word. For example, to most white Americans the words "police officer" connote a person who ensures safety. Unfortunately, because many black Americans have been treated roughly by police officers, the words now connote not feelings of safety but feelings of anxiety and fear for many black Americans. Speakers must become aware of the differences in meanings that various audience members may attach to certain words and work to avoid using words that trigger different meanings. Developing your language skills so that the messages you send are clear and sensitive will increase your communication effectiveness in every situation.

Jargon and Slang

Language is appropriate when it is free of jargon and slang with which audience members are unfamiliar. Many of us become so immersed in our work or hobbies that we forget that people who are not in our same line of work or who do not have the same hobbies may not understand specialized language that seems to be such a part of our daily communication. For instance, when a hacker gets into a conversation with a computer-illiterate friend about computers, the hacker will naturally speak about firewalls, back doors, and other jargon. But unless the hacker can express these ideas in language that his friend understands, little communication will take place. In short, anytime you are talking with people outside your specific work or hobby area, you need to carefully define or avoid jargon and speak instead in descriptive language that is recognized by the person to whom you are talking.

Show Sensitivity

Language is appropriate when it is sensitive to usages that others perceive as offensive. Some of the mistakes in language that we make result from using expressions that others perceive as sexist, racist, or otherwise biased—that is, any language that is perceived as belittling any person or group of people by virtue of their sex, race, age, handicap, or other identifying characteristic. Three of the most prevalent linguistic uses that communicate insensitivity are generic language, nonparallel language, and stereotyping.

Generic Language

Generic language uses words that may apply only to one sex, race, or gender as though they represent both sexes, races, or genders. Such use is a problem because it linguistically excludes part of the group of people it ostensibly includes. Let's consider some examples.

1. **Use of generic "he."** Traditionally, English grammar used the masculine pronoun "he" to stand for the entire class of humans regardless of sex. So, for example, in the past someone speaking standard English would say "When a person shops for food, *he* can save money by clipping coupons," even though most grocery shopping was done by women. Today, the use of generic "he" is inappropriate; we recognize it to be sexist because it excludes women. Despite traditional usage, it would be hard to maintain that we picture people of both sexes when we hear the masculine word *he*.

    Guideline: One way to avoid this problem is to use plurals. Instead of "Because a doctor has high status, his views may be believed regardless of topic," you can say, "Because doctors have high status, their views may be believed regardless of topic." Alternatively, you can use both the male and female pronouns: "Because a doctor has high status, his or her views may be believed regardless of topic." These changes, although small, may help you avoid alienating the people with whom you are speaking. Stewart, Cooper, Stewart, and Friedley cite research to show that using "he and she," and to a lesser extent "they," gives rise to listeners' including women in their mental images, thus increasing gender balance in their perceptions.[16]

2. **Generic "man."** A second problem results from the traditional reliance on the generic use of "man." Many words that have been part of our language are inherently sexist because they imply that they apply to only one gender. Consider the term *man-made*. What this really means is that a product was produced by human beings, but its underlying connotation is that a male human being made the item. Again, research has demonstrated that people usually visualize men (not women) when they read or hear these words. Moreover, when job titles end in "man," their occupants are assumed to have stereotypically masculine personality traits.[17]

    Guideline: Avoid using words such as *policeman, postman,* and *chairman;* instead, use *police officer, mail carrier,* and *chairperson.* Avoid the words *man-made* and *mankind* by substituting *made by hand* and *humankind.*

Nonparallel Language Use

Nonparallel language use occurs when terms are modified when the sex, race, or other characteristic of the individual differs from the dominant referent group. Because it treats groups of people differently, nonparallel language is also offensive. Two common forms of nonparallelism are marking and unnecessary association.

1. **Marking. Marking** means adding gender, race, age, or other designations unnecessarily to a verbal description. For instance, saying "Jones is an excellent female doctor" or "Smith is a superb black judge" would be marking. Marking is offensive to people because the speaker appears to be demeaning the person's qualifications. For instance, this usage seems to imply Jones is an excellent doctor for a woman or Smith is a superb lawyer for a black person.

    marking adding gender, race, age, or other designations unnecessarily to a general word

    Guideline: Avoid markers by treating all groups equally. Because you would be very unlikely to ever say "Jones is a good male doctor" and "Smith is a superb white lawyer," leave irrelevant references to sex, race, age, and other markers out of your speech.

2. **Unnecessary association.** Another form of nonparallelism is to emphasize a person's association with another when you are not talking about the other person. Often you will hear a speaker say something like this: "Gladys Thompson, whose husband is CEO of Procter and Gamble, is the chairperson for this year's United Way campaign." Using such unnecessary associations demeans the value of the person. In this example, it implies that Gladys Thompson is important not because of her own accomplishment but because of her husband's.

    Guideline: Avoid associating a person irrelevantly with his or her partner or family. If the person has done or said something noteworthy, you should recognize it alone.

Stereotyping

Stereotyping consists of assigning characteristics to people solely on the basis of their class or category. Stereotyping represents a shortcut in thinking. By developing an attitude or a belief about an entire group and then applying that attitude to every

stereotyping assigning characteristics to people solely on the basis of their class or category member of the group, a person no longer has to consider the potential for individual differences—the stereotype applies to all persons in the group.

Guideline: Avoid making statements that treat groups of people as if they can be identified by the same characteristics. Thus, in a speech, if you must make value judgments about people, make them about specific individuals, and make such a statement without reference to any group of people with which the person may be associated.

Effects of Insensitive Language Usage

You have heard children shout, "Sticks and stones may break my bones, but words will never hurt me." This rhyme may be popular among children even though they know it is a lie, because it gives them a defense against cruel name-calling. Whether we admit it or not, words do hurt, sometimes permanently. Insensitive language is often a sign of prejudice that results in efforts to discriminate and as a result may be considered unethical as well. Think of the great personal damage done to individuals throughout history as a result of being called "hillbilly," "nigger," "fag," "yid." Think of the fights started by one person calling another's sister or girlfriend a "whore." Of course, we all know that it is not the words alone that are so powerful; it is the context of the words—the situation, the feelings about the participants, the time, the place, or the tone of voice. You may recall circumstances in which a friend called you a name or used a four-letter word to describe you and you did not even flinch; you may recall other circumstances in which someone else made you furious by calling you something far less offensive.

Where does offensive racist language come from? According to Molefi Asante, an internationally known scholar, racist language has its roots in our personal beliefs and attitudes. To a great extent, these have been conditioned by the knowledge system to which we have been exposed. Until recently, this knowledge system has had a Eurocentric bias.[18] Thus the contributions to the development of humankind by cultures other than European ones have been ignored or minimized.

We should always be aware that our language has repercussions. When we do not understand or are not sensitive to our listeners' frame of reference, we may state our ideas in language that distorts the intended communication. Many times a single inappropriate sentence may be enough to ruin an entire interaction. For instance, if you say "And we all know the problem originates downtown," you may be alluding to the city government. However, if your listeners associate downtown not with the seat of government but with the residential area of an ethnic or social group, the sentence will have an entirely different meaning to them. Being specific will help you avoid such problems; recognizing that some words communicate far more than their dictionary meanings will help even more.

Summary

Your overall language goal is to develop a "personal" oral style that captures your uniqueness. Language usage should be guided by the knowledge that words are only representations of ideas, objects, and feelings. Meaning is often a product of word denotation, or dictionary meaning, word connotation, or the thoughts and feelings that words evoke, and complications arising from cultural differences.

One day after class, Heather, Terry, Paul, and Martha stopped at the Student Union Grill. They began talking about who was going to have to speak the first day of the round, when Martha mentioned that one of the people was a fellow who had given what appeared to be the best speech on the previous round.

"Yeah, he's a good speaker," Paul said. Then he added, "Do any of you really know Porky?"

"Who?" the group responded in unison.

"The fat guy you said gave the best speech last time. We've been in a couple of classes together—he's a pretty nice guy."

"What's his name?" Heather asked.

"Carl—but he'll always be Porky to me."

"Do you call him that to his face?" Terry asked.

"Aw, I'd never say anything like that to him—man, I wouldn't want to hurt his feelings."

"Well," Martha chimed in, "I'd sure hate to think that you'd call me 'skinny' or 'the bitch,' when I wasn't around."

"Come on—what's with you guys?" Paul retorted. "You trying to tell me that you never talk about another person that way when they aren't around?"

"Well," said Terry, "maybe a couple of times—but I've never talked like that about someone I really like."

"Someone you like?" queried Heather. "Why does that make a difference? Do you mean it's OK to trash talk someone so long as you don't like him?"

1. Sort out the ethical issues in this case. How ethical is it to call a person you supposedly like by an unflattering name that you would never call him if he were in your presence?

2. From an ethical standpoint, is whether you like a person or not what determines when such name-calling is OK?

Specific goals of language use are to state ideas clearly, vividly, emphatically, and appropriately. Ideas are clarified through precise, specific, concrete, simple language that is devoid of clutter. Precise words accurately depict your meaning. Specific and concrete words call up a single image. Simple words are the least pretentious but most precise words you can find. Avoid clutter by eliminating repetitions that do not add emphasis; eliminating empty phrases; editing long sentences into shorter, emphatic sentences; and combining sentences and phrases with like ideas. A speaker must also take into account how an audience might mistake meaning if they represent a different culture from the speaker.

Vividness means full of life, vigorous, bright, and intense. Increase the vividness of your language by using active rather than passive voice, using specific, active verbs that form sharp mental pictures, and using figurative language, especially similes and metaphors.

Emphasis means giving certain words and ideas more importance than others. One way to emphasize is through proportion, or spending more time on one point than another. A second way is through repetition. A third way is through transitions, words, and phrases that show relationships between ideas.

Appropriateness means using language that adapts to the audience's needs, interests, knowledge, and attitudes and that avoids alienating listeners. Appropriateness dictates formal versus informal language, using language meaningful to the speech community, freedom from jargon and unnecessary technical expressions, and sensitivity. Inappropriate and exclusionary language can be minimized by avoiding generic language, nonparallel language, and stereotyping.

CHALLENGE ONLINE

Use your Challenge of Effective Speaking CD-ROM for quick access to the electronic study resources that accompany this text. Included on your CD-ROM is access to the Challenge of Effective Speaking Web site featuring Speech Builder Express at Wadsworth Communication Café, InfoTrac College Edition, and a demo of WebTutor for *The Challenge of Effective Speaking*. The Challenge of Effective Speaking Web site offers chapter-by-chapter access to the Speech Preparation Action Step Activities, InfoTrac College Edition exercises, a digital glossary of key terms, Web links, Speech Preparation Forms, Speech Evaluation Checklists, and quizzes. Review the key terms and complete the InfoTrac College Edition exercise at
http://www.wadsworth.com/product/0534563856

InfoTrac College Edition Exercise

Using the Subject Guide, enter the search term "sexism in language" and select "periodical references." Locate the article titled "Does Alternating between Masculine and Feminine Pronouns Eliminate Perceived Gender Bias in Text?" by Laura Madson and Robert M. Hessling in *Sex Roles: A Journal of Research*, October 1999. Read the opening section and the "Discussion" section, which presents the analysis of answers to the question. The article reports a study of printed material, but what can you as a speaker learn from this study? How will you use pronouns in your speech? Why will you make this choice? Would your choice change if you spoke on a different topic? If you were a member of the opposite sex?

Key Terms

appropriateness *(191)*

brainstorming *(185)*

concrete words *(182)*

connotation *(180)*

context *(180)*

denotation *(180)*

familiar words *(183)*

figurative language *(187)*

internal transitions *(189)*

marking *(193)*

metaphor *(188)*

placement and
   sequencing *(188)*

precise words *(182)*

repetition *(189)*

restatement *(189)*

simile *(187)*

specific words *(182)*

stereotyping *(193)*

transitions *(189)*

vividness *(186)*

voice *(187)*

Challenge of Effective Speaking Web Site

Use your Challenge of Effective Speaking CD-ROM to access the book's Web site. There you will find activities to help you follow the suggestions offered in the text to practice speech wording and delivery.

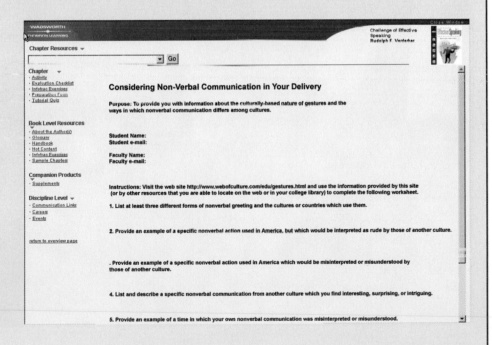

Practicing Delivery

Anne Dowie

Delivery I say has the sole and supreme power of oratory.
—Cicero, DeOratore, III, 56

As Nadia sat down, everyone in the audience burst into spontaneous applause.

"I don't understand it, Marv. I thought my speech was every bit as good as Nadia's, but when I got done all I got was the ordinary polite applause that everyone gets regardless of what they've done. Of course, I'm not as pretty as Nadia."

"Come on Syl, she's good looking but that's not why she got such a reception. Your speech was good. You had a good topic, lot's of good information and solid organization. But, truthfully? You just didn't deliver your speech anywhere near as well as she did."

Marv echoes what has been well known through the ages—good delivery is a hallmark of effective speaking. Why? Because the manner in which a speech is delivered greatly affects the audience's interest, understanding, and memory. Although delivery cannot change the ideas presented in a speech, it can make the most of those ideas. Even if you are not by nature a fluent, dynamic speaker, you can improve your delivery immensely if you are willing to practice.

Although speeches may be presented impromptu (on the spur of the moment without prior preparation), by manuscript (completely written out and then read aloud), or by memory (completely written out and then memorized), the material you have been reading is designed to help you present your speeches extemporaneously. An **extemporaneous speech** is carefully prepared and practiced, but the exact wording of each idea occurs as it is presented.

To deliver a speech extemporaneously, you will need to understand how the characteristics of voice, articulation, and bodily action affect delivery; how you can use your voice and bodily action to achieve a conversational quality; and how to practice the speech effectively. At the end of this chapter is the outline and text of a first graded speech given by a student in a beginning speaking course. In the margins of the speech text are our comments and critique.

extemporaneous speech a speech that is carefully prepared and practiced, but the exact wording of each idea occurs as it is presented

Components of Delivery

The components of delivery include voice, articulation, and bodily action.

Vocal Characteristics

Your voice is the vehicle that communicates the words of your speech to the audience. How you sound to your audience may emphasize the meaning, supplement the meaning, and at times even contradict the meaning of the words you speak. As a result, how you use your voice can make the difference between the success or failure of a speech. To use it well, it is important to understand how your voice works.

The four major characteristics of voice are pitch, volume, rate, and quality. Once you understand how to control these characteristics, you can create vocal variety and emphasis that will help communicate your meaning effectively.

pitch the highness or lowness of your voice

Pitch refers to the highness or lowness of your voice. Your voice is produced in the larynx by the vibration of your vocal folds. To feel this vibration, put your hand on your throat at the top of the Adam's apple and say "ah." Just as the pitch of a violin string is changed by making it tighter or looser, so the pitch of your voice is changed by tightening and loosening the vocal folds. Most people have a working pitch range of more than an octave—eight full notes on a musical scale.

Most people speak at a pitch level that is about right for them. A few, however, have pitch difficulties—that is, they talk using tones either too high or too low for their natural pitch. If you have questions about your pitch level, ask your instructor about it. If you are one of the few people with a pitch difficulty, your instructor can refer you to a speech therapist for corrective work. For most people, the question is not whether they have a satisfactory pitch range but whether they are making the best use of their pitch range.

volume the loudness of the tone you make

Volume is the loudness of the tone you make. When you exhale normally, your diaphragm relaxes and air is expelled through the trachea. When you speak, you supplement the force of the expelled air on the vibrating vocal folds by contracting your abdominal muscles. This greater force behind the air you expel increases the volume of your tone.

To feel how these muscles work, place your hands on your sides with your fingers extended over the stomach. Say "ah" in a normal voice. Now say "ah" as loudly as you can. If you are making proper use of your muscles, you should feel an increase in stomach contractions as you increase your volume. If you feel little or no stomach muscle contraction, you are probably trying to gain volume from the wrong source; such a practice can result in tiredness, harshness, and lack of sufficient volume to be heard in a large room.

Each person, regardless of size, can make his or her voice louder. If you have trouble talking loudly enough to be heard in a large classroom, work on increasing pressure from the abdominal area while exhaling.

rate the speed at which you talk

Rate is the speed at which you talk. Although most people utter between 130 and 180 words per minute in normal conversation, the rate that is best for anyone is a highly individual matter. An acceptable rate of speech is determined by whether listeners can understand what you are saying. Usually, even very fast talking is acceptable when words are well articulated and when there is sufficient vocal variety and emphasis.

If your instructor believes you talk too rapidly or too slowly, he or she will tell you and may suggest ways you can improve. If you want to change your speaking rate, start by working with written passages—it makes it easier to compute your speaking rate. First, read aloud for exactly three minutes. When you have finished, count the number of words you have read and divide by three to compute the number of words you read per minute. If you perceive your reading as too fast or too slow, reread the same passage for another three-minute period, consciously decreasing or increasing the number of words you read. Again, count the words and divide by three.

At first, it may be difficult to change speed significantly, but with practice you will see that you can read much faster or much slower when you want to. You may find that a different rate, whether faster or slower, will sound strange to you. To show improvement in your normal speaking, you have to learn to adjust your ear to a more appropriate rate of speed. If you practice daily, within a few weeks you should be able to accustom your ear to changes so that you can vary your rate with the type of material you read. As you gain confidence in your ability to alter your rate, you can practice with portions of speeches. You will talk faster when material is easy or when you are trying to create a mood of excitement; you will talk more slowly when the material is difficult or when you are trying to create a somber mood.

Quality is the tone, timbre, or sound of your voice. The best vocal quality is a clear and pleasant tone. Difficulties with quality include nasality ("talking through your nose" on vowel sounds), breathiness (too much escaping air during phonation), harshness (too much tension in the throat and chest), and hoarseness (a raspy sound). If your voice tends to have one of these undesirable qualities, consult your instructor. Although you can make some improvement on your own, significant improvement requires a great deal of work and extensive knowledge of vocal anatomy and physiology. Severe problems of vocal quality should be referred to a speech therapist.

quality the tone, timbre, or sound of your voice

Articulation

Articulation is shaping speech sounds into recognizable oral symbols that combine to produce a word. Articulation should not be confused with **pronunciation**—the form and accent of various syllables of a word. In the word statistics, for instance, articulation refers to shaping the ten sounds (s-t-a-t-i-s-t-i-k-s); pronunciation refers to grouping and accenting the sounds (sta-tis´-tiks). If you are unsure of how to pronounce a word in a speech, consult a dictionary for the proper pronunciation.

Many speakers suffer from minor articulation problems such as adding a sound where none appears (*athalete* for *athlete)*, leaving out a sound where one occurs (*libary* for *library)*, transposing sounds (*revalent* for *relevant)*, and distorting sounds (*truf* for *truth)*. Although some people have consistent articulation problems that require speech therapy (such as substituting *th* for *s* consistently in speech), most of us are guilty of carelessness that is easily corrected.

Two of the most common articulation faults for speakers are slurring sounds (running sounds and words together) and leaving off word endings. Spoken English always contains some running together of sounds. For instance, most people are likely to say "tha-table" for "that table." It is simply too difficult to make two *t* sounds in a row. But many people slur sounds and drop word endings to excess, making it difficult for listeners to understand us. "Who ya gonna see?" for "Who are you going to see?" illustrates both of these errors.

If you have a mild case of "sluritis" caused by not taking the time to form sounds clearly, you can make considerable improvement in articulation by taking ten to fifteen minutes three days a week to read passages aloud, trying to overaccentuate each sound. Some teachers advocate "chewing" your words—that is, making sure that lips, jaw, and tongue move carefully for each sound you make. As with most other problems of delivery, speakers must work conscientiously several days a week for months to improve significantly.

Because constant mispronunciation and misarticulation may suggest ignorance or carelessness (or both), it is important to correct mistakes. Exhibit 11.1 lists many common problem words that people are likely to mispronounce or misarticulate.

A major concern of speakers from different cultures and different parts of the country is their **accent**—the inflection, tone, and speech habits typical of the natives of a country, a region, or even a state or city. Thus, one doesn't have to be from a foreign culture to have an accent. In reality, nearly everyone speaks with some kind of an accent, since "accent" means any tone or inflection that differs from the way we and our neighbors speak. For instance, natives of a particular city or region will speak with inflections and tones that they believe are "normal" North American speech (for

articulation the shaping of speech sounds into recognizable oral symbols that combine to produce a word

pronunciation the form and accent of various syllables of a word

Slurring

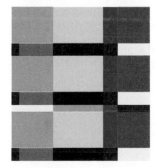

Articulation

accent the inflection, tone, and speech habits typical of the natives of a country, a region, or even a state or city

EXHIBIT 11.1 **Problem words**

Word	Correct	Incorrect
arctic	arc´-tic	ar´-tic
athlete	ath´lete	ath´a-lete
family	fam´-a-ly	fam´-ly
February	Feb´-ru-ary	Feb´-yu-ary
get	get	git
larynx	ler´-inks	lar´-nix
library	ly´brer-y	ly´-ber-y
particular	par-tik´-yu-ler	par-tik´-ler
picture	pic´-ture	pitch´-er
recognize	rek´-ig-nize	rek´-a-nize
relevant	rel´-e-vant	rev´-e-lant
theater	thee´-a-ter	thee-a´-ter
truth	truth	truf
with	with	wit *or* wid

instance, people from the Northeast who drop the *r* sound (saying *Havad* for *Harvard*) or people from the South who "drawl." But when they visit a different city or region, they will be accused of having an "accent," because the people living in the city or region they visit hear inflections and tones that they perceive as *different* from their own speech.

When should people work to lessen or eliminate an accent? Only when the accent is so "heavy" or different from audience members' expectations that they have difficulty in communicating effectively, or if they expect to go into teaching, broadcasting, or other professions where an accent may have an adverse effect on their performance.

Bodily Action

How effective you are in communicating your meaning also depends on how your nonverbal bodily actions supplement your voice. The principal nonverbal variables that affect meaning are facial expression, gestures, movement, poise, and posture.

facial expression eye and mouth movement

Facial expression refers to eye and mouth movement. The eyes and mouth communicate far more than we might realize. We need only recall the icy stare, the warm smile, or the hostile scowl we have received to understand that the eyes (and the mouth as well) mirror the mind. Your facial expression should be appropriate to what you are saying. If, for example, you get a stern look on your face when you say "City Council is not listening to the people," your facial expression adds power to your words. If, on the other hand, you smile or show no expression, your audience will be confused. Audiences look for facial expressions that seem to reflect your thoughts and feelings. Think actively about what you are saying, and your face will probably respond appropriately.

gestures movements of hands, arms, and fingers

Gestures are movements of hands, arms, and fingers. We use gestures consciously to describe or to emphasize. When a person says "about this high" or "nearly this round," we expect to see a gesture accompanying the verbal description. Likewise, when a person says, "Put that down" or "Listen to me," we look for a pointing finger, a pounding fist, or some other gesture that reinforces the point. If you gesture in conversation, you will usually gesture in speech. If you do not gesture in conversation, it

© Joel Gordon 1995

When a person speaks emphatically, we expect to see gestures and facial expression that reinforce the words.

is probably best not to force yourself to gesture in a speech. Leave your hands free at all times to help you "do what comes naturally." If you clasp your hands behind you, grip the sides of the speaker's stand, or put your hands in your pockets, then you are not free to gesture naturally even if you want to.

If you wonder what to do with your hands at the start of the speech so that they do not seem conspicuous, either rest them on the speaker's stand partially clenched or hold them relaxed at your sides—perhaps with one arm slightly bent at the elbow. Once you begin speaking, forget about your hands—they will be free for appropriate gestures. If, however, you discover that you have folded your arms in front of you or clasped them behind you, put them back in one of the two original positions. After you have spoken a few times, your instructor will suggest whether you need to be more responsive or somewhat restrained with your hands and arms.

Movement refers to motion of the entire body. Some speakers stand perfectly still throughout an entire speech. Others are constantly on the move. In general, it is probably best to remain in one place unless you have some reason for moving. A little movement, however, adds action to a speech, so it may help hold attention. Ideally, movement should help to focus on a transition, emphasize an idea, or call attention to a particular aspect of a speech. Avoid such unmotivated movement as bobbing and weaving, shifting from foot to foot, or pacing from one side of the room to the other. At the beginning of your speech, stand up straight on both feet. If you find yourself in some peculiar posture during the course of the speech, return to the upright position with your weight equally distributed on both feet.

movement motion of the entire body

Poise refers to assurance of manner. A poised speaker is able to avoid mannerisms that distract the audience, such as taking off or putting on glasses, jiggling pocket change, smacking the tongue, licking the lips, or scratching the nose, hand, or arm. As a general rule, anything that calls attention to itself is negative, and anything that helps reinforce an important idea is positive. Likewise, a poised speaker is able to control behaviors that accompany speech nervousness. All speakers show some amount of nervousness, but poised speakers have learned to control nervous

poise assurance of manner

behaviors by concentrating on communicating with the audience rather than focusing on themselves.

posture the position or bearing of the body, which gives further evidence of your poise

Posture refers to the position or bearing of the body. Good posture—upright stance and squared shoulders—communicates a sense of command to an audience. Speakers who slouch may be perceived as timid, self-conscious, or ill prepared.

Bodily action is a natural part of effective speaking. If you are relaxed and focused on what you are saying, your bodily action will probably be appropriate. If you tend to use either too much or too little bodily action, your instructor will notice and can give you pointers for limiting or accenting your normal behavior. Even though you discover minor problems, do not be concerned unless your bodily action takes away from your speaking effectiveness.

During speech practice sessions, try various methods to monitor or alter your bodily action. Videotape provides an excellent means of monitoring your bodily action. You may want to practice before a mirror to see how you look to others when you speak. (Although some speakers swear by this method, others find it a traumatic experience.) Perhaps the best method is to get a willing listener to critique your bodily action and help you improve. Once you have identified the behavior you want to change, tell your helper what to look for. For instance, you might say, "Raise your hand every time I begin to rock back and forth." By getting specific feedback when the behavior occurs, you can make immediate adjustments.

Achieving a Conversational Style

In your speech practice, as well as in the speech itself, the final measure of your presentation is how well you use your vocal and nonverbal components to develop a **conversational style**—an informal way of presenting a speech so that your listeners feel that you are talking with them, not at them. Five components of a conversational style are enthusiasm, vocal expressiveness, spontaneity, fluency, and eye contact.

conversational style an informal way of presenting a speech so that your listeners feel that you are talking with them

Enthusiasm

Enthusiasm is excitement or passion about your speech. If sounding enthusiastic does not come naturally to you, it will help if you have a topic that really excites you. Even normally enthusiastic people can have trouble sounding enthusiastic when they choose an uninspiring topic. Then, focus on how your listeners will benefit from what you have to say. If you are convinced that you have something worthwhile to communicate, you are likely to feel and show more enthusiasm.

enthusiasm the excitement or passion about the topic

To validate the importance of enthusiasm, think of how your attitude toward a class differs depending on whether the professor's presentation says "I'm really excited to be talking with you about geology (history, English lit)" or "I'd rather be anywhere than talking to you about this subject." A speaker who looks and sounds enthusiastic will be listened to, and that speaker's ideas will be remembered.

Vocal Expressiveness

Vocal expressiveness is the vocal contrast in pitch, volume, rate, and quality that affect the meaning audiences get from the sentences you present. Read the following sentence:

vocal expressiveness vocal contrast in pitch, volume, rate, and quality that affect the meaning audiences get from the sentences you present

We need to prosecute abusers.

We need to prosecute abusers.

We *need* to prosecute abusers.

We need to *prosecute* abusers.

We need to prosecute *abusers*.

What did the writer intend that sentence to mean? Without a context, who knows? Now, to illustrate how vocal expressiveness affects meaning, read the sentence aloud four times. The first time emphasize *We,* the second time emphasize *need,* the third time emphasize *prosecute,* and the fourth time emphasize *abusers* (see Exhibit 11.2).

When you emphasize *We,* it answers the question "Who will do it?" When you emphasize *need,* it answers the question "How important is it?" When you emphasize *prosecute,* it answers "What are we going to do?" When you emphasize *abusers,* it answers the question "Who will be prosecuted?" Thus, to ensure audience understanding, your voice must be expressive enough to delineate shades of meaning.

A total lack of vocal expressiveness produces a **monotone**—a voice in which the pitch, volume, and rate remain constant, with no word, idea, or sentence differing significantly from any other. Although few people speak in a true monotone, many severely limit themselves by using only two or three pitch levels and relatively unchanging volume and rate. An actual or near monotone not only lulls an audience to sleep but, more important, diminishes the chances of audience understanding. For instance, if the sentence "Congress should pass laws limiting the sale of pornography" is presented in a monotone, listeners will be uncertain whether the speaker is concerned with who should be responsible for the laws, what Congress should do with the laws, or what the subject of the laws should be.

monotone a voice in which the pitch, volume, and rate remain constant, with no word, idea, or sentence differing significantly from any other

Spontaneity

Spontaneity means being responsive to your ideas and their meaning while you are speaking. In a spontaneous speech, delivery is fresh; it sounds as if the speaker is really thinking about both the speech and the audience as he or she speaks. In contrast, a monotonous speech sounds like a rote recitation and decreases the audience's attention to both speaker and speech.

spontaneity being so responsive to your ideas that the speech seems as fresh as a lively conversation, even though it has been well practiced

Audiences often perceive a lack of spontaneity when speakers have memorized their speeches. Because people who try to memorize often have to struggle so hard to remember the words, their delivery tends to become monotonous. Although talented actors can make lines that they have spoken literally hundreds of times sound spontaneous and vocally expressive, most novice public speakers cannot.

How can you make your outlined and practiced speech still sound spontaneous? Learn the *ideas* of the speech—*don't memorize words.* Suppose someone asks you about the route you take on your drive to work. Because you are familiar with the route, you can present it spontaneously. You have never written out the route, nor have you memorized it—you "know it." You develop spontaneity in public speaking by getting to know the ideas in your speech as well as you know the route you take to work. Study your outline and absorb the material you are going to present, but do not try to memorize how you are going to present it. We will consider spontaneity further when we get to methods of speech rehearsal.

Fluency

Effective delivery is not only expressive and spontaneous, it is also **fluent**—devoid of hesitations and vocal interferences. Although most of us are occasionally guilty of using some **vocal interferences** (extraneous sounds or words that interrupt fluent speech), these interferences become a problem when they are perceived by others as excessive and when they begin to call attention to themselves and so prevent listeners from concentrating on meaning. The most common interferences that creep into our speech are *uh, er, well,* and *OK,* along with those nearly universal interrupters of Americans' conversation, *you know* and *like.*

Vocal interferences are difficult to eliminate from speech, but they can be reduced through awareness and practice. Vocal interferences often result from our fear of moments of silence that may lead to being interrupted. To avoid silent gaps in speaking, people learn to fill the "dead air time" with sounds such as *uh, er, well,* and *um.* Although the chance of being interrupted in conversation may be real (some people will seek to interrupt at any pause), the intrusion of an excessive number of fillers in a speech lead audience members to perceive the speaker as ill prepared or unconvincing.

Equally prevalent, and perhaps even more disruptive than filler sounds, is the incessant use of *you know* and *like.* The *you know* habit may begin as a way to find out whether what we are saying is already known by others. For some, *you know* may be an attempt to develop common ground—a way of showing that we and those to whom we are talking share common knowledge. For most people, however, flooding sentences with *you know* is simply a bad habit, resulting in such incoherent statements as "You know, Maxwell is, you know, a good, you know, lecturer."

Similarly, the use of *like* may start from making legitimate comparisons such as "He's hot, he looks *like* Tom Cruise." Soon the comparisons become shortcut, as in "He's like really hot!" Finally, the use of *like* becomes pure filler: "Like, he's really cool, like I can't really explain it, but I'll tell you he's like hot!" Most of us tolerate these fillers in daily conversation, but their use by speakers becomes annoying and detracts from the message.

Curiously, listeners are unlikely to acknowledge their irritation with a speaker's use of *you know* or *like,* even when the use affects their attention to the ideas. So, if you want to know whether your use of these interferences is excessive, you need to be proactive. The following steps can help you decrease your use of interferences.

1. **Train yourself to hear your interferences.** Even people with a major problem can be unaware of the interferences they use. You can train your ear in at least two ways:

   a. Tape-record yourself talking for several minutes about any subject—the game you saw yesterday, the course you plan to take next term, or anything else that comes to mind. Before you play it back, estimate the number of times you think you peppered your speech with *uh, you know,* and *like.* Then compare the actual number with your estimate. As your ear becomes trained, your estimates will be closer to the actual number.

   b. Have a close friend listen to you and raise a hand every time you use a filler such as *uh* or *you know.* The experience may be traumatic or nerve-wracking, but your own ear will soon start to pick up the vocal interferences as fast as the listener's.

2. **Practice seeing how long you can talk without using a vocal interference.** Begin by talking for fifteen seconds. Gradually increase the time until you can talk for two minutes without a single interference. Meaning may suffer, and you may spend a disproportionate amount of time avoiding interferences. Still, it is good practice.

HOW CAN WE JUSTIFY

If you're *not* using safety belts *now*, it's time to start. **Safety belts save lives!**

Variety: Which of these speakers would you rather listen to?

Don Klumpp/Getty Images

3. **Mentally note your interferences in conversation and in speech making.** You will make real headway when you can recognize your own interferences in real communication settings. When you reach this stage, you will find yourself avoiding and limiting interferences.

Eye Contact

Eye contact, also referred to as gaze, is the way we look directly at the people to whom we are speaking. In speech making, this involves looking at various groups of people in all parts of an audience throughout a speech. As long as you are looking at people (those in front of you, in the left rear of the room, in the right center of the room, and so on) and not at your notes or the ceiling, floor, or window, everyone in the audience will perceive you as having good eye contact with them.

Maintaining eye contact is important for several reasons.

1. **Maintaining eye contact helps audiences concentrate on the speech.** If speakers do not look at us while they talk, we are unlikely to maintain eye contact with them. This break in mutual eye contact often decreases concentration on the speaker's message.

2. **Maintaining eye contact increases the audience's confidence in you, the speaker.** Just as you are likely to be skeptical of people who do not look you in the eye as they converse, so too audiences will be skeptical of speakers who do not look at them. Eye contact is perceived as a sign of sincerity. Speakers who fail to maintain eye contact with audiences are perceived almost always as ill at ease and often as insincere or dishonest.[1]

3. **Maintaining eye contact helps you gain insight into the audience's reaction to the speech.** Because communication is two-way, your audience is speaking to you at the same time you are speaking to it. In conversation, the audience's response is likely to be both verbal and nonverbal; in public speaking, the audience's response is more likely to be shown by nonverbal cues alone. Audiences that pay attention are likely to look at you with varying amounts of intensity.

eye contact the way we look directly at the people to whom we are speaking

Listeners who do not pay attention are likely to yawn, look out the window, and slouch in their chairs. By monitoring your audience's behavior, you can determine what adjustments, additions, and deletions you should make in your plans. As speakers gain greater skill, they can make more and better use of the information they get about listeners through eye contact with them.

One way of ensuring eye contact during your speech is to think of your audience as a collection of groups sitting in various places in the room. Then, at random, talk for four to six seconds with each group. Perhaps start with a Z pattern. Talk with the group in the back left for a few seconds, then glance at people in the far right for a few seconds, and then move to a group in the middle, a group in the front left, and then a group in the front right, and so forth. Then perhaps reverse the order, starting in the back right. Eventually you'll find yourself going in a random pattern in which you look at all groups over a period of a few minutes. Using such a pattern helps you avoid spending a disproportionate amount of your time talking with those in front of you or in the center of the room.

Rehearsal

rehearsing   practicing the presentation of your speech aloud

Now that you have your outline and an overall plan of what you need to do to ensure interest and understanding, you are ready to begin **rehearsing**—practicing the presentation of your speech aloud. Too often, speakers believe that they are ready to present the speech once they have finished their outline. But if you are scheduled to speak at 9 A.M. Monday and you don't finish the outline until 8:45 A.M, the speech is likely to be far less effective than it would have been had you allowed yourself sufficient practice time. It is only through practicing the speech aloud that you can assure effective presentation.

In this section, we consider a timetable for preparation and practice, how to prepare and use speech notes, and some specific guidelines to make individual rehearsal sessions effective.

Timetable for Preparation and Practice

In general, you will need to complete your outline at least two days before a speech is due so that you have sufficient time for rehearsal sessions that include a practice, an evaluation of all aspects of the speech, and another practice. As the timeline in Exhibit 11.3 suggests, you should plan on working part of every day for a week as you prepare each classroom speech.

Is there really a relationship between practice time and speech effectiveness? A study by Menzel and Carrell offers tentative confirmation for the general hypothesis that more preparation time leads to better speech performance. They concluded, "The significance of rehearsing out loud probably reflects the fact that verbalization clarifies thought. As a result, oral rehearsal helps lead to success in the actual delivery of a speech."[2]

Preparing Speaking Notes

speech notes   a word or phrase outline of your speech, plus hard-to-remember information such as direct quotations and statistics

Prior to your first rehearsal session, you will want to prepare a draft of your speech notes. **Speech notes** are a word or phrase outline of your speech, plus hard-to-remember information such as direct quotations and statistics. Notes should consist of the fewest words possible, in lettering large enough to be seen instantly at arm's length.

EXHIBIT 11.3   Timetable for preparing a speech

7 days before	Select topic; begin research
6 days before	Continue research
5 days before	Outline body of speech
4 days before	Work on introduction and conclusion
3 days before	Finish outline; find additional material if needed; have all visual aids completed
2 days before	First rehearsal session
1 day before	Second rehearsal session
Due date	Give speech

Begin by reducing your speech outline to an abbreviated outline of key sentences, phrases, and words. Later, anything in the speech for which you must have a perfectly accurate representation—such as a specific example, a quotation, or a set of statistics—can be added in the appropriate spot in your final speaking notes. You will also indicate exactly where you will use visual aids.

Making an abbreviated outline helps in at least two ways. First, the act of compiling the abbreviated outline helps to cement the flow of the speech in your mind. Second, it gets you to think about key ideas and phrasings. Notice that this outline does not include all the developmental material (personal experiences, examples, illustrations, quotations, statistics, and so forth) that you will use to bring life to the speech and adapt to your audience.

For a speech in the three- to five-minute range, two or three 3 × 5-inch note cards are all you will need. For a speech in the five- to ten-minute range, three to four note cards should be sufficient: one card for goal and introduction, one or two cards for

Peter Chapman Photography

When a speaker's notes are really a complete outline or a manuscript, chances for effective delivery are lessened considerably. Prepare a few note cards that can be used to refresh memory, not as a crutch.

EXHIBIT 11.4 **Notecards**

1st C: Introduction

How many hounded by vendors?

Do they make CC sound like answer to dreams?

If yes, need criteria to evaluate

Three criteria: 1 IR, 2 Fee, 3 Perks

Body

Examine interest rates

IR's are % that a company charges to carry on balance

- Average of 18%
- As much as 21%
- Start as low as 6 to 8%—for periods—but restrictions

IR's variable or fixed

- Variable change month to month
- Fixed stay same

(Considered IR's, look at next criterion)

2d C: Examine the annual fee

AF is cost company charges to extend credit

AF varies widely

- Some cards no annual fee
- Most companies average around $25

(After considered interest and fees, weigh benefits)

Weigh the perks

Perks are extras

- Rebates.
- Frequent flier miles
- Discounts on items

Perks don't outweigh other criteria

Conclusion

So, 3 criteria: IR's, Annual Fees, Perks

the body, and one card for the conclusion. When your speech contains a particularly important and long quotation or a complicated set of statistics, you may want to write it in detail on a separate card. Exhibit 11.4 shows how Emming could represent his complete outline shown on pages 152–153 of Chapter 8 on two 3 × 5-inch note cards.

During practice sessions, use your note cards to prompt your memory, just as you would in the speech. Either place the note cards on the speaker's stand or hold them in one hand and refer to them only when needed. Speakers often find that the act of making a note card is so effective in helping cement ideas in their mind that during practice, or later during the speech itself, they do not need to refer to their notes at all.

Remember to make sure that you practice using visual aids in your rehearsals. As we said in Chapter 9, you should indicate on your notes exactly when you will use each visual aid (and when you will remove it). Work on statements for introducing the visual aids, and practice different ways of showing the visual aids until you are satisfied that everyone in the audience will be able to see them.

Rehearsal Sessions

The goals of your rehearsals are three fold. First, practice actually wording your ideas, making sure that you speak clearly, vividly, emphatically, and appropriately as we discussed in Chapter 10. Second, as you rehearse experiment with your voice and bodily action and work for a conversational style. Finally, during rehearsals practice using your visual aids until you are comfortable and satisfied that everyone in the audience will be able to see them. A good **rehearsal session** involves practicing the speech, analyzing it, and practicing it again.

rehearsal session involves practicing the speech, analyzing it, and practicing it again

First Practice

Your initial rehearsal should include the following steps.

1. Tape-record your practice session. If you do not own a recorder, try to borrow one. You may also want to have a friend sit in on your practice.

2. Read through your sentence outline once or twice to refresh ideas in your mind. Then put the outline out of sight.

3. Make the practice as similar to the speech situation as possible, including using the visual aids you've prepared. Stand up and face your imaginary audience. Pretend that the chairs, lamps, books, and other objects in your practice room are people.

4. Write down the time that you begin.

5. Begin speaking. Keep going until you have presented your entire speech.

6. Write down the time you finish. Compute the length of the speech for this first practice.

Analysis

Replay the tape. Look at your complete outline again. Did you leave out any key ideas? Did you talk too long on any one point and not long enough on another? Did you clarify each of your points? Did you try to adapt to your anticipated audience? Was your wording clear, vivid, emphatic, and appropriate? Did you sound conversational? Were there any problems with your delivery? If you had a friend or relative listen to your practice, then have that listener help with your analysis. Now list three specific things you will do differently in your next practice.

Rehearsing is an essential part of preparing an effective speech. To make your practice sessions most useful, try to make them as similar as possible to the actual speech situation.

Second Practice

Repeat the six steps outlined for the first practice. By practicing a second time right after your analysis, you are more likely to make the kind of adjustments that begin to improve the speech.

Additional Rehearsals

After you have completed one full rehearsal session, consisting of two practices and analyses, put the speech away until that night or the next day. Although you should rehearse the speech at least one more time, you will not benefit if you cram all the practices into one long rehearsal time. You may find that a final practice right before you go to bed will be very helpful; while you are sleeping, your subconscious will continue to work on the speech. As a result, you are likely to find significant improvement in your mastery of the speech when you practice again the next day.

How many times you practice depends on many variables, including your experience, your familiarity with the subject, and the length of your speech.

Ensuring Spontaneity and Conversational Style

When practicing, try to learn the speech ideas, not memorize specific phrasings. Recall that memorizing the speech involves saying the speech the same way each time until you can give it word for word without notes. **Learning the speech** involves

learning the speech understanding the ideas of the speech but having the freedom to word the ideas differently each time

understanding the ideas of the speech but having the freedom to word the ideas differently during each practice. We can illustrate the method of learning a speech using a short portion of Emming's speech outline, which reads as follows:

A. Interest rates are the percentages that a company charges you to carry a balance on your card past the due date.
1. Most credit cards carry an average of 18 percent.

Now let's consider three practices that focus on this small portion of the outline.

First practice: "Interest rates are the percentages that a company charges you to carry a balance on your card past the due date. Most credit cards carry an average of 18 percent. Did you hear that? 18 percent!"

Second practice: "Interest rates are the percentages that a company charges you when you don't pay the balance in full and thus still owe the company money. Most credit cards carry an average of 18 percent. Did you hear that? 18 percent! So, if you leave a balance, every month before you know it, you're going to be paying a lot more money than you thought you would."

Third practice: "Interest rates are the percentages that a company charges you when you don't pay the balance in full and thus still owe the company money. Most credit cards carry an average of 18 percent. Did you hear that? A whopping 18 percent, at a time when you can get about any kind of a loan for less than 10 percent. Of course, if you pay off your balance, there's no cost—but high percentages of credit card holders don't, and thus rack up a lot of extra costs."

Notice that points A and 1 of the outline are in all three versions; the essence of the outline will be part of all your practices. But because you have made slight variations each time, when you finally give the speech there will be that sense of spontaneity. In your speech, you will probably use wording that is most meaningful to you. To evaluate your practice sessions, complete Speech Preparation Activity 6.1. The Student Response to Activity 6.1 provides an example of how Emming rated his practice sessions.

Criteria for Evaluating Speeches

In addition to learning to prepare and present speeches, you are learning to analyze critically the speeches you hear. From a pedagogical standpoint, critical analysis of speeches not only provides the speaker with both an analysis of where the speech went right and where it went wrong but also gives you, the critic, insight into the methods that you want to incorporate, or perhaps avoid, in presenting your own speeches.

In the past several chapters, as you have been learning the steps involved in speech preparation, you have also learned the criteria by which speeches are measured. The critical assumption is that if a speech has good content, is well organized, and is well presented, it is more likely to achieve its goal. Thus, the critical apparatus for evaluating any speech comprises questions that relate to the basics of content, organization, and presentation.

For the first round of major speeches, we recommend that you use the Speech Evaluation Checklist, which includes a series of questions that cover the general criteria. But notice that the primary emphasis will be on clarity of goal, clarity and appropriateness of main points, and delivery.

Activity 6.1
Speech Rehearsals

The goal of this exercise is to help you analyze the effectiveness of your rehearsals. One complete rehearsal includes a practice, an analysis, and a second practice.

First Practice

1. Find a place where you can be alone to practice your speech. Follow the six points of the first practice as listed on page 211.

Analysis

2. Replay the tape. Look at your outline again and answer the following questions:

   Did introduction get attention and lead into the speech? ＿＿＿

   Were main points clearly stated? ＿＿＿

   Were main points well developed? ＿＿＿

   Was material adapted to the audience? ＿＿＿

   Were section transitions present? ＿＿＿ Clear? ＿＿＿

   Did the conclusion summarize the main points? ＿＿＿

   Leave the speech on a high note? ＿＿＿

   Were visual aids well used? ＿＿＿

   Were the ideas expressed

   clearly ＿＿＿

   vividly ＿＿＿

   emphatically ＿＿＿

   appropriately? ＿＿＿

   Did you have good eye contact? ＿＿＿

   Sound enthusiastic? ＿＿＿

   Show vocal expressiveness? ＿＿＿

   Sound spontaneous? ＿＿＿

   Speak fluently? ＿＿＿

3. List three specific changes you will make in your next practice session:

   a.

   b.

   c.

Second Practice

4. Repeat the six steps outlined for the first practice. Did you achieve the goals you set for the second practice?

Activity 6.1
Speech Rehearsals

(Emming's Response)

First Practice

1. Find a place where you can be alone to practice your speech. Follow the six points of the first practice as listed on page 211.

Analysis

2. Replay the tape. Look at your outline again and answer the following questions:

Did introduction get attention and lead into the speech? <u>Yes</u>

Were main points clearly stated? <u>Yes</u>

Were main points well developed? <u>OK</u>

Was material adapted to the audience? <u>Need more</u>

Were section transitions present? <u>Yes</u>   Clear? <u>Yes</u>

Did the conclusion summarize the main points? <u>Yes</u>

Leave the speech on a high note? <u>No</u>

Were visual aids well used? <u>OK</u>

Were the ideas expressed clearly <u>OK</u>

vividly <u>Need more</u>

emphatically <u>OK</u>

appropriately? <u>OK</u>

Did you have good eye contact? <u>Need more</u>

Sound enthusiastic? <u>Need more</u>

Show vocal expressiveness? <u>OK</u>

Sound spontaneous? <u>Too close to notes</u>

Speak fluently? <u>Too much "uh"</u>

3. List three specific changes you will make in your next practice session:

   a. Need more complete development of second point.

   b. Need to use more personalization for adaptation.

   c. Biggest weakness was in delivery, especially eye contact, enthusiasm, spontaneity, and reliance on notes.

Second Practice

4. Repeat the six steps outlined for the first practice. Did you achieve the goals you set for the second practice? <u>For the most part</u>

Explain: Delivery was a lot better. Doing the speech twice in a row really helped—I was able to show more enthusiasm. My eye contact was better because I didn't look at notes as much. Content was also better. I had a better grasp of the information. I still need more work on audience adaptation.

SPEECH EVALUATION checklist

Although the general criteria for evaluating any speech are included here, emphasis for this first speech is placed on the primary criteria shown in boldface (speech goal, all items of speech organization, and several items of speech presentation).

Check items that were accomplished effectively.

Content

_____ **1. Was the goal of the speech clear?**

_____ **2.** Did the speaker have high-quality information?

_____ **3.** Did the speaker use a variety of kinds of developmental material?

_____ **4.** Were visual aids appropriate and well used?

_____ **5.** Did the speaker establish common ground and adapt the content to the audience's interests, knowledge, and attitudes?

Organization

_____ **6. Did the introduction gain attention, gain good will for the speaker, and lead into the speech?**

_____ **7. Were the main points clear, parallel, and meaningful complete sentences?**

_____ **8. Did transitions lead smoothly from one point to another?**

_____ **9. Did the conclusion tie the speech together?**

Presentation

_____ **10.** Was the language clear?

_____ **11.** Was the language vivid?

_____ **12.** Was the language emphatic?

_____ **13. Did the speaker sound enthusiastic?**

_____ **14. Did the speaker show sufficient vocal expressiveness?**

_____ **15. Was the presentation spontaneous?**

_____ **16. Was the presentation fluent?**

_____ **17. Did the speaker look at the audience?**

_____ **18.** Were the pronunciation and articulation acceptable?

_____ **19.** Did the speaker have good posture?

_____ **20.** Was speaker movement appropriate?

_____ **21.** Did the speaker have sufficient poise?

Based on these criteria, evaluate the speech as (check one):

_____ excellent, _____ good, _____ satisfactory, _____ fair, _____ poor

assignment

Presenting Your First Speech

1. Prepare a four- to six-minute informative or persuasive speech. Use the Speech Preparation Activities to develop an effective adaptation plan based on the five questions you spoke to in Speech Preparation Activity 2.2 and the combined activities in Speech Preparation Activity 4.7

2. Criteria for evaluation include all the essentials of topic and purpose, content, organization, presentation, but special emphasis will be placed on clarity of goal, clarity and appropriateness of main points, and delivery (items that are in boldface on the checklist). Use the Speech Evaluation Checklist to critique your speech. As you practice your speech, you can use this critique to ensure that you are meeting the basic criteria in your speech. A sample student outline and speech follow.

speech

This section presents a sample speech adaptation plan, outline, and transcript given by a student in an introductory speaking course as his first major speech.

Catching, Throwing, and Cradling a Lacrosse Ball, by Anthony Masturzo[3]

Adaptation Plan

1. **Speaking directly.** My main way of speaking directly will be to use personal pronouns.

2. **Interest.** Since interest is not automatic, I will be using myself, an actual lacrosse stick, and ball as visual aids. I think the use of these in demonstration will help to perk audience interest.

3. **Understanding.** Since most of the class will never have participated or have knowledge of the game, I will focus on aspects of the game that they'll be able to understand even if they don't fully know how the game is played.

4. **Attitude toward speaker.** Since they don't know me, I will have to help them understand that I have played the game extensively and have in-depth knowledge.

5. **Attitude toward topic or speech goal.** Since there are more men than women in the class and since men are usually willing to be interested in talking about and listening for information on most any sport, I think the men will receive my sport topic favorably. My true test is gaining and retaining the interest of women.

Speech Outline

Specific Goal: I want my audience to learn the skills necessary to play the game of lacrosse.

Introduction

I. Although we think the national sport of Canada is hockey, it is actually lacrosse.

II. Lacrosse is similar to hockey in that it has similar rules and penalties but is played on a soccer field with the same number of position players.

Thesis Statement: Three skills necessary to play the game of lacrosse are catching, throwing, and cradling the ball.

Body

I. One skill necessary to play the game of lacrosse is catching the ball.
   A. Catching the ball is accomplished with a series of steps.
      1. Your feet should be shoulder length apart.
      2. You hold the stick in a ready position.
      3. You adjust the height and length of the stick to meet the ball.
      4. Once the ball is in the crosse, you give with the ball.
   B. The common problems that hinder your effectiveness are as follows.
      1. No hand-eye coordination.
      2. A tendency to swat at the ball.
      3. Improper hold on the stick.

II. The second skill necessary to play the game of lacrosse is throwing the ball.
   A. Throwing the ball is accomplished with a series of steps.
      1. Your feet should be shoulder length apart.
      2. Turn your body to give appropriate back swing.
      3. Step, twist body, release dominant arm and retrieve weak arm.
      4. Snap wrist.
      5. Follow through.
   B. The common problems that hinder your effectiveness are as follows.
      1. No follow through.
      2. Poor form.

III. The final skill necessary to play the game of lacrosse is to cradle the ball while running.
   A. Cradling the ball is accomplished with a series of steps.
      1. Hold the stick in a ready position.
      2. Twist your wrist in and out.
      3. Arm should move naturally.
   B. The common problems that hinder your effectiveness are as follows.
      1. Herky-jerky wrist and arm movement.
      2. Unbalanced stick.

Conclusion

I. The skills necessary to play the game are catching, throwing, and cradling.

II. Once you have mastered these, you can go on to strategy and shooting.

Sources
Personal Experience: 3 yr. Varsity Letterman, Walsh Jesuit Lacrosse Team.
Interview: Brian Masturzo, Defensive Captain, Walsh Jesuit Varsity Lacrosse Team.
Research: www.lacrossenetwork.com/outsidersguide/history

Speech and Analysis

Read this speech aloud at least once. Then analyze it on the basis of the primary criteria in the checklist on page 216: Clarity of goal and clarity of organization. Although Anthony used himself, a lacrosse stick, and a ball as visual aids throughout the speech, you will see only a few snapshots in this written version. To get a complete view of his use of visual aids and his good delivery skills, you can watch the speech under Speech Interactive on your Challenge of Effective Speaking CD-ROM.

Speech

When you think of Canadian sports, what's the first thing that comes to mind? You're right, it is hockey. But did you know that one of Canada's national sports is also lacrosse? Lacrosse network.com writes, "Created by indigenous Americans, this sport was considered an excellent practice for war. The sport pitted tribe against tribe in a game where each tried to place a feather stuffed deer skin ball past a goalie." Of course nowadays, we've Americanized the sport. We no longer use a deer skin stuffed ball—we use hard rubber. The sticks are actually made of graphite and plastic—no long sticks entwined. What I want to show you today are the three skills that are necessary to learn the game of lacrosse.

The first skill that's necessary is catching the lacrosse ball. Very simple. It all starts with proper form. You want your feet about shoulder length apart, you want good positioning on the stick, two hands with the cross facing out. As the ball comes in you need to give with the ball.

A lot of common mistakes occur with catching. The first is the absence of hand-eye coordination—if you have no coordination, this game becomes very difficult. The second is improper holding of the stick. You may have a turn, you may have too tight of a grip and you're not ready for the ball. The third problem is the tendency to swat at the ball rather than to give when you're trying to catch it.

The second skill that's necessary to learn the game of lacrosse is throwing the ball. Once again you have the

Analysis

Anthony opens with a rhetorical question to get the audience thinking with him.

In this introduction he contrasts current equipment with the original. Notice that both Anthony's outline and his adaptation plan mentioned his three years as a varsity letterman in lacrosse. For some reason, perhaps nervousness, he failed to mention it in the speech itself.

Here Anthony uses a transition to lead into the points of the body of the speech.
Anthony states his first main point in a clear, complete sentence.

Throughout the speech, Anthony uses himself, the stick, and the ball as visual aids.

Throughout the speech Anthony divides his main points into first explaining the process and then showing common mistakes.

Here Anthony needs a transition to lead into the second main point of the speech.

Again, his main point is stated clearly.

stick in a ready position. But this time since you have a ball in the net, you'll have a tendency to hold it a little farther back. Then you need to step with the opposite foot, snap your wrist, and follow through. The follow-through is what is the key with throwing the lacrosse ball.

The main problem when you throw—when you first start—is you tend to stop early with no follow through. You just want to get rid of the ball. Going through the complete process improves with experience.

The final skill necessary in playing the game of lacrosse is cradling the ball. Cradling means keeping the ball inside the stick—inside the crosse. The game of lacrosse is played on a soccer field with the same positions as in soccer. In order to advance the ball, a lot of the times you'll need to run with the ball. Now, defenders—the opponents—are going to attempt to knock the ball loose. They do that with stick checks and with body checks. You need to find a way to keep the ball in here no matter what occurs. So, in order to keep the ball in here, you need to do what's called a cradle. Notice, what you're doing is pulling the ball across your body and back, but you're doing it as you run. Just like this.

Problems with cradling. Uh, I would say the number one problem is a herky-jerky motion where you tend to snap the ball rather than to comfortably bring it across your body.

So, to summarize, throwing the ball, catching the ball, and cradling the ball are the three skills that are necessary to master in order to play the game of lacrosse. Once you've mastered these skills, you can then work on other skills such as strategy and shooting. ■

Notice that his explanations are very clear and easy to follow.

Here and throughout the speech Anthony does a good job of talking directly with the audience.
Again, he could use an internal transition.

Again, a clear statement of the main point.
Notice how he defines "cradling" to make sure that we can follow his explanation.
Comparison to soccer in this section helps us to get a better understanding of how Lacrosse is played.

He continues to be very conscious of his audience. He continues to be careful in showing us how these skills are accomplished.

"Problems with cradling" is a heading. He needs to build this into a meaningful complete sentence.

Good closing summary.

This is a strong first speech. The structure of the speech is especially good. His use of visual aids, including himself, helps us to follow his directions very easily. ■

Terry Weathers is running for Student-Body President and has asked her friend Megan to deliver the key speech of support at the All University Candidate's Meeting. Being a good friend, Megan agrees.

Megan works several days developing the speech, and she believes that she has prepared a really good one. The problem is that although Megan can prepare excellent speeches she suffers from stage fright. She is scared to death to give this one in front of such a large audience. So, she asks Donnell Gates, a guy in her speech class who wows audiences with his engaging manner, to deliver the speech she wrote at the event.

Donnell thought about her request and left the following message on her voice mail: "Listen, you know I'm not crazy about Terry, so I would never vote for her. But since I don't really care who wins this election, I'll give the speech. Hey, I just enjoy the power I have over an audience!"

1. Now that Megan knows that Donnell doesn't care for Terry, should she let him give the speech?

2. And what about Donnell? Should he give such a speech knowing that he wouldn't support Terry himself?

Summary

Delivery refers to the use of voice and body to communicate the message of the speech; it is what the audience sees and hears.

Although speeches may be delivered impromptu, by manuscript, or memorized, in this course we focus on speeches that are presented extemporaneously—prepared and practiced but with the exact wording determined at the time of speaking.

The physical elements of delivery include voice, articulation, and bodily action. The four major characteristics of voice are pitch, volume, rate, and quality. Pitch refers to the highness or lowness of a voice. Volume is the loudness of tone. Rate is the speed at which a speaker talks. Quality is tone, timbre, or sound of a voice.

Effective speakers also are careful with their articulation, the shaping of speech sounds and their pronunciation, and the form and accent of various syllables.

Nonverbal bodily actions affect a speaker's meaning. Facial expression, gestures, movement, poise, and posture all work together in effective speaking.

Effective speeches achieve a conversational quality, including enthusiasm, vocal expressiveness (variety, emphasis, and freedom from monotonous tone), spontaneity (sounding fresh, not memorized), fluency (freedom from such vocal interferences as *uh, um, well, you know,* and *like),* and eye contact.

Between the time the outline is completed and the speech is given, it is important to practice the speech several times, weighing what you did and how you did it after each practice. During these practice periods, you will work on presenting ideas spontaneously and using notes effectively.

Use your Challenge of Effective Speaking CD-ROM for quick access to the electronic study resources that accompany this text. Included on your CD-ROM is access of the Challenge of Effective Speaking Web site featuring Speech Builder Express at Wadsworth Communication Café, InfoTrac College Edition, and a demo of Web Tutor for *The Challenge of Effective Speaking*. The Web site offers chapter-by-chapter access to the Speech Preparation Action Step Activities, InfoTrac College Edition exercises, a digital glossary of key terms, Web links, Speech Preparation Forms, Speech Evaluation Checklists, and quizzes. Review the key terms and complete the InfoTrac College Edition exercises at
http://www.wadsworth.com/product/0534563856

InfoTrac College Edition Exercise

Using the Subject Guide, enter the search term "nonverbal communication" and select "periodical references." Locate the article titled "Do You Speak Body Language?" by Anne Warfield, *Training and Development*, April 2001, to learn more about nonverbal communication. How important are nonverbals to communication effectiveness? After reading this article, evaluate your own ability to speak at an appropriate volume. How adept are you at varying the volume at which you speak so that all members of your audience can hear you comfortably?

Key Terms

accent *(201)*

articulation *(201)*

conversational style *(204)*

enthusiasm *(204)*

extemporaneous speech *(199)*

eye contact *(207)*

facial expression *(202)*

fluency *(206)*

gestures *(202)*

learning the speech *(212)*

monotone *(205)*

movement *(203)*

pitch *(200)*

poise *(203)*

posture *(204)*

pronunciation *(201)*

quality *(201)*

rate *(200)*

rehearsal session *(211)*

rehearsing *(208)*

speech notes *(208)*

spontaneity *(205)*

vocal expressiveness *(204)*

vocal interferences *(206)*

volume *(200)*

Challenge of Effective Speaking Web Site

Access Speech Builder Express and complete the Speech Preparation Action Step Activities for your first major speech.

Speech Interactive

You can prepare for your own speech performance and refine your critiquing skills by viewing and assessing the speech by Anthony Masturzo, featured on pages 217–220, under Speech Interactive on your Challenge of Effective Speaking CD-ROM. After you have viewed the Lacrosse speech, complete the Speech Evaluation Checklist. You can compare your critique to that provided by a professor.

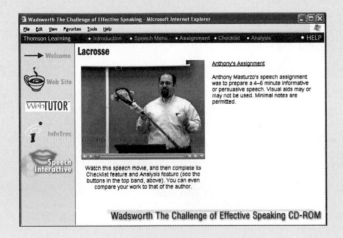

12 Principles and Practices of Informative Speaking

Joel Gordon

*Any piece of knowledge I acquire today has a value at this moment
exactly proportioned to my skill to deal with it.*
—Ralph Waldo Emerson, "Natural History of Intellect," 1871

For several months, a major architectural firm had been working on designs for the arts center to be built in the middle of downtown. Members of the city council and guests from various constituencies in the city, as well as a number of concerned citizens, were taking their seats as the long anticipated presentation was about to begin. As Linda Garner, mayor and presiding officer of the city council, finished her introduction, Donald Harper, the principal architect of the project, walked to the microphone to begin his speech.

Scenarios like this are played out every day as speakers try to increase our understanding of complex issues. In fact, it is difficult to conceive of professional people who do not use informative speaking in their jobs. In our opening quote, Ralph Waldo Emerson succinctly captures the challenge of adapting information to a specific audience: "Any piece of knowledge I acquire today has a value at this moment exactly proportioned to my skill to deal with it."

An **informative speech** is a public presentation whose goal is to convey facts, ideas, or theories without advocating them so that audience members understand and remember the information. Thus, as an informative speaker, your rhetorical goal is to present information in a way that holds interest, facilitates understanding, and increases the likelihood of remembering. We begin our discussion of informative speaking by presenting four principles of informing that should help you meet your rhetorical goal as you prepare any informative speech. The remainder of the chapter explains three types of informative speeches: speeches of demonstration or process, speeches of definition, and expository speeches.

informative speech speech that conveys facts, ideas, or theories without advocating a position

Principles of Informing

You will be more effective in meeting your rhetorical goals of creating and maintaining interest, developing understanding, and increasing remembering if you apply principles of intellectual stimulation, creativity, relevance, and emphasis.

Intellectual Stimulation

Principle 1 Audiences are more likely to listen to information they perceive to be intellectually stimulating.
Information will be perceived as **intellectually stimulating** when it is new to audience members and meets a deep-seated need to know. When we say "new," we mean information that most of the audience is not familiar with or that presents new insights or twists on familiar topics. If you really have analyzed your audience and researched your topic, you should have information that will be new to a majority of your audience.

intellectually stimulating information that is new to audience members and meets a deep-seated need to know

For example, a topic that should be of interest to college students—especially women—is the drug Rohypnol, also known as the "date rape" drug. On one hand, it gives a cheap but dangerous high; on the other hand, it can be used to lower the defenses and resistance of others. Even though a college audience has probably heard about the date-rape drug, they are unlikely to know much of its history, properties, and other dangers.

Even when you have chosen a topic that most of the people in your audience are familiar with, you can brainstorm new angles, new applications, or new perspectives. For instance, during the basketball season, a player (or a real aficionado) who first considers talking about how to shoot a jump shot would be wiser to brainstorm other topics that would give viewers a better understanding of the game as they watch it. For instance, the speaker might brainstorm "pick and roll," "matchup zone defenses," "using the press," or "breaking a press." These are topics casual fans may have heard of but may not really understand very well.

But just being new information is not enough. To intellectually stimulate, the information must also meet the audience's deep-seated hunger for knowledge and insight. Part of the informative speaker's job is to satisfy that hunger. Every day we are touched by ideas and issues that we don't fully grasp. Often we ignore these ideas and issues, partly because we don't have sufficient motivation to find additional information. For instance, several years ago scientists discovered an "ice man"—the well-preserved body of a man who lived between four and five thousand years ago—buried in a glacier of the southern Alps. Newspaper headlines announced the discovery and readers were excited by the information, but probably not many pursued the topic. The informative speaker who seizes this topic and links the ice man to an understanding of our own history and development may well stimulate our natural intellectual curiosity.

Let's consider a more typical example. Suppose you are planning a speech on new cars. From just the data you could draw from the April issue of *Consumer Reports* (the month in which comparative statistics and ratings are given for all new cars), you could find information that would be intellectually stimulating. For instance, we are aware that over time SUVs have captured an increasingly large share of the U.S. automobile market, at least in part because of their perceived adaptability. A speech that answered these questions would be of value to your audience: Do SUVs achieve high safety ratings? Are SUVs a good investment? Do SUVs get comparable gas mileage?

During the course, work off your brainstorming list to find a topic. But for an important informative speech, be sure to choose a topic that you know will challenge your audience intellectually.

Creativity

Principle 2 Audiences are more likely to listen to, understand, and remember information that is presented creatively.

creativity a person's capacity to produce new or original ideas and insights

Creativity can be defined as a person's capacity to produce new or original ideas and insights.[1] Although you may be thinking "I'm just not a creative person," all of us can be creative if we are willing to work at it. Let's consider some guidelines and procedures that can help you become a more creative speaker.

1. **Gather enough high-quality information to give you a broad base from which to work.** Contrary to what many people think, creativity is more likely a product of perspiration than inspiration. The greater your quantity of high-quality information, the greater your flexibility and choices.

2. **Give yourself enough time for the creative process to work.** Many students finish their outline just in time to "go over the speech" once before they present it—then they wonder why they are not able to "be creative." Your mind needs time to reflect on your outline and information. This is why we recommend completing your outline for a classroom speech at least two days before the actual presentation. With extra time available, you are likely to find that the morning after an uninspiring practice you suddenly have two or three fresh ideas to work with. While you were sleeping, your mind was still going over the material. When you awoke, the product of unconscious or subconscious thought reached your consciousness. You can facilitate creativity simply by giving your mind time to work with your information.

3. **Be prepared to pursue a creative idea when it comes.** Have you ever noticed how ideas seem to come at odd times, like while you're cleaning your room, mulching the garden, or waiting at a stoplight? Have you also noticed that when you try to recall those "great" ideas they are likely to have slipped away? Many speakers, writers, and composers carry pencil and paper with them at all times. When an idea comes, they make a note of it. Not all of these flights of fancy are flashes of creative genius, but some of them are good or at least worth exploring. If you do not make note of your ideas, you will never know whether they are good.

4. **Create alternative choices for specific goals or lines of development.** Suppose you are planning to give a speech on climatic variation in the United States and your research has uncovered the data shown in Exhibit 12.1. We will use these data to show that (1) one set of data can suggest several lines of development on one topic and (2) the same point can be made in many different ways.

EXHIBIT 12.1 Temperature and precipitation highs and lows in selected U.S. cities

City	Temperature (in degrees Fahrenheit)		Precipitation (in inches)	
	High	**Low**	**July**	**Annual**
Chicago	95	−21	3.7	35
Cincinnati	98	−7	3.3	39
Denver	104	−3	1.9	15
Los Angeles	104	40	trace	15
Miami	96	50	5.7	56
Minneapolis	95	−27	3.5	28
New Orleans	95	26	6.1	62
New York	98	−2	4.4	42
Phoenix	117	35	0.8	7
Portland, ME	94	−18	3.1	44
St. Louis	97	−9	3.9	37
San Francisco	94	35	trace	19
Seattle	94	23	0.9	38

One set of data can suggest several lines of development. Study the information in Exhibit 12.1, and ask what is unusual or noteworthy and why. Do you notice several unusual or noteworthy points? First, you might notice that the high temperatures in U.S. cities vary far less than the low temperatures. For instance, for the year shown, the summer temperature was 96 degrees in Miami and 95 degrees in Minneapolis. However, the winter low in Miami was 50 degrees, and the low was minus 27 degrees in Minneapolis—a 77-degree difference! Conventional wisdom would suggest that high temperatures should vary nearly as much as low temperatures. Why don't they?

You might also have noticed that it hardly ever rains on the west coast in the summer. Two of the three west coast cities, Los Angeles and San Francisco, show only a trace of rain in July, and a third, Seattle, often considered a rainy city, shows only 0.9 inch in July—less than one-third of any eastern city, and less than one-sixth of Miami. Why is there so little rain on the west coast in July? Why is there so much more in the east?

Finally, did you notice that July, a month thought to be hot and dry, actually accounts for more than the expected average of one-twelfth of annual precipitation for major cities cited in the east and midwest? Yet we think of July as the driest month of the year. Why do we perceive July to be a dry month? Why isn't it?

So, as we study the data in this one chart, we can raise questions that would enable us to create three different lines of development for a speech on climate: Why are highs so similar but lows so different? Why is there so much more rain in the summer in the midwest and east than in the west? Why is July wetter in most cities than we'd expect?

The same point can be made in many different ways. Using only the information from Exhibit 12.1, let's consider two ways of supporting the point that "Yearly high temperatures in U.S. cities vary far less than yearly low temperatures."

(a.) Of the thirteen cities selected, ten (77%) had yearly highs between 90 and 100 degrees. However, of the same thirteen cities, four (31%) had yearly lows above freezing; two (15%) had lows between 0 and 32 degrees; and seven (56%) had low temperatures below 0.

(b) Chicago, Miami, Minneapolis, New Orleans, Portland (ME), San Francisco, and Seattle—seven cities at widely varying latitudes—all had yearly high temperatures of 94 to 96 degrees. In contrast, the same seven cities had lows ranging from 50 degrees in Miami down to minus 27 degrees in Minneapolis.

Can you find another way of making the same point?

As we discussed previously, to be creative you must give yourself time to think.

5. **Force yourself to practice sections of the speech in different ways**. Too many times, when we have finished our outline, we act as if it is cast in stone. Then we keep going over it the same way, "to learn it." If you don't take the time to practice in different ways and allow yourself to be content with the first way of presenting material that comes to mind, you won't have an opportunity to consider alternatives that might be better. If, however, you purposely phrase key ideas in different ways in each of the first few practices, you give yourself choices. Although some of the ways you express a point may be similar, trying new ways will stretch your mind, and chances are good that one or two of the ways will be far superior and much more imaginative than any of the others.

All speakers need to demonstrate the relevance of their topic to the audience. Notice how these children are paying close attention to what the firefighters are saying.

Relevance

Principle 3 Audiences are more likely to listen to and remember information they perceive as relevant.

Rather than acting like sponges that absorb every bit of information, most of us act more like filters: We listen only to that information we perceive to be relevant. **Relevance** is the extent to which audience members find personal value in the information presented. Information will be seen as relevant when it relates to audience members needs and interests.

  Vital information—information the audience perceives as a matter of life or death—may be the ultimate in relevance. Police cadets, for instance, will see information explaining what they should do when attacked as vital. Similarly, students may perceive information that is necessary to their passing a test as vital. When a speaker shows listeners that information is critical to their well-being, they have a compelling reason to listen.

relevance   the extent to which audience members find personal value in the information presented

vital information   information the audience perceives as a matter of life or death

Of course, information does not have to be vital to be perceived as relevant. But always ask yourself in what way the material you plan to present is truly important to the audience, and emphasize that connection in your speech. For example, in a speech on Indonesia, a topic that may seem distant from the audience's felt needs and concerns, you can increase the perception of relevance by focusing on the importance of Indonesian manufacturing to the U.S. economy and local jobs. In a speech on the Egyptian pyramids, you can demonstrate relevance by relating their construction techniques to contemporary building construction. In any speech you give, it is up to you to show how the information relates to the audience's needs and interests.

Although you should demonstrate relevance throughout the speech, it is especially important to do so during your introduction when audience members are sure to ask themselves, "Why should I listen to a speech on . . . ?" Notice how the following opening for a speech on high-speed rail transportation establishes relevance:

> Have you been stuck in a traffic jam lately? Have you started what you hoped would be a pleasant vacation only to be trampled at the airport or, worse, to discover when you got to your destination that your luggage hadn't? We're all aware that every year our highways and our airways are getting more congested. At the same time, we are facing a rapidly decreasing supply of petroleum. Today, I'm going to tell you about one of the most practical means for solving these problems—high-speed rail transportation.

Emphasis

Principle 4 Audiences are more likely to understand and to remember information that is emphasized.
Audiences will remember only some of the information presented in a speech—the rest is likely to be forgotten. Part of your challenge is to determine what you want the audience to retain and then to emphasize that information. To meet this challenge, you must prioritize your information.

Ordinarily, the highest priority information in your speech includes the specific goal, the main points, and key facts that give meaning to the main points. So, if you were giving a speech on Roquefort cheese, you would want to make sure the audience remembered the following:

- **Goal**: to understand the three distinct elements of Roquefort cheese
- **Main points**: Roquefort cheese is trademarked, Roquefort cheese is made exclusively from ewe's milk, and Roquefort cheese is colored and flavored from molds grown only in caves located in Roquefort-sur-Soulzon.
- **Important facts**: For a salad dressing to be labeled "Roquefort," it must contain at least 15 percent legislated Roquefort. It takes 800,000 ewes to provide the milk necessary to keep Roquefort cheesemakers in business. The mold grown in caves is cultivated in bread, then ground and injected into the cheese to give the distinctive color and flavor.

Once you have prioritized your information, plan a strategy for increasing your audience's retention of these items. In previous chapters, we have discussed various methods of emphasizing information. Let's remind ourselves of the importance of visual aids, repetition, transitions, and humorous stories, and then add one more method, mnemonics.

1. **Use visual aids.** Visual aids emphasize, because we remember more when we can associate pictures with words. Especially for informative speeches, you will want to think very carefully about the kinds of visual aids that will work best for you.

2. **Repeat important words and ideas.** Just because a word is spoken does not necessarily mean that it is perceived. One of the best ways of breaking through is sheer repetition. You can repeat a word or you can restate an idea in a slightly different way, but remember that when repetition is overdone it loses its effectiveness. Repeating a few important words and ideas will pay dividends—but repeating too many words or ideas will backfire.

3. **Use transitions to direct audience thinking.** Since listeners cannot go back if they get lost, it is especially important for speakers to do what they can to help audiences see where they have been and where they are going. Thus, in the introduction of the speech on Roquefort cheese, you tell the audience what you will cover: "In this speech, we will look at the three distinct elements of Roquefort cheese." Then, as you proceed through a long main point, you might remind your listeners where you are going by saying, "So we've seen that Roquefort cheese is trademarked, now let's consider what it's made from." And before the end of the speech, you might review: "So, in this speech, we've seen that Roquefort cheese is trademarked, it's made exclusively from ewe's milk, and colored and flavored from molds grown only in caves located in Roquefort-sur-Soulzon."

   The value of such clarifying structure is tremendous. Because listeners' minds may wander, you must exercise control in how you want the audience to perceive what you say. I have heard listeners swear that a speaker never stated the second main point of the speech, when in reality the point was stated—but in a way that had no effect on the audience. Clarifying structure through transitions helps your audience recognize where you are in the speech and why your point is significant.

4. **Use humor to stress key points.** Of all the methods of presenting information, our own experience shows that we are most likely to remember information told in humorous story form. Suppose you were giving a speech on the importance of keeping things in perspective. One main point might be that a problem that seems enormous at the moment may turn out to be minor in a few days, so being able to put events into perspective saves a great deal of psychological wear and tear. To cement this point, you might tell the following story:

   A first-time visitor to the races bet two dollars on the first race on a horse that had the same name as his elementary school. The horse won, and the man was ten dollars ahead. In each of the next several races he bet on horses such as Apple Pie, his favorite, and Kathie's Prize, after his wife's name, and he kept winning. By the end of the sixth race, he was 700 dollars ahead. He was about to go home when he noticed that in the seventh race, Seventh Veil was scheduled in the number seven position, and was currently going off at odds of seven to one. The man couldn't resist—he bet his entire 700 dollars. And sure enough, the horse came in seventh. When he got home, his wife asked, "How did you do?" Very calmly he looked at his wife and said, "Not bad—I lost two dollars." That's keeping things in perspective!

5. **Develop memory aids for your audience.** You can help your listeners retain more of your speech by suggesting memory aids, formally called **mnemonics.** For example, in a speech on evaluating diamonds, your audience might remember that the four criteria are weight, clarity, tint, and shape. But they would be more likely to remember the criteria if you used the words "carat, clarity, color, and cutting." Why? Because you've created a memory aid—the four criteria all begin with C.

   Mnemonics also may be **acronyms**—words formed from initial letters of each of the successive parts of a compound term (NATO, North American Treaty Organization; OPEC, Organization of Petroleum Exporting Countries),

mnemonics   memory aids

acronyms   words formed from initial letters of each of the successive parts of a compound term, common words that comprise the first letters of objects or concepts, or sentences with each word starting with a letter that signals something else common words made up of the first letters of objects or concepts (HOMES for the five great lakes—Huron, Ontario, Michigan, Erie, Superior), or sentences made up of words whose initial letters signal something else (Every Good Boy Does Fine for the five musical notes on the lines in the treble clef of the scale). For example, in her speech on the healing power of listening, Carol Koehler, Professor of Communication and Medicine, offered the word *CARE* to reflect the qualities of the therapeutic communicator: C for concentrate, A for acknowledge, R for response, and E for emotional control.[2]

association the tendency of one thought to stimulate recall of another, similar thought

Most memory aids work on the basis of association. An **association** is the tendency of one thought to stimulate recall of another, similar thought. In the speech on evaluating diamonds, suppose we are trying to help the audience remember the value of color. If blue is the most highly prized tint and yellow or brown tints lower a diamond's value, we might associate blue tint with "the blue-ribbon prize" and yellow (or brown) tint with "a lemon." Thus, the best diamond gets the "blue ribbon," and the worst diamond is a "lemon."

Figurative associations are similes or metaphors. A simile is a comparison using *like* or *as:* "A computer screen is like a television monitor." A metaphor states an identity: "Laser printers are the Cadillacs of computer printers." The more striking you make your associations, the more likely your audience will be to remember your point.

Methods of Informing

In the first part of this chapter, we presented the fundamental principles of informative speaking. Now we turn our attention to how we use these principles in three common types of informative speeches: speeches of demonstration or process, speeches of definition, and speeches of exposition. Each of these types of speech relies on the use of several unique skills. At times, however, you may use skills from all of these types within a single speech.

For instance, in an informative speech on hurricanes Marta might use skills associated with each type of informative speech. For her first main point she *demonstrates* how a hurricane develops; for her second point she *defines* hurricanes and contrasts them with tornadoes and typhoons; in her third point she gives an *exposition* (or explanation) of the devastating effects of a hurricane on individual victims, business and industry, and the community. Alternatively, she might devote her entire speech to a *demonstration* of how hurricanes develop, a *definition* of hurricanes, or an *exposition* on the devastating effects of a hurricane on individual victims, business and industry, and the community.

Because the skills specific to demonstration, definition, and exposition differ, we will treat each type separately. We begin by describing each type and then give an example with a sample speech.

Demonstration or Process Explanation Speech

Many informative speeches involve either demonstrating or explaining a process—telling how to do something, how to make something, or how something works. For instance, a chef can explain the process of making a souffle, an airplane mechanic can explain how a turbojet works, or an author can explain how to get a book published. In the sample speech at the end of this section, the speaker explains the process of tablature.

Partial demonstrations are frequently used at industrial and commercial trade shows.

Whereas a **process explanation** tells how to do something, how to make something, or how something works, often with the help of visual aids, a **demonstration** involves a live, hands-on visual portrayal of the process. For instance, a computer trainer might demonstrate how to use new software, a chef might demonstrate how to bone a chicken, or a golf pro might demonstrate how to hit out of sand traps. Some of these demonstrations are completely hands-on, performing the entire step-by-step procedure; others are partial demonstrations, using various visual aids.

To explain or demonstrate a process effectively, you must begin your preparation by carefully delineating the individual steps in the process. If there are three to five steps, these will be the main points in the speech. If there are more than five steps, you will need to group and subordinate the steps so that they are easier to remember. For example, suppose a baker wanted to demonstrate how to make a pie. Because there are numerous steps, he or she might group them into three main steps, making the crust, preparing the filling, and assembling the pie.

When the task is relatively simple, such as how to get more power on a forehand table tennis shot, you may want to try a **complete demonstration**, going through the complete process in front of the audience. If so, practice until you can do it smoothly and easily under the pressure of facing an actual audience. Since the actual demonstration is likely to take longer than the practice (you may have to make some modifications during the speech to enable everyone in the room to see the demonstration), you may want to make sure that the final practice is somewhat shorter than the maximum time limit you will have for the speech.

For a relatively complicated or lengthy process, you may want to consider a **modified demonstration** in which you complete various stages of the demonstration beforehand and do only part of the actual work in front of the audience. Television chefs use this technique with great success. Suppose you were going to demonstrate construction of a floral display. Actually performing the construction from scratch is too complex and time-consuming for a speech-length presentation. Instead, you could prepare a complete set of materials to begin the demonstration, a mock-up of

process explanation telling how to do something, how to make something, or how something works

demonstration going through the complete process in front of the audience

complete demonstration going through the complete process in front of an audience

modified demonstration completing various stages of the demonstration beforehand so that you only show parts of the complete demonstration in front of the audience

Chapter Twelve: Principles and Practices of Informative Speaking **233**

the basic floral triangle, and a completed floral display. During the speech, you would describe the materials needed and then begin demonstrating how to make the basic floral triangle. Rather than trying to get everything together perfectly in a few seconds, you could remove, from a bag or some other concealed place, a partially completed arrangement illustrating the floral triangle. You would then use this in your demonstration, adding flowers as if you were planning to complete it. Then, from another bag, you could remove the completed arrangement to illustrate one of the effects you were discussing. Conducting a modified demonstration of this type is often easier than trying to complete an entire demonstration in a limited time.

Throughout a demonstration, speak slowly and repeat key ideas often. We learn best by doing, so if you can include audience participation, you may be even more successful. In a speech on origami, or Japanese paper folding, you could explain the principles, then pass out paper and have audience members each make a figure. Actual participation will increase interest and ensure recall. Finally, through other visual aids, you could show how these principles are used in more elaborate projects.

Although your audience may be able to visualize a process through vivid word pictures (in fact, in your impromptu explanations in ordinary conversation, it is the only way you can proceed), most effective demonstrations use visual aids. More than with any other kind of informative speech, carefully prepared visual materials are essential to listeners' understanding in demonstration or process speeches.

SPEECH **assignment**

Explaining or Demonstrating a Process

Prepare a three- to six-minute speech in which you show how something is made, how something is done, or how something works. An outline like that on pages 234–235 is required. Evaluation will focus on quality of the topic, getting and maintaining interest, facilitating understanding, increasing retention (including use of visual aids), clarity of organization, and quality of presentation. The following are the kinds of topics that would be appropriate for this assignment:

How to Do It	**How to Make It**	**How It Works**
racing start	spinach soufflé	zone defense
networking	fishing flies	helicopter
hanging wallboard	paper figures	compact disc
grading meat	wood carvings	photocopier

As you develop your plan for adapting the speech to your audience, be sure to include five short sections discussing how you will use your creativity to (1) speak directly to the audience, (2) build credibility, (3) get and maintain interest, (4) facilitate understanding, and (5) increase retention. Where appropriate comment on the use of demonstration and visual aids and the role of language and delivery techniques for implementing that plan.

checklist

Explaining Processes or Demonstrating

Write a critique for at least one of the informative speeches you hear in class. Outline the speech. As you outline, answer the following questions. Check all items that were accomplished effectively.

Primary Criteria

_____ **1.** Was the specific goal appropriate for a process explanation or demonstration?

_____ **2.** Did the speaker show expertise with the process?

_____ **3.** Did the speaker organize the steps of the process?

_____ **4.** Did the speaker have the necessary materials to demonstrate the process?

_____ **5.** Did the speaker demonstrate the process skillfully?

_____ **6.** Did the speaker select or construct useful visual aids?

_____ **7.** Did the speaker use the visual aids effectively?

_____ **8.** Did the speaker use any special strategies to help the audience remember main points and other key information necessary to demonstrate the process?

General Criteria

_____ **1.** Was the specific goal clear?

_____ **2.** Was the introduction effective?

_____ **3.** Was the organizational pattern appropriate for the intent and content of the speech?

_____ **4.** Was the conclusion effective?

_____ **5.** Was the language clear, vivid, emphatic, and appropriate?

_____ **6.** Was the speech delivered enthusiastically, with vocal expressiveness, fluently, spontaneously, and directly?

Evaluate the speech as (check one)

_____ excellent,   _____ good,   _____ average,   _____ fair,   _____ poor.

Use the information from your checklist to support your evaluation.

demonstration speech

Tablature by John Mullhauser[3]

This section presents a sample speech adaptation plan, outline, and transcript given by a student in an introductory speaking course as his first major speech.

Adaptation Plan

1. **Speaking directly to the audience:** Throughout the speech I will talk directly to the audience. I will use personal pronouns, and I will go slowly so that they will be able to follow my directions.

Speech Interactive
for Challenge

2. **Building credibility:** From the start I will show how I have mastered tablature. Then by explaining tablature carefully, the audience will see that I know what I'm talking about.

3. **Getting and maintaining interest:** I'll start the speech with a startling statement and then show that everyone in class can learn to do what I can do. I believe that as the class starts to understand, they will become even more interested.

4. **Facilitating understanding:** I will take the class through each step slowly and carefully. By using visual aids (the guitar itself and an example of tablature) to show the class the notes on paper and then to show where to pluck the strings, class members should be able to see themselves playing along with me. Although they may be doubtful at first, as we go along, they will come to understand how simple the process is.

5. **Increasing retention:** Again, use of visual aids should help retention. And I will also use repetition to make sure that they can follow.

Speech Outline

Specific Goal: I want my audience to understand the basics for learning and utilizing guitar tablature.

Introduction

I. If someone asked me to play a song on the guitar by almost any artist, I could.

II. I'm not a prodigy, but I do have a trick that allows me to play guitar music.

III. Today I want to share with you this trick called tablature.

Thesis Statement: The three steps that will enable audience to utilize tablature are getting the basic understanding of the guitar, learning tablature notation, and applying notation to the playing.

Body

I. The first step for utilizing tablature is holding the guitar.
  A. Hold the guitar on your right quad while in a sitting position
  B. Use your hands correctly.
    1. Your right hand holds the pick between your thumb and index finger.
    2. Your left hand lies along the neck of the guitar.

    C. Each of the metal bars on the neck divides the guitar into frets.

    D. The strings are plucked to play the guitar.

        1. There are six strings on a standard guitar.

        2. The notes of each string from lowest to highest are E, A, D, G, B, E.

(Now that you have a basic understanding of holding the guitar, let's examine tablature notation.)

II. The second step for utilizing tablature is to grasp tablature notation.

    A. Tablature is just a picture of the guitar from the player's viewpoint.

    B. Each line represents a string on the guitar verbatim.

        1. The first line represents the high E, the highest string on the guitar.

        2. The last line represents the low E, the lowest string on the guitar.

    C. The numbers on the lines of the tablature represent which string and which fret are to be played.

    D. Groups of notes are separated.

        1. A line separates the notes to be played into groups.

        2. This enables you to learn one part at a time.

(Now that you understand the basics of the guitar and tablature, it is time to apply tablature to playing a song.)

III. The third step for utilizing tablature is to play the notes.

    A. To demonstrate how tablature works, I will play a song.

    B. Notice how each tablature notation identifies a note on the guitar.

Conclusion

Now that you know the basics of the guitar, understand the nature of tablature, and how to use tablature to play the notes, you are now ready to play nearly any song you choose.

Sources

Dowland, John, *Lute Songs of John Dowland.* Mineola, NY: Dover, 1997.
Vogler, Leonard, "The Encyclopedia of Picture Chords," Amsco Publishing, 1990, p. 6.

Speech and Analysis

Read this speech aloud at least once. Then analyze it on the basis of the primary criteria in the checklist on page 233. Although John used himself, his guitar, and a visual aid of tablature throughout the speech, you will not see his visual aids in this written version. To get a complete view of his use of visual aids and his demonstration skills, watch the speech under Speech Interactive on your Challenge of Effective Speaking CD-ROM.

Speech

If someone asked me to play nearly any song on the guitar I could. I could play songs by almost any artist—I could play Dave Matthews band, Phish, Mettalica, Slayer, Negata, Spoon, Rick James, you name it, I could probably play it. I'm not a prodigy on the guitar, I'm not some kind of an evil genius or something, I just know the

Analysis

John begins with a startling statement.

    Then he mentions the trick that allows a person to play

nearly any tune—tablature.

He finishes his introduction with a preview of the three steps— a preview that serves as a transition to the body of the speech.

Here John states the first step.

Throughout the remainder of the speech he demonstrates the various steps.

During the first step he sat on the edge of the desk and showed the audience how to hold a guitar. Then he identified the frets and the strings.

Here he uses a transition to lead into the second step.

John presents his second main point clearly.

In this section, in addition to using his guitar, he uses a piece of paper with numbers that represent the frets and lines that represent the strings.

Here again John uses a transition to lead into the third step.

John presents a clear statement of the third step. In this section he goes slowly through the start of a song, clearly showing how anyone would know which string to pluck and where to pluck it by applying the tablature notations.

As he went along, everyone in class quickly recognized the song he was playing.

This section of the speech represents a true demonstration of tablature application.

In the conclusion, John summarizes the steps and assures us that we too can play the guitar by using tablature. ■

special trick that allows me to play nearly any tune. Um, today I'm going to share this trick with you, called tablature. There are three steps that can enable you to understand and utilize tablature.

The first step is a basic understanding of a guitar. The second step that will help you understand and use tablature is learning tablature notation. And the third step that will help you utilize tablature is applying tablature back to the guitar.

The first step that I want to look at is learning the basics of playing the guitar. This is a guitar. To properly hold the guitar, you place it on your right knee where it's ergonomically designed to fit. You place the pick in your right hand in between your thumb and your index finger. Your left hand will vary on the neck as to what you are playing. Each of these metal bars divides the guitar up into what are called frets. And on your standard guitar you're going to have six strings, which the notes respectively are E A D G B and E. Now that you have a basic understanding of a guitar, let's take a look at tablature notation.

The second step for understanding tablature is learning the notation. This is what tablature would look like. All it is is an exact copy of the guitar strings onto a piece of paper from a player's viewpoint. The first line on the tablature represents the highest string on the guitar—or the E string, the high E string. The last line on the guitar represents the lowest string on the guitar or the low E string and all the other ones respectively. The numbers 7 5 3 represent to play seventh fret, the fifth fret, and the third fret. And they also signify which string you're going to play on. For example, these are all on the D string so you know to play on the D string. This one right here, these two 5s mean you play the fifth fret on the G string or the third highest string. The lines which break the tablature up have nothing to do with the song. All it does is break the song down so that it is easier to learn—into smaller chunks. Now that you have a basic understanding of the guitar and you know something about tablature notation, let's take a look at applying tablature to playing the guitar.

The third step for utilizing tablature is applying your knowledge of tablature notation. To effectively show this, I'm going to take you through a song piece by piece and show you exactly how to do so. Right here it says to play 7 5 3 and again it's on the third lowest string here—so you want to find the third lowest string, which is the D string right here.

Then you want to look for the first note is the 7th fret so [counting up] 1, 2, 3, 4, 5, 6, 7, so there's your note 7 5 3. Next it says play 5 7 7 again all on the D string. So, 1, 2, 3, 4, 5, 5, 7 7 7. Then it says 5 5 5 again on the D string. Then this is where it changes. You have a 7 on the D string. Then you go up higher one note, one string to the G string and you play 5 5 5. So you start at the 7 and go up a string to the G—and play the 5, so it's 7 5 5. So I'll play this all over again—I'm sure you know what song this is: 7 5 3 5 7 7 7 5 5 5 7 5 5 as easy as that and I'm sure everyone knows what song that was.

In conclusion, now that you know some basics of guitar, and you know how to read basic tablature notation, and you can apply it all back to the guitar, you guys are ready to go out and play nearly any song of your choosing. ■

Speech of Definition

Richard Weaver, a major twentieth-century figure in rhetorical theory, believed definition to be the most valuable of all lines of speech development because it helps audience members understand and relate to key concepts.[4] Clear vivid definitions are essential in all effective speeches, and we begin by explaining the types of short definitions you can use. Then we show how extended definitions can be used as the basis for major informative speeches.

Short Definitions

Short definitions clarify concepts in just a few words. Effective speakers learn to define by using synonym and antonym, classification and differentiation, use or function, and etymological reference.

1. **Synonyms and antonyms.** Using a synonym or an antonym is the quickest way to define a word, for you are able to indicate an approximate, if not exact, meaning in a single sentence.

   Synonyms are words that have the same or nearly the same meanings; **antonyms** are words that have opposite meanings. Defining by synonym is defining by association: For a word that does not bring up an immediate concrete meaning, we provide one that does. Synonyms for *prolix* include *long*, *wordy*, and *verbose*. Its antonyms are *short* and *concise*. Synonyms are not duplicates for the word being defined, but they do give a good idea of what the word means. Of course, the synonym or antonym must be familiar to the audience or its use defeats its purpose.

   synonyms words that have the same or nearly the same meanings

   antonyms words that have opposite meanings

2. **Classification and differentiation.** When you define by classification, you give the boundaries of the particular word and focus on the single feature that differentiates that word from words with similar meanings. Most dictionary definitions are of the classification and differentiation variety. For instance, a dog may be defined as a carnivorous, domesticated mammal of the family Canidae. "Carnivorous," "mammal," and "family Canidae" limit the boundaries to dogs, jackals, foxes, and wolves. "Domesticated" differentiates dogs from the other three.

3. **Use or function.** A third short way to define is by explaining the use or function of the object represented by a particular word. Thus, when you say "A plane is a hand-powered tool that is used to smooth the edges of boards" or "A scythe is a piece of steel shaped in a half circle with a handle attached that is used to cut weeds or high grass," you are defining tools by indicating their use. Because the use or function of an object may be more important than its classification, this is often an excellent method of definition.

4. **Etymology. Etymology** is the history or derivation of a particular word. Because meanings of words change over time, origin may reveal very little about modern meaning. In some instances, however, the history of a word lends additional insight that will help the audience not only better remember the meaning but also bring the meaning to life. For instance, a censor was originally one of two Roman magistrates appointed to take the census and, later, to supervise public morals. The best source of word derivation is the *Oxford English Dictionary*.

   etymology the derivation or history of a particular word

5. **Example and comparison.** Regardless of which short definition form you use, most statements need to be supplemented with examples, comparisons, or both to make them understandable. That is especially true when you define abstract words. Consider the word *just* in the following sentence: "You are being *just* in your dealings with another when you deal *honorably* and *fairly*." Although *just* has been defined by synonym, listeners still may be unsure of the meaning. We might add, "If Paul and Mary do the same amount of work and we reward them by giving them an equal amount of money, our dealings will be just; if, on the other hand, we give Paul more money because he's a man, our dealings will be unjust." In this case, the definition is clarified with both an example and a comparison.

Defining

Prepare a four- to six-minute extended definition. An adaptation plan and outline are required. Evaluation will focus on the definition's clarity and on the organization and quality of the developmental material.

Some of the best topics for extended definition are general or abstract words, words that give you leeway in definition and allow for creative development. Here are examples of the kinds of words for which extended definitions are appropriate:

impressionism	rhetoric	logic
existentialism	Epicurean	acculturation
myth	fossil	extrasensory perception
epistemology	humanities	status

As you develop your plan for adapting the speech to your audience, be sure to include five short sections discussing how you will use your creativity to (1) speak directly to the audience, (2) build credibility, (3) get and maintain interest, (4) facilitate understanding, and (5) increase retention. Where appropriate, comment on the use of demonstration and visual aids and the role of language and delivery techniques for implementing that plan.

For some words, a single example or comparison will be enough. For other words or in communicating with certain audiences, you may need several examples and comparisons.

Extended Definitions

Often a word is so important to a speech that an extended definition is warranted. An extended definition is one that serves as an entire main point in a speech or, at times, an entire speech. Thus, an entire speech can be built around an extended definition of a term such as *freedom, equality, justice, love,* or *impressionistic painting.*

An extended definition begins with a single-sentence dictionary definition or stipulated definition. For example, *Webster's Third New International Dictionary* defines *jazz* as "American music characterized by improvisation, syncopated rhythms, contrapuntal ensemble playing, and special melodic features peculiar to the individual interpretation of the player." This definition suggests four topics ("improvisation," "syncopation," "ensemble," and "special melodies") that could be used as the main points for a topically ordered speech. Such a speech could be organized as follows.

> **Specific Goal:** I want my audience to understand the four major characteristics of jazz.
> I. Jazz is characterized by improvisation.
> II. Jazz is characterized by syncopated rhythms.
> III. Jazz is characterized by contrapuntal ensemble playing.
> IV. Jazz is characterized by special melodic features peculiar to the individual interpretation of the player.

Each main point would be developed through extended definition of each term. The selection and use of examples, illustrations, comparisons, personal experiences, and observations will give the speech its original and distinctive flavor.

Wendy Finkleman's sample speech "Impressionistic Painting," which follows, is an example of a speech of definition.

Speech of Definition

Write a critique for at least one of the informative speeches you hear in class. Outline the speech. As you outline, answer the questions on the informative speech checklist.

Check all items that were accomplished effectively.

Primary Criteria

_____ **1.** Was the specific goal appropriate for defining?

_____ **2.** Did the speaker use classification and differentiation, synonym, use or function, or etymology effectively?

_____ **3.** Did the speaker use examples to develop the definition?

_____ **4.** Did the speaker use any special strategies to help the audience remember main points and other key information necessary to demonstrate the process?

General Criteria

_____ **1.** Was the specific goal clear?

_____ **2.** Was the introduction effective?

_____ **3.** Was the organizational pattern appropriate for the intent and content of the speech?

_____ **4.** Was the conclusion effective?

_____ **5.** Was the language clear, vivid, emphatic, and appropriate?

_____ **6.** Was the speech delivered enthusiastically, with vocal expressiveness, fluently, spontaneously, and directly?

Evaluate the speech as (check one)

_____ excellent, _____ good, _____ average, _____ fair, _____ poor.

Use the information from your checklist to support your evaluation.

SAMPLE speech of definition

Impressionistic Painting by Wendy Finkleman[5]

This section presents a sample speech adaptation plan, outline, and transcript given by a student in an introductory speaking course for her descriptive speech assignment.

Plan for Adapting to Audience

1. **Speaking directly to the audience:** I will use personal pronouns and compare impressionistic technique to the audience members' experience of watching color TV at close distances.

2. **Building credibility:** I hope to build credibility through my sincere interest in and knowledge of impressionistic painting.

3. **Getting and maintaining interest:** I will begin the speech with an attention-getting quotation. In several places in the speech I will call for the listeners to refer to their experiences. In addition, I plan to deliver the speech in a sincere, enthusiastic manner.

4. **Facilitating understanding:** I will state each of the three aspects clearly and discuss them in what I believe will be easy-to-understand language. I am putting special emphasis on clear, vivid language to describe the points I am making.

5. **Increasing retention:** In addition to clear transitions before main points, I hope to use vivid examples and comparisons that will be memorable to my listeners.

Speech Outline

Specific Goal: I want the audience to understand the definition of impressionistic painting.

Introduction

I. "I paint as the bird sings"; this quote from Monet describes the light, vibrant nature of impressionistic painting.

II. Through the years, impressionism has become a highly appreciated art form.

III. *Impressionism* is defined as a practice in painting among French painters of the late 1800s in which subject matter was depicted in its natural setting and painted in vibrant hues of unmixed color and with broad, fragmented brush strokes.

Thesis Statement: Impressionistic painting involves unique subject matter, use of color, and technique.

Body

I. Impressionism involves the unique use of natural subject matter.
   A. Impressionistic painters painted visual impressions.
      1. The painters did not use conventional arrangements.
      2. They painted entirely out of doors.
   B. The painters used nature as their predominant source of subject matter.
      1. They painted the effects of light on water.
      2. They enjoyed painting landscapes.

(Now let's consider the second aspect of impressionistic painting.)

II. Impressionistic painting also involves a unique use of color.
   A. The painters tried to record colors as they appeared in natural light.
      1. They used vibrant colors.
      2. The use of colors was nontraditional.
   B. Impressionistic painters were first to use color in shadows.
      1. Colors tended to cast complementary tones on neutral backgrounds.
      2. Effects of shadow can be achieved by contrasts in color.

(Not only does impressionism involve unique subject matter and unique use of color, but most notably it involves unique technique.)

III. Most notably, impressionistic painting involves a unique technique.
   A. The painters developed the technique of using fragmented brush strokes.
      1. They blended colors by placing them side by side on canvas.
      2. The effect is similar to the dots of light in a television picture.
   B. They left their paintings "unfinished" by conventional standards.
      1. There were no clear outlines.
      2. This translated the immediacy and strength of the impression.

Conclusion

I. In its unique use of subject matter, color, and technique, impressionism has made quite an impression on the art world.

Sources

Hayes, Colin. *The Colour Library of Art.* London: Paul Hamlyn Limited, 1961.
Janson, David. *The History of Art.* New York: Harcourt Brace, 1985.
Martini, Alberto. *Monet.* New York: Avenel Books, 1978.
Rouart, Kenis. *Degas.* New York: Rizzoli International, 1988.

Speech and Analysis

Read this speech aloud at least once. Then analyze it on the basis of the primary criteria in the checklist on page 241.

CORBIS/Bettmann

Speech

"I paint as the bird sings." This quotation from Claude Monet describes the light, vibrant nature of impressionistic painting. When impressionism first emerged in the late 1800s, it was frowned upon by critics; however, as time has moved on, it has become a highly appreciated art form. Impressionism is defined as a practice in painting among French painters of the late 1800s depicting subject matter in its natural setting, painted in vibrant hues of unmixed color, with broad, fragmented brush strokes. Let's consider each of these three aspects of impressionism.

The first aspect that makes impressionism unique is that it involves natural subject matter. Contrary to the practice of the time of arranging a basket of fruit or a basket of flowers or posing a model, impressionists painted natural objects primarily outdoors. In fact, impressionists were the first artists to both start and finish a painting outdoors. They didn't bring the painting inside the studio at all, nature was the predominant source of

Analysis

After using an attention-getting quotation from Monet, Wendy gives a complete definition of impressionism, focusing on the three key aspects that differentiate it from other styles of painting.

Notice the good transition leading into the body of the speech.

Because the definition includes three specific aspects that differentiate impressionism from other painting styles, each main point focuses on one aspect.

The first main point focuses on the use of natural subject matter. In developing the definition, Wendy emphasizes that not only were the subjects natural objects but the paintings were done in a natural environment.

This second main point develops the second aspect of impression-ism, the use of color.

their subjects. Many of their paintings featured land-scape views. And since impressionists were particularly fascinated with the effect of light on water, they often painted water scenes.

Now let's consider the second aspect of impressionis-tic painting. A second aspect of impressionism that defines it is the unique use of color. Again, in contrast to the typical practice of the time, instead of using muted tones impressionists captured the natural colors of nature by using more vibrant hues. More distinctive than just their selection of color was their use of color in shadows.

Notice how Wendy uses clear examples to explain how colors are perceived in shadows.

Claude Monet, who was one of the originators of impressionistic painting, found that a color when cast on a neutral background would tend to cast in complemen-taries. For example, a red when cast on a gray background will tend to cast a bluish-green hue, because red is oppo-site blue-green on the color wheel. Yellow, on the other hand, would tend to cast a violet hue since yellow is oppo-site violet on the color wheel. Monet found that this same effect occurred in nature. Thus there was no longer a need to render shadows as dark harsh tones when you could render shadows by using complementary colors. This unique aspect of impressionistic painting was a signifi-cant artistic advancement.

Régates à Argenteuil by Claude Monet, CORBIS/Edimédia

Regates a Argenteuil
by Claude Monet

Not only does impressionism involve unique subject matter and unique use of color, but most notably it involves unique technique. A third aspect of impression-ism that defines it is the technique of using broad, frag-mented brush strokes. On canvas, these brush strokes looked a little bit similar to a comma or a semicolon. Instead of mixing the colors on a palette or on a plate before putting them on a canvas, impressionists blended them by putting separate flashes of color on the canvas. Their effect was similar in manner to the way a television screen works. When you sit very close to a television screen, you see different tiny dots of color, and when you move away, those tiny dots of color form a solid visual impres-sion. Because of the nature of these fragmented brush strokes, the paintings looked very unfinished by conven-tional standards. They didn't have the sharp clear outline that is characteristic of the painting of the time; nor did they leave a smooth appearance. Again this method was often frowned upon by the critics of the time, but it added to the originality of impressionism and it created a sense of immediacy and strength of the impressionists, which was the primary goal of their painting.

Here the good transition reviews the first two aspects and leads into the third, the use of broad, fragmented brush strokes.

This comparison of the perception of brush strokes and commas is a good one. Likewise, the comparison to the way we perceive color on a television screen helps the audience to understand the point.

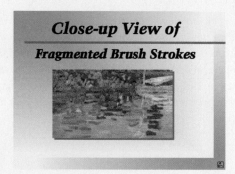

Close-up View of
Fragmented Brush Strokes

So, the next time you hear people refer to impres-sionistic painters, you can picture paintings depicting subject matter in its natural setting, painted in vibrant hues of unmixed color, with broad, fragmented brush strokes. ■

In her conclusion, Wendy reveiws the three major parts of her definition.

This speech is a good example of using the aspects of a definition as the framework for an entire speech. ■

Expository Speech

When a speaker draws on extensive research and uses a variety of developmental techniques to inform an audience, the speaker is giving an **expository speech.** Most classroom lectures are expository presentations. Expository speeches make extensive use of source material to give the speech depth. For example, expository speeches on "The Causes of Teen Violence," "The Practice of Islamic Religion," and "The Origin and Classifications of Nursery Rhymes" would present up-to-date information drawn from a variety of sources.

An expository speech embodies all of the principles that we discussed in the first part of the chapter, and may include demonstrating and defining, but the distinguishing characteristic of an expository speech is the quantity and quality of the research material that is used to create a stimulating informative speech. It is an excellent assignment for a major informative speech.

SPEECH EVALUATION checklist

Expository Speech

Primary Criteria

_____ **1.** Was the specific goal designed to increase audience information?

_____ **2.** Did the speaker show creativity in idea development?

_____ **3.** Was the speaker effective in establishing his or her credibility on this topic?

_____ **4.** Was the information intellectually stimulating?

_____ **5.** Did the speaker show the relevance of the information?

_____ **6.** Did the speaker emphasize the information?

_____ **7.** Was the organizational pattern appropriate for the intent and content of the speech?

General Criteria

_____ **1.** Was the specific goal clear?

_____ **2.** Was the introduction effective?

_____ **3.** Were main points clear?

_____ **4.** Was the conclusion effective?

_____ **5.** Was the language clear, vivid, emphatic, and appropriate?

_____ **6.** Was the speech delivered enthusiastically, with vocal expressiveness, fluently, spontaneously, and directly?

Evaluate the speech as (check one)

_____ excellent _____ good _____ average _____ fair _____ poor.

Use the information from this checklist to support your evaluation.

Expository Speaking

Prepare a five- to eight-minute general informative speech. An outline and a list of sources are required. Criteria for evaluation include quality of resource material, including citing sources for key information, means of ensuring audience interest, understanding information, and retaining information.

As you develop your plan for adapting the speech to your audience, be sure to include five short sections discussing how you will use your creativity to (1) speak directly to the audience, (2) build credibility, (3) get and maintain interest, (4) facilitate understanding, and (5) increase retention. Where appropriate, comment on the use of demonstration and visual aids and the role of language and delivery techniques for implementing that plan.

SAMPLE expository speech

Speech Interactive for Challenge

This section presents a sample expository speech adaptation plan, outline, and transcript given by a student in an introductory speaking course.

Women in World War II by Lindsey Degenhardt[6]

Adaptation Plan

1. **Speaking directly to members of the audience:** I will use rhetorical questions and personal pronouns to show audience I am talking to them directly.

2. **Building credibility:** I will use documented sources to show that I have good information, and I will use an example of my grandmother's experience to show that I have personal knowledge of events.

3. **Getting and maintaining interest:** Since the audience interest level will not be high, I will compare the 1940s to now and show that some of the fads now are the same as the fads then. I will try to show that although World War II happened a long time ago, the results have affected our current culture. I will also try to make my delivery enthusiastic.

4. **Facilitating understanding:** I will present the information clearly. I will use repetition and transitions to make my points clearer. I will also use examples and show visual aids.

5. **Increasing retention:** I will repeat my main points three times throughout the speech, in the introduction, in the body, and in the conclusion. I will use sectional transitions to reinforce retention of main points. I will tell stories and use visual aids to help the audience retain the information. I will also tell how the 1940s has had an impact on our culture today.

Speech Outline

Specific Goal: I would like the audience to understand the three ways that women helped the war effort during World War II.

Introduction

I. Do you think that World War II happened so long ago that it has no effect on us now?

II. Some of our music is based on 1940s swing and several recent movies are based on 1940s events.

III. Today I am going to share with you the roles that women played during World War II.

Thesis Statement: Three ways in which women helped the war effort during World War II were by working at home, working outside of the home, and enlisting in the military.

Body

I. One way in which women helped the war effort was by working at home.
  A. Women rationed food and supplies.
    1. They cut back on their use of sugar, canned goods, silk, and gasoline.
    2. They donated their pots and pans.
  B. Women planted "Victory Gardens."

(Now that we have seen how women helped from their homes, let's see how they helped outside of their homes.)

II. A second way in which women helped the war effort was by working outside of the home.
  A. Before the war, very few women were employed.
  B. During the war, women took a variety of jobs.
    1. In 1945, almost 19 million women were working.
    2. Women made up 40% of the workforce in aircraft assembly in 1944.

(We have now seen how women helped the war effort by getting jobs. Let me tell you the third way in which women helped.)

III. A third way in which women helped the war effort was by enlisting in the military.
  A. The Army and Navy Nurse Corps were started in the early 1900s.
    1. During World War II, 31.3% of all active nurses were women.
  B. By January 1943, all branches of the United States military included women.
    1. There were three positions that women could be trained in: radio operators, storekeepers, and secretaries.
    2. To be in the WAVES, women had to meet higher standards and be older than males to enlist.
    3. My grandmother was in the WAVES, the women's branch of the Navy.

Conclusion

I. Women helped at home, at work, and in the military.

II. If women had not helped in the war, there might not be so many women enrolled in college right now.

Sources

Creedy, Brooks Spive, *Women Behind the Lines*. New York: The Women's Press, 1949.

Hartmann, Susan M., *Home Front and Beyond*. Boston: Twain Publishers, 1982.

Historical Statistics of the United States Colonial Times to 1957. U.S. Bureau of the Census.

O'Neill, William L., *A Democracy at War*. New York: The Free Press, 1993.

Statistical Abstract of the United States. U.S. Census Bureau, 2000.

Stein, Conrad R., *World at the Home Front*. Chicago: Children's Press, 1986.

Weatherford, Doris, *American Women and World War II*. New York: Facts on File, 1990.

Speech and Analysis

Read this speech aloud at least once. Then analyze it on the basis of the primary criteria in the checklist on page 245. You can watch, listen to, and evaluate the following informative speech by Lindsey Degenhardt under Speech Interactive on your Challenge of Effective Speaking CD-ROM. As you watch the speech, what recommendations would you suggest to help her make the delivery of the speech even better?

Analysis

Lindsey begins her speech with a rhetorical question.

Her goal in this part of the introduction is to get the class to wondering what she is going to talk about in the speech.

After stating her goal, Lindsey clearly previews the three ways women helped the war effort.

Here Lindsey states her first subpoint, that women rationed food and supplies. She then supports this point with specific examples.

Now she introduces her second subpoint, that another way women helped at home was to grow Victory gardens.

Speech

When someone mentions World War II, do you groan and think, "I don't want to hear about World War II, that happened such a long time ago and it doesn't have anything to do with me"? Did you know that swing dancing and swing music similar to that played by Big Daddy Little Daddy was popular in the 1940s? Even some recent movies such as *Pearl Harbor* are based on 1940s events. Since so many more movies are portraying the roles that men played during the war, I'm going to share with you the roles women played during World War II. There are three ways in which women helped the war effort during World War II. They worked at home, worked outside of the home, and enlisted in the military.

One way in which women helped the war effort was by working at home. To help the soldiers, women rationed food and supplies. They cut back on their use of sugar, canned goods, soap, and gasoline. The canned goods and sugar went to feed the soldiers. The soap was used to make parachutes. And the gasoline was used to fuel tanks and airplanes. When the military had a shortage of aluminum, women donated pots and pans so that the military could make tanks, planes, and artillery.

Another way in which women helped at home was—they grew Victory gardens. Victory gardens are just normal vegetable gardens, um carrots, beans, cucumbers—that sort of thing. But the reason that women planted these was they thought that if they grew their own food, they wouldn't buy so much food from the store, and the surplus could be used to feed the soldiers. Now that we've seen how women helped from their homes, let's see how they helped outside of their homes.

A second way in which women helped the war effort was working outside of their homes. Before the war started, not very many women were employed. According to the New York Census, less than 14 million women were employed in 1940 compared to 42 million men. When women worked during this time they were usually teachers, secretaries, or librarians. But during the war a lot of men were either drafted or enlisted, so a lot of the factory jobs opened up and no one but women were there to work. So women became crane operators, hydraulic press operators, tractor drivers, and miners. According to Conrad Stein, author of *World at the Home Front,* by 1944 40% of the workforce was made up of women and 12% in shipyards. In 1945, 19 million women worked compared to 46 million men.

So now the ratio is getting a little closer. And compare that to today when 65 million women worked in 1999 compared to 75 million men. Now we have seen how women helped on the home front by getting jobs, let me tell you about another way women helped.

A third way that women helped the war effort was by enlisting in the military. In the early 1900s the Army/Navy Nurse Corps was started. And according to Susan Hartmann, author of *Home Front and Beyond,* during World War II, 31.3% of all active nurses were women. And Doris Weatherford, author of *American Women and World War II,* stated in her book that by January 1943 all of the branches of the United States military included women. Now not only could they be nurses, they could also be radio operators, secretaries, and storekeepers. But although women were now allowed in the military, they had to be of higher standards and also had to be older to enlist. And they couldn't actually use guns and fight in other countries. For instance, my grandmother was in the WAVES, and she was positioned in Texas. But she couldn't be, even though she went to two years of college, she couldn't be a commissioned officer. She had to have a degree to be a commissioned officer—but she was a non-commissioned officer.

On January 26, 1945, Japan surrendered. This defeat might not have been possible without the help of women at home, at work, and in the military. Not only did women have an effect on the outcome of the war, women also, the women of the '40s also had an effect on our culture today. Because if women had just gone back to their housewife positions after working in factories there might not be so many women with college degrees today. ■

After defining "Victory gardens," she shows how this effort helped the war effort.

Here's a good transition to the second main point.
  Here Lindsey clearly states the second way women helped.
  She shows how women not only retained traditional roles but also stepped in to do jobs that were held by the men who were drafted or who enlisted.

In this section she documents the statistics she uses to develop her main point.

Here is another good transition.

Now, Lindsey clearly states her third main point.

In this section she gives examples of the kinds of roles women filled in the military to help free men to engage in the fighting. Notice the use of specific examples to support her point.

Here Lindsey presents the ironic point that although women did the necessary work, they were prevented from becoming commissioned officers.

After a short review of the three roles women fulfilled, she concludes with a statement that shows that doing this kind of work opened many occupational possibilities for women from then on.
  This is a very good expository speech. She has a good introduction that captures attention and leads into the speech; she gives three clearly stated and well-developed main points using high-quality information; and she provides a good conclusion that not only summarizes the main points but also shows the effects of their efforts on our culture today. ■

As Jason was practicing his speech, he found that he had some statistics that were important to his point, but he couldn't remember where he had gotten them. He recalled that during the two hours he had spent at the library he had found several articles from which he had taken information. He had tried to be very careful about identifying the sources from which specific information came. But as he looked through his notes he discovered at least three sets of information for which there were no references. Fortunately, two of the three weren't that important, but this one set of statistics was. As he pondered the problem, he concluded, "I know I didn't make these up—I'm pretty sure that I copied the statistics accurately," but of course neither the source nor the date of the statistics was included. He thought, "I could go back through all the sources I have written down, but not only would this take me a very long time, I can't be sure that this particular set of statistics is from any of those."

The more he considered it the more convinced he became that even though he hadn't written down the source, he knew the statistics were valid, so there was no reason he shouldn't use them. He decided that what he'd say is, "A recent magazine article included the following statistics."

1. Does Jason face an ethical problem here? If so, what it is it?

2. If you had been in the same position, what would you have done? Explain why your solution would be a good one.

Summary

Informative speeches are those in which the primary goal is to create understanding. As an informative speaker, your rhetorical challenge is to present information in a way that facilitates attending, understanding, and remembering.

To accomplish these goals, speakers can learn to incorporate several principles: Audiences are more likely to show interest in, understand, and remember information (1) if they perceive the information to be intellectually stimulating, (2) if it is presented creatively, (3) if they perceive it to be relevant, and (4) if it is emphasized.

Information is seen as intellectually stimulating when it is new to audience members and meets a deep-seated need to know. Creativity involves using material in an imaginative way. Information is perceived as relevant if it is vital or important to audience members. Information is likely to be remembered if it is presented with the help of visual aids, if it is repeated, if it is introduced with external transitions, if it is presented humorously, or if it includes mnemonic devices.

Methods of informative speaking include process explanation or demonstration, definition, and exposition.

Process explanation or demonstration involves showing how to do something, how to make something, or how something works. Both full and modified demonstrations are often enhanced by visual aids.

Defining is giving the meaning of a word or concept through synonym and antonym, classification and differentiation, use or function, or etymological reference, and is enhanced by the use of examples and comparisons.

Exposition is a general informative speech using outside sources of information.

CHALLENGE ONLINE

Use your Challenge of Effective Speaking CD-ROM for quick access to the electronic study resources that accompany this text. Included on your CD-ROM is access to the Challenge of Effective Speaking Web site featuring Speech Builder Express at Wadsworth Communication Café, InfoTrac College Edition, and a demo of Web Tutor for *The Challenge of Effective Speaking*. The Web site offers chapter-by-chapter access to the Speech Preparation Action Step Activities, InfoTrac College Edition exercises, a digital glossary of key terms, Web links, Speech Preparation Forms, Speech Evaluation Checklists, and quizzes. Review the key terms and complete the InfoTrac College Edition exercise at **http://www.wadsworth.com/product/0534563856**

InfoTrac College Edition Exercise

Neuroscience, the study of brain functioning, is helping teachers and speakers understand and improve audience learning. Using PowerTrac, search "author" Perry, Bruce. Look for the article titled "How the Brain Learns Best" by Bruce Perry. Read this short article. How does Perry's "Bob and Weave" lecture advice relate to organizing an informative speech? Do you use the fact, concept, narrative Bob and Weave to improve your audience's ability to remember the main points of your speech? If not, revise your speech plan so that you do. How do Perry's comments reinforce strategies discussed in this chapter? What particular bit of his advice stands out for you?

Key Terms

acronyms *(231)*

antonyms *(239)*

association *(232)*

complete demonstration *(233)*

creativity *(226)*

demonstration *(233)*

etymology *(239)*

expository speech *(245)*

informative speech *(225)*

intellectually stimulating *(225)*

mnemonics *(231)*

modified demonstration *(233)*

process explanation *(233)*

relevance *(229)*

synonyms *(239)*

vital information *(229)*

Challenge of Effective Speaking Web Site

Use your Challenge of Effective Speaking CD-ROM for quick access to Speech Builder Express on the book's Web site. Complete the Speech Preparation Action Step Activities to help you prepare to give the informative speech you have been assigned.

13 Principles of Persuasive Speaking

David Young-Wolff/PhotoEdit/PictureQuest

Speech is power: speech is to persuade, to convert, to compel.

—Ralph Waldo Emerson, "Social Aims," 1875

As she finished her powerfully persuasive speech in favor of the motion to strike, the entire assembly rose as a body and cheered. Over the din, the local union president shouted, "All those in favor, say 'aye'" and as one, the members roared "aye." As she walked to her seat, people reached to pat her on the back, and those who could not touch her chanted her name: "Sheila . . . Sheila . . . !"

"Sheila! Wake up," Denny chided as he shook her shoulder, "you're supposed to be working on your speech."

Perhaps you've been stirred by an issue and imagined yourself giving such a rousing speech that your audience cheered wildly and was moved to act. Although it is easy to fantasize this scenario, our real-life attempts to persuade require careful planning and diligent preparation. **Persuasive speaking** is a process in which a speaker presents a message intended to affect beliefs or move audience members to act. It is the most demanding speech challenge, because it requires not only the skills necessary for effective informative speaking but additional skills needed to change attitudes and behavior. To become an effective persuasive speaker, you need to understand how basic principles of persuasive speaking are used during your speech preparation process.

persuasive speaking a process in which a speaker presents a message intended to affect an audience in a way that is likely to reinforce a belief, change a belief, or move an audience to act

Choose an Ethical Speech Goal

Principle 1   You are more likely to persuade audience members when they understand that you believe in your goal and that your goal is in their best interests.
To be ethical, a speech goal must meet three tests. First, a goal is ethical if it does not compromise the integrity of the speaker. Integrity, consistency between what one believes and how one acts, is the opposite of hypocrisy. Thus, if Cameron believes capital punishment is morally wrong, it would be unethical for him to deliver a speech in support of capital punishment. Second, an ethical speech goal respects audience members' rights of free choice. Richard Weaver, a leading scholar in ethical speaking issues, said many years ago that ethical speech is based on choice. An audience must be allowed to accept the appeal to persuade on its merits. Third, Weaver went on to say, "As rhetoric [speech] confronts us with choices involving values, the rhetorician [speaker] is a preacher to us, noble if he tries to direct our passion toward noble ends and base [unethical] if he uses our passion to confuse and degrade us."[1] So, an ethical goal leads audience members toward choices that are in their own best interest and those of the larger society rather than just in the self-interest of the speaker. Thus, to meet the ethical test, a speech goal must do the following:

- Embody the honest belief of the speaker
- Honor audience choice
- Be in the best interests of the audience

proposition a persuasive speech goal

You will begin your persuasive speech preparation by writing a persuasive speech goal (often called a **proposition**), which must meet the criteria discussed in Chapter 4. The goal should be a complete sentence that uses an infinitive to show the nature of the desired response. Consider these three examples of goal statements for persuasive speeches that meet these tests:

> I want my audience to believe the city should build a downtown entertainment center.

> I want my audience to believe late-term abortions should be prohibited.

> I want my audience to donate money to the United Way.

Persuasive goal statements can be classified into two types: (1) goals whose purpose is to strengthen or change a belief and (2) goals whose purpose is to move audience members to act. Correctly identifying the type of goal is important, because each type of goal requires a different approach to how arguments are developed.

strengthen or change a belief desiring to have listeners agree with you that the belief you present is reasonable

Although a speech goal that is phrased to **strengthen or change a belief** may result in listeners' acting upon that belief, the primary emphasis is on having audience members adopt the belief you espouse. Here are some examples of speech goals that seek to strengthen or change beliefs:

> I want the audience to believe it is in the best interests of our country for the federal government to finance stem cell research.

> I want the audience to believe fluency in a foreign language should be required of all high school graduates.

> I want the audience to believe America's children are being overmedicated.

Notice that in each case the speech goal advocates what should or ought to be believed—not what audience members should or ought to do as a result of that belief.

move an audience to action desiring to have listeners actually do what you want them to

Speech goals that are designed to **move an audience to action** go beyond gaining agreement on a belief—they state exactly what you want your audience to do. The following goals all seek action:

> I want the audience to donate money to the food bank drive.

> I want the members of my audience to write to their congressional representatives to support legislation in favor of gun control.

> I want the audience members to attend the school's production of *Grease*.

Once you have completed the speech assignment exercise, you will have a clear goal and thesis statement for your persuasive speech. Exhibit 13.1 provides an example completed by a student from this course.

Adapt to Attitude of Audience

Principle 2   You are more likely to be able to persuade when you direct your goal and your information to the audience's attitude.

Persuasion is more likely to take place when your arguments are fitted to the initial attitude of members of your audience, so it is crucial to assess the direction and strength of audience members' attitudes before you speak. An **attitude** is "a general or enduring positive or negative feeling about some person, object, or issue."[2] An attitude is expressed in evaluative terms—you like or dislike something, something is

attitude a general or enduring positive or negative feeling about some person, object, or issue

Writing a Persuasive Speech Goal and Thesis Statement

The goal of this activity is to develop an effective persuasive speech specific goal and thesis statement.

1. Check the type of persuasive goal you have for this speech: ___ change or strengthen a belief ___ move to action

2. Write a first draft of your speech goal using a complete sentence that specifies the type of response you want from the audience:

3. Review what you have written. Underline the infinitive phrase. Does the infinitive phrase express precisely the specific audience reaction desired? If not, revise the infinitive phrase:

4. Review what you have written. Does the statement clearly express the complete response you want from your audience? If not, revise the infinitive phrase until it has this clarity, and write your final draft of your speech goal:

5. Identify and list the specific issues you will cover to reach your speech goal:

6. After reviewing the issues, write a thesis statement that incorporates these issues:

E X H I B I T 13.1 **Writing a persuasive speech goal and thesis statement**

1. Check the type of persuasive goal you have for this speech: _X_ change or strengthen a belief ___ move to action

2. Write a first draft of your speech goal using a complete sentence that specifies the type response you want from the audience: I want to convince the audience that capital punishment doesn't work.

3. Review what you have written. Underline the infinitive phrase. Does the infinitive phrase express precisely the specific audience reaction desired? If not, revise the infinitive phrase: Yes

4. Review what you have written. Does the statement clearly express the complete response you want from your audience? If not, revise the infinitive phrase until it has this clarity: I want to convince the audience that capital punishment isn't effective in meeting criteria.

5. Identify and list the specific issues you will cover to reach your speech goal: whether death penalty is applied only to guilty, whether it reduces prison overcrowding and expenses, whether it deters crime.

6. After reviewing the issues, write a thesis statement that incorporates these issues: Capital punishment is not effective because it is used in cases where guilt is in question; it does not reduce prison overcrowding and expenses, and it does not deter violent crime.

When you know that your audience is already leaning in your favor, you can focus your speech on a specific course of action.

good or bad, effective or ineffective, moral or immoral, and so forth. For instance, if a person believes it is appropriate to spank misbehaving children, this person has a positive attitude toward corporal punishment.

We have said that the goal of a persuasive speech is to affect audience beliefs or behavior. But how do beliefs and behaviors relate to attitudes? Most psychologists define **belief** as the cognitive, or mental, aspect of an attitude; that is, we believe something to be true if someone can prove it to our satisfaction. On the subject of corporal punishment, I might believe spanking children helps to give them respect for school rules. If I hold a positive attitude toward corporal punishment in general, it will be easier for me to hold a belief that spanking children will increase their respect for school rules.

An **opinion** is a verbal expression of an attitude or a belief that is expressed with little or no evidence to support it. "I think corporal punishment is important" is an opinion that reflects a favorable attitude (important rather than unimportant) about corporal punishment. "I think spanking children who disobey helps to give them respect for school rules" is an opinion reflecting the belief that spanking is related to developing obedience.

There is a difference between an opinion and a behavior. A **behavior** is an action related to or resulting from an attitude or a belief. As a result of their attitudes or beliefs, people behave in certain ways. For instance, people who believe corporal punishment is a valuable tool in training children may be inclined to spank children who have disobeyed rules. Spanking is the behavior that results from the belief.

Usually behavior reflects opinions and attitudes held. For instance, a person who has a favorable attitude toward corporal punishment may then express the opinion that corporal punishment is important and, as a result of that attitude and opinion, spank children when they misbehave. Of course, it is possible for discrepancies to occur. A person may voice the opinion that corporal punishment is important but never actually spank a child who disobeys rules.

belief the cognitive, or mental, aspect of an attitude

opinion verbal expression of a belief or attitude

behavior an action related to or resulting from an attitude or belief

EXHIBIT 13.2 Opinion continuum

Hostile (negative)	Opposed	Mildly Opposed	Neither in favor nor opposed	Mildly in favor	In favor	Highly in favor (positive)
2	3	24	1	2	2	1

Because much of the success of a speech depends on determining how an audience is likely to react to your goal, you must find out where the audience stands. As we learned in Chapter 4, you can make these judgments based on demographic information and/or opinion polls. The more data you have about your audience and the more experience you have in analyzing audiences, the better your chances of judging audience attitudes accurately.

Audience attitudes (expressed by opinions) about your speech goal will be distributed along a continuum from very positive to very negative (Exhibit 13.2). Although an audience may have individual opinions at nearly every point along the continuum, a significant number of audience members will hold opinions that cluster near each other. For purpose of adapting to the audience, you will want to consider that cluster to be the general audience attitude toward your speech goal. This will enable you to classify your audience's initial attitude as predominantly "in favor" (already agreeing with or holding a positive attitude toward your goal), "no opinion" (uninformed, neutral, or apathetic), or "opposed" (holding a negative attitude or an opposite point of view).

Exhibit 13.2 shows a distribution of individual member's attitudes toward a specific persuasive speech goal. Notice that individual members vary widely in the attitude held, but of the thirty-five members surveyed, twenty-four were mildly opposed to the speaker's goal. The speaker could classify this audience as opposed to the specific goal. To adapt to your audience, you will need to develop a strategy based on how you categorize the audience's attitude.

Suppose this is your goal: "I want audience members to believe that lowering their intake of saturated fats can reduce the risk of heart attacks." In your research, you may have found that consumption of high amounts of saturated fats in the teen years establishes life-long eating habits and begins slow vascular deterioration that people may not begin to notice until later in life. As you will see, your assessment of audience attitude is likely to affect (1) how you phrase your goal and/or (2) how you determine the way you will use your information.

In Favor

When your audience has a positive attitude toward your speech goal, your task is to reinforce their beliefs or motivate them to act. Because beliefs are spread along a continuum, an audience that is generally in favor of your specific goal may still need to be reminded of the reasons for holding this belief. By providing additional or new arguments and evidence that support the belief, you can help the audience become further committed to this belief. If your audience poll shows that most audience members accept the idea that lowering saturated fats reduces heart disease, then you may want to reinforce this belief by providing evidence from the most recent studies and theories. Some of your audience will be familiar with some of your arguments, but the current evidence you provide will reinforce and strengthen audience attitudes.

At times, if you believe your listeners strongly support your belief, then you may want to change your specific goal to motivating the audience to act on their belief. For instance, if members of your audience strongly support that their intake of saturated fats will reduce heart disease, then you might change your specific goal to motivating them to adopt a specific diet that is low in saturated fats. When you believe your listeners are on your side, try to crystallize their attitudes, recommit them to a particular direction, or suggest a specific course of action that will serve as a rallying point. The presentation of a thoughtful and specific solution increases the likelihood of audience action.

No Opinion

If your audience analysis indicates that your listeners have no opinion about your specific goal, you will want to figure out whether it is because they are uninformed, neutral, or apathetic. This will enable you to choose arguments that are likely to move audiences to support your belief. If you find your audience has no opinion because it is *uninformed,* you will need to provide enough information to help your audience understand the subject before you develop persuasive appeals that are directed toward establishing a belief or moving your listeners to action. For instance, if you believe your audience is uninformed about the need to lower saturated fat intake, then early in the speech you need to define "saturated fat," talk about how cholesterol is formed, and share medical evidence about its effects on the human body. Then the audience will be equipped to listen to the arguments you make. Novice speakers sometimes spend so much time explaining the basics to an uninformed audience that they shortchange the time they can devote to developing the reasons for believing.

You may find that your audience is informed but has no opinion because it is *neutral.* A neutral audience is able to reason objectively and accept sound reasoning. It is not prejudiced, holds no preconceived opinions, and is open minded. In this case, you will present the strongest arguments and support them with the best information you can find.

You may find that your audience members have no opinion because they are *apathetic.* An apathetic audience has no opinion because it is uninterested, unconcerned, or indifferent to your goal. To convince this audience type, you will begin by motivating them to recognize the importance or urgency of your topic. By using the adaptation technique of personalizing, members of an apathetic audience may begin to identify with your speech goal. For example, if members of your audience know what saturated fat is, know how cholesterol is formed, and even understand the medical information on negative effects—but do not seem to care—you can overcome their apathy by personalizing statistics, by choosing stories about people they can identify with, and by choosing material that is directed to your listeners' personal needs.

Opposed

If you find that your listeners are opposed to your speech goal, then you need to determine whether their attitude is slightly negative or totally hostile. If you believe your listeners are *slightly opposed* to your goal, you can approach them directly with

© Paul Conklin/PhotoEdit, Inc.

If you believe your listeners are opposed to your proposal, your strategy should include presenting arguments in ways that lessen your listeners' negative attitudes and do not increase their hostility.

your arguments, hoping that the weight of your evidence will be sufficient to change their attitudes and swing them to your side. If your audience is slightly opposed to your goal of lowering their saturated fat intake by eliminating all fried foods, you can present good reasons and strong evidence to support the proposal.

If an audience is mildly opposed to your goal, present your arguments carefully so that you reduce your listeners' negative attitudes without arousing their hostility. Take care to present your arguments objectively and make your case clearly enough that those members who are only mildly negative will consider the proposal and those who are very negative will at least understand your position.

If you believe your audience is *hostile* toward your specific speech goal, you will want to approach the topic indirectly or to consider a less ambitious goal. A complete shift in attitude or behavior as a result of one speech is probably unrealistic. Instead, present a modest proposal that seeks a slight change in attitude. With this strategy you will be able to get an audience to consider your arguments. In later speeches, you can try to move the audience further. For instance, suppose the audience is comprised of obese people who have tried diet after diet and who are "fed up" with appeals to restrict their food intake. Trying to convince them that they should eliminate all saturated fat from their diet would be a hopeless task. You might, however, convince them to avoid French fries cooked in animal fat.

Exhibit 13.3 on page 260 summarizes the strategy choices we have reviewed for audiences with different attitudes toward your topic. Later in this chapter, we will discuss patterns of speech organization that are appropriate for each type of audience.

Since audience attitude toward your persuasive speech goal can be especially important, take time to complete the speech assignment on assessing audience attitudes. Exhibit 13.4 on page 261 provides an example of an audience assessment made by a student from this course.

EXHIBIT 13.3 Adapting persuasive speech goals to audience attitudes

AUDIENCE ATTITUDES		STRATEGY CHOICES
If audience members are …	then they may …	so that you can …
Strongly in favor	■ be ready to act	■ provide practical suggestions
		■ put emphasis on motivation rather than on information and reasoning
In favor	■ already share many of your beliefs	■ crystallize and reinforce existing beliefs and attitudes to lead them to a course of action
Mildly in favor	■ be inclined to accept your view, but with little commitment	■ strengthen positive beliefs by emphasizing supporting reasons
Neither in favor nor opposed	■ be uninformed	■ emphasize information relevant to a belief or move to action
	■ be neutral	■ emphasize reasons relevant to belief or action
	■ be apathetic	■ concentrate on motivating them to see the importance of the proposition or seriousness of the problem
Mildly opposed	■ have doubts about the wisdom of your position	■ give them reasons and evidence that will help them to consider your position
Opposed	■ have beliefs and attitudes contrary to yours	■ emphasize sound arguments
		■ concentrate on shifting beliefs rather than on moving to action
		■ be objective to avoid arousing hostility
Hostile	■ be totally unreceptive to your position	■ plant the "seeds of persuasion"
		■ try to get them to understand your position

Provide Good Reasons and Sound Evidence

Principle 3   You are more likely to persuade an audience when the body of your speech contains good reasons and strong evidence that support your speech goal. Human beings take pride in being rational; we seldom do anything without some real or imagined reason. Since the 1980s, persuasive speech theory has focused sharply on persuasion as a cognitive activity; that is, people form cognitive structures or mental maps and use these to create meaning for experiences.[3] To help audience members develop a way to think about the speech goal, effective speakers state the main points of a persuasive speech as reasons.

Assessing Audience Attitudes

1. Based on the results of a survey or other evidence, is your audience's attitude toward your speech goal in favor ___, neutral ___, or opposed ___ to your speech goal?

2. Write the speech strategy you will use to adapt to that attitude.

Identifying Good Reasons

Reasons are statements that answer *why* you should believe or do something. For most persuasive speeches, you will want to do research to verify and/or discover reasons that support your specific goal. For example, for a speech goal phrased "I want the audience to believe that home ownership should be encouraged," you might discover these six reasons:

reasons statements that tell why a proposition is justified

 I. Home ownership builds strong communities.
 II. Home ownership reduces crime.
 III. Home ownership increases individual wealth.
 IV. Home ownership increases individual self-esteem.
 V. Home ownership improves the value of a neighborhood.
 VI. Home ownership is growing in the suburbs.

Once you have a list of possible reasons, weigh and evaluate them and select the three or four best based on these criteria.

1. **Is the reason supportable?** Some reasons that sound impressive are not supported with facts. For example, the first reason, "Home ownership builds strong communities," sounds like a good one; but what facts can you find to support it directly? Reasons like this one are sometimes only supported by opinions of prominent people, and little systematic study may have been made to verify the claim. In these cases, the reason shouldn't be presented in the speech.

EXHIBIT 13.4 Assessing audience attitudes

1. Based on the results of a survey or other evidence, is your general audience's attitude in favor ___, neutral _X_, or opposed ___ to your speech goal.

2. Write the speech strategy you will use to adapt to that attitude:
Since at least a few members of the class may hold strong views, I will want to be careful to present solid information to support the conclusions I draw.

2. **Is the reason relevant to the proposition?** Some statements may look like reasons but don't supply much proof. For instance, "Home ownership is growing in the suburbs" may sound like a reason for encouraging home ownership, but why suburban growth in ownership is related to encouraging all home ownership is unclear.

3. **Will the reason have an impact on the intended audience?** Suppose you have a great deal of factual evidence to back up the statement "Home ownership increases self-esteem." Even if it is a well-supported reason, it will not be an ineffective reason to use in a speech if the majority of the audience are bankers who do not view this as an important outcome. It might be a compelling reason, however, if the audience includes many members from the helping professions.

Finding Evidence to Support Your Reasons

By themselves, reasons are only unsupported claims. Although some reasons are self-explanatory and occasionally have a persuasive effect without further support, most listeners want to hear evidence—factual information and expert opinions—to support the reasons before they will either accept or act on them.

As we learned in Chapter 6, the best supporting material for main points are verifiable factual statements. In a speech designed to motivate people to donate money to Alzheimer's research, suppose you give the reason "Alzheimer's disease is a major killer." The statement "According to statistics presented in last month's *Time* magazine, Alzheimer's disease is the fourth leading cause of death for adults" would be factual support for that reason.

Statements from people who are experts on a subject can also be used as evidence to support a reason. For example, expert opinion support for the reason "Alzheimer's disease is a major killer" might be the statement, "According to the Surgeon General, 'By 2050 Alzheimer's disease may afflict 14 million people a year.'"

Let's look at an example of how both fact and opinion evidence can be used to support a proposition:

Proposition: I want the audience to believe television violence has a harmful effect on viewers.

Reason: Television violence desensitizes people to violence.

Evidence by fact: In a survey of 50 children between the ages of 5 and 10 in Los Angeles, California, the children were asked after watching *Teenage Mutant Ninja Turtles* whether or not violence was acceptable. Thirty-nine of them responded "Yes, because it helps you to win fights."

Evidence by expert opinion: According to Kirsten Houston, a well-regarded scholar writing in the July 1997 *Journal of Psychology*, "Repeated exposure to media violence is a major factor in the gradual desensitization of individuals to such scenes. This desensitization, in turn, weakens some viewers' psychological restraints on violent behavior."

Whether your evidence is a factual statement or an opinion, you'll want to ask at least three questions to assure yourself that what you present is "good" evidence.

1. **What is the source of the evidence?** This question involves both the people who offered the opinions or compiled the facts and the book, journal, or Internet sources where they were reported. Just as some people's opinions are more

SPEECH assignment

Selecting Reasons

1. Write the specific goal that you will use for your first persuasive speech.

2. Write at least six reasons that support your specific goal.

3. Place stars next to the three or four reasons you believe are the best.

reliable than others, so are some printed and Internet sources more reliable than others. As we stated in Chapter 6, be especially careful of undocumented information that comes from the Internet. If evidence comes from a poor source, an unreliable source, or a biased source, verify it through other sources or drop it from your speech.

2. **Is the evidence recent?** Products, ideas, and statistics are best when they are recent. You must ask when the particular evidence was true. Five-year-old evidence may not be true today. Furthermore, an article in last week's newsmagazine may be using five-year-old evidence in the story.

3. **Is the evidence relevant?** Just as reasons need to be relevant to the proposition, evidence needs to be relevant to the reason. Make sure your evidence directly supports the reason. If it does not, then do not include it. In the next chapter, we will look at forms of reasoning and fallacies of reasoning and offer some specific guidelines for testing the relevance of evidence.

To be certain that your reasons match your speech goal, complete the speech assignment on selecting reasons. Exhibit 13.5 shows how one student completed this assignment.

EXHIBIT 13.5 Selecting reasons

1. Write the specific goal that you will use for your first persuasive speech: I want to convince the audience that capital punishment doesn't work.

2. Write at least six reasons that support your specific goal:

   It is inhumane.

   ✳ It is used in cases where guilt is in question.

   ✳ It doesn't reduce overcrowding and expenses.

   Only a very few are ever executed.

   Frivolous appeals waste time and money.

   ✳ It does not deter crime.

3. Place stars next to the three or four reasons you believe are the best.

Organize Reasons to Meet Audience Attitudes

Principle 4   You are more likely to persuade an audience when you use an organizational pattern for your reasons that is tailored to your audience's initial attitude toward your speech goal.

Statement of logical reasons, problem solutions, comparative advantages, criteria satisfaction, and motivational are organizational patterns for persuasive speeches designed to be used with specific types of audiences and propositions. For each pattern, we will describe it, illustrate it, show the audience attitudes for which it is most applicable, and describe the logic of the order. So that you can contrast the patterns and better understand their use, we will illustrate each pattern using the same proposition (specific goal) and the same (or similar) reasons.

Statement of Logical Reasons Pattern

statement of logical reasons a straightforward organization in which you present the best-supported reasons you can find

The **statement of logical reasons** is a straightforward organization in which you use the best-supported reasons you can find, presenting the second strongest reason first, the strongest reason last, and other reason(s) in between. This pattern is used when your listeners have no opinion on the subject, are apathetic, or are perhaps mildly in favor or opposed.

> **Proposition:** I want my audience to vote in favor of the school tax levy on the November ballot.
>
> I. The income will enable the schools to restore vital programs. (second strongest)
>
> II. The income will enable the schools to give teachers the raises they need to keep up with the cost of living.
>
> III. The actual cost to each member of the community will be very small. (strongest)

The assumption underlying the use of the statement of logical reasons pattern is this: When good reasons and evidence are presented supporting a proposal, the proposal should be adopted.

Problem Solution Pattern

problem solution pattern an organization that provides a framework for clarifying the nature of the problem and for illustrating why a given proposal is the best one

The **problem solution pattern** is a framework that clarifies the nature of the problem and provides evidence to support a specific proposal as the best solution to the problem. The problem solution pattern is organized around three general reasons: (1) There is a problem that requires action. (2) The proposal will solve the problem. (3) The proposal is the best solution to the problem because it will lead to positive consequences. This pattern works well for a topic that is relatively unfamiliar to an audience—one in which they are unaware that a problem exists—or for an audience that has no opinion or is only mildly pro or con. A problem solution organization for the school tax proposition might look like this:

> **Proposition:** I want my audience to vote in favor of the school tax levy on the November ballot.
>
> I. The shortage of money is resulting in serious problems for public education. (statement of problem)
>
> II. The proposed increase is large enough to solve those problems. (solution)
>
> III. For now, a tax levy is the best method of solving the schools' problems. (consequences)

Effective speakers vary their organizational patterns depending on attitudes of their different audiences.

The assumption underlying the problem solution pattern is this: When a problem is presented that is not or cannot be solved with current measures and the proposal can solve the problem practically and beneficially, then the proposal should be adopted.

Comparative Advantages Pattern

The **comparative advantages pattern** is an organizational pattern in which a proposed change is compared to the status quo and demonstrated to be superior. Rather than presenting the proposition as a solution to a grave problem, the comparative advantage form of organization presents the proposition as one that ought to be adopted solely on the basis of the advantages of that proposition when compared to what is currently being done. Although this pattern can work for any audience attitude, it works best when the audience agrees that change may be necessary. A comparative advantages approach to the school tax proposition would look like this:

comparative advantages pattern an organization that allows you to place all the emphasis on the superiority of the proposed course of action

> **Proposition**: I want my audience to vote in favor of the school tax levy on the November ballot.
>
> I. Income from a tax levy will enable schools to raise the standards of their programs higher than the current program. (advantage 1)
>
> II. Income from a tax levy will enable schools to hire better teachers than the current program. (advantage 2)
>
> III. Income from a tax levy will enable schools to bring the educational environment to a higher level than the current program. (advantage 3)

The assumption underlying the use of the comparative advantages pattern is this: When reasons are presented that show a proposal is a significant improvement over what is being done, then the proposal should be adopted.

Criteria Satisfaction Pattern

criteria satisfaction pattern
an indirect organization that seeks
audience agreement on criteria
that should be considered when
evaluating a particular proposition
and then shows how the proposition
satisfies those criteria

The **criteria satisfaction pattern** is an organizational method that presents evidence to support specific criteria that should be considered when evaluating a particular proposal and then provides evidence about how the specific proposal advocated by the speaker satisfies those criteria. When your audience is opposed to your propositions, you need a pattern of organization that will not aggravate their hostility. The criteria satisfaction pattern will work in this situation because it approaches the proposal indirectly by first focusing on the criteria the audience may find agreeable prior to introducing the specific proposition. A criteria satisfaction organization for the school tax proposition would look like this:

Proposition: I want my audience to vote in favor of the school tax levy on the November ballot.

I. We all want good schools. (a community value)
   A. Good schools have programs that prepare our youth to function in society. (one criterion of good schools)
   B. Good schools are those with the best teachers available. (a second criterion of good schools)
II. Passage of the school tax levy will guarantee good schools.
   A. Passage will enable us to increase the quality of vital programs. (satisfaction of one criterion)
   B. Passage will enable us to hire and keep the best teachers. (satisfaction of the second criterion)

The assumption underlying the criteria satisfaction pattern is this: When a proposal meets a set of agreed-on criteria, it should be adopted.

Motivational Pattern

motivational pattern an
organization that combines problem
solving and motivation, following
a problem solution pattern but
including required steps designed to
heighten the motivational effect of
the organization

The **motivational pattern**, articulated by Allan Monroe who was a professor of Speech at Purdue University, combines problem solving and motivation. It follows a problem solution pattern but includes required steps designed to heighten the motivational effect of the organization. Motivational patterns usually include a five-step, unified sequence that replaces the normal introduction–body–conclusion model: (1) an attention step, (2) a need step that fully explains the nature of the problem, (3) a satisfaction step that explains how the proposal solves the problem in a satisfactory manner, (4) a visualization step that provides a personal application of the proposal, and (5) an action appeal step that emphasizes the specific direction listener action should take. A motivational pattern for the school tax proposition would look like this:

Proposition: I want my audience to vote in favor of the school tax levy on the November ballot.

I. Comparisons of worldwide test scores in math and science have refocused our attention on education. (attention)
II. The shortage of money is resulting in cost-saving measures that compromise our ability to teach basic academic subjects well. (need, statement of problem)
III. The proposed increase is large enough to solve those problems in ways that allow for increased emphasis on academic need areas. (satisfaction, how the proposal solves the problem)

Selecting an Organizational Pattern

1. Write reasons you are planning to use:

2. Select a pattern of organization:

3. State your reasons for choosing this pattern based on your audience analysis and proposed reasons:

    IV. Think of the contribution you will be making not only to the education of your future children but also to efforts to return our educational system to the world level it once held. (visualization of personal application)

    V. Here are "Vote Yes" buttons you can wear to show you are willing to support this much-needed tax levy. (action appeal showing specific direction)

Because motivational patterns are variations of problem solution patterns, the underlying assumption is similar: When the current means are not solving the problem, a new solution that does solve the problem should be adopted.

    Examine your speech goal and review the reason you selected in the previous exercise, then complete the speech assignment and select the pattern of organization you feel would be most effective for you to use. Exhibit 13.6 shows how one student completed this assignment.

EXHIBIT 13.6 Selecting an organizational pattern

1. Write reasons you are planning to use:

    Capital punishment is used in cases where guilt is in question.

    Capital punishment doesn't reduce overcrowding and expenses.

    Capital punishment does not deter crime.

2. Select a pattern of organization: statement of logical reasons

3. State your reasons for choosing this pattern based on your audience analysis and proposed reasons: Audience attitude is generally neutral. Thus no need to develop an organization intended for negative audiences.

Use Emotion to Motivate Audience

motivation forces acting on or within an organism to initiate and direct behavior

emotions subjective experiences triggered by actions or words that are accompanied by bodily arousal and by overt behavior

Principle 5   You are more likely to be able to persuade audiences when you motivate them through appeals to their emotions.

Motivation, the "forces acting on or within an organism to initiate and direct behavior,"[4] results from the use of vivid images and emotional language. Motivation, to a large extent, is based on what Aristotle called *pathos,* or emotional appeal.

Emotions, such as anger, fear, surprise, and joy, are subjective experiences triggered by actions or words that are accompanied by bodily arousal and by overt behavior.[5] Effective persuasive speech development entails both logical and emotional elements that act interdependently, so we need to look for good reasons and for support that will, if properly phrased, arouse these emotions.

As you work on your speeches, think about the kind of emotions you want to arouse, the information necessary to arouse those emotions, and how the information can be phrased for maximum effect. Let's consider each of these.

1. **What emotions do you want your audience to experience as you make your point?** The emotions you want to arouse will differ from speech to speech. For instance, in a speech calling for more humane treatment of the elderly, you may decide that you want your listeners to feel sadness, anger, grief, caring, and perhaps, guilt. In contrast, in a speech designed to get the audience to attend your school's production of a musical, you may want your listeners to feel anticipation, excitement, and enthusiasm.

2. **What information do you have that could be used to stimulate those emotions?** For the speech on the elderly, suppose you have determined that you want your listeners to feel sad about how people in nursing homes are treated. Your information might include data from interviews with elderly individuals whose only talk of the future is the inevitability of death; accounts of social workers explaining that many elderly live totally in the past and are reluctant to talk about or even think about the future; or statistics that show few nursing homes have programs that give their clients anything to look forward to.

3. **Keeping ethical considerations in mind, how can you phrase your information to elicit those emotions?** How well you motivate is likely to depend on how vividly you phrase your information. For instance, for the speech on the elderly you might say:

    Currently, elderly people are alienated from society. A high percentage live in nursing homes, live on small fixed incomes, and exist out of the mainstream of society.

    But with the addition of a question and some language that creates more vivid pictures, you could make this statement more emotionally powerful:

    Currently, elderly people are alienated from the very society that they devoted their entire lives to build. What happens to elderly people in America? They become the forgotten, hidden, silent segment of society. They are warehoused in "old people's homes" so that they can live out their lives and die without being "a bother" to their sons and daughters. Because they must subsist on small fixed incomes, most don't enjoy the fruits of their labor in the bosom of their families. Rather they are robbed of their dignity and forced to live among strangers out of our sight and out of our minds.

    Meaningful emotional appeals can be valid and valuable parts of the introduction and conclusion of your speech. Notice how emotional appeals heighten the power of this introduction and conclusion in a student speech on euthanasia.[6] The student began her speech as follows:

Credibility is important in persuasive speaking. Colin Powell built his credibility through his personal integrity and demonstration of character. The audience's perception of your trustworthiness results from their assessment of your character and your apparent motives for presenting the information.

> Let's pretend for a moment. Suppose that on the upper right-hand corner of your desk there is a button. You have the power by pushing that button to quickly and painlessly end the life of one you love: your brother or father. This loved one has terminal cancer and will be confined to a hospital for his remaining days. Would you push the button now? His condition worsens. He is in constant pain, and he is hooked up to a life-support machine. He first requests, but as the pain increases he pleads for you to help. Now would you push that button? Each day you watch him deteriorate until he reaches a point where he cannot talk, he cannot see, he cannot hear—he is only alive by that machine. Now would you push that button?

After giving reasons for changing our laws on euthanasia, she concluded her speech as follows:

> I ask again, how long could you take walking into that hospital room and looking at your brother or father in a coma, knowing he would rather be allowed to die a natural death than be kept alive in such a degrading manner? I've crossed that doorstep—I've gone into that hospital room, and let me tell you, it's hell. I think it's time we reconsider our laws concerning euthanasia. Don't you?

Regardless of your beliefs about the subject of euthanasia, you would be likely to experience pain as you empathize with her feelings.

In the next chapter, we will take a more detailed look at motivation, incentives, and basic needs.

Develop Your Credibility

Principle 6   You are more likely to persuade your listeners when they have faith in your credibility.

Most studies confirm that speaker credibility has a major effect on audience belief and attitude.[7] In earlier chapters, we outlined the nature of credibility, showing that you will be perceived as a credible speaker if audiences perceive you as knowledgeable, trustworthy, and personable. In a persuasive speech, part of your credibility hinges on whether audience members perceive that you "walk your talk"—

that you really believe in and are personally committed to your goal. For example, Tony wants to give a speech that will motivate class members to choose an "alternative spring break" trip with Habitat for Humanity to help build homes. It will be more credible and persuasive if he has already gone on this trip or if he is signed up to participate this spring break.

Present the Speech Convincingly

Principle 7   You are more likely to persuade an audience if you develop an effective oral presentation style.
Previous chapters have addressed characteristics of presentation that you must develop to increase your effectiveness, including the importance of practicing your speech until your presentation (language and delivery) enhances it. Regardless of how well you apply the previous six principles, convincing presentation is a necessity for effective persuasive speaking.

Critical Thinking and the Persuasive Principles

How do we know that following these principles of persuasion during speech preparation will really help us be effective? To answer this question, you need to understand how critical thinking by audience members affects attitude change. The elaboration likelihood theory developed by social psychologists Richard Petty and John Cacioppo suggests that sometimes people evaluate information in an elaborate way using their critical thinking—and sometimes people process information in a simpler, less critical manner.[8]

SPEECH assignment

Persuasive Speaking

1. Prepare a four- to seven-minute speech in which you affect audience belief or move your audience to action. An outline is required.

2. As an addendum to the outline, you may wish to write a persuasive plan for adapting to your specific audience that includes the following:

   a. How your goal adapts to whether your prevailing audience attitude is in favor, no opinion, or opposed.

   b. What reasons you will use and how the organizational pattern you selected is fitting for your topic and audience.

   c. How you will establish your credibility with this audience.

   d. How you will motivate your audience by using incentives or by appealing to their emotions.

Petty and Cacioppo believe people sometimes process information via a **central route** (using critical thinking) and sometimes via a **peripheral route** (using simple cues). When an issue is really important to us, we are likely to use the central route, looking for good reasons and sound evidence in support. When an issue is less important, or if we don't believe we have the time or energy to really "dig into" the issue, we'll take the peripheral route and accept what is said on the basis of the credibility of the source or appeal of motivational techniques (so well known and used by advertising agencies).

When attitudes are changed as the result of critical thinking, these scholars suggest that the change is likely to last. When attitudes change based on simple cues—such as the credibility of the source or emotional response—the attitude is more

central route using critical thinking to analyze persuasive messages

peripheral route using simple cues to analyze persuasive messages

SPEECH EVALUATION checklist

Persuasive Speech

For one or more of the speeches you hear during a round of persuasive speeches, complete the checklist and then write a two- to five-paragraph evaluation of the speech. See the sample outline and speech that follows.

Check items that were accomplished effectively.

Primary Criteria

_____ **1.** Was the specific goal designed to affect a belief or move to action?

_____ **2.** Did the speaker present clearly stated reasons?

_____ **3.** Did the speaker use facts and expert opinions to support these reasons?

_____ **4.** Was the organizational pattern appropriate for the type of goal and assumed attitude of the audience?

_____ **5.** Did the speaker use emotional language to motivate the audience?

_____ **6.** Was the speaker effective in establishing his or her credibility on this topic?

General Criteria

_____ **1.** Was the specific goal clear?

_____ **2.** Was the introduction effective?

_____ **3.** Were the main points clear?

_____ **4.** Was the conclusion effective?

_____ **5.** Was the language clear, vivid, emphatic, and appropriate?

_____ **6.** Was the speech delivered enthusiastically, with vocal expressiveness, fluently, spontaneously, and directly?

_____ **7.** Was the speaker ethical in handling information?

Evaluate the speech as (check one)

_____ excellent, _____ good, _____ average, _____ fair, _____ poor.

Use the information from your checklist to support your evaluation.

likely to fade. Can you recall times when you listened to a persuasive message, seemed totally drawn to the power of the message, yet within a day or two forgot why you were so enthralled and so changed your mind? This is a sign that you were affected through the peripheral route. Likewise, can you think of times when you listened to a persuasive message, thought about the strengths of the reasons and evidence and changed your mind, and days later could still give the sound reasons in support of that message and your new belief? This is a sign of being affected through the central route of critical thinking.

The speech planning process you have been learning and the persuasive principles focus on providing audience members with sound reasons and solid evidence as the basis for their change of belief or decision to act. But, understanding human nature, we also study how to motivate through emotional appeals and through establishing our personal credibility. As Woodward and Denton report, "the peripheral route of persuasion, although short-term, is still very effective. This is why advertising repetition and use of emotional appeals is very successful."[9]

Finally, Herbert Simons reminds us that both critical and emotional thinking are useful: "Central and peripheral processing are not mutually exclusive; much of the time we use them in combination." He goes on to say, "When we genuinely need information and we know we need it—the lure of a free gift or of a pretty face isn't as likely to work on us. This has been demonstrated in numerous experiments."[10]

SAMPLE persuasive speech

Capital Punishment by Eric Wais[11]

This section presents a sample speech adaptation plan, outline, and transcript given by a student in an introductory speaking course as his first major speech.

Adaptation Plan

A. **How your goal adapts to whether your prevailing audience attitude is in favor, no opinion, or opposed.** I believe that, being college students, most of the audience will lean toward a slightly more liberal view of the topic of capital punishment. While I believe that it is the majority opinion in this country to be in favor of the death penalty, I think most of the audience will at worst be toward the liberal end of that opinion and not be strongly opposed to my goal. But since I do expect the audience to oppose my goal, I plan on focusing on hard statistics rather than opinion. It is hard for the audience's preexisting opinions to get in the way of accepting facts from reputable sources such as the FBI and the Department of Justice.

B. **What reasons you will use, and how the organizational pattern you have selected is appropriate to your topic and audience**. Again, I chose the logical reasons pattern because I feel the best way to deal with an audience I expect to be mildly opposed to my proposition is to keep it as straightforward as possible. I chose the reasons that were least emotional and most logical so that I could back them up with as many facts and statistics as possible without losing their impact.

C. **How you will establish your credibility with this audience.** Since I have no personal credibility myself, I will have to rely on finding the most reliable and reputable sources I can. While some of my more opinionated points are supported by more partisan sources (Death Penalty Information Center, etc.), all of my hard facts come from the FBI and the Department of Justice, which are the most reliable sources of such information available and difficult to dispute.

D. **How you will motivate your audience by appealing to their emotions**. Even though I have chosen to make my speech as logical as possible, I still believe there is a strong element of emotion to the topic of capital punishment. I will try to contain all of my emotional appeals to the introduction and conclusion to avoid conflicting with the hard facts in the body of my speech. But in the introduction and conclusion I will try to appeal to the idea that capital punishment amounts to state-sanctioned murder and that any act of the state is an act of its people and, therefore, an act of the audience themselves. I think this is an element of the topic often overlooked and will therefore appeal to the audience's emotions.

Outline

Specific Goal: I want to convince the audience that capital punishment is not effective.

Introduction

I. It is natural to feel anger toward murderers and to want vengeance.

II. But can we really justify the state-sanctioned murder that capital punishment amounts to?

Thesis Statement: Capital punishment should be abolished because it is not used only in cases of clear guilt, it does not help reduce prison overcrowding and expenses, and it does not deter violent crime.

Body

I. The death penalty is not used only in the cases of clear guilt.
   A. Large numbers of people have been released when their convictions have been overturned.
   B. Some people have been released because they did not have a fair trial.
   C. Many other people sitting on death row may be innocent.

II. The death penalty does not help reduce prison overcrowding and expenses.
   A. Since reinstatement of the death penalty in 1977, only 722 people have been executed.
   B. The cost of incarceration is much less than the cost of execution.

III. The death penalty does not deter crime.

    A. Murder rates in death penalty states are highest per capita.

        1. In 1999, murder rates per capita were 3.6 in non–death penalty states as compared to 5.5 in death penalty states. (FBI)

        2. In neighboring states, the non–death penalty neighbor always has a lower murder rate. (FBI)

    B. Death penalty may actually increase murder rates due to a brutalizing effect.

    C. That death penalty does not deter crime is believed by over 80 percent of criminologists.

Conclusion

I. All of these (not used only in cases of clear guilt, not reducing prison overcrowding and expenses, and not deterring crime) show that capital punishment is ineffective.

II. The real issue then is a moral one: the state is an extension of your will and power—when the state executes someone, you are responsible.

III. Webster defines murder as "the unlawful taking of a human life"—when you lawfully take a human life it is vengeance, not justice.

Sources

Akers, Ronald L., and Michael L. Radelet, "Deterrence and the Death Penalty? The Views of the Experts," *Journal of Criminal Law and Criminology, 87,* February 1996, pp. 1–16.

Death Penalty Information Center, http://www.fbi.gov/

FBI Uniform Crime Reports, http://www.fbi.gov/publish/crime.htm

Hoppe, Christy, "Executions Cost Texas Millions," *Dallas Morning Star,* March 8, 1992, p. 1A.

Isikoff, Michael, and Evan Thomas, "Waiting for Justice," *Newsweek,* May 21, 2001, p. 23.

Thomson, Ernie, "Deterrence versus Brutalization," *Homicide Studies,* May 1977.

U.S. Department of Justice, Bureau of Justice Statistics, http://www.ojp.usdoj.gov/bjs/

Speech and Analysis

Read this speech aloud at least once. Then analyze it on the basis of the primary criteria in the checklist on page 271. To get a complete view of his delivery skills, you can watch the speech under Speech Interactive on your Challenge of Effective Speaking CD-ROM.

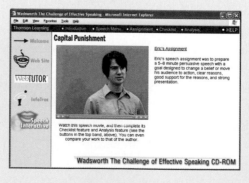

Speech

I know it's natural to feel anger and to want vengeance toward people who commit murder, violent crimes, and horrible atrocities that we hear about in the news: Timothy McVeigh and people like this. And they're all human emotions—we all feel them from time to time. And there's nothing wrong with that, but as a modern society can we really justify the state-sanctioned murder that capital punishment amounts to? You're going to hear three major arguments from supporters of the death penalty as to why it should exist in this country. But I'm going to try to show you today that the death penalty is not used only in cases of clear guilt, that it does not help overcrowded prisons and expenses, and it does not deter violent crime. And for these reasons it should be abolished in this country.

One thing you'll hear often is that the death penalty is only handed down in cases where we're sure of the suspect's guilt. Now I know that even being raised in a conservative family, one of the things I always had a problem with even as a child about the death penalty is what happens if they've got the wrong guy. They can't really fix that, they can't correct their mistakes, and you're all probably aware that the government does not like to admit its mistakes and it certainly doesn't like to publicize its mistakes, but does make them. Since 1977 when the death penalty was reinstated by the Supreme Court, 93 people have been released, 35 since 1994 alone, all after being proven innocent of the crimes they were originally convicted of. I'll give you a couple of good examples. Donald Paradese was convicted in Idaho of murder in 1981. He was scheduled for execution three times. Each time he came within days of being killed. He was finally released this year after twenty years in prison when it was found that prosecutors and police had destroyed key evidence that had showed his innocence. And that his court appointed attorney who put on a three-hour defense in his original trial had never tried a case or had never studied criminal law before.

Some people aren't so lucky. Leo Jones was convicted of murdering a police officer in Florida, also in 1981. He was executed in 1998 by lethal injection. He was convicted only because of a confession he signed after eight hours of police interrogation by an officer who was later convicted of physically torturing suspects to coerce false confessions. These are the people we know about. There are many other cases—and we have no idea how many other mistakes we might have made or how many people are sitting on death row right now who may be innocent of what they were accused of. But some people say that these

Analysis

In this introduction, Eric tries to get the audience to share common feelings.

Notice the strategy Eric uses to frame his reasons for abolishing capital punishment. First, he presents the reasons that are most widely used to justify capital punishment. Then he gives counter-arguments for each of these reasons.

Eric presents the first reason that is often mentioned in support of capital punishment. Then working with his own personal experience, he begins to show that many times the death penalty is handed down in cases where the accused is not really guilty.

In this section Eric provides statistics to show that many mistakes have been made in the past.

Then he moves to two specific examples to dramatize his argument. But to clarify his reasoning he needed to state that in one example the person was saved, but in the other example the person was executed before it could be shown that he was innocent.

Notice how Eric is able to dramatize his examples enough so that we empathize with the suffering of the people involved.

Eric's statement of another reason offered by supporters of capital punishment serves as a transition to his next argument.

are the rare cases and that the death penalty serves other functions and is still viable.

One of the things they say is that our prisons are overcrowded and that it costs too much to house these convicted murderers for forty or fifty years at a time. But the statement really doesn't make a whole lot of sense, especially when dealing with prisoner overcrowding. It's so amazing when I hear that argument, and I do still hear that argument because since 1977 only 722 people have been executed in this country. Last year alone there were over a million people in our prison systems. Seven hundred and twenty-two beds over twenty-five years is not making all the difference in the world. And that's not to mention that our prisons right now in this country as of 2000 according to the U.S. Department of Justice are only at 94 percent capacity and have not been above capacity in almost a decade. And it's actually steadily going down.

The other thing you hear is that we shouldn't be expected to pay for these people who sit in prison for forty or fifty years. What you don't hear about is the price of executions themselves. The price of building the execution equipment, of maintaining the execution equipment, of manning these death houses, of actually performing executions. According to a *Dallas Morning Star* article in 1992, in Texas, a single execution cost 2.3 million dollars. That's three times what it costs to imprison someone for forty years at a maximum security prison in a single cell. Three times what it costs to imprison someone for life in a maximum security prison just to kill them.

Now a lot of people will say, it's not about the money—it's not about prison debts, a death penalty performs a very significant task in our society, it deters violent crime—it helps keep people from committing murders. And this sounds logical to everyone. I know it sounds logical to me. If you tell me, "you do this and you'll be killed," I'm certainly going to think twice about it. Unfortunately when it comes to homicides, statistics just don't connect it up.

According to the FBI, over 75 percent of homicides in this country are aggravated. That means they're not cold, calculated, premeditated crimes. They're crimes of passion, and they're crimes where people aren't thinking about the consequences of their actions. It doesn't mean they don't deserve to be punished and be held responsible for those actions. But it means that they're really not taking into consideration, you know, "I wonder if the death penalty may be applied toward my case later on in this." In 1999, according to the FBI's crime reports in non–death penalty states, of which there are 12 in this country, murders per capita were 3.6 compared to 5.5 in the rest of the thirty-eight states that did have capital

---

In this section he raises questions about the argument that because of overcrowding it costs too much to house convicted murderers.

First, Eric does a good job of emphasizing the small number of those actually put to death.

Notice how his repetition emphasizes the point he is making.

Then he quotes a Department of Justice statistic to show that jails are not overcrowded.

Here Eric moves into the second part of his argument, the costs involved.

Eric uses an example of a Texas execution to show that a single execution costs three times as much as keeping a person in jail for forty years. He then repeats the thrust of his point for emphasis. Still, his argument would be stronger if he could show that this one example truly reflects the costs of executions.

In this third point, Eric counters the argument that the presence of the threat of capital punishment deters crime. Notice how this final reason is the strongest and most important.

He begins with statements that seem to support the argument. Then he announces the real problem—that capital punishment is not a deterrent.

Then he shows that most capital crimes are those of passion, where the guilty aren't thinking about what they've done.

Then he goes on to compare statistics of those states with capital punishment to those states without showing that the murder rates are actually lower in states without capital punishment!

punishment. This has been consistent ever since the death penalty was reinstated in 1977.

Non–death penalty states have always had lower murder rates than death penalty states. There have been some studies such as one done by Dr. Ernie Thompson of the University of Arizona that have shown that there may actually be a brutalizing effect from capital punishment that actually increases murder rates in death penalty states. He's shown that in months after executions, murder rates in these states skyrocket. It has something to do with the state's use of violence against people, which somehow desensitizes and almost encourages violence in its citizens. Now, according to a poll done by Homicide Studies in the *National Criminology Journal,* in 1999, over 80 percent of professional criminologists do not believe that the death penalty effectively deters violent crime. That's 80 percent of professionals who study crime and the psychology of crime, all saying that executing prisoners does not deter violent crime.

Here Eric adds further strength to his argument by presenting a reason why capital punishment may even have an opposite effect—it may make murder more likely.

Now all of these are logical reasons why the death penalty doesn't do the job it's supposed to. It's flawed. It often is used against people when we are not positive of their guilt, it does not help overcrowding of prisons, it does not cut down on expenses, and all signs point to the fact that it does not effectively deter violent crime. But the real issue here is a moral one. You have to remember that when a state executes someone, it's an extension of your will and your power. And if you wouldn't be comfortable flipping a switch or pulling a trigger, or putting the noose around the neck yourself, how can you really justify having the state do it for you? Webster defines murder as the unlawful taking of a human life. The lawful taking of human life is vengeance—not justice. ■

In this speech, Eric does a good job of presenting reasons that show why capital punishment should be abolished.

In his conclusion, Eric reviews his arguments and concludes with an emotional appeal linking capital punishment not with justice but with vengeance. ■

Summary

Persuasive speeches are designed to establish or change a belief or motivate an audience to act. The principles governing persuasive speeches are similar to those presented for informative speeches, as are the steps of speech preparation.

First, write a clear persuasive speech goal, or proposition, stating what you want your audience to believe or do. Second, analyze your audience's interest and knowledge levels and attitude toward your goal. Third, build the body of the speech with good reasons—statements that answer why the proposition is justified. Support reasons with facts and expert opinions. Fourth, create an organization for the speech that suits your goal and your analysis of the audience. Five organizational patterns for persuasive speeches are statement of logical reasons, problem solution, comparative advantages, criteria satisfaction, and motivational. Fifth, motivate your audience by reworking language to appeal to the emotions, especially in your introduction and

Christie had promised to give a speech in support of her good friend Mary Anne for student body president. Although Mary Anne is a good friend, Christie doesn't really believe she is qualified for the office. Still, though, when a friend is in need, you help her.

Christie has good support for her reasons that Mary Anne is a high-energy person and that she is honest. But what Mary Anne wants her to stress are her job qualifications. Although Mary Anne had held an office of class vice president in eleventh grade, she hasn't really been involved in any leadership roles in college.

Christie thought she would talk about what Mary Anne had done in high school and act as if it related to college experience. She was careful so that at no time did she really say that she was talking about college experience, but she worded the material in a way that left that impression. When she finished, she said, "Well, that's the best I can do," and she began practicing the speech.

1. Was Christie's behavior ethical?
2. What might Christie have done to avoid any question of unethical behavior?

conclusion. Sixth, use your credibility advantageously. Especially in persuasive speaking, one of the most important ways of building credibility is to behave in an ethical manner. Seventh, deliver the speech convincingly. Good delivery is especially important in persuasive speaking.

The elaboration likelihood theory developed by social psychologists Richard Petty and John Cacioppo suggests that sometimes people evaluate information in an elaborate way using their critical thinking—and sometimes people process information in a simpler, less critical manner. Central and peripheral processing are not mutually exclusive; much of the time we use them in combination.

CHALLENGE ONLINE

Use your Challenge of Effective Speaking CD-ROM for quick access to the electronic study resources that accompany this text. Included on your CD-ROM is access to the Challenge of Effective Speaking Web site featuring Speech Builder Express at Wadsworth Communication Café, InfoTrac College Edition, and a demo of WebTutor for *The Challenge of Effective Speaking*. The Web site offers chapter-by-chapter access to the Speech Preparation Action Step Activities, InfoTrac College Edition exercises, a digital glossary of key terms, Web links, Speech Preparation Forms, Speech Evaluation Checklists, and quizzes. Review the key terms and complete the InfoTrac College Edition exercise at **http://www.wadsworth.com/product/0534563856**

InfoTrac College Edition Exercise

Using the Subject Guide enter "Three Good Reasons to Just Say No." When you have opened this short article from *Church & State*, September 2000, read the three reasons. Using material you learned from this chapter, consider whether or not the three reasons presented are "good ones." If you believe they are good reasons, what makes them good? If you believe they do not meet the tests of good reasons, what needs to be done to make them good reasons?

Key Terms

attitude *(254)*

behavior *(256)*

belief *(256)*

central route *(271)*

comparative advantages pattern *(265)*

criteria satisfaction pattern *(266)*

emotions *(268)*

motivation *(268)*

motivational pattern *(266)*

move an audience to action *(254)*

opinion *(256)*

peripheral route *(271)*

persuasive speaking *(253)*

problem solution pattern *(264)*

proposition *(254)*

reasons *(261)*

statement of logical reasons *(264)*

strengthen or change a belief *(254)*

Challenge of Effective Speaking CD ROM

Use your Challenge of Effective Speaking CD-ROM to access Speech Interactive. You can also access Speech Builder Express. Complete the Speech Preparation Action Step Activities for your speech.

You can also use your CD-ROM to access Speech Interactive. There you can view "Becoming an Entrepreneur!" for a different approach to persuasive speaking.

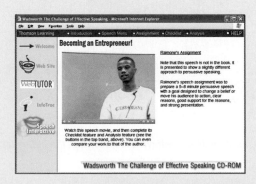

14 Practicing Persuasive Speaking Skills

© David Young-Wolff/PhotoEdit, Inc.

There is nothing to be afraid of if you believe and know that the cause for which you stand is right.
—Martin Luther King Jr., Speech, Savannah, Georgia, January 1, 1961

"Kelly, congratulations! I hear you landed a really plum internship with a political organization for next term."

"Well thanks. In some ways I'm really excited, but in other ways I'm kind of scared."

"What do you mean?"

"The exciting part is that it gives me experience working with really knowledgeable people in a real political campaign. But, what scares me is that they want me to provide ideas for various public speaking situations."

"That sounds great. What's the problem?"

"I'm concerned about whether I've got the background and skills. Not only do they want someone who understands persuasion—you know the whole ethos, logos, pathos bit—but also they expect me to be able to develop the arguments to support our policy positions."

"So? Kelly, you always seem to win the arguments you have with people!"

"Come on—this is different. Not only will I prepare stump speech material, but I'll be preparing material to refute our opponent's arguments and rebut their attacks on ours."

Effective speaking demands that you become skilled in all aspects of persuasion. In the first section of this chapter, Reasoning with Audiences, we describe the basic reasoning process and explain several types of arguments. In the second section, Motivating Audiences, we explain two theoretical perspectives that suggest lines of development that can increase the likelihood of audiences' acting favorably. In the final section of this chapter, Refuting Persuasive Claims, we discuss how you can analyze and then build counterarguments to ill-conceived or unwarranted proposals presented by others.

Reasoning with Audiences

In the previous chapter, we explained that in public speaking reasoning with an audience means presenting reasons and evidence in support of a speech goal. A reason with its supporting evidence is called an **argument**.

argument reason with its supporting evidence

In this section, we describe how to form several types of logical arguments. Then we present an example of a speech (with outline and speech plan) that illustrates how multiple arguments are used when presenting a speech.

Sound reasoning is essential to persuasive speakers like former New York City mayor Rudy Giuliani, who know that their evidence and reasoning will be closely scrutinized in public debate.

Essentials of Reasoning: The Toulmin Method

reasoning the mental process of drawing inferences from factual information

arguing the process of proving a conclusion you have drawn with factual information

Reasoning is the mental process of drawing inferences (conclusions) from factual information. **Arguing** is the process of proving conclusions you have drawn with factual information—reasons and evidence. Thus, when we observe that the engine of our friend's car is "missing" at low speeds and stalling at stoplights, we can reason (draw the inference) that the car needs a tune-up. When we talk with our friend, however, we may need to argue (prove to him) that the car needs a tune-up, because it is "missing" at low speeds and stalling at stoplights.

As you prepare your speeches, you need a method for analyzing the soundness of the reasons or arguments that you are planning to make. The basic elements of an argument are the claim, the support, and the reasoning process, called the warrant.

Claim

claim the proposition or conclusion to be proven so that the audience will believe

The **claim** is the proposition or conclusion to be proven so that the audience will believe. We may call the claim a speech goal (or proposition), conclusion, or inference to be proven. In our example, the claim is "The car needs a tune-up."

Support

data reasons and evidence (facts, opinions, observations, evidence, assumptions, or assertions) that provide the basis for a conclusion of an argument

From our discussion in the previous chapter, we know that we support a claim (the specific goal of our speech) with reasons and evidence. The **data** that support a claim can include both the reasons and the evidence—the facts, opinions, experiences, and observations—that supports the reasons. In the car example, the support for our argument includes two reasons, "missing at low speeds" and "stalling at stoplights," as well as the evidence that supports each of these reasons. In outline form, our example looks like this:

> **Specific Goal (Claim):** I want the audience to believe that the car needs a tune-up.
>
>   **I.** The car misses at low speeds.
>
>   (supported with examples)

II. The car stalls at stoplights.
   (supported with examples)

But how can we know whether this argument's reasoning is sound? To determine the soundness of our arguments, we need to understand the reasoning process.

Reasoning Process

The **reasoning process** is the conscious or subconscious logic that connects the support (reasons and evidence) to the claim (speech goal or proposition). This logic can be verbalized in a sentence that explains how the support is related to the claim. The verbalization of the reasoning process is called a **warrant**.[1] For instance, a person who argues (makes the claim that) "the car needs a tune-up" on the basis of "missing" and "stalling at stoplights" may verbalize the reasoning process with this warrant: "Missing at low speeds and stalling at stoplights *are common indications or signs* that the car needs a tune-up."

Although the warrant may not be verbalized during the speech itself, speakers need to identify the warrant during speech preparation to analyze and test the soundness of their reasoning. Later we will identify the questions to ask to weigh the strength of the warrant (reasoning process).

Stephen Toulmin,[2] a philosopher/rhetorician, developed a system for analyzing arguments that begins by outlining and labeling each part of the argument. Using **C** for claim, **S** for support (reason and evidence, including events), and **W** for warrant or explanation of the reasoning process, we can write the reasoning for our example in outline form as follows:

C I want the owner to believe that the car needs a tune-up. (specific goal)

S **I.** The engine misses at low speeds.
   (plus evidence in support)

   II. The car stalls at stoplights.
   (plus evidence in support)

W (I believe this reasoning is sound because missing and stalling are *major indicators— signs*—of the need for a tune-up.)

The warrant is written in parentheses because it may not actually be stated when the speech is given.

Types and Tests of Arguments

Although an oral argument always includes a claim and support (reasons and/or evidence), different logical relationships can exist between support and claims. The six types of arguments presented here are commonly used in persuasive speeches.

Arguing from Example

When you **argue from example**, you support your claim by providing one or more individual examples. Because you will discover numerous examples in your research for nearly any topic, you are likely to use arguing from example quite frequently. The warrant for an argument from example is this: "What is true in the examples provided is (or will be) true in general or in other instances."

Suppose you are supporting Juanita Martinez for president of the local neighborhood council. Your claim is that "Juanita is electable." In examining her résumé to find support for this claim, you find several examples of her previous victories. She was elected treasurer of her high school junior class, chairperson of her church youth group, and president of her college sorority. Each of these is an example that gives support to the claim. How are the claim and the examples related? We could say,

---

reasoning process the conscious or subconscious logic that leads from the data to the claim

warrant the verbalization of the reasoning process

arguing from example supporting a claim by providing individual examples

"What was true in several instances (Juanita has been elected in four previous races) is true or will be true in general or in other instances (she will be electable in this situation)." Let's look at this argument in speech analysis form:

C   Juanita Martinez is electable.
S   Juanita has won previous elections.
    A.   Juanita won the election for treasurer of her high school junior class.
    B.   Juanita won the election for chairperson of her church youth group.
    C.   Juanita won the election for president of her sorority.
W   (Because Juanita Martinez was elected to previous offices, she is electable for this office.)

But how do we know whether an argument from example is valid? To test the strength of this type of argument answer the following questions.

1. **Are enough examples cited?** Are three elections (junior class treasurer, youth group chairperson, and sorority president) enough examples? Because the instances cited should represent most or all possibilities, enough must be cited to satisfy the listeners that the instances are not isolated or handpicked.

2. **Are the examples typical?** Are the three examples typical of all of her campaigns for office? Typical means that the examples cited must be similar to or representative of most or all within the category. If examples are not typical, they do not support the argument. For instance, since all three of these successes came in youth organizations, they may not be typical of election dynamics in communication organizations. If the three examples are not typical, then the logic of the argument can be questioned. As a speaker, you might search for additional examples that are typical.

3. **Are negative examples accounted for?** In searching for supporting material, we may find one or more exceptions to the argument we wish to make. If the exceptions are minor or infrequent, then they do not necessarily invalidate the argument. For instance, in college Juanita may have run for and lost the chairpersonship of the chess club. That one failure does not necessarily invalidate the argument. If, however, negative examples prove to be more than rare or isolated instances, the validity of the argument is open to serious question. For instance, if you found that Juanita had run for office twelve times and was successful on only the three occasions cited, then the argument would be fallacious. If you believe the negative examples are too common, and you question the logic of the argument, then you will want to use a different type of argument.

Arguing from Analogy

arguing from analogy supporting a claim with a single comparable example that is significantly similar to the subject of the claim

When you **argue from analogy,** you support a claim with a single comparable example that is significantly similar to the subject of the claim. The general statement of the warrant of an argument from analogy is this: "What is true for situation A will also be true in situation B, which is similar to situation A, or will be true in all similar situations." Suppose you wanted to prove that Northwest High should conduct a raffle to raise enough money to buy band uniforms. You could support the claim by analogy with a single example: "East High, a school that is significantly similar to Northwest, conducted a raffle and raised enough money to purchase uniforms for its entire band." The form for this argument from analogy looks like this:

C   Northwest High should conduct a lottery to raise money for band uniforms.
S   East High, which is very similar to Northwest High, raised money through a lottery.
W   (What worked at a very similar school, East High, will work at Northwest High.)

Let us return to the claim that Juanita is electable for president of the senior class. If you discover that Juanita has essentially the same characteristics as Paula Jefferson, who was elected president two years ago (both are very bright, both have a great deal of drive, and both have track records of successful campaigns), then you can use the single example of Paula to form a reason: "Juanita has the same characteristics as Paula Jefferson, who was elected two years ago." Let's look at how the Martinez argument would look in outline form:

C   Juanita Martinez is electable.

S   Juanita has the same characteristics as Paula Jefferson, who was elected two years ago.

    A.   Juanita and Paula are both very bright.

    B.   Juanita and Paula both have a great deal of drive.

    C.   Juanita and Paula both have won other campaigns.

W   (What was true for Paula will be true for Juanita, who has similar characteristics.)

So, the claim is supported by an analogous example; then additional support is offered to validate the analogy.

To test the strength of an argument from analogy, answer the following questions.

1.   **Are the subjects being compared similar in every important way?** Are Paula and Juanita similar in intelligence, drive, and track records in elected offices? If subjects do not have significant similarities, then they are not comparable. If the subjects being compared are not similar in important ways, then you can question the reasoning on that basis.

2.   **Are any of the ways that the subjects are dissimilar important to the outcome?** If Paula is a native of the community but Juanita has only been in the area for a year, is this dissimilarity important? When the dissimilarities outweigh the subjects' similarities, then conclusions drawn from the comparisons may be invalid. So, when you prepare to argue from analogy, be sure to consider dissimilarities.

Arguing from Causation

When you **argue from causation,** you support a claim by citing events that have occurred that bring about the claim. Reasoning from causation says that one or more of the events cited always (or at least usually) bring about a predictable effect or set of effects. The general warrant for arguments from cause can be stated as follows: "If an event (A) came before another event (B) and is associated with that event (A), then we can say that it (A) is the cause of the event (B). For instance, you could develop a causal argument based on the relationship between mortgage interest rates and home sales: "Home sales are bound to increase during the next three months (claim), because mortgage interest rates have dropped markedly recently (causal event)." Let's look at this type of argument in outline form:

arguing from causation   citing events that have occurred that bring about the claim

C   Home sales will increase.

D   Mortgage interest rates have dropped.

W   (Lower interest rates generally lead to higher home sales.)

In researching Juanita's election campaign, you might discover that (1) she has campaigned intelligently and (2) she has won the endorsement of key community leaders. If these two events can be seen as causes for victory, then you can form the argument that Juanita has engaged in behavior that leads to campaign victories, thus supporting the claim that she is electable. The argument would look like this:

Persuasive speakers such as politicians must be as careful with their reasoning and evidence when speaking to a group of supporters as they would be when addressing a more neutral or hostile audience.

AP/Wide World Photos

C   Juanita Martinez will be elected.
S   **A.**   Juanita has campaigned intelligently.
    B.   Juanita has key endorsements.
W   (Intelligent campaigning and getting key endorsements bring about [cause] electoral victory.)

To test the strength of an argument from causation, answer the following questions.

1.   **Are the events alone sufficient to cause the stated effect?** Are intelligent campaigning and key endorsements important enough by themselves to result in winning elections? If the events are truly causes, it means that if these events were eliminated, then the effect would be eliminated as well. If the effect can occur without these events occurring, then you can question the causal relationship.

2.   **Do other events accompanying the cited events actually cause the effect?** Are other factors (such as luck, drive, friends) more important in determining whether a person wins an election? If the other events appear equally or more important in bringing about the effect, then you can question the causal relationship between the data cited and the conclusion. If you believe other data caused the effect, then you can question the reasoning on that basis.

3.   **Is the relationship between the causal events and the effect consistent?** Do intelligent campaigning and key endorsements always (or usually) yield electoral victories? If there are times when the effect has not followed the cause, then you can question whether a causal relationship exists. If you believe the relationship between the cause and the effect is not consistent, then you can question the reasoning on that basis.

Arguing from Sign

arguing from sign   supporting a claim by citing data that signal or indicate the claim

When certain events, characteristics, or situations always or usually accompany something, those events, characteristics, or situations are signs. **Arguing from sign** is supporting a claim by citing information that signals the claim. For instance, your doctor may claim that you have had an allergic reaction because you have hives and are running a slight fever.

The general warrant for reasoning from sign can be stated as follows: "When phenomena usually or always accompanying a specific situation occur, then we can expect that specific situation is occurring (or will occur)." So, the warrant for the allergy argument can be stated as follows: "Hives and a slight fever are indicators (signs) of an allergic reaction." Let's look at this argument in outline form:

C You have had an allergic reaction.

S A. You have hives.

   B. You have a slight fever.

W (Hives and a slight fever are signs of an allergic reaction.)

Signs should not be confused with causes; signs accompany a phenomenon but do not cause it. In fact, signs may actually be the effects of the phenomena. A rash and fever don't cause an allergic reaction; they are indications, or effects, of a reaction.

In analyzing Juanita's campaign, if you notice that Juanita has more campaign workers than all other candidates combined and that a greater number of people from all segments of the community are wearing "Juanita for President" buttons, you may reason that "Juanita's campaign has the key signs of an election victory." A speech outline using this sign argument would look like this:

C Juanita Martinez will be elected.

S A. Juanita has more campaign workers than all other candidates combined.

   B. A greater number of community members are wearing her campaign buttons.

W (The presence of a greater number of campaign posters and buttons than the opponents have is a sign/indicator of victory.)

To test the strength of an argument from sign, answer the following questions.

1. **Do the signs cited always or usually indicate the conclusion drawn?** Do large numbers of campaign workers and campaign buttons always (or usually) indicate election victory? If the data can occur independently of the conclusion, then they are not necessarily indicators. If the signs cited do not usually indicate the conclusion, then you can question the reasoning on that basis.

2. **Are a sufficient number of signs present?** Are campaign workers and buttons enough to indicate a victory? Events or situations are often indicated by several signs. If enough signs are not present, then the conclusion may not follow. If there are insufficient signs, then you can question the reasoning on that basis.

3. **Are contradictory signs in evidence?** Are campaign buttons thrown away in great numbers? If signs usually indicating different conclusions are present, then the stated conclusion may not be valid. If you believe that contradictory signs are evident, then you can question the reasoning on that basis.

Arguing from Definition

When you **argue from definition**, you support a claim by citing supporting evidence that proves the claim has the distinguishing characteristics commonly associated with similar phenomena. The general warrant for an argument from definition is this: "If the characteristics that are primary criteria for describing a particular phenomenon are present in the claim, then we can call the claim by that phenomenon's name." For instance, you may wish to argue that a movie is of Academy Award caliber on the basis of its outstanding plot, superior acting, and excellence in direction. The warrant for this argument is that excellence in plot, acting, and directing are primary criteria that define "Academy Award caliber."

arguing from definition supporting a claim by citing as supporting evidence that the claim has the distinguishing characteristic commonly associated with similar phenomena

In researching Juanita's campaign, if you notice that Juanita uses good judgment, that her goals are in the best interests of the community, and that she is decisive, you may argue that "Juanita is a leader." In outline form, the argument would look like this:

C Juanita is a leader.
S **A.** Juanita shows good judgment.
   B. Juanita's goals are in the best interests of the group.
   C. Juanita is decisive.
W (Good judgment, consideration of group interests, and decisiveness are key characteristics in the definition of leadership.)

To test the strength of an argument from definition, answer the following questions.

1. **Are the characteristics cited the most important ones in identifying the phenomenon?** Are judgment, consideration of group interests, and decisiveness the important distinguishing criteria for describing leadership? If other criteria are considered to be more important, then the reasoning is questionable.

2. **Are all important aspects of the definition included in the statement of the characteristics?** For example, even if the three criteria mentioned are important, are other criteria, such as drive, even more important? If a more important criterion is not mentioned, then the reasoning may be questionable.

3. **Are the characteristics cited better described by some other term?** For instance, are the three criteria cited better descriptions of followers than leaders? If the characteristics or criteria are most often associated with another word, then the reasoning may be questionable.

Arguing from Authority

arguing from authority supporting a claim with the opinions of one or more experts

When you **argue from authority,** you support a claim with the opinions of one or more experts. Reasoning from authority says that one or more expert opinions are enough to establish the claim. The general form of the warrant for arguments from authority can be stated as follows: "If these experts believe the claim to be true, then it must be true." For instance, you could claim that the United States has to become more conservation conscious based on waste management authority Gina Gordan's statement that "We have been a throwaway society—we simply have to change our ways." The warrant for this argument might be stated as follows: "If an authority on waste disposal favors limiting throwaway items, it should be done." In outline form, the argument would look like this:

C The United States has to be more conservation conscious.
S Statement of waste management authority: "We have been a throwaway society—we simply have to change our ways."
W (Expert opinion supports the claim.)

If, in analyzing Juanita's campaign, you notice that an influential editorial writer for the local paper predicts her election, then you can form an argument that "Juanita is supported by a local opinion leader." In outline form, the reasoning would look like this:

C Juanita will be elected.
S An influential editorial writer for the local paper has said, "Because Juanita Martinez is the best-qualified candidate, she should be elected president of the community council."
W (If an authority supports a candidate's election, it is likely to occur.)

To test the strength of an argument from authority, answer the following questions.

1. **Is the source of the testimony a recognized authority?** For instance, is an editorial writer for the local paper an authority on community voting patterns?

2. **Is the opinion consistent with that of other authorities?** The more authorities that support an idea, the stronger the support is. If you find other authorities that disagree with the claim, then you should question the claim on that basis.

Combining Arguments in a Speech

An effective speech usually contains several reasons, which are based on various types of arguments. For a speech with the goal "I want my audience to believe that Juanita is electable," you might choose to present three of the reasons we've been working with. Suppose you selected the following:

   I. Juanita has run successful campaigns in the past. (argued by example)
      A. Juanita was successful in her campaign for treasurer of her high school class.
      B. Juanita was successful in her campaign for chairperson of her church youth group.
      C. Juanita was successful in her campaign for president of her sorority.
  II. Juanita has engaged in procedures that result in campaign victory. (argued by cause)
      A. Juanita has campaigned intelligently.
      B. Juanita has key endorsements.
 III. Juanita is a strong leader. (argued by definition)
      A. Juanita shows good judgment.
      B. Juanita always considers the best interests of the group.
      C. Juanita is decisive.

Just as each of our reasons is presented as an argument, so too is the overall speech. We need to determine what type of argument we are making. What relationship do all three of these reasons have with the overall claim? That is, how do running successful campaigns in the past, being engaged in procedures that result in victory, and being a strong leader relate to whether Juanita is electable? Are they examples of electability? Do they cause one to be elected? Are they signs that usually accompany election? Do they distinguish a person who is electable from one who is not? As you study this example, you will recognize that the warrant is best stated this way: "Running successful campaigns in the past, being engaged in procedures that result in victory, and being a strong leader are all signs of electability." Now you can test the soundness of the overall argument by using the tests of sign argument listed earlier.

Avoiding Fallacies of Reasoning

When you think you have finished constructing your reasons, take a minute to make sure you haven't been guilty of any of these four common fallacies.

1. **Hasty generalization**. Because the supporting instances cited should represent most or all possibilities, enough must be cited to satisfy the listeners that the instances are not isolated or handpicked. A very common fallacy of reasoning, hasty generalization, means presenting a generalization (perhaps a reason) that is either not supported with evidence or perhaps supported with only one weak example.

hasty generalization presenting a reason or other generalization supported by a single weak example or none at all

2. **False cause.** False cause means attributing causation to an event that is not related to, or does not produce, the effect. It is human nature to look for causes for events, but identifying something that happened or existed before the event

false cause attributing causation to an event that is not related to, or does not produce, the effect

or at the time of the event and labeling it as the cause is often a fallacy. Think of the people who blame loss of money, sickness, and problems at work on black cats that ran in front of them, or mirrors that broke, or ladders they walked under. We recognize these as false cause superstitions.

appeal to authority relying on the testimony of someone who is not an expert on the issue at hand

3. **Appeal to authority.** When an argument from authority relies on testimony from a famous person who is not really an expert on the issue, the result is a fallacy known as appeal to authority. For instance, advertisers are well aware that the public idolizes athletes, movie stars, and television performers, and are likely to accept their word on subjects these stars may know little about. When a celebrity tries to get the viewer to purchase a car based on the celebrity's supposed "expert" knowledge, the argument is a fallacy.

ad hominem argument an attack on the person making the argument rather than on the argument itself

4. **Ad hominem argument.** An ad hominem argument is an attack on the person making the argument rather than on the argument itself. Literally, ad hominem means "to the man." For instance, if Michael Jordan presented the argument that athletics are important to the development of the total person, the reply "Great, all we need is some jock justifying his own existence" would be an example of an ad hominem argument.

Such a personal attack is often made as a smokescreen to cover a lack of good reasons and evidence. Ad hominem name-calling is used to try to encourage the audience to ignore a lack of evidence, and it is often used in political campaigns. Make no mistake, ridicule, name-calling, and other personal attacks are at times highly successful, but they almost always are fallacious.

Write a critique of one or more of the speeches given to meet this assignment. Because the focus of this assignment is on reasoning, use the Speech of Reasons Checklist.

SPEECH assignment

A Speech of Reasons

Prepare a four- to six-minute speech in which the focus or force of your persuasion rests on the presentation and development of two to four reasons.

The speech goal may be to affect a belief or to move to action. Thus, the emphasis in this assignment is not on the type of proposition but on the arguments supporting it. Each main point should be a reason that is supported with good evidence. Select your reasons on the basis of soundness of argument and potential impact on the intended audience. The main points of your outline are likely to follow a statement of logical reasons, problem solution, or comparative advantages pattern.

As you develop your plan for adapting the speech to your audience, be sure to discuss the following questions:

1. How will you get, build, and maintain audience interest in your topic?
2. How much background information will you need to present to prepare the audience to understand your reasons?
3. Why did you organize your reasons in this way?
4. How will you establish your credibility with this audience?

Speech of Reasons

Check all items that were accomplished effectively.

Primary Criteria

_____ **1.** Was the specific goal clear?

_____ **2.** Was the specific goal designed to affect a belief or move to action?

_____ **3.** Did the speaker present clearly stated reasons?

_____ **4.** Did each reason directly support the specific goal?

_____ **5.** Was each reason important to the audience's acceptance of the goal?

_____ **6.** Did the speaker use facts and expert opinions to support these reasons?

_____ **7.** Was the evidence for the reasons well documented?

General Criteria

_____ **1.** Was the specific goal clear?

_____ **2.** Was the introduction effective?

_____ **3.** Was the organizational pattern appropriate for the intent and content of the speech?

_____ **4.** Was the conclusion effective?

_____ **5.** Was the language clear, vivid, emphatic, and appropriate?

_____ **6.** Was the delivery convincing?

Evaluate the speech as (check one)

_____ excellent, _____ good, _____ average, _____ fair, _____ poor.

Use the information from your checklist to support your evaluation.

SAMPLE **speech**

Dangerous Trucks
by Charone S. Frankel[3]

This section presents a sample persuasive-speech adaptation plan, outline, and revised speech delivered by Charone S. Frankel from San Francisco State University at a speech contest.

Adaptation Plan

Audience Analysis: My audience ranges in age from late teens to mid-twenties and are all college students.

1. **Creating and maintaining interest.** I will try to motivate them by beginning with a vivid example that I believe will get their attention and get them emotionally involved. Then, throughout the speech, I will try to relate my information to audience experiences.

2. **Background knowledge.** My perception is that my audience is neutral on the subject of truck safety—largely because they are not familiar with the extent of the problem. But since most of us have had occasion to be fearful of the number of trucks and the way they're driven on major highways, I think the audience will be willing to listen to me. I will attempt to build a positive attitude by using information that they can relate to and understand.

3. **Organization.** I have organized my speech following a problem solution order. Since I believe that my audience will be at least neutral at the start, I think this straightforward organization will work.

4. **Building credibility.** I plan to build credibility by showing my familiarity with material that illustrates the problems in the trucking industry. I have good sources, and I will document key information throughout the speech.

Outline

Specific Goal: I want my audience to believe that we should solve the problem of highway deaths caused by unsafe trucks.

Introduction

I. On the night Heidi Jorgenson was killed in a truck accident, she had been planning her wedding.

II. The trucking industry must be held accountable for their increasing number of accidents.

Thesis Statement: Unsafe trucking is a growing problem that should be corrected before more people lose their lives needlessly.

Body

I. Trucking safety is a major problem.

    A. The more than 75 million trucks traveling in the United States are involved in some 250,000 crashes and 6,000 fatalities every year.

    B. While fatality rates for most vehicles have remained constant, truck-related deaths have risen 20 percent since 1992.

(Now that we've seen the extent of the problem, let's look at why it exists.)

II. The trucking industry has some terrible safety habits.

    A. Worst is the practice of making truckers drive too many hours.

        1. Thirty percent of truck wrecks are caused by driver fatigue.

        2. Truckers drive 66 to 75 hours a week even though they are supposed to be limited to 60 hours.

        3. The American Trucking Association wants changes in laws to allow truckers to stay on the road longer.

    B. Nearly as bad is the fact that the trucking industry is not bothering to use new safety equipment that is available.

       1. Trucking companies are skeptical of the costs.

       2. Moreover, trucking companies refuse to recognize the safety benefits.

(The problem is great, but the cure is relatively easy.)

III. The problem can be greatly reduced in two ways.

    A. First, the government needs to take a more active role.

       1. The government needs to be prodded to enforce laws that are already on the books.

       2. The government needs to pass legislation that would increase fines for safety violations.

       3. The government needs to pass legislation requiring companies to install safety equipment.

    B. Second, we as individuals can help.

       1. We can lobby Congress to act.

       2. We can take a more active role in following safety practices.

Conclusion

I. We have seen the seriousness of the problem.

II. We must work to solve the problem if we think our lives are worth more than the paltry $2,400 the trucking company was fined for the accident that killed Heidi.

Sources

Chappell, Lindsay. "Push for Big Rig Safety May Benefit Suppliers." *Automotive News*, September 6, 1999, p. 20.

Lavelle, Marianne. "The Killer Trucks: Lax Safety Rules, Long Hours Wreak Havoc on the Roads." *U.S. News & World Report*, September 13, 1999, pp. 12–18.

"Big Rig Crash." KTVU News, Channel 2, January 24, 2000.

"McCain-Schuster Motor Carrier Bill." *Congressional Daily*, May 27, 1999.

Speech and Analysis

Read this speech aloud at least once. Then analyze it on the basis of the primary criteria in the checklist on page 291. This is an edited version of the speech as it was originally given. On the Challenge of Effective Speaking CD-ROM, under Speech Interactive, listen to the speech as it was originally given and then compare it with this revised version.

Speech

At 10 P.M. on May 27th of last year, Heidi Jorgenson and her fiancé, Doug, were driving home after a meeting with their priest at which they planned their upcoming wedding. Without warning, a 300-pound steel blade fell off a tractor-trailer coming toward them in the opposite lane and sheared off the top passenger side of Doug and Heidi's car, killing Heidi instantly.

Later it was discovered that the trucker was driving illegally, for his company had failed to obtain an oversized-load permit. The driver and company were fined

Analysis

Charone begins with an emotional anecdote designed to get attention and to arouse an emotional reaction from her audience.

twenty-four hundred dollars. Twenty-four hundred dollars for taking a human life! Does that sound like justice? Probably not, but according to the *U.S. News & World Report,* September 13, 1999, the trucking industry has been blatantly breaking the law and getting away with it for years. Minimally enforced safety regulations and nearly nonexistent punishment of violators have caused heavy trucks to become by far the most dangerous vehicles on the road.

Unsafe trucking is a growing problem that must be corrected before more people lose their lives. In addressing this issue we will examine the problem, show why it exists, and look at the solutions that must be enacted if we are to solve this problem.

Let's start with the point that trucking safety is a major problem. According to the *U.S. News & World Report,* there are about 75 million trucks traveling more than 160 trillion miles a year throughout the United States. According to the *Journal of Safety and Health,* these trucks are involved in close to 250,000 crashes and 6,000 fatalities every year.

Let's get a mental picture of what 6,000 fatalities really means. Take the total number of people here at this tournament (500), and multiply that by twelve. And while fatality rates for most types of vehicles have remained constant over the years, truck-related deaths have actually risen 20 percent since 1992, hear that—20 percent, according to the May 27, 1999, issue of *Congress Daily.*

So the question a reasonable person might ask, then, is "Why have trucks become so dangerous?" By taking a close look at the current system, we'll see how the trucking industry practically invites tragedies like Heidi Jorgensen's.

My point? The trucking industry has some terrible safety habits. Worst of all is the widespread practice of making truckers drive . . . and drive . . . and drive until they are barely conscious. Jim Hall, Chairman of the National Transportation Safety Board, says that 30 percent of all truck wrecks are actually caused by driver fatigue. Numerous studies have shown that truckers routinely dust past the federal limit of 60 hours a week on the road. In fact, a study done last year for the Department of Transportation shows that truckers are averaging 66 hours on the road behind the wheel and 75 hours if they don't belong to a union. Can you imagine driving 75 hours a week? And that's apparently still not enough because the American Trucking Association says that its top priority is to change the laws to allow truckers to stay on the road longer!

But in addition to staying on the road too much, most of the trucking industry is simply not bothering to use a multitude of new safety equipment that is available. The reason, according to the September 6th, 1999, *Automotive News,* is that trucking companies are skeptical about the costs and benefits of safety devices. To put it another way, trucking companies don't feel that saving lives of people like you and me is enough of a "benefit" to justify spending money on safety equipment. Clearly it is the attitudes and policies of both our government and the trucking industry that are causing these 6,000 deaths every year.

The good news is that solving this problem is a fairly straightforward process. Since we cannot rely on the trucking industry to regulate itself, our government needs to step in and start forcing trucking companies to clean up their acts.

First of all, current legislation needs to be enforced a lot more strictly. No more 75-hour weeks for drivers! We also need to pass new legislation that would increase fines for safety violations and make it mandatory that truckers rest for 10 to 14 hours between hauls. Furthermore, it is imperative that trucking companies be required by law to install safety equipment in their vehicles. According to the *Automotive News,* for about an additional 15 percent of what trucks currently cost, they can have new anti-rollover technology, more powerful disc brakes, a crash avoidance sensor system, and an onboard computerized data recorder that would prevent speedy drivers from falsifying their logbooks.

More importantly, we as individuals need to realize that we have a vested interest in making trucks safer. We all must support truck safety legislation. One thing you can do is lobby in favor of former President Clinton's proposal to increase fines and make 10- to 14-hour rests between hauls mandatory. Another thing you can do that may have a direct impact on how safe the roads are for you is to take an active role in protecting yourself. Make sure to give those big trucks plenty of clearance. Don't follow them too closely, and remember: if you can't see their mirrors, they can't see you. These things will help make the roads safer for all of us.

We have now taken a look at the problem of unsafe trucking. We have seen how both industry carelessness and government apathy have caused close to 6,000 deaths each year, and we have seen that there is a clear solution. Unsafe trucking is a growing problem, and it must be corrected before more people lose their lives. Heidi Jorgensen was supposed to have been married last October. Instead, she is in the ground. The trucking industry has been getting away with murder, and it is going to continue until we decide to put an end to it. I certainly hope you think that your life is worth more than 2,400 dollars. ∎

Motivating Audiences

Reasoning provides a logical base for persuasion and a rationale for changing an audience's attitude; motivation brings an audience to action. In the previous chapter, we defined motivation as "forces acting on or within an organism to initiate and direct behavior,"[4] and we discussed how language that arouses emotions can motivate. In this section, we look at two specific approaches for motivating audiences: weighing incentives and meeting needs.

Weighing Incentives

People are more likely to act when the speech goal presents incentives that outweigh costs.

An **incentive** is "a goal objective that motivates."[5] Incentives (rewards) include economic gain, good feelings, prestige, or other positive outcomes. If you can earn money by turning in cans and bottles to a recycling center, then you might see earning money as an incentive to recycle. Earning money may be a meaningful incentive for someone short of cash, but not necessarily meaningful for someone who has money or who doesn't care about earning relatively small amounts of money.

People are more likely to be motivated by incentives (rewards) if they outweigh the costs.[6] **Costs** are units of expenditure such as time, energy, money, or other negative outcomes.

According to Thibaut and Kelley, the originators of incentive theory, each of us seeks situations in which our behavior will yield us rewards in excess of the costs; or, conversely, each of us will continue our present behavior unless we are shown that either lower costs or higher rewards will come from changing a particular behavior. Consider an example. Suppose you are asking your audience to volunteer an hour a

incentives (rewards) goal objectives that motivate, such as economic gain, good feelings, prestige, or other positive outcomes

costs units of expenditure such as time, energy, money, or other negative outcomes

When Bill Gates talks about using Microsoft® products, he is likely to give his audience incentives to motivate their behavior.

© Gary Nolan/CORBIS

week to help adults learn to read. The time you are asking them to give is likely to be perceived as a *cost* rather than as an incentive; however, you may be able to describe volunteering in a way that is perceived as a **reward**, a meaningful incentive. That is, you may be able to get members of the audience to feel civic-minded, responsible, or helpful as a result of volunteering time for such a worthy cause. In the speech, if you can show that those rewards or incentives outweigh the cost, you can increase the likelihood of volunteering.

reward a meaningful incentive

In your speech, then, you must achieve one of the following:

1. Show that the time, energy, or money investment is small.
2. Show that the benefits in good feelings, prestige, economic gain, or other possible rewards are high.

The speech at the end of this section is an excellent example of the use of this strategy.

Using Incentives to Meet Needs

People are more likely to act when incentives satisfy a strong but unmet need. Many theorists who take a humanistic approach to psychology have argued that incentives are most powerful when they meet basic needs. Early work on needs theory was done by Abraham Maslow. He suggested that people are more likely to act when a speaker's incentive satisfies a strong unmet need in members of the audience.

hierarchy of needs five categories arranged in order of importance moving from physiological needs, safety needs, belongingness and love needs, esteem needs, to self-actualization needs

Maslow suggested a **hierarchy of needs** that is particularly useful in providing a framework for needs analysis. Maslow divided basic human needs into five categories arranged in a hierarchy that begins with the most fundamental needs. The five categories illustrated in Exhibit 14.1 are (1) physiological needs, including food, drink, and life-sustaining temperature; (2) safety and security needs, including long-term

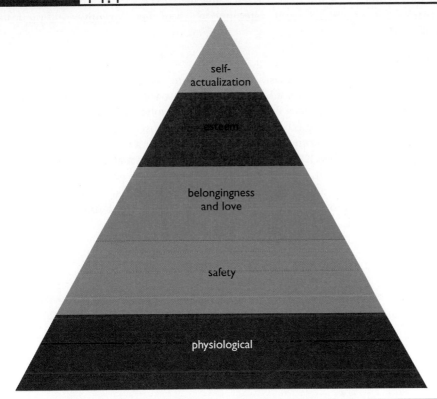

survival and stability; (3) belongingness and love needs, including the need to iden-tify with friends, loved ones, and family; (4) esteem needs, including the quest for material goods, recognition, and power or influence; and (5) self-actualization needs, including the need to develop one's self to realize one's full potential.[7] By placing these needs in a hierarchy, Maslow suggested that one set of needs must be met or satisfied before the next set of needs emerges. In theory, then, a person will not be motivated to meet an esteem need of gaining recognition until basic physio-logical, safety, and belongingness and love needs have been met.

What is the value of this analysis to you as a speaker? First, it suggests the kinds of needs you may want to appeal to in your speeches. Second, it enables you to under-stand why a line of development will work on one audience and fail with another. For instance, in difficult economic times, people are more concerned with physiological and safety needs and will be less responsive to appeals to affiliation and altruism. Thus, in recessionary times, fund-raisers for the arts experience far more resistance to giving than they do during economic upswings. Third, and perhaps most crucial, it alerts you to the need for analysis. When your proposition conflicts with a felt need, you have to be prepared with a strong alternative in the same category or in a more fundamental category. For instance, if your proposal is going to cost people money (higher taxes), you will have to show how the proposal satisfies a comparable need (perhaps by increasing their security).

Let us make this discussion more specific by looking at just a few powerful incentives for action. Once you have selected a specific speech goal and have determined reasons for its acceptance, try to determine which of these incentives will motivate your audience.

Wealth

The desire for wealth—the acquisition of money and material goods—is an incentive that grows out of an esteem need. For example, those with little money for a car can perhaps be motivated to buy a Ford Escort or a Chevrolet Geo because these cars get good gas mileage and are economical to operate. Those who have a great deal of money can perhaps be motivated to buy a Rolls Royce or a Cadillac because they are prestigious. If your speech goal affects audience wealth or material goods positively, you may want to stress it. On the other hand, if your speech goal requests money, be prepared to cope with an audience's natural resistance. You may be able to appeal to another motive from the same category (esteem) or from a more fundamental category to override any money the audience will have to give up.

SPEECH assignment

Motivating Action

1. Prepare a four- to seven-minute persuasive speech designed to bring your audience to action.

2. As an addendum to the outline, write a persuasive plan for adapting to your specific audience. For this particular assignment, the plan should have short sections in which you answer the following questions:

   a. How will you get, build, and maintain audience interest in your topic?

   b. How much background information will you need to present to prepare the audience to understand your speech?

   c. What organizational pattern will you follow? For this speech you are likely to select the pattern (statement of logical reasons, comparative advantages, problem solution, criteria satisfaction, or motivational) that you believe is most likely to increase your chance of motivating this audience.

   d. How will you establish your credibility with this audience?

   e. What overall strategy will you use in motivating your audience to act? You are likely to want to show incentives for the action that outweigh costs of time, energy, or money invested, and show that incentives meet such major needs, motives, or values as wealth, power, conformity, pleasure, and so on.

Power

Another esteem need incentive is power. For many people, personal worth depends on their power over their own destiny, power over others, and the recognition and prestige that come from the exercise of power. If your proposition enables a person, group, or community to exercise power, it may be worth emphasizing. On the other hand, if your speech takes power away from some or all of your listeners, you will need to provide strong compensation to motivate them.

Conformity

Conformity is a major belongingness need incentive for nearly everyone. Conformity grows out of a need for belongingness. People often behave in a given way because a friend, a neighbor, an acquaintance, or a person in the same age bracket behaves that way. Although some people will be more likely to do something if they can be the first to do it or if it makes them appear distinctive, most people feel more secure when they act in ways that conform with others of their kind. The old saying that there is strength in numbers certainly applies to conformity. If you can show that many people similar to the members of your audience favor your plan, that argument may well provide motivation.

Pleasure

When people are given a choice of actions, they often pick the one that gives them the greatest pleasure, enjoyment, or happiness. On at least one level, pleasure is a self-actualizing need; however, it also operates as an esteem need. If your speech relates to something that is novel, promises excitement, is fun to do, or offers a challenge, you can probably motivate your audience on that basis.

These are only four possible incentives for action growing out of basic audience needs. Sex appeal, responsibility, justice, and many others operate within each of us. If you discover that you are not relating your material to basic audience needs, then you probably need to revise your procedure.

Knowing which needs an audience has and appealing to those needs are two different things. To maximize your effectiveness, you must understand how to trigger these needs.

What happens when your specific goal does not meet a specific audience need? Either you can change the wording of your goal so that it is in tune with audience needs, or you can work to create or uncover an audience need that the specific goal will meet. For instance, if you are giving a speech intended to motivate the audience to go to dinner at Le Parisien (a very expensive restaurant), your goal may meet a need to eat out occasionally but be in opposition to most people's need to eat for a reasonable price. For this speech to be effective, you must either change the specific goal to recommend a more modest restaurant or arouse some needs that would be met by going to Le Parisien.

In planning strategy in terms of basic needs, ask yourself these questions:

1. What needs does this audience have at this time?
2. How can I develop my reasons so that they relate to the dominant needs of this audience?

Write a critique of one or more of the speeches given to meet this assignment. Because the focus of this assignment is on motivation, use the Speech of Motivation Evaluation Checklist.

Speech of Motivation

Check all items that were accomplished effectively.

Primary Criteria

_____ **1.** Did the speech goal call for a specific audience action?

_____ **2.** Were the reasons stated clearly and vividly?

_____ **3.** Were the reasons directed to the needs of this audience?

_____ **4.** Did the speaker use facts and expert opinions to support these reasons?

_____ **5.** Was the speaker effective in establishing his or her credibility on this topic?

_____ **6.** Did the speaker lead the audience to believe that the benefits to be gained from the action far outweigh costs of time, energy, or money invested; or

_____ **7.** Did the speaker create dissonance in the audience that could only be relieved by the action of the specific goal; or

_____ **8.** Was the speaker ethical in handling material?

General Criteria

_____ **1.** Was the specific goal clear?

_____ **2.** Was the introduction effective?

_____ **3.** Was the organizational pattern appropriate for the intent and content of the speech?

_____ **4.** Was the conclusion effective?

_____ **5.** Was the language clear, vivid, emphatic, and appropriate?

_____ **6.** Was the delivery convincing?

Evaluate the speech as (check one)

_____ excellent, _____ good, _____ average, _____ fair, _____ poor.

Use the information from your checklist to support your evaluation.

SAMPLE speech

This section presents a sample speech adaptation plan, outline, and transcript given by a student in an introductory speaking course for her speech of motivation.

Notes to Neighbors by Dana Bowers[8]

Adaptation Plan

Audience Analysis: My audience ranges in age from late teens to mid-twenties. They are all college students of varying majors and classes.

1. **Creating and maintaining interest.** I plan to begin the speech by getting my audience to see the extent of the problem. Throughout the speech I will rely on personal experiences to maintain interest. And wherever possible I will try to identify with audience experience.

2. **Background knowledge.** I do not believe the information I will present is difficult to understand. Early in the speech I will outline what participating in Notes to Neighbors requires.

3. **Organization.** I have organized my speech following a motivational pattern. I will get attention in the introduction. I will show the nature of the problem as well as show that student participation is an easy way of helping to solve the problem. Then I will help the class visualize the nature of the problem—this will serve to motivate them to follow through with their volunteering time.

4. **Building credibility.** I plan to build credibility primarily by sharing my experiences in working with the program.

5. **Motivation.** During my preparation I found that my audience was sympathetic with the needs of supporting cancer research, so I am focusing on motivating them to act. Not only will I show that the requirements of participation are easy to meet, but also that spending the little time and money will do so much.

Outline

Specific Goal: I want the audience to sign up for the American Cancer Society's Notes to Neighbors.

Introduction

I. I bet all of you know that cancer is a leading cause of death.

II. And I know from talking with you that many of you know the helpless feeling of dealing with a person with cancer.

III. But there's a very easy way that you can help.

Thesis Statement: I want all of you to sign up for the Notes to Neighbors program because the demand for donations is tremendous and Notes to Neighbors is a realistic way for students to contribute in the fight against cancer.

Body

I. The American Cancer Society is only able to meet a small amount of the demand for private research funding.

    A. Of the more than 2,000 applications for research grants, the American Cancer society was only able to fund 491 of them.

    B. This means that there are more willing researchers than there is money available to fund the research.

        1. Our efforts through Notes to Neighbors would help increase the amount of money available for researchers.

        2. The more research that is done, the closer we get to a cure that may stop the suffering.

II. Notes to Neighbors is an easy, realistic way for students to contribute to the fight against cancer.

A. Notes to Neighbors costs the volunteer a maximum of a five-dollar book of stamps.

    1. know that there are times when I've only had five dollars to get through the rest of the week.

    2. Last year I persuaded my boss to donate five dollars for my book of stamps so that helping didn't really cost me anything.

B. The Notes to Neighbors program takes a maximum of two hours, once a year, to complete.

    1. I know all of our time is precious.

    2. Last year I was able to address my envelopes in only forty-five minutes.

    3. Moreover, I was able to accomplish the task in my spare time at work.

Conclusion

I. So we see that research is necessary and the Notes to Neighbors program is easy to complete.

II. But if I still have not convinced you, let me ask how many of you have actually taken care of someone with cancer?

A. Let me tell you about my experience.

B. Isn't it worth the small amount of money and time that might reduce that half a million people who now die of cancer?

C. Remember those people are somebody's children, mothers, fathers, or siblings—Won't you help?

Sources

Experience: Last spring I participated in the Notes to Neighbors campaign.
American Cancer Society Web site, http://www.cancer.org/ See progress Newsletter, Fall, 1998, Funding
Ohio Department of Health Web site, http://www.odh.state.oh.us/ See "Data and Statistics" then "Cancer Incidence"
Telephone interview: Cincinnati Chapter of American Cancer Society

Speech and Analysis

Read this speech aloud at least once. Then analyze it on the basis of primary criteria on the checklist on page 300.

Analysis

Dana uses a series of statistics to get audience attention.

Here she identifies with the audience.

Speech

Cancer is a leading cause of death. Nationally it kills over half a million people a year. In Ohio, according to the Ohio Department of Health, more than 25,000 people have cancer. And, in Hamilton County, where a lot of us work and live and go to school, over 2,000 people have cancer.

Now I know from asking that a lot of you have said that you know someone that had or now has cancer. And, so I think you know how I feel. It's a strange feeling, it's a very helpless feeling watching someone you love suffer from cancer. And I've discovered something that helps me fight this feeling and that's volunteering for the American Cancer Society's fund-raising program called Notes to Neighbors.

This program asks its volunteers to address and mail form letters asking for donations from people in their own area, and they also provide the addresses and forms and lists for these letters. All the volunteer has to do is send out the notes, receive the donations, and then send the total donations to the American Cancer Society. I wish you'd all sign up for Notes to Neighbors because the demand for donations is tremendous. And doing this for neighbors is a really great way to fight against cancer.

Why should you participate in this program? First, because the American Cancer Society is able to meet only a small amount of the demand for private research funding. As you can see (visual aid) out of 2,225 applications for grants (these are private grants mind you), only 491 were able to be funded by the American Cancer Society. That's only 21 percent. Another 231 (about 11%) of the applications were accepted, but they weren't funded because the Society ran out of money—so again, only 21 percent got funded. And of the total of 2,225 applicants, 1,503 were rejected—a great many of these because of lack of money. So, that's 79 percent of all proposals, a great many of which were worthy, didn't get funded. This means that there are more willing researchers to do the work than there is money that the American Cancer Society has to give. What I want you to do is help with Notes to Neighbors in order to increase the amount of money the Cancer Society has to give to researchers, thereby moving along the fight against cancer.

Notes to Neighbors is an excellent way for you to participate because it is an easy and realistic way for you to contribute to the fight against cancer. The dollar cost for participating in the Notes to Neighbors program for one person is really only the cost of one book of stamps. All you have to do is buy one five-dollar book of stamps to participate in this program. Now I know as students we really don't have a lot of money to throw around—there have been weeks when I had only five dollars to eat on all week. And I know everyone has gone through this at least once. So you might be saying, "I can't even afford five dollars!" But there are ways of getting around this cost. If you want to do it, you can do it. There are ways. For instance, last year when I did this, I asked my boss at work to donate a book of stamps so that I could complete this program, and he did—so it really cost me nothing. And I bet you can think of a way too.

In addition to costing only a few dollars at most, Notes to Neighbors takes you only two hours, once a year, to complete. That's only two hours! And that's at a maximum. I know all of you work, because I've asked, and obviously we're all here at school, so I know your time is precious. Most days you don't have a lot of time to contribute to volunteer work because you're here trying to get an education. Last year when I got my envelopes, it took me only forty-five minutes. Moreover, I was able to do this in my spare time while I was at work. Let me explain. You see, I work as a waitress at a restaurant—and when I was waiting for people to come in, I used that time that I ordinarily spent just waiting to write my addresses on the forms. Now everybody has some time during nearly every day where you're waiting, whether it be at your job, at school, or whatever. I'm talking about times when you're not really doing anything. My example was at work waiting for people to come into the restaurant. I'm sure you have times just like mine. By using those times it doesn't cut into your free time. You're not actually taking time away from work or your social life to do this—but you're still helping people.

Now, I hope I've made this pretty clear that the money and the time it will take to do this is really inconsequential to those of us who really don't have a lot of spare time or money to give. But, if I haven't convinced you that this program is easy to do

Dana states the name of the program and briefly states what people have to do.

Dana makes her initial appeal to her audience.

Her first reason focuses on the problem—lack of money for research.
  Good use of statistics to show how few of the proposals got funded.

She shows that researchers are ready and able—they just need money to do the work.

Dana's second reason shows that students can participate for little or no real monetary cost.
  Good use of reiteration.

Here she identifies with students' hesitancy to commit themselves. But then she uses her own experience to show that the monetary problem can be overcome.

Dana's third reason also focuses on the ease of completing the task.
  Again, she shows the ability to identify with student concerns— lack of time.
  Another excellent use of personal experience to show how any of us can make the time.

She reviews the points that the program costs little in the way of money or time. But then she *recognizes that people may still not be motivated to follow through. To provide motivation, she returns again to her own experience.*

Here Dana vividly shows what cancer can do to people.

The details of this experience help the audience visualize what it's like to suffer from cancer.

Dana now relates her experience to the entire audience. Throughout the speech Dana blends logical information and emotional appeal quite well. This is a good persuasive speech that follows the motivational pattern.

or that it's important to do, I want to ask you a couple of questions. How many of you have taken care of someone who has cancer? How many of you have seen the agony of cancer first hand? For those of you who haven't, I want to tell you a little bit of what it's like.

My father was diagnosed with brain cancer two years ago this January. He went directly into the hospital a week later for a couple of rounds of radiation and chemotherapy. Since then, I've watched him go from 190 pounds to weighing less than I do—that's more than 70 pounds gone. The problem is, he's not able to eat and this is due to a lot of the damage done by the radiation to his rib muscles. His salivary glands are destroyed—there's swelling in his throat, and he's not able to eat solid foods. He has to drink Ensure for every meal every day for two years. Also the swelling in his throat has closed his windpipe completely, so they had to do a tracheotomy to relieve the swelling so he can breathe and not suffocate. My father is fifty-seven years old, and in the last two years he hasn't been able to work because of his illness. Last week he was forced out of his business that took him fifteen years to build. And now he's living on disability—and wasting away in front of the television.

What I want you to understand is that the half a million people who die a year from cancer belong to other people—they belong to mothers, daughters, siblings, and fathers. This disease can be cured, but it will take research to find the cures. Please help. Please sign up for Notes to Neighbors to help the American Cancer Society fund that research that is so necessary.

Refuting Persuasive Claims

When you are confronted with a speech that makes a claim, you can accept it, reject it, or perhaps suspend judgment. If you reject the speech, you can sit quietly and fume, or you can take issue with the speaker who made the claim. The goal of this section is to give you the expertise to evaluate arguments critically and to refute those that you believe are faulty or not in the best interests of the audience. **Refutation** is the process of proving that an argument or series of arguments, or the conclusion drawn from that argument or those arguments, is false, erroneous, or at least doubtful.

In this section, we consider the steps involved in refuting arguments. The section concludes with a speech assignment that enables you to put refutation into practice, along with a sample refutation speech.

refutation the process of proving that an argument or series of arguments, or the conclusion drawn from that argument or those arguments, is false, erroneous, or at least doubtful

Outline What Your Opponent Says and Your Reaction

Divide a piece of paper in half vertically, and outline your opponent's speech in one column. Use the other column to note your refutation of each point. Exhibit 14.2 illustrates notes on one point of the speaker's argument. Notice that the specific goal is written in full, the main point is written as a complete sentence as nearly as possible to the actual words used, and the subpoints include enough words to reflect the content. Accurate notes will help you avoid distorting what your opponent actually said.

Bob Daemmrich/Stock, Boston/PictureQuest

The better you anticipate your opponent's arguments, the more effective you'll be in refuting them.

Outline of Argument	**Comments**
Specific Goal: To prove that students should purchase insurance while they are young.	
I. Buying insurance while you are young provides systematic compulsory savings.	True, but are these necessarily beneficial?
A. Each due period you get a notice—banks, etc., don't provide service.	True, but what if you miss a payment?
B. Once money is invested it is saved—there's no deposit and withdrawal with insurance.	True, but what if you need money? You can borrow, but you have to pay interest on your own money! Cash settlement results in loss of money benefits.

In the comments column, sketch your thoughts related to each point made. Thoughts will come to mind as you outline. If you sketch your reactions as you listen, you will be in a much better position to respond.

Analyze the Evidence and Arguments

At this stage, you will have a reasonably accurate account of all your opponent has said. Now, how will you reply? Base your refutation on your analysis of the weaknesses in the speaker's evidence and arguments.

Evaluating Evidence

If the speaker presented little or no evidence, then you will point this out. Although you can occasionally find reasons that are unsupported, it's more likely that your opponent has given supporting evidence. So, you might question the quality of the material.

For each piece of evidence that is presented, answer the following questions:

1. Is the evidence fact or opinion?

2. Does the evidence come from high-quality sources?

3. Is the evidence out of date?

4. Is the evidence relevant to the argument being made?

Once you have evaluated the quality of the evidence, you can move on to testing the argument.

Evaluating the Reasoning (Warrants)

Although attacks on evidence can be an effective means of refutation, a more convincing form of refutation is to attack the reasoning from the evidence. Even if all the facts are true, the conclusion fails if the reasoning is unsound.

As we saw earlier in this chapter, each argument presented in a persuasive speech is composed of claims or propositions and data (reasons and evidence). To refute another's reasoning, first identify the type of argument: example, analogy, causation, sign, definition, or authority; then answer the questions relevant to testing each type of warrant (see pages 283–289). Then determine what if any fallacies are present (see pages 289–290).

Organize and Present Your Refutation

Once you have discovered the weaknesses in the evidence and arguments, organize your refutation. Although you may not have long to consider exactly what you will say, your refutation must be organized nearly as well as your planned speeches. Think of refutation points as units of argument. Organize each as follows:

1. State the argument or evidence you are going to refute clearly and concisely.

2. State what you will prove; tell your listeners how you plan to proceed so that they can follow your thinking.

Refuting Arguments

Work with a classmate to select a debatable topic and to phrase a speech goal that establishes or changes a belief, such as "The United States should establish mandatory, periodic drug tests for all military personnel" or "The United States should withdraw all troops from Afghanistan." Clear the wording with your instructor. Phrase the specific goal so that the first speaker (you or your classmate) is in favor of the proposal. The first speaker then will give a three- to six-minute persuasive speech presenting at least three arguments for the proposal. The second speaker will give a three- to six-minute speech opposing the specific arguments presented by the first speaker.

3. Present the reasons and data completely and with documentation (a brief reference to source).

4. Draw a conclusion; do not rely on the audience to draw the proper conclusion for themselves. Never go on to another reason/argument before you have drawn your conclusion.

To illustrate this method, let us examine a short unit of refutation directed to the first argument presented in Exhibit 14.2. In the following abbreviated statement, notice how the four steps of refutation (stating the argument, stating what you will prove, presenting proof, and drawing a conclusion) are incorporated:

1. Mr. Jackson has said that buying insurance provides systematic, compulsory savings.

2. His assumption is that systematic, compulsory saving is a benefit of buying insurance while you are young. But I believe just the opposite is true; I believe that it has at least two serious disadvantages.

3. First, the system is so compulsory that if you miss a payment you stand to lose your entire savings and all benefits. Most insurance contracts include a clause giving you a thirty-day grace period, after which the policy is canceled (evidence). Second, if you need money desperately, you have to take a loan against your policy. The end result of such a loan is that you have to pay interest in order to borrow your own money (evidence).

4. From this analysis, I think you can see that this systematic, compulsory saving is more disadvantageous than advantageous for people who are trying to save money.

Write a critique of one or more of the debates you hear in class. Use the Speech of Reasons Checklist (page 291) to evaluate the first speech. Then use the questions in the Speech of Refutation Checklist as a basis for your analysis of the speech of refutation.

Supporting and Refuting: Two Sides of a Debate

The following two speeches are presented to illustrate a debate format, with one supporting a speech goal and the second refuting the arguments presented in the first speech.[9]

SPEECH EVALUATION *checklist*

Speech of Refutation

Check items that were accomplished effectively.

_____ **1.** Did the speaker state the argument to be refuted clearly and concisely?

_____ **2.** Did the speaker clearly state his or her position on that argument?

_____ **3.** Did the speaker document evidence in support of his or her position?

_____ **4.** Did the speaker draw a clear conclusion?

_____ **5.** Did the speaker follow these four steps for each unit of refutation?

Evaluate the speech as (check one)

_____ excellent, _____ good, _____ average, _____ fair, _____ poor.

SAMPLE *speech in favor*

Instead of analyzing the first speech on the basis of its effectiveness as a speech, analyze it as if you were to give the speech of refutation. That is, consider its strengths and weaknesses, but do so in a context of how you would develop your refutation. After you have determined a strategy for refuting the speech, read the analysis.

Prohibiting the Use of Lie Detector Tests by Sheila Kohler

Analysis

The negative speaker should outline as clearly as possible the key affirmative points. Special care

Speech

Lie detector or polygraph tests used either to screen job applicants or to uncover thefts by employees have become a big business. Hundreds of thousands are given each year, and the number is steadily rising. What I propose to you today is that employers should be prohibited from administering lie detector tests to their employees either as a condition of employment or as a condition of maintaining their job. I support this proposition for two reasons. First, despite technological improvement in equipment, the accuracy of results is open to question; and second, even if the tests are accurate, use of lie detector tests is an invasion of privacy.

First, let's consider their accuracy. Lie detector tests just have not proved to be very accurate. According to Senator Birch Bayh, tests are only 70 percent accurate. And equally important, even the results of this 70 percent can be misleading. Let's look at two examples of the kinds of harm that come from these misleading results.

One case involves a young girl named Linda Boycose. She was at the time of the incident a bookkeeper for Kresge's. One day she reported $1.50 missing from the previous day's receipts. A few weeks later, the store's security man gave her a lie detector test. He first used the equipment with all its intimidating wiring, and then he used persuasion to get information. He accused her of deceiving him and actually stealing the money. After this test, Boycose was so upset she quit her job—she then spent the next two years indulging in Valium at an almost suicidal level. A Detroit jury found Boycose's story so convincing that it ordered the department store chain to award her $100,000. Now, almost six years later, she is still afraid to handle the bookkeeping at the doctor's office she manages.

The next example is of a supermarket clerk in Los Angeles. She was fired after an emotional response to the question "Have you ever given discount groceries to your mother?" It was later discovered that her mother had been dead for five years, thus showing that her response was clearly an emotional one.

Much of the inaccuracy of the tests has to do with the examiner's competence. Jerry Wall, a Los Angeles tester, said that out of an estimated 3,000 U.S. examiners, only 50 are competent. Some polygraph operators tell an interviewee that he or she has lied at one point even if the person has not, just to see how the person will handle the stress. This strategy can destroy a person's poise, leading to inaccuracies. With these examples of stress situations and inefficient examiners, the facts point to the inaccuracy of polygraph test results.

My second reason for abolishing the use of these tests is that they are an invasion of privacy. Examiners can and do ask job applicants about such things as sexual habits and how often they change their underwear. The supposed purpose of lie detector tests is to determine whether an employee is stealing. These irrelevant questions are an invasion of privacy, and not a way to indicate whether someone is breaking the law.

Excesses are such that the federal government has been conducting hearings on misuse. Congress is considering ways to curtail their use.

That they are an invasion of privacy seems to be admitted by the companies that use them. Employers are afraid to reveal too much information from tests because they have a fear of being sued. Because of an examiner's prying questions on an employee's background, and because government has shown such concern about the continued use of polygraphs, we can conclude that they are an invasion of privacy.

In conclusion, let me ask you how, as an employee, you would feel taking such a test. You'd probably feel nervous and reluctant to take the test. Couldn't you see yourself stating something that would be misconstrued, not because of the truth but because of your nervousness? Also, how would you feel about having to answer very personal and intimate questions about yourself in order to get a job?

Because lie detector tests are inaccurate and an invasion of privacy, I believe their use should be prohibited. ∎

should be taken to write affirmative reasons accurately. Accuracy of tests is critically important. Is there confirmation for this estimate? If so, accept it, work around it, or both. If not, correct it.

A decision on how to deal with "misleading" will depend on development. These two examples are highly emotional and may be persuasive, but: (1) Only two examples have been given. Nothing has been presented to show that the examples are representative. (2) The examples do not necessarily indicate a problem with the mechanics of testing.

Assuming that testers are relatively incompetent, how does this information affect the negative case? Can this be either admitted or ignored? If not, how can it be refuted? Reemphasis of importance of level of accuracy. Can instances of abuse be admitted without concluding that tests should be abolished? How?

This material demonstrates a threat of government intervention. But has government intervened? Has government determined what constitutes "invasion of privacy"?

Some emotional appeal in this summary. How can the effect of this be countered? ∎

SAMPLE speech of refutation

In the speech of refutation, we would expect the speaker to say something about the two reasons that were presented in the first speech. In your analysis, look to see how the groundwork for refutation is laid; then look for the use of the four-step method of refutation.

Using Lie Detector Tests by Martha Feinberg

<table>
<tr><td>

Analysis

Good opening. Speaker has clearly stated her position and has laid the groundwork for her negative position.

This material establishes a need for some measures to be taken against theft. It shows that tests are not being used without good reason.

This represents further clarification of what affirmative has done and what negative proposes to do. It helps to place the affirmative attack in proper perspective.

Good direct attack on level of accuracy. Notice tht she states opponent's point, states her position on the point, and then presents the evidence. But why are Kelly's figures better than Bayh's? The speaker needs to show us with a concluding statement of refutation.

Good job of debating the conclusion to be drawn from the examples. Still, we would like to have heard her make a closer examination of the examples themselves.

That businesses use the tests does not prove that businesses are convinced they are accurate. Need more factual data here.

This is a further attempt to put the affirmative argument into proper perspective. Judge's ruling gives strong support to her opinion.

</td><td>

Speech

My opponent has stated that the use of lie detector tests by employers should be abolished. I strongly disagree; I believe employers have to use these tests. Before examining the two reasons she presented, I'd like to take a look at why more than 20 percent of the nation's largest businesses feel a need to use these tests and why the number is growing each year.

Employers use lie detector tests to help curb employee theft. According to the National Retail Merchants Association, employees steal as much as $40 billion of goods each year. Moreover, the figure increases markedly each year. The average merchant doesn't recognize that he loses more to employees than to outsiders—50 to 70 percent of theft losses go to employees, not to shoplifters. This use of lie detector tests is a necessity to curb this internal theft.

Now, I do not believe that my opponent ever tried to show that there is not a problem that lie detector testing solves; nor did she try to show that lie detector testing doesn't help to deter internal theft. Notice that the two reasons she presented are both about abuses. Let's take a closer look at those two reasons.

First, my opponent said that the accuracy of results is open to question; in contrast, I would argue that these tests are remarkably accurate. She mentioned that Senator Bayh reported a 70-percent level of accuracy. Yet the literature on these tests as reported by Ty Kelley, vice president of government affairs of the National Association of Chain Drug Stores, argues that the level is around 90 percent, not 70 percent.

She went on to give two examples of people who were intimidated and/or became emotional and upset when subjected to the test. And on this basis she calls for them to be abolished. I would agree that some people do become emotional, but this is hardly reason for stopping their use. Unless she can show a real problem among many people taking the test, I think we'll have to go along with the need for the tests.

If these tests are so inaccurate, why are one-fifth of the nation's largest companies using them? According to an article in *Business Week*, "Business Buys the Lie Detector," more and more businesses each year see a necessity for using the tests because they deter crime. These tests are now being used by nearly every type of company—banks, businesses, drug stores, as well as retail department stores.

Her second reason for why the tests should be abolished is that they are an invasion of privacy. I believe, with Mr. Kelley, whom I quoted earlier, that there must be some sort of balance maintained between an individual's right to privacy and an employer's right to protect his property. In Illinois, for instance, a state judge ruled that examiners could ask prying questions—there has yet to be any official ruling that the use is "an invasion of privacy."

</td></tr>
</table>

My opponent used the example of asking questions about sexual habits and change of underwear. In that regard, I agree with her. I think that a person is probably pretty sick who is asking these kinds of questions—and I think these abuses should be checked. But asking questions to screen out thieves, junkies, liars, alcoholics, and psychotics is necessary. For instance, an Atlanta nursing home uses polygraph tests to screen out potentially sadistic and disturbed nurses and orderlies. Is this an invasion of privacy? I don't think so.

It is obvious to me that some type of lie detector test is needed. Too much theft has gone on, and something must be done to curtail this. I say that lie detector tests are the answer. First, they are accurate. Companies have been using them for a long time, and more and more companies are starting to use them. And second, it is only an invasion of privacy when the wrong types of questions are asked. I agree that these abuses should be curbed, but not by doing away with the tests. Employers cannot do away with these tests and control theft; the benefits far outweigh the risks. ■

Good line of argument. Any attempt at refuting alleged abuses would be damaging to the negative position.

Here the speaker does a nice job of bringing emphasis back to the need for the tests.

This is a good speech of refutation. It illustrates the importance of showing the negative position before launching into refutation; it illustrates good form for refutation; and it provides several approaches to refutation. ■

REFLECT ON ethics

Alexandro, a student who had worked full time for three years before returning to college for his sophomore year, decided that for his final speech he would motivate the members of his class to donate money to the Downtown Food Bank. He was excited about this topic because he had begun volunteering for the Food Bank during those last three years and had seen firsthand the face of hunger in this community.

He planned to support his speech with three reasons: (1) that an increasing number of people in the community needed food; (2) that government agencies were unable to provide sufficient help; and (3) that a high percentage of every donated dollar at the food bank went into food. As he researched these points, he discovered that the number of families who were in need in the community had not really risen in the past two years and that government sponsorship of the Food Bank had increased. Then, when he examined the Food Bank's financial statements, he discovered that only 68 percent of every dollar donated was actually spent on food. Faced with this evidence, he just didn't think his reasons and evidence were very strong.

Yet, because of his experience, he still thought the Food Bank was a cause that deserved financial support, so he decided to focus his entire speech on the heartwarming case of the Hernandez family. Ineligible for government assistance, over the years this family of ten had managed to survive because of the aid they received from the Food Bank. Today, several of the children had graduated from college, and one was a physician working in the barrio. By telling this heart-wrenching story of the struggle to survive, Alexandro thought he would be successful in persuading the class.

1. Would it be ethical for Alexandro to give his speech in this way? If so, why?

2. If not, what would he need to do to make the speech ethical?

Summary

A speech argument is the product of three essential elements: claim, data, and warrant. A claim is the proposition or conclusion to be proven. Data constitute the reasons and evidence that provide the basis for a claim. A warrant is a statement that explains the relationship between the evidence (facts and opinion) and the claim (the reason).

Common forms of argument are arguing by example, analogy, causation, sign, definition, and authority. Test reasoning by answering questions about the warrant for the particular argument.

The catalyst for arousing the imagination, inspiring commitment, and moving people to action is the psychological aspect of persuasion called motivation. Two theories of motivation address issues of incentives and basic needs.

Audiences are more likely to be motivated to act when the speech goal presents incentives that create a favorable cost/reward ratio. Costs are units of expenditure; rewards are the benefits received from a behavior. The goal is to have low costs and high rewards.

Audiences are more likely to act when the proposition satisfies a strong, but unmet, need. To use needs strategy in a speech, the speaker can help the audience identify certain unmet needs and then show how acting on the specific speech goal will fulfill those needs.

Refutation is the process of proving that an argument or series of arguments, or the conclusion drawn from that argument or those arguments, is false, erroneous, or at least doubtful. Refutation can be handled systematically. Take careful notes of what your opponent says, note your reaction to each argument, plan your procedure, and present your refutation following the four-step method.

CHALLENGE ONLINE

Use your Challenge of Effective Speaking CD-ROM for quick access to the electronic study resources that accompany this text. Included on your CD-ROM is access to the Challenge of Effective Speaking Web site featuring Speech Builder Express at Wadsworth Communication Café, InfoTrac College Edition, and a demo of WebTutor for *The Challenge of Effective Speaking*. The Web site offers chapter-by-chapter access to the Speech Preparation Action Step Activities, InfoTrac College Edition exercises, a digital glossary of key terms, Web links, Speech Preparation Forms, Speech Evaluation Checklists, and quizzes. Review the key terms and complete the InfoTrac College Edition exercise at **http://www.wadsworth.com/product/0534563856**

InfoTrac College Edition Exercise

This chapter has presented many ideas about motivation. Using the term "persuasion," search the "periodical references" for Persuasion (Psychology). Look for the article titled "Tactical Tips for Persuading Effectively from 3 Steps to Yes" by Gene Bedell, *Manage*, May 2001. Consider the suggestions listed under the three steps. What does Bedell suggest that supplements what you've read in the chapter? List three suggestions you believe will help you be more persuasive.

Key Terms

ad hominem argument *(290)*

appeal to authority *(290)*

arguing *(282)*

arguing from analogy *(284)*

arguing from authority *(288)*

arguing from
    causation *(285)*

arguing from definition *(287)*

arguing from
    example *(283)*

arguing from sign *(286)*

argument *(281)*

claim *(282)*

costs *(295)*

data *(282)*

false cause *(289)*

hasty generalization *(289)*

hierarchy of needs *(296)*

incentives (rewards) *(295)*

reasoning *(282)*

reasoning process *(283)*

refutation *(304)*

reward *(296)*

warrant *(283)*

Challenge of Effective Speaking Web Site

Use your Challenge of Effective Speaking CD-ROM to access the book's Web site. Then access the Forms and Speech Evaluation Checklist for Chapter 14.

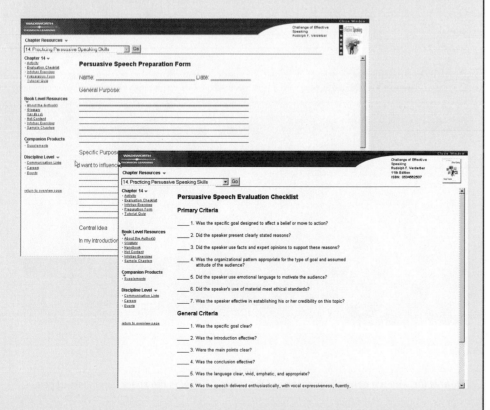

CHAPTER 15 Adapting to Special Occasions

Ritual is the way we carry the presence of the sacred. Ritual is the spark that must not go out.
—Christina Baldwin, *Life's Companion, Journal Writing as a Spiritual Quest,* 1990

Steve Dunwell/Getty Images/The Image Bank

It was a warm, beautiful spring day. Thousands of people were overflowing the school Green Place, where temporary stands were set up in honor of the U.S. senator who had been selected by the school to deliver the annual address.

Dignitaries are often called upon to meet the needs of a variety of special occasions, and some of the speaking you may do will be under circumstances that are best described as ceremonial. In these speeches, whether you give information or persuade, you must meet the conventions of the particular occasion. The guidelines for speech preparation we have studied throughout this book will serve you well, but you must also be familiar with the needs that these occasions serve.

Although no speech can be given by formula, certain occasions require at least the knowledge of conventions that various speakers observe and that audiences may expect. Speakers should always use their own imagination to determine how to develop the theme and should never adhere slavishly to those conventions. Still, you must know the conventions before you can decide whether to deviate from or ignore them entirely. In addition, you may sometimes be called upon to speak, or be motivated to speak, on the spur of the moment.

This chapter gives the basics of preparing and presenting five common types of special speeches—introductions, presentations, acceptances, welcomings, and tributes—as well as speeches for other special occasions. It concludes with sections on impromptu and manuscript speaking.

Introductions

A **speech of introduction** is designed to pave the way for the main speaker. If you make the introduction in a way that psychologically prepares the audience to listen to the speech, then you have accomplished your purpose.

speech of introduction speech designed to pave the way for the main speaker

Procedure

Your listeners want to know who the speaker is, what the person is going to talk about, and why they should listen. Sometime before the speech, consult with the speaker to ask what he or she prefers that you say. Usually, you want the necessary biographical information that will show who the speaker is and why he or she is qualified to talk on the subject. The better known the person is, the less you need to say about him or her. For instance, the introduction of the U.S. president is simply, "Ladies and gentlemen, the president of the United States."

Ordinarily, you want enough information to allow you to talk for at least two or three minutes. Only on rare occasions should a speech of introduction last longer than three or four minutes; the audience is assembled to hear the speaker, not the introducer. During the first sentence or two, establish the nature of the occasion; in the body of the speech, establish the speaker's credibility. The conclusion usually includes the name of the speaker and the title of the talk.

SPEECH assignment

Speech of Introduction

Prepare a two- to three-minute speech of introduction. Assume that you are introducing the featured speaker for a specific occasion. Criteria for evaluation include creativity in establishing speaker credibility and presenting the name of the speaker and the speech title.

Considerations

Some special cautions apply when preparing a speech of introduction. First, do not overpraise the speaker. If expectations are too high, the speaker will never be able to live up to them. For instance, an overzealous introducer might be inclined to say, "This man [woman] is undoubtedly one of the greatest speakers around today. You will, I am sure, agree with me that this will be one of the best speeches you've ever heard." Although such an introduction may seem complimentary, it does the speaker a disservice by emphasizing comparison rather than speech content.

A second caution is to be familiar with what you have to say. Audiences question sincerity when introducers have to read their praise. Many of us have been present when an introducer said "And now, it is my great pleasure to present that noted authority . . ." and then had to look at some notes to recall the name. Finally, get your facts straight. The speaker should not have to spend time correcting your mistakes.

A typical speech of introduction might go like this:

> Fellow club members, it is my pleasure to introduce Susan Wong, the new president of our finance club. I've worked with Susan for three years and have found her to have a gift for organization, insight into the financial markets, and an interest in aligning our club with financial leaders in our community. Susan, as you may not know, has spent the last two summers working as an intern at Salomon Smith Barney and has now laid the groundwork for more college internships for club members this summer. She is a finance major, with a minor in international business. Susan is ready to lead our finance club for the next year, and we are lucky to have her. Let's give a warm welcome to our new president, Susan Wong!

Presentations

presentation speech   speech designed to present an award, a prize, or a gift to an individual or a group

A **presentation speech** is designed to present an award, a prize, or a gift to an individual or a group. Sometimes, a presentation accompanies a long tribute to an individual. Usually, the speech is a fairly short, formal recognition of an accomplishment.

Procedure

Your speech usually has two goals: (1) to discuss the nature of the award, including its history, donor, or source, and the conditions under which it is made; and (2) to discuss the recipient's accomplishments. If a competition was held, describe what the person did in the competition. Under other circumstances, discuss how the person has met the criteria for the award.

Obviously, you must learn all you can about the award and about the conditions under which such awards are made. Although the award itself may be a certificate,

© Michael Newman/PhotoEdit, Inc.

When presenting an award, discuss the nature of the award and the recipient's accomplishments.

plaque, or trophy symbolizing an achievement, the contest may have a long history and tradition that must be mentioned. Because the audience wants to know what the recipient has done, you must know the criteria that were met. For a competition, this includes the number of contestants and the way the contest was judged. If the person earned the award through years of achievement, know the particulars of that achievement.

Ordinarily, the speech is organized to show what the award is for, gives the criteria for winning or achieving the award, and states how the person won or achieved the award. If the announcement of the recipient's name is meant to be a surprise, what is said should build up to the climax—naming the winner.

Considerations

For the speech of presentation, there are only two special considerations. First, avoid overpraising; do not explain everything in such superlatives that the presentation lacks sincerity and honesty. Second, if you are going to hand the award to the recipient, be careful to hold the award in your left hand and present it to the

SPEECH assignment

Speech of Presentation

Prepare a three- to five-minute speech in which you present a gift, a plaque, or an award to a member of your class. Criteria for evaluation include showing what the award is for, the criteria for winning, and how the person met the criteria.

recipient's left hand. At the same time, you want to shake the right hand in congratulations. With practice, you will be able to present the award and shake the person's hand smoothly and avoid those embarrassing moments when the recipient does not know what he or she is supposed to do.

Acceptances

acceptance speech   a response to a presentation speech

An **acceptance speech** is a response to a presentation speech. The purpose of the acceptance speech is to give brief thanks for receiving the award.

Procedure

The speech usually has two parts: (1) a brief thanks to the group, agency, or people responsible for giving the award; and (2) thanks to those who share in the honor if the recipient was aided by others.

Considerations

Unless the acceptance is the lead-in to a major address, the acceptance should be brief. (A politician accepting a gift from the Chamber of Commerce may launch into a speech on government, but the audience will probably be expecting it.) As the Academy Awards program so graphically illustrates, however, when people are honored, the tendency is to give overly long and occasionally inappropriate speeches. The audience expects the recipient to show his or her gratitude to the presenter of the award; it does not expect a major address.

Here is an example of an appropriate speech of acceptance:

> On behalf of our Board of Directors, thank you for this award, the Largest Institutional Benefactor in Second Harvest's 1998 Food Drive. It is an honor to be part of such a worthwhile cause, and it is really our board who should be thanking you, Second Harvest, for all the wonderful work you have done over the years. You continue to collect and distribute food to thousands of needful families and individuals, especially to our senior citizens and single mothers. Without your work, many would otherwise go hungry. You are a model of community sharing and caring.
>
> I would also like to thank our company staff—Juanita Alverez, Su Lin, Al Pouzorek, Linda Williams, and Jesus Washington—for their efforts in organizing the collection of food and money to go to Second Harvest. They were tireless in their work, persistent in their company memos and meetings requesting donations, and consistent in their positive and upbeat attitude throughout the drive. We could not have won this award without them! Let's give them a round of applause too.
>
> Finally, thank you, Second Harvest, for this honor—and we hope to be back next year to receive it again!

SPEECH assignment

Speech of Acceptance

This assignment can go together with the speech of presentation assignment. Prepare a one- to two-minute speech of acceptance in response to another speaker's speech of presentation. The criterion for evaluation is how imaginatively you can respond in a brief speech.

Welcoming Speech

Prepare a speech welcoming a specific person to your city, university, or social organization. Criteria for evaluation include how well you explain the nature of the institution and how well you introduce the person being welcomed.

Welcomings

A **welcoming speech** is one that expresses pleasure for the presence of a person or an organization. In a way, the speech of welcome is a double speech of introduction. You introduce the newcomer to the organization or city, and you introduce the organization to the newcomer.

welcoming speech speech that expresses pleasure for the presence of a person or an organization

Procedure

You must be familiar with both the person or organization you are welcoming and the situation to which you are welcoming the person. It is surprising how little many members of organizations, citizens of a community, and students at a college or university really know about their organization or community. Although you may not have the knowledge on the tip of your tongue, it is inexcusable not to find the material you need to give an appropriate speech. Likewise, you want accurate information about the person or organization you are introducing. Although the speech will be brief, you need accurate and complete information from which to draw.

After expressing pleasure in welcoming the person or organization, give a little information about your guest and about the place or organization to which he or she is being welcomed. Usually the conclusion is a brief statement of your hope for a pleasant and profitable visit.

Considerations

Again, the special caution is to make sure the speech is brief and honest. Welcoming guests does not require you to gush about them or their accomplishments. The speech of welcome should be an informative speech of praise.

Tributes

A **speech of tribute** is designed to praise someone's accomplishments. The occasion may be, for example, a birthday, accepting an office, a wedding toast, or retirement. A formal speech of tribute given in memory of a deceased person is called a eulogy.

speech of tribute speech designed to praise someone's accomplishments

Procedure

The key to an effective tribute is sincerity. Although you want the praise to be apparent, you do not want to overdo it.

You must have in-depth biographical information about your subject. Audiences are interested primarily in new information and specifics that characterize your

Special occasions such as weddings, birthdays, and retirements call for speeches and toasts. A short, well-prepared speech given with sincerity and sensitivity to the setting and occasion can make the celebration more meaningful and memorable for everyone concerned.

V.C.L./Getty Images

assertions, so you must have a mastery of much detail. Focus on the person's laudable characteristics and accomplishments. It is especially noteworthy if you find that the person has had to overcome a special hardship or meet a particularly trying condition. All in all, be prepared to make a sound, positive appraisal.

One way to organize a speech of tribute is by focusing on the subject's accomplishments. How detailed you make the speech will depend on whether the person is well known. If the person is well known, be more general in your analysis. If the person is little known, provide many more details so that the audience can see the reasons for the praise. In the case of distinctly prominent individuals, you may be able to show their influence on history.

Considerations

Remember, however, that no one is perfect. Although you need not stress a person's less glowing characteristics or failures, some allusion to this kind of information may make the person's positive features even more meaningful. Probably the most important guide is for you to keep your objectivity. Excessive praise is far worse than understatement. Try to give the person his or her due, honestly and sincerely.

SPEECH assignment

Speech Paying Tribute

Prepare a four- to six-minute speech paying tribute to a person, living or dead. Criteria for evaluation include how well you develop the person's laudable characteristics and accomplishments.

Other Ceremonial Occasions

Other occasions that call for ceremonial speeches are graduations, conferences or conventions, and holidays or events.

Nearly every educational institution includes a **commencement address**—a speech presented by a major political, business, or social figure, or a prominent alumnus/a—in its graduation ceremonies. The goal of most commencement speeches is to praise members of the graduating class and to inspire them in their future work. Although in some instances the commencement speech is a platform for a prominent figure to make a major policy statement, the best commencement speeches are ones that the graduating class can identify with.

Most organizations schedule a **keynote address** near the beginning of their conferences or conventions. Most of us are familiar with the keynote addresses presented at the national Democratic and Republican Party Conventions. The word itself gives us insight into the primary goal of the speech: to present a keynote intended to inspire participants in their work. Some keynotes, like those at national political conventions, are given as much or even more for the benefit of the television or radio audience. In these cases, the goal is to inspire listeners to support the particular political party and its candidates for office. Although there are no set guidelines for a keynote speech, the goal is to inspire—to generate enthusiasm among participants and those watching television or listening to the radio.

Commemorative addresses are presented to celebrate national holidays or anniversaries of important dates or events. Thus, Memorial Day, the Fourth of July, and Labor Day evoke countless speeches across the United States. Likewise, we hear speeches commemorating the tenth, twenty-fifth, or fiftieth anniversary of significant events such as D-Day, integration of schools, or the founding of organizations. The goals of such speeches often include reminding the audience of the background for the particular holiday, date, or event and then, ultimately, drawing some conclusion about its significance that inspires the audience.

commencement address
a speech presented by a major political, business, social figure, or a prominent alumnus/a during graduation ceremonies

keynote address   a speech presented near the beginning of a conference or convention that is designed to inspire participants in their work

commemorative address
speech presented to celebrate a national holiday or the anniversary of an important date or event

Impromptu Speeches

Up to this point, we've been operating under the assumption that you are aware that you will be called upon to speak, and thus have time to prepare. But occasionally, your speaking will be **impromptu,** on the spur of the moment. Whether you have attended a meeting and suddenly feel the urge to make a statement, or a reporter corners you and asks you for a statement, you still need to speak with confidence and make sense.

In short, any speech uses all the action steps and guidelines for effective speaking that we have considered except preparing visual aids and practicing. Let's consider these steps in terms of impromptu speaking.

impromptu speech   speech given on the spur of the moment

1. **Determine a goal.** Even on the spur of the moment, you should be able to articulate a specific goal. For instance, if you're motivated to speak at a social organization meeting at which the topic of raising dues is being considered, you will quickly think, "I want the organization to support the increase in dues." At the same time, you'll remind yourself of the nature of this organization.

2. Adapt material to the audience. Time prevents a careful survey of materials and how you can use them. Still, if you keep the audience in mind, ideas for adapting will come to you as you speak. You should certainly be able to use personal pronouns and rhetorical questions—and you should be able to relate any example, illustration, or story to the specific audience.

3. Gather information. For a formal speech you may spend hours at the library. For this impromptu occasion, take a few seconds to call up information that you know; perhaps you will rely on observation or your own experience. In any event, impromptu or not, you still need good information to support your views. Perhaps you'll think about some really good ideas members of the organization had that couldn't be implemented for lack of money.

4. Organize the material. For an impromptu speech, consider common organizational patterns. A persuasive speech requires reasons and evidence. What are the one or two reasons that come to mind in support of the goal to increase dues? From your experience, one reason might be that the money is needed to fund creative programs. Perhaps your experience also suggests that dues haven't been raised for several years. As an introduction, you might just tell the group what you will cover. Yet even in the nanoseconds you have before you actually begin speaking, an idea may come to you. For the conclusion, you may just summarize your reasons and make an appeal.

Although you don't have time to really consider composition when speaking extemporaneously, remind yourself to be as clear and vivid as possible.

How do you get better at impromptu speaking? Through practice. Don't back away from opportunities to speak. And in the privacy of your own quarters, you might actually talk for a minute or two about a subject that is near to you. We all fantasize about what we might say if we were called upon. Instead of fantasizing, do it.

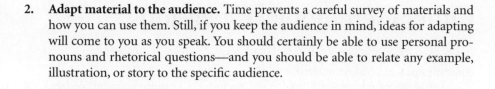

SPEECH **assignment**

Impromptu Speech

The best topics for impromptu speeches are those that each of you in class will be able to talk about without going beyond your own knowledge and experience. Your instructor will have words and phrases on 3-by-5-inch cards, such as "uses of computers," "the ideal mate," or "sex on television." At the beginning of the round, a student (usually a volunteer) draws three topics, selects one, and begins preparation. The first person to speak has three minutes to prepare. The second person in the round draws three cards just before the first person begins talking. The second person (and each subsequent speaker) also has three minutes. If the previous speech was less than three minutes, use the extra time to comment on the speech.

Manuscript Speeches

Throughout this book, we have been emphasizing extemporaneous speaking. Nevertheless, you may be called upon to give a manuscript speech on a ceremonial occasion when the precise wording of the speech is critical. A **manuscript speech** is written out completely and then read aloud.

manuscript speech speech that is written out completely and then read aloud

The final draft of your manuscript should be extremely well worded. You will want to show all that you have learned about making ideas clear, vivid, and appropriate. In your preparation, proceed as if you were giving an extemporaneous speech. Then record what you would ordinarily consider your final speech practice. Type the manuscript from your recorded practice, and work on polishing the language. This procedure will ensure that you are working from an oral style rather than from a written essay style.

After the manuscript has been completely written, practice using it effectively. You want to be sufficiently familiar with the material so that you do not have to focus your full attention on the manuscript as you read. Go over the manuscript at least three times in these final stages of practice. You will discover that even when you are reading you can have some eye contact with your audience. By watching audience reaction, you will know when and if to deviate from the manuscript.

So that the manuscript will be of maximum value to you, here are some tips for preparing it.

1. The manuscript should be typed, preferably on a computer or on a typewriter that has print that is pica-sized (12 points) or larger. Whatever size type you use, it is wise to double, or even triple, space the manuscript.

This practice sentence, a nice size for reading, is 14 point.

REFLECT ON ethics

"What's the matter Chet?—you really look as if something is bothering you!"

"Well, you know I'm introducing Rick at the University Convocation for those running for office. He's my friend and I told him I'd be happy to introduce him. So I asked him to give me some information that he'd like me to include. I thought he'd summarize some of the stuff he's done, but instead he wrote out an introduction that includes stuff about him that's largely fiction! I really feel like I'm in a pickle, Ken."

"So, he's the one who's running for office. You're just giving the introduction he wants you to give. Don't worry about it—nobody's going to pay attention to what you're saying anyway."

"Still, I'm giving the speech. I'm afraid that I'm going to be the one who gets blamed when and if people find out that what I've said isn't true."

"I'm telling you—your job is to do what Rick wants. You asked him to give you information and he did."

"I guess you're right—but I'm not going to like doing it."

1. Is Chet violating ethical principles by agreeing to give the opening Rick wants as written?

2. If so, what should Chet do about it? If not, explain your position.

2. For words that you have difficulty pronouncing, use phonetic spelling, accents, or diacritics to help your pronunciation.

3. Make marks that will help you determine pauses, places of special emphasis, or where to slow down or speed up. Also, be sure that the last sentence on each page is completed on that page to prevent any unintended pauses.

4. Number the pages boldly to keep them in their proper order. You may also find it valuable to bend the corner of each page slightly to help you turn pages easily.

5. Double-check to be sure that there will be a lectern or a speaker's stand on which the manuscript can be placed.

Summary

In addition to informative and persuasive speeches, you are likely to have occasion to give speeches of introduction, presentation, acceptance, welcome, and tribute. You may also have occasion to present a commencement address, a keynote speech, or a speech commemorating a particular event or occasion. Moreover, at times you may need to speak impromptu or from a manuscript.

Introductions are speeches that introduce a speaker. A presentation is a speech in which you present an award, a prize, or a gift to an individual or to a group. An acceptance is a response to a speech of presentation. A welcome is a speech that expresses pleasure at the presence of a person or an organization. A tribute is a speech that praises someone's accomplishments.

Commencement speeches are those that praise the graduating class and turn them toward the future. A keynote address, as its title indicates, offers a keynote for a conference or convention. Commemorative speeches celebrate national holidays or anniversaries of important dates.

Impromptu speeches are those that are given on the spur of the moment. Manuscript speeches are written out in full and read.

CHALLENGE ONLINE

Use your Challenge of Effective Speaking CD-ROM for quick access to the electronic study resources that accompany this text. Included on your CD-ROM is access to the Challenge of Effective Speaking Web site featuring Speech Builder Express at Wadsworth Communication Café, InfoTrac College Edition, and a demo of WebTutor for *The Challenge of Effective Speaking.* The Web site offers chapter-by-chapter access to the Speech Preparation Action Step Activities, InfoTrac College Edition exercises, a digital glossary of key terms, Web links, Speech Preparation Forms, Speech Evaluation Checklists, and quizzes. Review the key terms and complete the InfoTrac College Edition exercise at **http://www.wadsworth.com/product/0534563856**

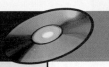

InfoTrac College Edition Exercise

The goal of most commencement speeches is to praise members of the graduating class and to inspire them in their future work. In "subject guide," type in either Jeanne Hey or "Inheritances of the Past" to bring up Jeanne Hey's commencement speech, *Vital Speeches*, July 1, 2001. Read the speech and then answer these questions: What does she do to (1) praise members of the graduating class and (2) inspire them in their future work? Based on these two criteria, how would you evaluate this commencement speech?

Key Terms

acceptance speech *(318)*

commemorative address *(321)*

commencement address *(321)*

impromptu speech *(321)*

keynote address *(321)*

manuscript speech *(323)*

presentation speech *(316)*

speech of introduction *(315)*

speech of tribute *(319)*

welcoming speech *(319)*

Challenge of Effective Speaking CD-ROM

Use your Challenge of Effective Speaking CD-ROM to access the book's Web site. You can view this impromptu speech by Amy Wood and then complete the Speech Improvement Plan.

16 Increasing the Effectiveness of Problem-Solving Discussions

© Michael Newman/PhotoEdit, Inc.

Men are never so likely to settle a question rightly as when they discuss it freely.

—Thomas Babington, Lord Macaulay (Southey's Colloquies)

Members of the Alpha Production Team at Meyer Foods were gathered to review their hiring policies. As the meeting began, Kareem, the team leader, said, "You know why I called you together. Each production team has been asked to review its hiring practices. So, let's get started." After a few seconds of silence, Kareem asked, "Drew, what have you been thinking?"

"Well, I don't know," Drew replied. "I haven't really given it much thought." There were nods of agreement all around the table.

"Well," Jeremy said, "I'm not sure I even remember what our current policies are."

"When I sent you the email notice of this meeting, I attached a preliminary analysis of our practices and some questions I hoped each of us would think about before this meeting," Kareem replied.

"Oh, is that what that was?" Byron asked. "I read the part about the meeting, but I guess I didn't get back to look at the attachment."

"Kareem, anything you think would be appropriate would be OK with me," Dawn added.

"Well, how about if we each try to come up with some ideas for next time," Kareem suggested. "Meeting adjourned."

As the group dispersed, Kareem overheard Drew whisper to Dawn, "These meetings sure are a waste of time, aren't they?"

Perhaps you have been part of a problem-solving discussion at school, at work, or at your church. Have you ever wondered why some of these discussions end up—as Drew described—as a waste of time? When problem-solving discussions are effective, they usually result in decisions that are useful. Because most of us will take part in problem-solving discussions, we need to learn how group process works and how to participate in ways that maximize effective problem solving.

In this chapter, we explain how problem-solving discussions can be structured to be both effective and efficient. We begin by examining the characteristics of effective problem-solving discussions. Next we consider the steps in an effective problem discussion. Then, we describe the essential responsibilities of both leaders and group members before, during, and after the discussion. Finally, we describe three formats used in public problem-solving discussions.

Bob Daemmrich/Stock, Boston

Effective problem-solving groups are composed of members who are committed to a common goal and who have diverse personalities, knowledge bases, skills, and viewpoints.

Characteristics of Effective Problem-Solving Discussions

problem-solving discussion a structured dialogue between individuals who interact and influence one another in order to develop a plan that will overcome an identified difficulty

A **problem-solving discussion** is a structured dialogue between individuals who interact and influence one another in order to develop a plan that will overcome an identified difficulty. Effective problem-solving discussions are characterized by clearly defined goals to which members are committed; an optimum number of members who have diverse personalities, knowledge bases, skills, and viewpoints; appropriate levels of cohesiveness; rules and norms that facilitate the open exchange of information, ideas, and opinions; and a physical setting that encourages interaction.

Develop Clearly Defined Goals to Which Members Are Committed

problem-solving goal a future state of affairs desired by enough members of the group to motivate the group to work toward its achievement

A **problem-solving goal** is a future state of affairs desired by enough members of the group to motivate the group to work toward its achievement.[1] Goals become clearer to members—and members become more committed to goals—when they are discussed. Through these discussions, members are able to make problem-solving goal statements more specific, consistent, challenging, and acceptable.

Optimum Number of Diverse Members

Effective discussion groups are composed of enough members to ensure good interaction but not so many members that discussion is stifled. In general, as the size of a discussion group grows, so does the complexity it must manage.

What is the "right" size for a problem-solving discussion group? It depends. In general, research shows that the best size for a group is the smallest number of people capable of effectively achieving the goal;[2] for many situations this might mean as few as three to five people. As the size of the group increases, the time spent discussing and deciding increases as well. This argues for very small groups because they will be able to make decisions more quickly. However, as the goals, problems, and issues become complex, it is unlikely that very small groups will have the diversity of information, knowledge, and skill needed to make high-quality decisions. For many situations, then, a group of five to seven or more might be most desirable.

More important than having a certain number of people in a group is having the right combination of people in the group. Notice the heading of this section was "optimum number of *diverse* members." Effective groups are likely to be composed of people who bring different but relevant knowledge and skills to the group discussion.[3] In homogeneous groups, members are likely to know the same things, come at the problem from the same perspective, and, consequently, be likely to overlook some important information or take shortcuts in the problem-solving process. In contrast, heterogeneous groups are likely to discuss ideas more thoroughly and have different information, perspectives, and values, and, consequently, discuss issues more thoroughly before reaching a decision.

Cohesiveness

Cohesiveness is the degree of attraction members have to one another and to the problem-solving goal. In a highly cohesive group, members genuinely like and respect each other, work cooperatively to reach the group's goals, and generally perform better than noncohesive groups.[4]

Research has found that several factors lead to developing cohesiveness in groups: attractiveness of group's purpose, voluntary membership, feeling of freedom to share opinions, and celebration of accomplishments.[5]

cohesiveness the degree of attraction members have to one another and to the group's goal

Rules and Norms

Norms are shared expectations for the way group members will behave during the discussion. Effective groups develop norms that support goal achievement[6] and cohesiveness.[7] Norms begin to be developed early in the life of the group. They grow, change, and solidify as people get to know one another better. Group members usually comply with norms and are sanctioned by the group when they do not.

Some groups choose to formulate explicit **ground rules**, prescribed behaviors designed to help the group meet its goals and conduct its conversations. These may include sticking to the agenda, refraining from interrupting others, actively listening to others, requiring full participation, focusing argument on issues rather than personalities, and sharing decision making. In most groups, however, norms evolve informally. When group members violate a group norm, they are usually sanctioned.

norms shared expectations for the way group members will behave while in the group

ground rules prescribed behaviors designed to help the group meet its goals and conduct its conversations

The Physical Setting

A good **working environment** is important for discussion group effectiveness. The physical setting in which a group works should be located conveniently for most members. The space should be at a comfortable temperature and be of appropriate size for the size and work of the group. Most important, the space should be comfortably furnished with all the resources the group needs to perform its tasks. Seating should be arranged to facilitate group interaction.

The temperature of the room in which a group meets affects the way in which the group interacts. People in rooms they perceive to be too warm are not only

working environment the physical setting in which a group works

uncomfortable but may feel crowded, which results in negative behaviors. Similarly, when the temperature of a room or meeting place is too cold, group members tend to become distracted.

The space in which a group meets should be appropriate for the size and composition of the group and the nature of what they are trying to accomplish during their time together. When the space is too big for the group, members will feel overwhelmed and distant from each other. In some cases they may even have trouble hearing one another. When the space is too small, the group will experience feelings of crowding. We've all found ourselves in situations where the room size contributed to negative experiences.

Seating arrangements can affect both group interaction and decision making. Seating can be too formal. When it approximates a board of directors seating style (Exhibit 16.1a), a dominant–submissive pattern emerges that can inhibit group interaction. The person at the head of the table is likely to be looked to for leadership and to be seen as having more influence than those members who sit on the sides. People who sit across the table from one another interact more frequently, but they also find themselves disagreeing with one another more often than they disagree with others at the table.

EXHIBIT 16.1 Which group's members will be able to arrive at a decision easily?

Seating that is excessively informal can also inhibit interaction. For instance, in Exhibit 16.1b, the three people sitting on the couch form their own little group; the two people seated next to each other form another group; and two members have placed themselves out of the main flow. In arrangements such as these, people are more likely to discuss with the people adjacent to them than with others. In such settings, it is more difficult to make eye contact with every group member.

The circle, generally considered the ideal arrangement for group discussions and problem solving, is depicted in Exhibit 16.1c. Circle configurations increase participant motivation to speak because sight lines are better for everyone and everyone appears to have equal status. When a round table is unavailable, the group may be better off without a table or with an arrangement of tables that makes a square, which approximates the circle arrangement (Exhibit 16.1d).

The Problem-Solving Discussion Process

Groups follow many different approaches to problem solving. Whether groups move in something approximating an orderly pattern or go in fits and starts, those groups that arrive at high-quality decisions are likely to accomplish certain tasks during their deliberations. These tasks include identifying a specific problem, analyzing the problem, arriving at criteria that an effective solution must meet, identifying possible alternative solutions to the problem and comparing the alternatives to the criteria, determining the best solution or combination of solutions, implementing the chosen solution, and monitoring the results.

Define the Problem

Much wheel-spinning takes place during the early stages of group discussion as a result of members not understanding their specific goal. It is the duty of the person, agency, or parent group that forms a particular discussion group to give the group a charge, such as "work out a new way of selecting people for merit pay increases," but rarely will the charge be stated in such a way that the group does not need to clarify its precise goal. Even when the charge seems clear, effective groups will want to make sure they are focusing on the real problem and not just symptoms of the problem.

Even when a group is given a well-defined charge, it will need to gather information before it can accurately define the specific problem. Accurately defining the problem requires the group to understand and discuss the background, history, and status of the problem. This means collecting and understanding a variety of information.

As early as possible, the group should develop a formal written statement of the problem. Unless the group has a formal definition of the problem, its discussion may be inefficient because each member may be addressing a slightly different problem.

Effective problem definitions have the following characteristics.

1. **They are stated as questions.** Because problem-solving discussions begin from the assumption that solutions are not yet known, problems should be stated as questions to be answered. For example, "What are the most important criteria for determining merit pay increases?"

2. **They contain only one central idea.** If the charge includes two questions— "Should the college abolish its foreign language and social studies require-

As early as possible, the group should develop a formal written statement of the problem.

ments?"—the group should break it down into two separate questions for discussion: "Should the college abolish its foreign language requirement? Should the college abolish its social studies requirement?"

3. **They use specific and precise language.** For instance, the problem definition "What should the department do about courses that aren't getting the job done?" may be well intentioned, and participants may have at least some idea about their goal, but such vague wording as "getting the job done" can lead to problems later. Notice how this revision of the preceding question makes its intent much clearer: "What should the department do about courses that receive low scores on student evaluations?"

4. **They can be identified as a question of fact, value, or policy.** How we organize our problem-solving discussion will depend on the kind of question we are addressing.

questions of fact questions concerned with discovering what is true or to what extent something is true

Questions of fact are concerned with discovering what is true or to what extent something is true. Implied in such questions is the possibility of determining truth through the process of examining facts by way of directly observed, spoken, or recorded evidence. "Do the sales figures from last year support our introduction of a new model next year?" is a question of fact. The group will discuss the validity of the evidence it has to determine what is true.

Questions of value concern subjective judgments of what is right, moral, good, or just. Questions of value can be recognized because they often contain evaluative words such as *good, reliable, effective,* or *worthy.* For instance, the program development team for a TV sitcom aimed at young teens may discuss "Is the proposed series of ads too sexually provocative?" Although we can establish criteria for "too sexually provocative" and measure material against those criteria, the criteria we choose and the evidence we accept depend on our judgment. A different group of people using different values might come to a different decision.

Questions of policy concern what courses of action should be taken or what rules should be adopted to solve a problem. "Where should the new landfill be built?" is a question of policy. The inclusion of the word *should* in questions of policy makes them the easiest to recognize and the easiest to phrase of all problem statements.

questions of value   questions that concern subjective judgments of what is right, moral, good, or just

questions of policy   questions that concern what courses of action should be taken or what rules should be adopted to solve a problem

Analyze the Problem

Analysis of a problem entails finding out as much as possible about the problem and determining the criteria that must be met to find an acceptable solution. Just as in speech making, three types of information can be helpful in analyzing problems. Most groups begin by sharing the information individual members have acquired through their experience. The second source of information that should be examined includes published materials available through libraries, electronic databases, and the Internet. The third source of information about a problem can be gleaned from other people. At times, the group may want to consult experts for their ideas about a problem or conduct a survey to gather information from a particular target group.

Once group members have gathered information, it must be shared with other members. It is important for group members to share new information they have found in order to fulfill the ethical responsibility that comes with participating in a problem-solving discussion. A study by A. R. Dennis revealed that groups tend to spend more time discussing information common to all group members if those members with unique information don't work to get their information heard.[8] The tendency to discuss common information while ignoring unique information leads to less effective decisions. To improve the group's ability to consider the information effectively, members should discuss information they have uncovered that seems to contradict their personal beliefs about the issue or the beliefs that have thus far been discussed by the group. When addressing complex issues, groups should separate information sharing from decision making by holding separate meetings, spaced far enough apart to enable members to think through their information.

Determine Solution Criteria

Once a group understands the nature of the problem, it is in a position to discuss the tests a solution must pass to solve the problem. The criteria selected should be ones that the information gathered has suggested are critical to successfully solving the problem. These criteria will be used to screen alternative solutions. Solutions that do not meet the test of all criteria are eliminated from further consideration. For example, a local citizens' committee is charged with selecting a site for a new county jail. The group arrives at the following phrasing for the problem: "Where should the new jail be located?" After the group agrees on this wording, they can then ask the question, "What are the criteria for a good site for a new jail?"

In discussion, suppose members contribute information related to the county's budget, the need for inmates to maintain family contact, concerns about proximity to schools and parks, and space needs. After considering this kind of information, the group might then choose the following criteria for selecting a site:

1. Maximum cost of $500,000 for purchasing the land.
2. A location no more than three blocks from public transportation.
3. A location that is one mile or more from any school, day-care center, playground, or youth center.
4. A lot size of at least ten acres.

Author Kathryn Young and her colleagues suggest that when groups discuss and decide on criteria before they think about specific solutions they increase the likelihood that they will be able to avoid becoming polarized and will be more likely to come to a decision that all members can accept.[9]

Identify Possible Solutions

For most policy questions, many solutions are possible. The trick is to tap the creative thinking of group members so that many ideas are generated. At this stage of discussion, the goal is not to worry about whether a particular solution fits all the criteria but to come up with a large list of ideas.

brainstorming a technique for generating as many ideas as possible by being creative, suspending judgment, and combining or adapting the ideas of others

One way to identify potential solutions is to brainstorm for ideas. **Brainstorming,** you'll recall, is an uncritical, nonevaluative process of generating ideas by being creative, suspending judgment, and combining or adapting the ideas of others. It involves verbalizing your ideas as they come to mind, without stopping to evaluate their merits. Members are encouraged, however, to build on the ideas presented by others. In a ten- or fifteen-minute brainstorming session, a group may come up with twenty or more possible solutions depending on the nature of the problem.

Evaluate Solutions

Once the group has a list of possible solutions, it needs to compare each solution alternative to the criteria that were developed. During this phase, the group must determine whether each of the criteria are equally important or whether certain criteria should be given more weight in evaluating the alternative solutions. Whether a group more heavily weights certain criteria or not, it should use a process that ensures that each alternative solution is thoroughly assessed against all of the criteria.

Decide

A group brought together for problem solving may or may not be responsible for making the actual decision, but it is responsible for presenting its recommendation. **Decision making** is the process of choosing among alternatives. The following five methods differ in the extent to which they require that all members agree with the decision and the amount of time it takes to reach a decision.

decision making the process of choosing among alternatives

1. **The expert opinion method.** Once the group has eliminated those alternatives that do not meet the criteria, the group asks the member who has the most expertise to select the final choice. Obviously, this method is quick and is useful when one member is much more knowledgeable about the issues or has a greater stake in the implementation of the decision.

expert opinion method asking the group member who has the most expertise to select the final choice

2. **The average group opinion method.** When using this approach, each member of the group ranks each of the alternatives that meet all the criteria. Their rankings are then averaged, and the alternative receiving the highest average ranking becomes the choice. This method is useful for routine decisions or when a deci-

average group opinion method accepting the alternative receiving the highest average ranking as the choice

sion needs to be made quickly. It can also be used as an intermediate straw poll that enables the group to eliminate low-scoring alternatives before moving to a different process for making the final decision.

3. **The majority rule method.** When using this method, the group votes on each alternative and the one that receives the majority of votes (50% + 1) is selected. Although this method is considered democratic, it can create problems. If the majority voting for an alternative is slight, then there may be nearly as many members who do not support the choice as there are those that do. If these minority members strongly object to the choice, they may sabotage implementation of the solution either through active or passive means.

majority rule method selecting the alternative that receives the majority of votes (50% + 1)

4. **The unanimous decision method.** In this method the group must continue deliberation until every member of the group believes the same solution is the best. As you would expect, it is very difficult to arrive at truly unanimous decisions, and to do so takes a lot of time. When a group reaches unanimity, however, it can expect that each member of the group will be fully committed to selling the decision to others and helping to implement the decision.

unanimous decision method every member of the group believes the same solution alternative is the best

5. **The consensus method.** This method is an alternative to the unanimous decision method. In consensus the group continues deliberation until all members of the group find an acceptable variation, one they can support and are committed to helping implement. Some members of the group may believe there is a better solution than the one that has been chosen, but they feel they can "live with" the one they have agreed to. Arriving at consensus, although easier than reaching unanimity, is still difficult. Although the majority rule method is widely used, going with the consensus method is a wise investment if the group needs everyone's support to implement the decision successfully.

consensus method the process of determining a solution that all members of the group find acceptable, can support, and are committed to helping implement

Implement and Monitor Decisions

In some cases, a decision made by a group requires some or all members of the group to take action to implement it. When this is the case, the group continues to use the problem-solving process to determine how action will be taken and who will be responsible for specific acts. In other cases, decisions made by the group may not require it to take action but may direct the work of others. For example, the citizens' site selection committee's choice for locating the new jail will not be implemented by the committee but by county officials. In either case, however, the group retains an ethical responsibility for monitoring how well the alternative that was chosen has been implemented and whether the original problem has been resolved. This monitoring responsibility can be delegated to one member of the group, or in the case of an ongoing group the results of decisions can be scheduled for regular review.

Leading Problem-Solving Discussions

How many times have you complained that a meeting you attended was a waste of time? Good problem-solving discussions don't just happen. They are intentionally planned, facilitated, and followed up. One of the principal duties formal discussion leaders perform is to plan and run effective problem-solving sessions. The following guidelines can help leaders make discussions productive.

Leaders of formal discussions should begin meetings by reviewing the goals and agenda for the session.

Preparing for the Meeting

1. **Prepare the agenda.** An agenda is an organized outline of the items that need to be covered during the meeting. Items for the agenda come from where the goup is in its problem-solving process and can be determined by reviewing the minutes of the previous meeting. What steps did the group agree to take? What new issues have arisen since the last meeting? Effective discussion leaders make sure the agenda is appropriate for the length of the meeting. Exhibit 16.2 shows an agenda for a group meeting to decide which one of three courses to offer over the Web next semester.

2. **Decide who should attend the meeting.** In most cases, all of the members of a problem-solving group will attend meetings. At times, however, one or more members of the group may not need to attend a particular meeting but may only need to be informed of the outcomes of the meeting.

3. **Arrange for an appropriate location and meeting time.** Be sure the location has all of the equipment and supplies the group will need to work effectively. This may include arranging for audiovisual equipment, computers, and other specialized equipment. Discussion groups become less effective when meetings go on too long. Ideally, a meeting should last no more than ninety minutes. If a meeting requires a longer period of time, then hourly breaks should be planned.

4. **Distribute the agenda.** The agenda should be in the hands of participants several days before the discussion. Unless group members get an agenda ahead of time, they won't be able to prepare for the meeting.

5. **Speak with each participant prior to the meeting to understand his or her positions and personal goals.** Spending time pre-working issues helps the leader anticipate conflicts that are likely to emerge during discussion and to plan how to manage them so that the group makes effective decisions and maintains cohesiveness.

EXHIBIT 16.2 Agenda for Web course committee

March 1, 2002

To: Campus commuter discussion group

From: Janelle Smith

Re: Agenda for discussion group meeting

Date: March 8

Place: Student Union, Conference Room A

Time: 3:00 P.M. to 4:30 P.M. (Please be prompt)

Meeting Objectives:

We will familiarize ourselves with each of three courses that have been proposed for Web-based delivery next semester.

We will evaluate each course against the criteria we developed last month.

We will use a consensus decision process to determine which of the three courses to offer.

Agenda for Group Discussion:

Review of Philosophy 141

    Report by Justin on Philosophy 141 proposal

    Committee questions

    Comparison of PHIL 141 to criteria

Review of Art History 336

    Report by Marique on Art History 336 proposal

    Committee questions

    Comparison of ARTH 336 to criteria

Review of Communication 235

    Report by Kathryn on Communication 235

    Committee questions

    Comparison of COMM 235 to criteria

Consensus building discussion and decision.

    Which proposals fit the criteria?

    Are there noncriteria-related factors to consider?

    Which proposal is more acceptable to all members?

Discussion of next steps and task assignments.

Set date of next meeting.

Leading Discussion

1. **Review and modify the agenda.** Begin the meeting by reviewing the agenda and modifying it per member suggestions. Because things can change between the time an agenda is distributed and when the discussion is held, reviewing the agenda ensures that the group is working on items that are still important and relevant. Reviewing the agenda also gives members a chance to control what is to be discussed.

2. **Provide task direction and manage interpersonal dynamics.** The role of the leader during a discussion is to provide the task or procedural direction and relationship management that the group lacks. Leaders need to maintain awareness of what the group needs at a specific time to facilitate productive discussion. For example, if the leader notices that some people are talking more than their fair share, and no one else is trying to draw out quieter members, the leader should try to balance the discussion by asking a reluctant member to comment.

3. **Monitor the time so that the group stays on schedule.** It is easy for a group to get bogged down in a discussion. Although a group member may serve as an expediter, it is the leader's responsibility to make sure the group stays on schedule.

4. **Monitor conflicts and intervene as needed.** A healthy level of conflict should be encouraged in the discussion so that issues are fully examined. But if the conflict level becomes dysfunctional, the leader may need to mediate so that relationships are not unduly strained.

5. **Periodically check to see if the group is ready to make a decision.** The leader of the group should listen for agreement and move the group into a formal decision process when the leader senses that discussion is no longer adding insight.

6. **Implement the group's decision rules.** The leader is responsible for overseeing that the decision-making rules the group has agreed to are used. If the group is deciding by consensus, the leader needs to make sure that each member feels that the chosen alternative is one that he or she can support. If the group is deciding by majority rule, the leader calls for the vote and tallies the results.

7. **Before ending the meeting summarize decisions, task responsibilities that have been assigned, and next steps that have been planned.** To bring closure to the meeting and to make sure that each member leaving the meeting is clear about what has been accomplished, the leader should summarize what has happened in the meeting.

8. **Ask the group to decide if and when another meeting is needed.** Continuing groups should be careful not to meet just for the sake of meeting. Leaders should clarify with members when and if future meetings are necessary. The overall purposes of future meetings will dictate the agenda that will need to be prepared.

Following Up

1. **Review the discussion outcomes and process.** A good leader learns how to be more effective at running discussions by reflecting on and analyzing how well the previous meeting went. Leaders need to think about whether the discussion accomplished its goals and whether group cohesion was improved or damaged in the process.

2. **Prepare and distribute a summary of discussion outcomes.** Some groups have a member who serves as the recorder and who distributes minutes, but many groups rely on their leaders for this. A written record of what was agreed to, accomplished, and next steps serves to remind group members of the work they have to do. If the group has a recorder, the leader should check to make sure that minutes are distributed in a timely manner.

3. **Repair damaged relationships through informal conversations.** If the debate during the discussion has been heated, it is likely that some people have damaged their relationships with others and left the meeting angry or hurt. Leaders can help repair relationships by seeking out these participants and talking with them. Through empathetic listening, we can soothe hurt feelings and spark a recommitment to the group.

4. **Follow up with participants to see how they are progressing on items assigned to them.** When participants have been assigned specific task responsibilities, the leader should check with them to see if they have encountered any problems in completing what was assigned.

Member Responsibilities

Members of effective problem-solving discussions also assume common responsibilities for making their meetings successful. The following guidelines were prepared by a class of university students. These guidelines describe how problem-solving group members should prepare for, behave in, and follow up the discussion so that problem-solving effectiveness is increased.[10]

Preparing for the Meeting

As the chapter opening vignette illustrated, too often people think of group discussions as a happening that requires attendance but no particular preparation. Countless times we've observed people who bring the packets of material about a discussion with them, but have spent little, if any, time studying the material. The reality is that problem-solving discussions should not be treated as impromptu events but as activities that pool information from well-prepared individuals. Before the meeting, prepare yourself by following these guidelines.

1. **Study the agenda.** Determine the purpose of the discussion and what you need to do to be prepared. Consider the agenda as an outline for preparation.
2. **Study the minutes.** If this is one of a series of meetings, study the minutes and your own notes from the previous discussion. Each meeting is not a separate event. What happened at one meeting should provide the basis for preparation for the next meeting.
3. **Prepare for your contributions.** Read handouts and do the research to become better informed about items on the agenda. If no handouts are given, it is up to you to find sources of information that you will need to be a contributing member of the discussion. Bring any materials you have uncovered that will aid the group in reaching a decision. If appropriate, discuss the agenda with others who will not be attending the meeting and solicit their ideas concerning issues to be discussed in the meeting.
4. **List questions.** Make a list of questions related to agenda items that you would like to have answered during the discussion.

Participating in the Discussion

Go into the discussion with the expectation that you will be a full participant. If there are five people in the group, all five should be participating.

1. **Listen attentively.** Concentrate on what others are saying so that you can use your material to complement, supplement, or counter what has been presented.
2. **Stay focused.** In a group setting, it's easy to get the discussion going in nonproductive directions. Keep your comments focused on the specific agenda item under consideration. If others have gotten off the subject, do what you can to get people back on track.

3. **Ask questions.** "Honest" questions whose answers you do not already know help to stimulate discussion and help to build ideas.

4. **Play devil's advocate.** When you think an idea has not been fully discussed or tested, be willing to voice disagreement or encourage further discussion.

5. **Monitor your contributions.** Especially when people are well prepared, they have a tendency to dominate discussion. Make sure you are neither dominating the discussion nor abdicating your responsibility to share insights and opinions.

6. **Take notes.** Even if someone else is responsible for providing the official minutes, you'll want notes that help you follow the line of development. Also, these notes will help you remember what has been said.

Following Up

Too often when discussions end, people leave and forget about what took place until the next meeting. What happens in one discussion provides a basis for what happens in the next, so it is important to follow up.

1. **Review and summarize your notes.** Try to do this shortly after you've left the meeting while ideas are still fresh in your mind. Make notes of what needs to be discussed next time.

2. **Evaluate your effectiveness.** How effective were you in helping the group move toward achieving its goals? Where were you strong? Where were you weak? What should you do next time that you didn't do in this discussion?

3. **Review decisions.** Make note of what your role was in making decisions. Did you do all that you could have?

4. **Communicate progress.** Inform others who need to know about information conveyed and decisions that were made by the group.

5. **Follow up.** Make sure you complete any assignments you received in the meeting.

6. **Review minutes.** Compare the official minutes of the meeting to your own notes, and report any significant discrepancies that you find from your own notes.

When the Discussion Goes Public

Although most of your group problem solving will be done in private and without the presence of an onlooking or participating audience, occasionally a discussion takes place in a public forum. Sometimes this means conducting your discussion with nonparticipating observers present; at other times this means presenting your group's conclusions to another group. In a public discussion, the group's discussion provides information for the listening audience as much as it provides the basis for members to analyze or solve a problem. As such, public discussions have much in common with traditional public speaking. Three common forms of public discussion are the symposium, the panel discussion, and the town hall meeting.

symposium a discussion in which a limited number of participants present individual speeches of approximately the same length dealing with the same subject, then discuss their reactions to what others have said and answer questions from the audience

Symposium

A **symposium** is a discussion in which a limited number of participants (usually three to five) present individual speeches of approximately the same length dealing with the same subject. After delivering their planned speeches, the participants in the symposium may discuss their reactions with one another or respond to questions

AP/Wide World Photos

Town Hall style meetings are often used by communities to discuss controversial issues that affect the well-being of residents.

from the audience. Despite the potential for interaction, a symposium often is characterized by long, sometimes unrelated speeches. Moreover, the part designated for questions may be shortened or canceled because "our time is about up." A symposium often omits the interaction necessary for a good discussion. If the participants make their prepared speeches short enough so that at least half of the available time can be spent on real interaction, a symposium can be interesting and stimulating. A good symposium that meets the goals of discussion is much more difficult to present than it appears; as a public-speaking assignment, however, the symposium may be beneficial. Rather than solving a problem, a symposium is more effective in shedding light on or explaining various aspects of a problem.

Panel Discussion

A **panel discussion** is a problem-solving discussion in front of an audience. After the formal discussion, the audience often is encouraged to question the participants. The discussion thus can be seen and heard by the audience: The group is seated in a semicircle, with the chairperson in the middle, to get a good view of the audience and the panelists. Because the discussion is for an audience, the panelists are obliged to make good use of traditional public-speaking skills. And because a panel discussion encourages spontaneity and interaction, it can be stimulating for both the audience and the participants. The panel works as a form of problem-solving discussion.

panel discussion a problem-solving discussion in front of an audience

Town Hall Meeting

A **town hall meeting** is an event in which a large number of people who are interested in a topic are convened to discuss and at times to decide an issue. In the New England states, many small towns use town hall meetings of residents to decide community-wide issues. In a town hall meeting, one person who is repected by other participants is selected to lead the discussion. The leader announces the ground rules

town hall meeting an event in which a large number of people who are interested in a topic are convened to discuss and, at times, decide an issue

for the discussion, introduces the issues to be discussed, calls on participants for comments, ensures that divergent opinions are expressed, periodically summarizes the discussion, and oversees the decision making. Because town hall meetings involve large numbers of people, turn taking is strictly controlled by the leader. Many town hall meetings follow *Roberts Rules of Order* so that the discussion remains focused and all participants' views are heard.

Summary

Effective problem-solving discussion groups share five characteristics: they develop clearly defined goals, have an optimum number of diverse members, work to develop cohesiveness, establish rules and norms, and meet in an appropriate setting.

Problem solving is a process that includes defining the problem as a question of fact, value, or policy; analyzing the problem; determining solution criteria; identifying possible solutions; evaluating solutions; deciding; and implementing and monitoring the decision.

Both members and leaders can improve the effectiveness of the meetings they attend by pre-meeting preparations, during meeting behaviors, and postmeeting activities.

Three common forms of public discussion are the symposium, the panel discussion, and the town hall meeting.

CHALLENGE ONLINE

Use your Challenge of Effective Speaking CD-ROM for quick access to the electronic study resources that accompany this text. Included on your CD-ROM is access to the Challenge of Effective Speaking Web site featuring Speech Builder Express at Wadsworth Communication Café, InfoTrac College Edition, and a demo of WebTutor for *The Challenge of Effective Speaking*. The Web site offers chapter-by-chapter access to the Speech Preparation Action Step Activities, InfoTrac College Edition exercises, a digital glossary of key terms, Web links, Speech Preparation Forms, Speech Evaluation Checklists, and quizzes. Review the key terms and complete the InfoTrac College Edition exercise at **http://www.wadsworth.com/product/0534563856**

InfoTrac College Edition Exercise

In Subject Guide enter "Democracy, Performance, and Outcomes in Interdisciplinary Health Care Teams" by Stephany J. Coopman, *Journal of Business Communication*, July 2001. Scroll down to the heading "Pragmatic Applications" near the end of the article. Read the first five paragraphs. What is the importance of all members of a team (a group) participating? What can you do in groups to which you belong to ensure participation in decision making by all members?

Key Terms

average group opinion method *(334)*

brainstorming *(334)*

cohesiveness *(329)*

consensus method *(335)*

decision making *(334)*

expert opinion method *(334)*

ground rules *(329)*

majority rule method *(335)*

norms *(329)*

panel discussion *(341)*

problem-solving discussion *(328)*

problem-solving goal *(328)*

questions of fact *(332)*

questions of policy *(333)*

questions of value *(333)*

symposium *(340)*

town hall meeting *(341)*

unanimous decision method *(335)*

working environment *(329)*

Appendix: Sample Speeches

All the sample speeches included in this main text were given by students. The speeches cited in this appendix illustrate how contemporary speakers have met the challenge of effective speaking. First are two speeches printed in their entirety. Each of them contains enough examples of the successful application of basic principles to make them worthy of attention. Your goal is not to copy what these speakers have done but to read and analyze them in order to better test the value of what you are planning to do in your own speeches. Then follow several titles of additional speeches you can access through InfoTrac College Edition.

The Purpose of Life: Where Have All the Heroes Gone?[1]

A speech by Janice Thayer, President of the Excel Corporation, delivered to the YMCA Woman of Distinction Annual Dinner, Grand Island, Nebraska, August 17, 2000. This speech is given at a special occasion, and Janice Thayer begins by identifying key people involved and thanking the organization for inviting her to be the Keynote Speaker. After further recognizing Aileen Gruendel for her award, she moves into her speech. Some features to look for are her means of identifying with this specific audience, her method of organization, her use of specific examples and illustrations, and her challenge "to make a difference."

Good Evening: Honored Guest, Aileen Gruendel, Dave, All Past Honorees, Executive Director, Anita, Your Executive Officers, Board Members, Volunteers and Members of the Grand Island YWCA, Ladies and Gentlemen:

Thank you very much for the recognition you've afforded me by inviting me to be your Keynote Speaker tonight. With sincerity, I say that it is an honor for me. And, to you, Aileen, my heartfelt Congratulations!

Since the announcement was made that Aileen was named as this year's Woman of Distinction, I have personally heard from people who were delighted with the news. Among them, Aileen, are your clients, friends and acquaintances—all so pleased and proud of you!

Columnist Leo Rosten wrote, "The purpose of life is to matter, to count, to have it make some difference that we lived at all."

I have been blessed to have been given the opportunity to spend my professional life in the company of mostly octogenarians—and many years beyond that at times. In the end, they all wanted to have mattered, to count, to have made a difference that they lived at all.

What kind of challenge is facing us that we might look at individually and collectively so that we might find a way to make that difference? I have always known that when women of the YWCA and women everywhere are faced with a challenge, a solution will be found and the problem will be fixed. Sometimes it takes just a while.

Sometimes it takes a little longer. But just for a moment, think about some truly notable and courageous women—Florence Nightingale and Susan B. Anthony and Amelia Earhart and Rosa Parks and Mother Theresa. Heroes all! They faced almost unsurmountable challenges and they faced them down because they all believed in their mission, and one person with a belief is worth more than ninety-nine with an opinion.

Since the time that those women were born, many battles have been fought and won—but some have been lost and among those that I fear we are losing is that of the hearts, minds and souls of our children—of our people to what has been called "The Coarsening of America."

Where have all the heroes gone?

Remember the old fashioned western movies? The hero was square-jawed and clean-shaven and he wore a white hat that he removed in the presence of women.

The villain, of course, had whiskers, wore a black hat and never removed it for anyone. But, even he didn't indulge in foul-mouthed language and the blood and guts destruction of another human being.

It used to be easier. We learned our ethical ideals from our parents and the message was simple: Virtue Triumphed. The Good Guys Won!

And the Hero or Heroine was the paragon of honesty, integrity, and trustworthiness. Where have all the heroes gone?

Even today, in the world of cynicism that surrounds us, when *Star Wars* was released again, it played to record crowds. We knew who the good guys were and the good guys won.

But, in real life, heroes are in short supply. Most Americans think that politicians today are characterized by glib rhetoric, empty promises, corruption and moral bankruptcy.

Ask people who work on a production line and they are likely to tell you that corporate executives embrace a balance sheet mentality which encourages bribery, price fixing, and defective products and services—and places no value on the worker as a person with needs and wants and dreams.

Police and firefighters and teachers and nurses in some cases abandon their posts to picket.

In the past they were the heroes, but now even the most honored, prized, professional athlete is too often revealed to be just a muscled mass whose annual salary is more than a dozen of my family members will together earn in a lifetime.

Where have all the heroes gone? I believe they are right here, right now, in this room.

They are you, the women who believe in the mission and the values of this organization who can confront our ills. And, it is the men who will work beside you. The mothers and fathers in America will have to speak up because when you are silent about a wrong, you condone it.

Where do we begin? Where we are is important, but in which direction we're moving is critical.

We must begin with our own thoughts. I once read that you become what you think, and I must say that for a moment I had my doubts, because if that were entirely true, all 7th grade boys would have become girls. We have to begin with our thoughts—our beliefs and this is what I believe.

We must bring back, not just to our own families, but to our schools and our workplaces, our organizations, our community and our country the value of:

RESPONSIBILITY

RESPECT

RELIGION AND
RIGHT—DOING WHAT'S RIGHT!

We must teach these principles and we must live them for it is not so much what we say as what we do.

Responsibility

Do you think that Florence Nightingale would picket? What would she say about responsibility; for to be responsible means to be accountable for our actions.

To practice responsibility is to do what we said we would do. To understand responsibility is to learn it when you are young. As a child, you must be taught to apologize to your neighbors when you pick their flowers, even if it is for the noble purpose of presenting a bouquet to your mother.

Children need to have work—and it should be appropriate for their age and ability. It is to have household chores and to contribute to the family unit by doing their share. We help foster a mature sense of responsibility in children in the same way that we cultivate other desirable traits: by practice and by example. Homework, extracurricular activities, after-school jobs, and volunteer work all contribute to maturation if parental example and expectations are clear, consistent and commensurate with the developing powers of the child.

It is a truism that everything which has ever been done in the world has been done by somebody. It was Adam, who when he ate the forbidden fruit in the Garden of Eden, laid the responsibility on Eve. And it was Eve, who in turn laid it on the beguiling serpent. "She made me do it/He made me do it" is a drama reenacted in every generation where siblings and playmates are called upon to answer for their misdeeds.

I can no longer bear to hear grown-ups talk about "mistakes that were made" and then expect the comforting calm of forgiveness to shower down on them like a gentle, warm and welcome rain in a summer evening—while they have been exhibiting the same pattern of behavior all of their lives.

I think a mistake is when you add two and two and get five on a math test. A mistake is when you read a map and turn a block too soon. I think a mistake is when you have made an error, but you learned from it and never repeat it again. To blame unseemly actions as a mistake is to never have learned responsibility.

That's not how it should be, and you can do something about it.

When I was the administrator every day at Riverside Lodge, whenever we hired a student, I had the opportunity to give them what I later learned my office staff termed her "Mother Superior Speech." It was the perfect time to talk about the responsibilities of holding a job; of contributing to the team; of coming to work as scheduled and on time. It would mean that you would probably have to work on a Saturday evening when your friends were going to a party. It would mean that your mother shouldn't call and make excuses for you so that you could go to that party, too.

When our son, Dan, was in Junior High School, I needed to attend a board meeting and participate in a work session in San Francisco. Ernie and I decided that it would be a wonderful opportunity for the entire family to travel with me and he and the boys could enjoy the city while I attended the meeting during the day. We told the boys to talk with their teachers and we called the schools to tell the principals that we felt this would be a very educational trip and would like them to excuse our sons. All gave that permission.

But, then Dan also needed to talk with his basketball coach. His coach said, "Yes, you may go, but if you go there will be consequences. You will not be practicing with your team, therefore you won't be prepared for our next game; you won't be a starter and I cannot guarantee how much you will play."

Dan came home to tell us about his talk with Coach Traudt and we said, "What do you want to do?" He said, "I want to go with you, but I'm going to stay home. My team needs me and I want to start and I want to play." My eyes filled with tears that I hoped he wouldn't see. I wanted him to go with us, but I knew that a grandparent or trusted friend would look after him and we were exceedingly proud of his decision.

That's responsibility. Maybe it was because he had to apologize to a neighbor when he picked her flowers to give his mother a bouquet. We must teach that in the end, we are all answerable for the kinds of persons we have become. That is how it should be and you can do something about it.

Respect

Where has it gone the heroes would ask. "The Coarsening of America" has crept up on us, and it is as vulgar as gutter language in a living room. On the Jerry Springer Show people reveal the most ugly things about each other, are verbally and physically abusive and the audience cheers!

Road rage leads to violent behavior and children are brought up to believe that it's normal when they are berated and belittled and somewhere every day the death of a child is reported—sometimes at the hand of a trusted adult and sometimes at the hand of another child.

I am disappointed in myself that I no longer recoil as viscerally as I once did when I hear four letter words in a movie. I watch so little of the network television programs, but when I do I am still amazed at the foul language that is spewed without so much as a blush.

Some of you will remember the collective gasp in movie theaters all across the country when Scarlett O'Hara said, "Oh, Rhett, what am I going to do?" and he replied, "Frankly, my dear, I don't give a damn!" There was a time when profanity and the use of the repulsive "f" word in movies and television, in homes and in schools was as alien as a stalk of corn in a field of rice. But, now it seems to be accepted in all manner of speech.

It should not be and you can do something about it. You can disapprove and write letters and send e-mail; stop buying the products of the sponsors who pay for the creation of this kind of trash and sell it as entertainment.

Where is respect for the police, for teachers and preachers, for parents and grandparents, for each other and for ourselves. It has to be taught. Just think about what a child learns from an adult who makes an obscene gesture to the driver in the car ahead of him because of a forgotten turn signal. Think about what a child learns from a parent who threatens to sue the teacher because the child was disciplined.

Good manners have disappeared from political discourse and there is more emphasis placed on human failure than on success.

Religion

Some of our churches' leaders believe that one of the reasons people seem to be going astray when it comes to values is that families don't give them the attention they once did. Some people want a religion that will make them feel respectable but does not require them to be. Daniel Webster said that, "If we abide by the principles taught in the Bible, our country will go on prospering."

There are blatant attempts to make ours a Godless society and for the past 30 years, our Supreme Court uses the Constitution and The Bill of Rights to gird the argument. But, what the First Amendment really says is that "Congress shall make no law respecting an establishment of religion or prohibiting the free exercise thereof."

Many countries have made one religion the Established official church and supported it with government funds. This amendment forbids Congress to set up or in any way provide for an established church. It has been interpreted to forbid government endorsement of, or aid to, religious doctrines.

But, has this interpretation been carried too far? Which of the Ten Commandments are harmful to our actions? Does the Golden Rule lift us to a better way of conducting our lives? Is it art to smear cow dung on a picture of the Virgin Mary, then force you to pay for it with your tax dollars?

We have been fortunate to have traveled recently to Athens and to the seat of the Roman Empire. The excesses of the past are still there to see and to imagine yet today. And as you walk through the coliseum your mind tricks you into thinking that you can see and hear and smell man's inhumanity to man and beast.

Edward Gibbon in 1788, set forth in his famous book, Decline and Fall of the Roman Empire, five reasons why that great civilization withered and died.

The undermining of the dignity and sanctity of the home, which is the basis for human society.

Higher and higher taxes; the spending of public money for free bread and circuses for the populace.

The mad craze for pleasure, with sports and plays becoming more exciting, more brutal and more immoral.

The building of great armaments when the real enemy was within—decay of individual responsibility.

The decay of religion whose leaders lost touch with life and their power to guide.

It's a sobering paragraph, isn't it? Regardless of the protesters and those who discount it, we must continue to keep faith as the foundation of our society, for those who pray as they ought, will endeavor to live as they pray.

Right—Do what is right

Rosa Parks knew that it was not right to have to go to the back of the bus. She would say that little by little we have learned that women—that all people—must be treated more equally, and that racial progress has been steady, yet too slow.

She'd say that we must value the world in which we live and celebrate our differences because the melting pot is being supplanted by a gumbo pot; and rather than trying to boil everything down to make this one soup, all of these ingredients are needed to make it interesting. It is right for America to accept itself.

Children are not born knowing prejudice. As the song says, "They've got to be taught to hate and fear—they have to be carefully taught!" It is essential to teach youngsters right from wrong as they grow up. There has been a myth that children can create their own values, but of course, children have precious little chance to do that. Does it make sense for parents to remain neutral bystanders when everyone else from script writers, to entertainers, to advertisers, to sex educators insist on selling their values to our children?

A study conducted by the Search Institute showed that children whose parents express and enforce standards thrive at twice the rate of children who don't have values promoted in a similar way.

With kids there is too much sex and seduction too soon and it is promoted both in overt and subtle ways. When do they have time to be innocent? They don't unless we protect them.

There are times when it is right to tell children no—and they want to be; they want to have limits; they want their moms and dads to care enough to make the rules. They want and need to be loved. They need to have the joy and the conversation and the companionship of the family eating dinner together. That's not done very much anymore, you know—the forum where the family can talk together about their day— what they learned and what they should have learned.

There was an article written by Dottie Enrico in *USA Today* called "Survey: Fallen Heroes Among Most Admired Athletes." It came out during O. J. Simpson's criminal trial for murder. The article reported on a survey performed by Sponsorship Research International of Stamford, Connecticut, and the results were astounding.

Among the top twenty athletes listed as most admired were Mike Tyson, O. J. Simpson, and Tonya Harding. The article went on to say, "Behavioral specialists say the presence of Tyson (a convicted rapist), Simpson, (on trial for murder) and Harding (who pleaded guilty to conspiracy) on the list is a disturbing statement about American values."

What can be right about a teenager on MTV asking the President of the United States if he wears boxers or briefs and what can be right about the President of the United States answering the question!

Have you and I always done the right thing? Of course not. In the future will we always do the right thing? Of course not, and there are times that those decisions have caused us great anguish. And that is good because anguish is the result of a conscience.

Barbara Bush must have been heartened when, in his acceptance speech her son said, "I believe in grace, because I have seen it . . . In peace, because I have felt it . . . In forgiveness, because I have needed it."

Ladies and Gentlemen, this is our challenge—yours and mine. To make a difference. Not by the conspicuousness of our silence, but by speaking out when things are wrong. The philosopher Maimonedes said, "If not now, when? If not me, who?"

Let's sum it up like this:

Fortunate are the persons,
Who in this life can find
A purpose that can fill their days
And goals to fill their mind.
For in this world there is a need
For those who'll lead the rest,
To rise above the "average" life
By giving of their best!
Will you be one, who dares to try
When challenged by the task,
To rise to heights you've never seen,
Or is that too much to ask?

Where have all the heroes gone? They who dared, who dreamed, who lifted and inspired us to understand that in the end the purpose of life is to matter, to count, to have it make some difference that we lived at all!

As so many of you here have added to my life, I hope I've added to yours in some small way. Good Night.

The Music in Your Soul: A Celebration of Life[2]

A speech by Francis J. McClain, Livingstone Professor of Music at Queens College, delivered at the Fall Convocation of Students, Faculty, and Staff of Queens College, Charlotte, North Carolina, September 18, 2001. After opening her speech with the recognition of the impact of the terrorist attack on September 11, Francis McClain focuses on the necessity of celebrating each day to its fullest. Some features to look for are her means of building her credibility on the topic, her way of showing the relevance of her topic, her means of adapting to her audience, her method of organization, and her use of quotations, examples, and illustrations.

The horrific terrorist attack on our country taught us how in a single minute, we can be hurled from order into chaos, from joy into sorrow, and from life into death. Shouldn't we, therefore, learn to appreciate life more, to view each day as the blessing it is, and to celebrate each day to its fullest? So then, on this Fall Convocation at Queens College, let us celebrate life and this day. As students, faculty, and staff, let us observe this occasion as a time of new beginnings, new goals, and new opportunities for the attainment of worthwhile endeavors.

As a music therapist, I know that the power of music can not only comfort and console us, it can also inspire, unify, and uplift our spirits. So I thought, wouldn't it be appropriate if I could place the concept of celebration within a musical framework? Now we all know that most celebrations—whether weddings, parties, dances, receptions—are more festive, more engaging, more memorable with just the right type of music. After all, most of us love, or at least, like music. WE MOVE, SOOTHE, AND GROOVE TO IT, RIGHT?

In fact, music is not just a part of our lives, it is a part of our language, as well. Don Campbell, the author of *The Mozart Effect,* states that "Music is rapidly becoming the common tongue of the modern world." Musical metaphors now dominate our language. For example:

- When people are in agreement, We are in tune, or in harmony with each other.
- When we want to make a good impression, We want to set the right tone, strike a sympathetic chord, or communicate on the same wavelength.
- When you hear good news, it is music to your ears!
- And when we don't know what to expect, we play it by ear.

And of course, the list could go on.

So then, like the musical qualities we have adopted into our language, there are also music qualities and characteristics we can utilize in our lives. Now when I speak of musical qualities, I am not referring to how well you may or may not sing or play, or what you know or don't know about music, or what type or style of music you like or dislike, or how much you loved or hated your music lessons. Regardless of this, you all have some of the same elements in you that are in music. And these musical qualities, which emanate from the soul, are essential to the celebration of life!

Think of what you respond to most in the music you enjoy—not the lyrics, but the music itself. Is it the melody, the harmony, the rhythm, the tempo or the dynamics? Whichever of these elements it is, each of us has some of these same musical qualities in us and we can use them daily.

Melody

First of all, like music, each of us has a unique melody. Just as we identify a song by its melody, each of us is identified by our melody, which I like to think of as our musical personality.

For example, some personalities are like melodies. Some of you are quiet, soft, and lyrical. Others are rhythmic and energetic. Some are majestic and somber. Yet others may be whimsical and funny. Still others are cool and mellow. And truthfully, some of you are like the new styles of music, you are just way out there.

Regardless, your melody is your own sound, your own style, your essence, your identity. You know this is true because when a person tells us something about someone else, we often say that sounds just like him or her. In other words, we recognize the melody of that individual. Whatever the sound or style of your melody, use it to celebrate life. Like the film classic with Julie Andrews, you have your own Sound of Music. So find a job, a career, a hobby, a dream that suits your music—that will let you play your melody to its fullest.

You know, you can't really be happy when you're playing someone else's song. Mama Cass Elliot, a singer my colleagues remember from their youthful days, phrases it this way: "Make your own kind of music. Sing your own special song. Make your own kind of music, even if nobody else sings along."

In the work setting especially, you need a job that will allow you the joy of expressing your melody, your creativity. As Duke Ellington, the famous African-American jazz composer and performer, said, "People who make a living doing something they don't enjoy wouldn't even be happy with a one-day work week." So find an atmosphere and environment that welcomes and nurtures your melody.

Harmony

Just as the melody is the solo or single line, the harmony involves other voices or instruments that complement and add beauty to the melody. Bringing harmony does not only refer to singing a particular voice part, such as soprano, alto, tenor, or bass, or playing given notes on a particular instrument. It also refers to how you bring various people and ideas together. You truly celebrate life when you are able to help individuals work together, care about each other, and share with each other.

I suspect that some of you as RAs in the dorm, and officers of various clubs and organizations may get plenty of practice this year in the art of harmony—of getting people to work cooperatively together and to live peacefully together, to support, complement, and genuinely care about each other.

So take heart, and remember the words of Jesus when he said, "Blessed or happy are the peacemakers, for they shall be called the children of God."

Rhythm

Well, besides melody and harmony, there is also rhythm. Many of you may respond to the rhythm of music because it organizes the music. It brings energy and vitality to the music. The rhythm gives us the beat that causes us to clap our hands and tap our feet.

Some of you have the gift of rhythm. You know how to get people organized, energized, enthusiastic, and motivated. For some of you, it will be your energy, your encouragement that will keep people from giving out or giving up. The enthusiasm you display can truly be contagious and can inspire others to go the extra mile.

Like the rhythm of nature and the rhythm of our own bodies, some of you will show a dependability and regularity in everything you do. You won't miss a single beat in anything you do to achieve your goal.

Tempo

Now just as a melody has rhythm, it also has a tempo. The element of tempo refers to the speed or pace of the music—how fast or slow the music will go. As you know, a fast tempo can stimulate us to move in a certain way, to put pep in our step, give us a boost, and energize us. In contrast, a slow tempo can help us relax, reduce stress, slow down our heart rate, help us focus more, cause us to be more introspective.

As you celebrate life, you will learn the art of tempo. Things happen to us at different times and tempos. They are not always at the expected or desired time. Some things come quickly, others far more slowly. Learn to accept and appreciate where you are right now in your life.

Some of you know how to use the element of tempo. You know how to move quickly or slowly, depending on what is needed. During this year, you may be asked to move quickly on a decision, or to do a job in a very short period of time. You will be asked to step in—at a moment's notice. And some of you will be successful because you will be able to quickly assess a situation, make a plan, stay with it, and keep a steady tempo until the task is completed.

Yet others may need to move a little slower. Perhaps take the time to listen, weigh the issues, or think through a problem. You will be successful because you were patient, because you waited, because you did not act in haste.

Some of you have perhaps already decided that the tempo of four years to complete a degree is a little too fast for you. It doesn't fit your melody—so you are going to slow down the pace. Don't be afraid to make this decision if it is appropriate for you. Remember that sometimes by slowing down the pace, we can avoid decisions or actions that could later on have detrimental results. The tempo of life can become so hectic, so complex that we can't enjoy where we are for thinking about where we want to be or think we should be. So perhaps we could all benefit by slowing down a little.

On the other hand, however, sometimes you can slow down the tempo of life a little too much. In fact, there is a proverb that I like from the book *Leaves of Gold* that states "laziness travels so slowly that poverty soon overtakes him." A word to the wise!

In all sincerity, concerning the tempo and timing of life, remember the words of King Solomon in Ecclesiastes: "To every thing there is a season, and a time to every purpose under heaven."

Dynamics

Well after melody, harmony, rhythm, tempo, the last element is that of dynamics, which refers to the volume—the loudness or softness of your melody.

Over the years, I see freshmen come in quiet, reserved, and a little shy about using their melodies and in leading others. But by the senior year, they crescendo to become leaders with loud, vibrant, and stimulating melodies. Therefore, I encourage you to use the opportunities at Queens to turn up your volume, to grow, and to be a leader. So when it is your time to be heard, be a strong soloist, sound off. Raise the volume. Show others the love and passion you have for something. Don't be afraid to put yourself out there for a cause. As Martin Luther King would say, "Be a drum major for justice."

However, when others need to be heard, let your melody float softly in the background. Those of you who have ever sung in a choir, played in a band or orchestra know how the beauty of the music can be destroyed by just one person playing or singing louder than everyone else. So learn to blend, to complement, to sustain the efforts of others. Like the element of dynamics, learn when to be loud enough to be heard and soft enough to hear others.

Well, in summary, I sincerely hope you will

- Use your unique melody in a very meaningful way throughout your life;
- Blend your voice with others to create harmony;
- Find a rhythm that organizes and energizes your life;
- Select a tempo that is comfortable for you and your goals.
- Decide when the dynamics of your melody should be loud or soft.

When you discover and develop your musical qualities, your life will truly take on a new dimension that will honor your Creator and enhance your interactions with others.

In closing, I say thank you and may God bless as you use the music in your soul to celebrate life!

Other Speeches

You can learn a great deal from reading contemporary speeches presented by a variety of speakers in many settings. Here is a list of speeches that you can download. To access these speeches using InfoTrac College Edition, click on PowerTrac. Press on Key Word and drag down to Title. Then enter one of the following titles:

Richard A. Abdoo, "Coal Is Not a Four Letter Word: A Necessity in the U.S. Energy Portfolio," *Vital Speeches* (January 1, 2002): 176–179.

Antoinette M. Bailey, "Bow Wave: Women Leaders Coming to the Fore in High Tech Businesses," *Vital Speeches* (June 1, 2002): 502–504.

William R. Brody, "The Intellectual Climate in the U.S.: Perceptions of Winners and Losers," *Vital Speeches* (July 1, 2002): 559–563.

John A. Challenger, "How to Downsize: Doing It with Dignity," *Vital Speeches* (December 1, 2000): 114–117.

George C. Fraser, "Rebuilding the Extended Family: The Power and Importance of Effective Networking," *Vital Speeches* (November 1, 2001): 48–57.

Charles M. Reed, "Reading as if for Life: Preparing Young Women for the Real World," *Vital Speeches* (November 15, 2001): 84–87.

Notes

Chapter 1

1. Daniel Golman, *Working with Emotional Intelligence* (New York: Bantam Books, 1998), pp. 12–13.

2. Larry Samovar and Richard E. Porter, "Understanding Intercultural Communication: An Introduction and Overview." *Intercultural Communication: A Reader,* 9th ed. (Belmont, CA: Wadsworth, 2000), p. 7.

3. Lee Gardenswartz and Anita Rowe, *Diverse Teams at Work* (Burr Ridge, IL: Irwin Professional Publishing, 1994), p. 32.

4. Richard L. Johannesen, *Ethics in Human Communication,* 3d ed. (Prospect Heights, IL: Waveland Press, 1990), p. 1.

5. Carl Wellman, *Morals and Ethics,* 2d ed. (Englewood Cliffs, NJ: Prentice-Hall, 1988), p. 305.

6. M. S. Pritchard, *On Becoming Responsible* (Lawrence: University of Kansas Press, 1991), p. 39.

7. Susan Neiburg Terkel and R. Shannon Duval, eds., *Encyclopedia of Ethics* (New York: Facts on File, 1999), p. 122.

8. Brian Spitzberg, "A Model of Intercultural Communication Competence," in L. A. Samovar and R. E. Porter, eds., *Intercultural Communication: A Reader,* 9th ed. (Belmont, CA: Wadsworth, 2000), p. 375.

9. Gerald M. Phillips, *Communication Incompetencies: A Theory of Training Oral Performance Behavior* (Carbondale, IL: Southern Illinois University Press, 1991).

Chapter 2

1. Virginia P. Richmond and James C. McCroskey, *Communication: Apprehension, Avoidance, and Effectiveness,* 4th ed. (Scottsdale, AZ: Gorsuch Scarisbrick, 1995), p. 98.

2. R. R. Behnke and L. W. Carlile. "Heart Rate as an Index of Speech Anxiety," *Speech Monographs* 38 (1971): 66.

3. Michael J. Beatty and R. R. Behnke, "Effects of Public Speaking Trait Anxiety and Intensity of Speaking Task on Heart Rate During Performance," *Human Communication Research* (1991): 18.

4. Michael J. Beatty, James C. McCroskey, and Alan D. Heiser, "Communication Apprehension as Temperamental Expression: A Communibiological Paradigm," *Communication Monographs* 65 (September 1998): p. 200.

5. James C. McCroskey and Michael J. Beatty, "Communication Apprehension," in James C. McCroskey, John A.

Daley, Michael M. Martin, and Michael J. Beatty, eds., *Communication and Personality: Trait Perspectives* (Cresshill, NJ: Hampton Press, 1998), p. 229.

6. John A. Daly, John P. Caughlin, and Laura Stafford, "Correlates and Consequences of Social-Communicative Anxiety," in John A. Daly, James C. McCroskey, Joe Ayres, Tim Hopf, and Debbie M. Ayres, eds., *Avoiding Communication: Shyness, Reticence, and Communication Apprehension,* 2d ed. (Cresskill, NJ: Hampton Press, 1997), p. 27.

7. Lynn Kelly, Gerald M. Phillips, and James A. Keaton, *Teaching People to Speak Well: Training and Remediation of Communication Reticence* (Cresskill, NJ: Hampton Press, 1995), p. 11.

8. Gerald Phillips, "Rhetoritherapy versus the Medical Model: Dealing with Reticence," *Communication Education* 26 (1977): 37.

9. Michael Motley, "COM Therapy," in John A. Daly, James C. McCroskey, Joe Ayres, Tim Hopf, and Debbie M. Ayres, eds., *Avoiding Communication: Shyness, Reticence, and Communication Apprehension,* 2d ed. (Cresskill, NJ: Hampton Press, 1997), p. 27.

10. Phillips, "Rhetoritherapy versus the Medical Model," p. 37.

11. Theodore Clevenger Jr., "A Synthesis of Experimental Research in Stage Fright," *Quarterly Journal of Speech,* 45 (April 1959): 136.

12. Kathleen Ellis, "Apprehension, Self-Perceived Competency, and Teacher Immediacy in the Laboratory-Supported Public Speaking Course: Trends and Relationships," *Communication Education* 44 (January 1995): 73.

13. Heidi M. Rose, Andrew S. Rancer, and Kenneth C. Crannell, "The Impact of Basic Courses in Oral Interpretation and Public Speaking on Communication Apprehension," *Communication Reports* 6 (Winter 1993): 58.

14. Motley, "COM Therapy," p. 382.

15. Ibid., p. 380.

16. Joe Ayres and Theodore S. Hopf, "The Long-Term Effect of Visualization in the Classroom—A Brief Research Report," *Communication Education* 39 (January 1990): 77.

17. Phil Scott, "Mind of a Champion," *Natural Health* 27 (January–February 1997): 99.

18. Joe Ayres, Tim Hopf, and Debbie M. Ayres, "An Examination of Whether Imaging Ability Enhances the

Effectiveness of an Intervention Designed to Reduce Speech Anxiety," *Communication Education* 43 (July 1994): 256.

19. Virginia P. Richmond and James McCroskey, *Communication: Apprehension, Avoidance, and Effectiveness,* 4th ed. (Scottsdale, AZ: Gorsuch Scarisbrick, 1995), p. 98.

20. Lynne Kelly, Gerald M. Phillips, and James A. Keaten, *Teaching People to Speak Well: Training and Remediation of Communication Reticence* (Cresskill, NJ: Hampton Press, 1995), p. 11.

21. Ibid., pp. 11–13.

22. Karen Kangas Dwyer, "The Multidimensional Model: Teaching Students to Self-Manage High Communication Apprehension by Self-Selecting Treatments," *Communication Education,* 49 (January 2000): 79.

23. Delivered in speech class, University of Cincinnati. Used with permission of Eric Wais.

Chapter 3

1. Andrew Wolvin and Carolyn Gwynn Coakley, *Listening,* 4th ed. (Dubuque, IA: Brown & Benchmark, 1996), p. 69.

2. Michel Purdy, "What Is Listening?" in Michael Purdy and Deborah Borsoff, eds., *Listening in Everyday Life: A Personal and Professional Approach,* 2d ed. (New York: University Press of America, 1997), p. 4.

3. Lyman K. Steil, Larry L. Barker, and Kittie W. Watson, *Effective Listening* (Reading, MA: Addison-Wesley, 1983), p. 51. See also C. Day, "How Do You Rate as a Listener?" *Industry Week* 205 (April 28, 1980): 30–35; and R. W. Rasberry, "Are Your Students Listening? A Method for Putting Listening Instruction into the Business Communication Course," *Proceedings,* Southwest American Business Communication Association Spring Conference (1980): 215.

4. Joan Gorham, "The Relationship between Verbal Teacher Immediacy Behaviors and Student Learning," *Communication Education* 37 (1988): 51.

5. Roni S. Lebauer, *Learning to Listen, Listen to Learn: Academic Listening and Note-Taking,* 2nd ed. (White Plains, NY: Longman, 2000), p. 49.

6. Wolvin and Coakley, *Listening,* p. 239.

7. Charles U. Larson, *Persuasion: Reception and Responsibility,* 8th ed. (Belmont, CA: Wadsworth, 1998), p. 12.

Chapter 4

No notes in this chapter.

Chapter 5

1. *The World Almanac and Book of Facts* (Mahwah, NJ: World Almanac Books, 2001), p. 803.

Chapter 6

1. M. Miller, *The Lycos Personal Internet Guide* (Indianapolis, IN: Que Corporation, 1999), p. 187.

2. R. A. Sherman, *Mr. Modem's Internet Guide for Seniors* (San Francisco: CA: Sybex, 1999), p. 137.

3. N. Snell, *Teach Yourself the Internet in 14 Hours,* 2d ed. (Indianapolis, IN: Sams.Net., 1998), p. 258.

4. David Munger, Daniel Anderson, Bret Benjamin, Christopher Busiel, and Bill Pardes-Holt, *Researching Online,* 3d ed. (New York: Longman, 2000), p. 5.

5. Ibid.

6. "Using Cyber Resources." [Web page] DeVry/Phoenix, March 15, 2000. URL: http://www.devry-phyx.edu//rnresrc//dowsc/integrity.htm [Accessed October 17, 2001]

7. Jim Kapoun, "Teaching Undergraduates WEB Evaluation: A Guide for Library Instruction." [Web page] January 25, 2000. URL: http://www.ala.org/acrl/undwebev.htm. [Accessed October 17, 2001]

8. Munger, Anderson, Benjamin, Busiel, and Pardes-Holt, *Researching Online,* p. 17.

9. Esther Grassian, "Thinking Critically about World Wide Web Resources." [Web page] June 1995; URL: http//www.library.ucla.edu/libraries/college/help/critical/index.htm. [Accessed October 17, 2001]

10. Craig T. Tengler and Frederic M. Jablin, "Effects of Question Type, Orientation, and Sequencing in the Employment Screening Interview," *Communication Monographs* 50 (1983): 261.

11. Shirley Biagi, *Interviews That Work: A Practical Guide for Journalists,* 2d ed. (Belmont, CA: Wadsworth, 1992), p. 94.

12. Susan Paddock, "Campaigning for Peace: Preventing Youth Violence in America," *Vital Speeches of the Day* (May 15, 2001): 469.

13. John Ahladas, "Global Warming," *Vital Speeches of the Day* (April 1, 1989): 382.

14. Jerry Yelverton, "Nuclear Engineering: An Exciting Future Ahead," *Vital Speeches of the Day* (August 15, 2001): 656.

15. Donald Baeder, "Chemical Wastes," *Vital Speeches of the Day* (June 1, 1980): 497.

16. William E. Franklin, "Careers in International Business: Five Ideas or Principles," *Vital Speeches of the Day* (September 15, 1998): 719.

17. J. A. Howard, "Principles in Default: Rediscovered and Reapplied," *Vital Speeches of the Day* (August 1, 2000): 618.

18. Steven Trachtenberg, "Five Ways in Which Thinking Is Dangerous," *Vital Speeches of the Day* (August 15, 1986): 653.

19. G. Michael Durst, "The Manager as a Developer," *Vital Speeches of the Day* (March 1, 1989): 309–310.

20. Hans Becherer, "Enduring Values for a Secular Age: Faith, Hope and Love," *Vital Speeches of the Day* (September 15, 2000): 732.

21. Cynthia Opheim, "Making Democracy Work: Your Responsibility to Society," *Vital Speeches of the Day* (November 1, 2000): 60.

Chapter 7

No notes in this chapter.

Chapter 8

1. Wendy Liebermann, "How America Shops," *Vital Speeches of the Day* (July 15, 1998): 595.

2. Earnest W. Deavenport, "Walking the High Wire: Balancing Stakeholder Interests," *Vital Speeches of the Day* (November 15, 1995): 49.

3. Dana G. Mead, "Courage to Grow: Preparing for a New Commercial Century," *Vital Speeches of the Day* (May 15, 1998): 465.

4. Susan Morse, "The Rap of Change: A New Generation of Solutions," *Vital Speeches of the Day* (January 1, 2001): 186.

5. Nancy W. Dickey, "Packing My Bag for the Road Ahead: Everyone's Access to Medicine," *Vital Speeches of the Day* (September 15, 1998): 717.

6. Edward E. Crutchfield Jr., "Profitable Banking in the 1980's," *Vital Speeches of the Day* (June 15, 1980): 537.

7. Richard C. Harwood, "Thought My Soul Would Rise and Fly: Creating a New Public Story," *Vital Speeches of the Day* (July 1, 2001): 558.

8. Richard Lamm, "Unexamined Assumptions: Destiny, Political Institutions, Democracy and Population," *Vital Speeches of the Day* (September 15, 1998): 714.

Chapter 9

1. Michael E. Patterson, Donald F. Danscreau, and Dianna Newbern, "Effects of Communication Aids on Cooperative Teaching," *Journal of Educational Psychology* 84 (1992): 453–461.

2. Barbara Tversky, "Memory for Pictures, Maps, Environments, and Graphs," in David G. Payne and Frederick G. Conrad, eds., *Intersections in Basic and Applied Memory Research* (Mahwah, NJ: Laurence Erlbaum, 1997), pp. 257–277.

3. Joe Ayres, "Using Visual Aids to Reduce Speech Anxiety," *Communication Research Reports* (June–December 1991): 73–79.

4. Judith Humphrey, "Executive Eloquence: A Seven-Fold Path to Inspirational Leadership," *Vital Speeches of the Day* (May 15, 1998): 470.

Chapter 10

1. C. K. Ogden and I. A. Richards, *The Meaning of Meaning* (London: Kegan, Paul, Trench, Trubner, 1923).

2. M. W. Cornog, *Merriam Webster's Vocabulary Builder* (Springfield, MA: Merriam Webster, 1998).

3. W. B. Gudykunst and Y. Matsumoto, "Cross-Cultural Variability of Communication in Personal Relationships," in W. B. Gudykunst, S. Ting-Toomey, and T. Nishida, eds., *Communication in Personal Relationships across Cultures* (Thousand Oaks, CA: Sage, 1996), p. 21.

4. G. Hofstede, *Cultures and Organizations: Software of the Mind* (New York: McGraw-Hill, 1991), p. 67.

5. D. Levine, *The Flight from Ambiguity* (Chicago: University of Chicago Press, 1985), p. 28.

6. Beverly Chiodo, "Choose Wisely," *Vital Speeches of the Day* (November 1, 1987): 42.

7. For instance, in his analysis of language, Walter Nash discusses more than twenty figures of syntax and semantics. Walter Nash, *Rhetoric: The Wit of Persuasion* (Cambridge, MA: Basil Blackwell, 1989), pp. 112–129.

8. Robert H. Schertz, "Deregulation: After the Airlines, Is Trucking Next?" *Vital Speeches of the Day* (November 1, 1977): 40.

9. Carl Wayne Hensley, "Speak with Style and Watch the Impact: Make Things Happen," *Vital Speeches of the Day* (September 1, 1995): 703.

10. Gerry Sikorski, "Will and Vision," *Vital Speeches of the Day* (August 1, 1986): 615.

11. Ronald W. Roskens, "Webs of Sand," *Vital Speeches of the Day* (February 1, 1986): 233.

12. Reed E. Hundt, "Serving Kids and the Community: Do We Want TV to Help or Hurt Children?" *Vital Speeches of the Day* (September 1, 1995): 675.

13. James N. Sites, "Chemophobia," *Vital Speeches of the Day* (December 15, 1980): 154.

14. Sheridan Baker, *The Complete Stylist and Handbook* (New York: Thomas Y. Crowell, 1966), pp. 73–74.

15. M. L. Hecht, M. J. Collier, and S. A. Ribeau, *African American Communication: Ethnic Identity and Cultural Interpretation* (Newbury Park, CA: Sage, 1993), p. 84.

16. L. P. Stewart, P. J. Cooper, A. D. Stewart, and S. A. Friedley, *Communication and Gender,* 3d. ed. (Boston, MA: Allyn & Bacon, 1998), p. 63.

17. S. B. Gmelch, *Gender on Campus: Issues for College Women* (New Brunswick, NJ: Rutgers University Press, 1998), p. 51.

18. M. K. Asante, *The Afrocentric Idea* (Philadelphia, PA: Temple University Press, 1998), pp. 95–96.

Chapter 11

1. Judee K. Burgoon, Deborah A. Coker, and Ray A. Coker, "Communicative Effects of Gaze Behavior: A Test of Two Contrasting Explanations," *Human Communication Research* 12 (1986): 495–524.

2. K. E. Menzel and L. J. Carrell, "The Relationship between Preparation and Performance in Public Speaking," *Communication Education* 43 (1994): 23.

3. Delivered in speech class, University of Cincinnati. Used with permission of Anthony Masturzo.

Chapter 12

1. H. J. Eysenck, "The Measurement of Creativity," in M. A. Boden, ed., *Dimensions of Creativity* (Cambridge, MA: MIT Press, 1994), p. 200.

2. Carol Koehler, "Mending the Body by Lending an Ear: The Healing Power of Listening." *Vital Speeches of the Day* (June 15, 1998): 543–544.

3. Delivered in speech class, University of Cincinnati. Used with permission of John Mullhauser.

4. Richard Weaver, "Language Is Sermonic," in R. L. Johannesen, R. Strickland, and R. T. Eubanks, eds., *Language Is Sermonic* (Baton Rouge: Louisiana State University Press, 1970), p. 212.

5. Delivered in speech class, University of Cincinnati. Used with permission of Wendy Finkleman.

6. Delivered in speech class, University of Cincinnati. Used with permission of Lindsey Degenhardt.

Chapter 13

1. Richard Weaver, "Language Is Sermonic," in James L. Golden, Goodwin F. Berquist, and William E. Coleman, eds., *The Rhetoric of Western Thought*, 6th ed. (Dubuque, IA: Kendall Hunt, 1997), p. 178.

2. Richard E. Petty and John Cacioppo, *Attitudes and Persuasion: Classic and Contemporary Approaches* (Boulder, CO: Westview, 1996), p. 7.

3. Kay Deaux, Francis C. Dane, and Lawrence S. Wrightsman, *Social Psychology in the '90s*, 6th ed. (Pacific Grove, CA: Brooks/Cole, 1993), p. 19.

4. Herbert L. Petri, *Motivation: Theory, Research, and Applications*, 4th ed. (Belmont, CA: Wadsworth, 1996), p. 3.

5. Wayne Weiten, *Themes and Variations* (Pacific Grove, CA: Brooks/Cole, 1995), p. 711.

6. Betsy Burke, speech on euthanasia delivered in speech class, University of Cincinnati. Portions used with permission of Betsy Burke.

7. Kenneth E. Anderson and Theodore Clevenger Jr., "A Summary of Experimental Research in Ethos," *Speech Monographs* 30 (1963): 59–78.

8. Stephen W. Littlejohn, *Theories of Human Communication*, 7th ed. (Belmont, CA: Wadsworth/Thomson, 2002), p. 132.

9. Gary C. Woodward and Robert E. Denton Jr. *Persuasion and Influence in American Life*, 4th ed. (Prospect Heights, IL: Waveland Press, 2000), p. 168.

10. Herbert W. Simons, Joanne Morreale, and Bruce Gronbeck, *Persuasion in Society* (Thousand Oaks, CA: Sage, 2001), p. 35.

11. Delivered in speech class, University of Cincinnati. Used with permission of Eric Wais.

Chapter 14

1. Stephen Toulmin, *The Uses of Argument* (Cambridge: Cambridge University Press, 1958).

2. Ibid.

3. Delivered at speech contest. Used with permission of Charone S. Frankel.

4. Herbert L. Petri, *Motivation: Theory, Research, and Applications*, 4th ed. (Belmont, CA: Wadsworth, 1996), p. 3.

5. Ibid., p. 185.

6. John W. Thibaut and Harold H. Kelley, *The Social Psychology of Groups* (New York: Wiley, 1959), p. 10.

7. Abraham H. Maslow, *Motivation and Personality* (New York: Harper & Row, 1954), pp. 80–92.

8. Delivered in speech class, University of Cincinnati. Used with permission of Dana Bowers.

9. The following two speeches are based on a debate between Sheila Kohler and Martha Feinberg, presented at the University of Cincinnati, and are used here with their permission.

Chapter 15

No notes in this chapter.

Chapter 16

1. D. Johnson and F. Johnson, *Joining Together: Group Theory and Group Skills*, 7th ed. (Boston: Allyn and Bacon, 2000).

2. E. Sundstrom, K. P. DeMeuse, and D. Futrell, "Work Teams: Applications and Effectiveness," *American Psychologist* (February 1990): 120–133.

3. J. S. Valacich, J. F. George, J. F. Nonamaker Jr., and D. R. Vogel, "Idea Generation in Computer Based Groups: A New Ending to an Old Story," *Small Group Research* 25 (1994): 83–104.

4. C. Evans and K. Dion, "Group Cohesion and Performance: A Meta-Analysis," *Small Group Research* 22, (1991): 175–186.

5. W. N. Widmer and J. M. Williams, "Predicting Cohesion in a Coacting Sport," *Small Group Research* 22 (1991): 548–570; P. R. Balgopal, P. H. Ephross, and T. V. Vassil,

"Self-Help Groups and Professional Helpers," *Small Group Research* 17 (1986): 123–137.

6. M. Shimanoff, "Group Interaction and Communication Rules," in R. Cathcart and L. Samovar, eds., *Small Group Communication: A Reader* (Dubuque, IA: Wm. C. Brown, 1992).

7. M. E. Shaw, *Group Dynamics: The Psychology of Small Group Behavior,* 3d ed. (New York: McGraw-Hill, 1981).

8. A. R. Dennis, "Information Exchange and Use in Small Group Decision Making," *Small Group Research* 27 (1996): 532–550.

9. K. S. Young, J. T. Wood, G. M. Phillips, and D. J. Pederson, *Group Discussion: A Practical Guide to Participation and Leadership,* 3d. ed. (Prospect Heights, IL: Waveland Press, 2000).

10. "Guidelines for Meeting Participants" developed by students in BAD 305: Understanding Behavior in Organizations, Northern Kentucky University, Fall 1998.

Appendix

1. Janice Thayer, "The Purpose of Life: Where Have All the Heroes Gone?" *Vital Speeches of the Day* (April 15, 2001): 404–408. Reprinted by permission of *Vital Speeches of the Day* and Janice Thayer.

2. Frances J. McClain, "The Music in Your Soul: A Celebration of Life," *Vital Speeches of the Day* (November 1, 2001): 59–61. Reprinted by permission of *Vital Speeches of the Day* and Frances J. McClain.

Glossary

accent the inflection, tone, and speech habits typical of the natives of a country, a region, or even a state or city

acceptance speech a response to a presentation speech

acronyms words formed from initial letters of each of the successive parts of a compound term, common words that comprise the first letters of objects or concepts, or sentences with each word starting with a letter that signals something else

active listening specific behaviors that turn a speech into a kind of dialogue

adaptation relating to audience interests and needs verbally, visually, and vocally

adaptation reaction the gradual decline of your anxiety level that begins about one minute into the presentation and results in your anxiety level declining to its prespeaking level in about five minutes

ad hominem argument an attack on the person making the argument rather than on the argument itself

anecdotes brief, often amusing stories

anticipation reaction the level of anxiety you experience prior to giving the speech, including the nervousness you feel while preparing and waiting to speak

antonyms words that have opposite meanings

appeal describes the behavior that you want your listeners to follow after they have heard the arguments

appeal to authority relying on the testimony of someone who is not an expert on the issue at hand

appropriateness using language that adapts to the needs, interests, knowledge, and attitudes of the listener and avoiding language that alienates

arguing the process of proving a conclusion you have drawn with factual information

arguing from analogy supporting a claim with a single comparable example that is significantly similar to the subject of the claim

arguing from authority supporting a claim with the opinions of one or more experts

arguing from causation citing events that have occurred that bring about the claim

arguing from definition supporting a claim by citing as supporting evidence that the claim has the distinguishing characteristic commonly associated with similar phenomena

arguing from example supporting a claim by providing individual examples

arguing from sign supporting a claim by citing data that signal or indicate the claim

argument reason with its supporting evidence

articulation the shaping of speech sounds into recognizable oral symbols that combine to produce a word

association the tendency of one thought to stimulate recall of another, similar thought

attending paying attention to what the speaker is saying regardless of extraneous interferences

attitude a general or enduring positive or negative feeling about some person, object, or issue

audience a specific group of people to whom the speech message is directed

audience adaptation the active process of developing a strategy for tailoring the material to your specific speech audience

audience analysis the study of the specific audience for a speech

average group opinion method accepting the alternative receiving the highest average ranking as the choice

bar graph chart with vertical or horizontal bars to show relationships between two or more variables at the same time or at various times on one or more dimensions

behavior an action related to or resulting from an attitude or belief

belief the cognitive, or mental, aspect of an attitude

brainstorming a technique for generating as many ideas as possible by being creative, suspending judgment, and combining or adapting the ideas of others

central route using critical thinking to analyze persuasive messages

channel both the route traveled by the message and the means of transportation

chart graphic representation that presents information in an easily interpreted format

claim the proposition or conclusion to be proven so that the audience will believe

clarity of main points when main point wording is likely to call up the same images in the minds of all audience members

closed questions narrowly focused questions ranging from those that require yes or no to short answers

cohesiveness the degree of attraction members have to one another and to the group's goal

commemorative address speech presented to celebrate a national holiday or the anniversary of an important date or event

commencement address a speech presented by a major political, business, social figure, or a prominent alumnus/a during graduation ceremonies

communication competence the impression that communication behavior is appropriate and effective

communication orientation views a speech as just an opportunity to talk with a number of people about a topic that is important to the speaker and to the audience

communication orientation motivation (COM) techniques techniques designed to reduce anxiety by helping the speaker adopt a "communication" rather than a "performance" orientation toward the speech

comparative advantages pattern an organization that allows you to place all the emphasis on the superiority of the proposed course of action

comparisons illuminate a point by showing similarities

complete demonstration going through the complete process in front of an audience

concrete words words that are likely to appeal to our senses or conjure up a picture

confrontation reaction the surge in your anxiety level that you feel as you begin to speak

connotation the feelings or evaluations we associate with a word

consensus method the process of determining a solution that all members of the group find acceptable, can support, and are committed to helping implement

context the interrelated conditions of communication; the position of a word in a sentence and its relationship to other words around it

contrasts highlight differences

conversational style an informal way of presenting a speech so that your listeners feel that you are talking with them

costs units of expenditure such as time, energy, money, or other negative outcomes

creative thinking the ability to transcend traditional ideas and find new ideas, forms, methods, and interpretations

creativity a person's capacity to produce new or original ideas and insights

credibility the level of trust that an audience has or will have in the speaker

criteria satisfaction pattern an indirect organization that seeks audience agreement on criteria that should be considered when evaluating a particular proposition and then shows how the proposition satisfies those criteria

critical analysis the means of analyzing and evaluating a speech

critical thinking an analytical and evaluative process using logic or reasoning to present information in a way that is likely to provide understanding, change a belief, or uncover problems in another person's informative or persuasive message

cultural setting the beliefs, values, attitudes, meanings, social hierarchies, religion, notions of time, and roles of a group of people

data reasons and evidence (facts, opinions, observations, evidence, assumptions, or assertions) that provide the basis for a conclusion of an argument

decision making the process of choosing among alternatives

decoding the process the audience uses to transform messages back into ideas and feelings

demonstration going through the complete process in front of the audience

denotation the direct, explicit meaning a language community formally gives a word

diversity differences between and among people that affect nearly every aspect of the communication process

emotions subjective experiences triggered by actions or words that are accompanied by bodily arousal and by overt behavior

encoding the process the speaker uses to transform ideas and feelings into words, sounds, and actions

enthusiasm the excitement or passion about the topic

ethical issues focus on degrees of rightness and wrongness in human behavior

etymology the derivation or history of a particular word

examples specific instances that illustrate or explain a general factual statement

expert opinion method asking the group member who has the most expertise to select the final choice

expert opinions interpretations and judgments made by authorities in a particular subject area

extemporaneous speech a speech that is carefully prepared and practiced, but the exact wording of each idea occurs as it is presented

external noises the sights, sounds, and other stimuli that draw people's attention away from the intended meaning

eye contact the way we look directly at the people to whom we are speaking

facial expression eye and mouth movement

factual statements those that can be verified

false cause attributing causation to an event that is not related to, or does not produce, the effect

familiar words words that your specific audience will understand

feedback verbal and nonverbal responses to messages

figurative language using a word or words in an imaginative rather than a literal sense

flow chart symbols and connecting lines used to diagram a complex system or procedure

fluency devoid of hesitations and such vocal interferences as "uh," "er," "well," "okay," "you know," and "like"

follow-up questions questions designed to pursue the answers given to primary questions

general criteria those skills that are required for all speeches

general goal the intent of your speech

gestures movements of hands, arms, and fingers

graph a diagram that compares information

ground rules prescribed behaviors designed to help the group meet its goals and conduct its conversations

hasty generalization presenting a reason or other generalization supported by a single weak example or none at all

hierarchy of needs five categories arranged in order of importance moving from physiological needs, safety needs, belongingness and love needs, esteem needs, to self-actualization needs

historical setting previous communication episodes

impromptu speech speech given on the spur of the moment

incentives (rewards) goal objectives that motivate, such as economic gain, good feelings, prestige, or other positive outcomes

informative speech speech that conveys facts, ideas, or theories without advocating a position

intellectually stimulating information that is new to audience members and meets a deep-seated need to know

internal noises the thoughts and feelings that interfere with meaning

internal transitions words and phrases that link parts of a sentence in ways that help people see the relationships of the parts

Internet an international electronic network of networks

interviewing skillfully asking and answering questions

keynote address a speech presented near the beginning of a conference or convention that is designed to inspire participants in their work

knowledge and expertise qualifications or capability—a track record

leading questions questions phrased in a way that suggests the interviewer has a preferred answer

learning the speech understanding the ideas of the speech but having the freedom to word the ideas differently each time

line graph chart that indicates changes in one or more variables over time

listening the process of receiving, attending to, and assigning meaning to aural and visual stimuli

logical reasons order organizing the main points of a persuasive speech by the reasons that support the speech goal

main points complete-sentence representations of the ideas you have used in your thesis statement

majority rule method selecting the alternative that receives the majority of votes (50% + 1)

manuscript speech speech that is written out completely and then read aloud

marking adding gender, race, age, or other designations unnecessarily to a general word

meaningful main points when main points are informative

message ideas and feelings presented to an audience through words, sound, and action symbols selected and organized by the speaker and interpreted by members of the audience

metaphors like a simile, but instead of a direct comparison using like or as, build a direct identification between the objects being compared

mnemonics memory aids

modified demonstration completing various stages of the demonstration beforehand so that you only show parts of the complete demonstration in front of the audience

monotone a voice in which the pitch, volume, and rate remain constant, with no word, idea, or sentence differing significantly from any other

motivation forces acting on or within an organism to initiate and direct behavior

motivational pattern an organization that combines problem solving and motivation, following a problem solution pattern but including required steps designed to heighten the motivational effect of the organization

move an audience to action desiring to have listeners actually do what you want them to

movement motion of the entire body

multiple-choice questions respondents choose from a number of alternative answers

narrative a tale, an account, or a personal experience

neutral questions questions phrased without direction from the interviewer

noise any stimulus that gets in the way of sharing meaning

norms shared expectations for the way group members will behave while in the group

open-ended questions broad-based questions that ask the interviewee to provide whatever information he or she wishes; ask for opinions without directing respondents to answer in a predetermined manner

opinion verbal expression of a belief or attitude

panel discussion a problem-solving discussion in front of an audience

parallel structure of main points when main point wording follows the same structural pattern, often using the same introductory words

paraphrase a statement in your own words of the meaning you have assigned to a message

passive listening making no conscious effort to remember what is being said

performance orientation views public speaking as a situation demanding special delivery techniques in order to impress an audience aesthetically

periodicals magazines and journals that appear at fixed periods

peripheral route using simple cues to analyze persuasive messages

personableness the impression you make on your audience based on such traits as enthusiasm, friendliness, warmth, and a ready smile

personalize relate it to audience references

personal pronouns words that refer directly to members of the audience

persuasive speaking a process in which a speaker presents a message intended to affect an audience in a way that is likely to reinforce a belief, change a belief, or move an audience to act

physical setting the location, time of day, light, temperature, distance between communicators, and seating arrangements

pie graph chart that helps audiences to visualize the relationships among parts of a single unit

pitch the highness or lowness of your voice

placement and sequencing constructing a list of items in a way that the most important comes last

plagiarism to steal and pass off the ideas and words of another as one's own or to use a created production without crediting the source

poise assurance of manner

posture the position or bearing of the body, which gives further evidence of your poise

precise words words that most accurately or correctly capture the sense of what we are saying

presentation speech speech designed to present an award, a prize, or a gift to an individual or a group

primary criteria the most important elements for consideration in a particular type of speech

primary questions questions the interviewer plans ahead of time that serve as the main points for the interview outline

problem solution pattern an organization that provides a frame-work for clarifying the nature of the problem and for illustrating why a given proposal is the best one

problem-solving discussion a structured dialogue between individuals who interact and influence one another in order to develop a plan that will overcome an identified difficulty

problem-solving goal a future state of affairs desired by enough members of the group to motivate the group to work toward its achievement

process explanation telling how to do something, how to make something, or how something works

pronunciation the form and accent of various syllables of a word

proposition a persuasive speech goal

proximity a relationship to personal space

psychological setting the manner in which people perceive both themselves and those with whom they communicate

public speaking apprehension the level of fear a person experiences when anticipating or actually speaking to an audience

public speaking skills training systematically teaching the skills associated with the processes involved in preparing and delivering an effective speech with the intention of improving speaking competence as a means of reducing public speaking apprehension

quality the tone, timbre, or sound of your voice

questions of fact questions concerned with discovering what is true or to what extent something is true

questions of policy questions that concern what courses of action should be taken or what rules should be adopted to solve a problem

questions of value questions that concern subjective judgments of what is right, moral, good, or just

rate the speed at which you talk

reasoning the mental process of drawing inferences from factual information

reasoning process the conscious or subconscious logic that leads from the data to the claim

reasons statements that tell why a proposition is justified

refutation the process of proving that an argument or series of arguments, or the conclusion drawn from that argument or those arguments, is false, erroneous, or at least doubtful

rehearsal session involves practicing the speech, analyzing it, and practicing it again

rehearsing practicing the presentation of your speech aloud

relevance the extent to which audience members find personal value in the information presented

repetition saying the same words again

restatement echoing the same idea using different words

retaining storing information in memory and using techniques that will help you identify and recall that information

reward a meaningful incentive

rhetorical question a question phrased to stimulate a mental response rather than an actual spoken response on the part of the audience

scaled questions questions that allow for a range of responses

section transitions complete sentences that link major sections of a speech

semantic noises alternate meanings aroused by a speaker's symbols

serious having physical, economic, or psychological impact

setting the location for a speech

simile a direct comparison of dissimilar things

skimming a method of rapidly going through a work to determine what is covered and how

speaker the source or originator of the communication message

specific goal a complete sentence that specifies the exact response the speaker wants from the audience

specific words words that clarify meaning by narrowing what is understood from a general category to a particular group within that category

speech goal what you want your listeners to know, believe, or do

speech notes a word or phrase outline of your speech, plus hard-to-remember information such as direct quotations and statistics

speech plan a strategy for achieving your speech goal

speech of introduction speech designed to pave the way for the main speaker

speech of tribute speech designed to praise someone's accomplishments

speeches oral presentations usually given without interruptions

spontaneity being so responsive to your ideas that the speech seems as fresh as a lively conversation, even though it has been well practiced

statement of logical reasons a straightforward organization in which you present the best-supported reasons you can find

statistics numerical facts

stereotyping assigning characteristics to people solely on the basis of their class or category

strengthen or change a belief desiring to have listeners agree with you that the belief you present is reasonable

subject a broad area of knowledge, such as the stock market, cognitive psychology, baseball, or the Middle East

survey gathering information directly from people

symposium a discussion in which a limited number of participants present individual speeches of approximately the same length dealing with the same subject, then discuss their reactions to what others have said and answer questions from the audience

synonyms words that have the same or nearly the same meanings

systematic desensitization a technique in which people first learn procedures for relaxation, then learn to apply these to the anxiety they feel when they visualize participating in a series of anxiety producing communication situations, so that they can remain relaxed when they encounter anxiety-producing situations in real life

thesis statement a sentence that outlines the specific elements of the speech supporting the goal statement

time order organizing the main points of the speech by a sequence of ideas or events, focusing on what comes first, second, third, and so on

timely relating to now

topic some specific aspect of a subject

topic order organizing the main points of the speech by categories or divisions of a subject

town hall meeting an event in which a large number of people who are inter-ested in a topic are convened to discuss and, at times, decide an issue

transitions words, phrases, and sentences that show relationships between and among ideas or that create bridges to other words, phrases, or sentences

trustworthiness both character and apparent motives for speaking

two-sided questions questions that call for a yes/no or true/false response

unanimous decision method every member of the group believes the same solution alternative is the best

understanding the ability to decode a message by correctly assigning a meaning to it

visual aid a form of speech development that enables the audience to see as well as to hear information

visualization techniques reduces apprehension by helping speakers develop a mental picture of them giving a masterful speech

vital information information the audience perceives as a matter of life or death

vividness full of life, vigorous, bright, and intense

vocal expressiveness vocal contrast in pitch, volume, rate, and quality that affect the meaning audiences get from the sentences you present

vocal interferences extraneous sounds or words that interrupt fluent speech

voice the form of a transitive verb that tells whether the grammatical subject performs the action stated in the verb or is acted upon

volume the loudness of the tone you make

warrant the verbalization of the reasoning process

welcoming speech speech that expresses pleasure for the presence of a person or an organization

word chart a summary, list, or outline

working environment the physical setting in which a group works

Photo Credits

This page constitutes an extension of the copyright page. We have made every effort to trace the ownership of all copyrighted material and to secure permission from copyright holders. In the event of any question arising as to the use of any material, we will be pleased to make the necessary corrections in future printings. Thanks are due to the following authors, publishers, and agents for permission to use the material indicated.

Chapter 1 2: Joel Gordon 7: (top) Dennis Brack / Black Star / PictureQuest (middle) © IT Int'l/ eStock Photography / PictureQuest (bottom) © Michael Newman / PhotoEdit, Inc. 10: Alex Wong / Newsmakers 12: Christopher Morris / Black Star / PictureQuest 14: Terrence Miele

Chapter 2 18: Joel Gordon 23: Joel Gordon 25: © Jeff Greenberg / PhotoEdit, Inc. 29: © Spencer Grant / PhotoEdit, Inc.

Chapter 3 38: Tom McCarthy / corbisstockmarket.com 40: Bob Daemmrich / Stock, Boston 41: © David Weintraub / Stock, Boston Inc. / PictureQuest 46: © Billy E. Barnes / PhotoEdit / PictureQuest

Chapter 4 52: © Jeff Greenberg / PhotoEdit, Inc. 57: Joel Gordon 60: Joel Gordon 61: Tom Bean / AllStock / PictureQuest

Chapter 5 70: Bob Daemmrich / Stock, Boston 72: AP / Wide World Photos 76: © David Young-Wolff / PhotoEdit, Inc. 82: Joel Gordon

Chapter 6 90: © David Young-Wolff / PhotoEdit, Inc. 91: © Richard Hamilton Smith / CORBIS 94: InfoTrac 97: © David Young-Wolff / PhotoEdit, Inc. 99: Sierra Club 101: Jason Harris / © Wadsworth Publishing. All rights reserved. 106: © Jon Feingersh / corbisstockmarket.com

Chapter 7 116: Peter Chapman Photography 124: © Bill Bachmann / PhotoEdit, Inc. 125: © Steve Dunwell / Getty Images / The Image Bank

Chapter 8 136: Joel Gordon 138: Charles Gupton / corbisstockmarket.com 145: Jeffry Myers / Stock, Boston

Chapter 9 158: © Michael Newman / PhotoEdit, Inc. 160: © Jack Hollingsworth / CORBIS 167: Courtesy of InFocus Systems, Inc.

Chapter 10 178: Peter Holst / Getty Images 181: Pablo Corral V / CORBIS 184: Elle Schuster / Getty Images 186: © Michael Newman / PhotoEdit, Inc.

Chapter 11 198: Anne Dowie 203: © Joel Gordon 1995 207: Don Klumpp / Getty Images 209: Peter Chapman Photography 212: © Myrleen Ferguson / PhotoEdit, Inc.

Chapter 12 224: Joel Gordon 229: © Tom Prettyman / PhotoEdit, Inc. 233: © Jeff Greenberg / PhotoEdit, Inc. 243: CORBIS / Bettmann 244: (both): Regates à Argenteuil by Claude Monet, CORBIS / Edimedia

Chapter 13 252: David Young-Wolff / PhotoEdit / PictureQuest 256: © Jose Carrillo / PhotoEdit, Inc. 259: © Paul Conklin / PhotoEdit, Inc. 265: Harvey Finkle 269: © Jacques M. Chenet / CORBIS

Chapter 14 280: © David Young-Wolff / PhotoEdit, Inc. 282: AP / Wide World Photos 286: AP / Wide World Photos 296: © Gary Nolan / CORBIS 305: Bob Daemmrich / Stock, Boston / PictureQuest

Chapter 15 314: Steve Dunwell / Getty Images / The Image Bank 317: © Michael Newman / PhotoEdit, Inc. 320: V.C.L. / Getty Images

Chapter 16 326: © Michael Newman / PhotoEdit, Inc. 328: Bob Daemmrich / Stock, Boston 332: © LWA-Dann Tardif / corbisstockmarket.com 336: © IFA Bilderteam/ eStock Photography/ PictureQuest 341: AP / Wide World Photos

Index